AGENCY AND JOINT ATTENTION

Agency and Joint Attention

Edited by Janet Metcalfe
and Herbert S. Terrace

OXFORD
UNIVERSITY PRESS

OXFORD
UNIVERSITY PRESS

Oxford University Press is a department of the University of Oxford.
It furthers the University's objective of excellence in research, scholarship,
and education by publishing worldwide.

Oxford   New York
Auckland   Cape Town   Dar es Salaam   Hong Kong   Karachi
Kuala Lumpur   Madrid   Melbourne   Mexico City   Nairobi
New Delhi   Shanghai   Taipei   Toronto

With offices in
Argentina   Austria   Brazil   Chile   Czech Republic   France   Greece
Guatemala   Hungary   Italy   Japan   Poland   Portugal   Singapore
South Korea   Switzerland   Thailand   Turkey   Ukraine   Vietnam

1007087173

Oxford is a registered trademark of Oxford University Press in the UK and certain other
countries.

Published in the United States of America by
Oxford University Press
198 Madison Avenue, New York, NY 10016

Library of Congress Cataloging-in-Publication Data
Agency and joint attention/edited by Janet Metcalfe, Herbert S. Terrace.
    pages cm
Includes bibliographical references and index.
ISBN 978-0-19-998834-1
1. Joint attention.   2. Intentionalism.   3. Human behavior.   4. Psychology, Comparative.
I. Metcalfe, Janet.   II. Terrace, Herbert S., 1936–
BF323.J63A44 2013
153.7´33—dc23
2013003697

9 8 7 6 5 4 3 2 1
Printed in the United States of America
on acid-free paper

Contents

Contributors

Howard Andrews
NYS Psychiatric Institute
New York, NY

Lorraine Bahrick
NYS Psychiatric Institute
Florida International University
Miami, FL

Beatrice Beebe
NYS Psychiatric Institute
New York, NY

Anne Böckler
Max Planck Institute for Human
 Cognitive and Brain Sciences,
Leipzig, Germany

Rechele Brooks
Institute for Learning & Brain Sciences
University of Washington
Seattle, WA

Karen Buck
NYS Psychiatric Institute
New York, NY

Josep Call
Department of Developmental and
 Comparative Psychology
Max Planck Institute for Evolutionary
 Anthropology
Leipzig, Germany

Malinda Carpenter
Department of Developmental and
 Comparative Psychology
Max Planck Institute for Evolutionary
 Anthropology
Leipzig, Germany

Peter Carruthers
Department of Philosophy
University of Maryland
College Park, MD

Henian Chen
NYS Psychiatric Institute
New York, NY

Patricia Cohen
NYS Psychiatric Institute
New York, NY

Christiane Diefenbach
Max Planck Institute for Human
  Cognitive and Brain Sciences
Leipzig, Germany

Logan Fletcher
Department of Philosophy
University of Maryland
College Park, MD

Fabia Franco
Department of Psychology
Middlesex University
London, UK

Vittorio Gallese
Department of Neuroscience
University of Parma
IIT Brain Center for Social and Motor
  Cognition
Parma, Italy

György Gergely
Cognitive Development Center
Central European University
Budapest, Hungary

Stefanie Hoehl
Psychology Department
University of Heidelberg
Heidelberg, Germany

Joseph Jaffe
NYS Psychiatric Institute
New York, NY

Günther Knoblich
Donders Institute for Brain, Cognition,
  and Behaviour
Radboud University
Nijmegen, The Netherlands
Cognitive Science Department
Central European University
Budapest, Hungary

Frank Lachmann
Institute for the Psychoanalytic Study of
  Subjectivity
New York, NY

Hakwan Lau
Department of Psychology
Columbia University
New York, NY

Margaret T. Lynn
Department of Experimental Psychology
Ghent University
Ghent, Belgium

Sara Markese
NYS Psychiatric Institute
New York, NY

Janet Metcalfe
Department of Psychology
Columbia University
New York, NY

Andrew N. Meltzoff
Institute for Learning & Brain Sciences
University of Washington
Seattle, WA

Tanaz Molapour
Department of Clinical Neuroscience
Karolinska Institute
Stockholm, Sweden

Ezequiel Morsella
Department of Psychology
San Francisco State University
Department of Neurology
University of California, San Francisco
San Francisco, CA

Kristine H. Onishi
Department of Psychology
McGill University
Montreal, Quebec, Canada

Elisabeth Pacherie
Institut Jean Nicod
Paris, France

Derek C. Penn
Cognitive Evolution Group
University of Louisiana
Lafayette, LA
The Reasoning Lab
University of California, Los Angeles
Los Angeles, CA

Daniel J. Povinelli
Department of Biology
University of Louisiana
Lafayette, LA

Wolfgang Prinz
Max Planck Institute for Human
    Cognitive and Brain Sciences
Leipzig, Germany

Elizabeth Redcay
Department of Psychology
University of Maryland
College Park, MD

Rebecca Saxe
Department of Brain & Cognitive Sciences
Massachusetts Institute of Technology
Cambridge, MA

Natalie Sebanz
Department of Cognitive Science
Central European University
Budapest, Hungary
Donders Institute for Brain, Cognition,
    and Behaviour
Radboud University
Nijmegen, The Netherlands

Corrado Sinigaglia
Department of Philosophy
University of Milan
Milan, Italy

Anne Springer
Max Planck Institute for
    Human Cognitive and
    Brain Sciences
Leipzig, Germany

Sara Steele
Center for Neural Science
New York University
New York, NY

Herbert S. Terrace
New York Psychiatric Institute
Department of Psychology
Columbia University
New York, NY

Robrecht van der Wel
Donders Institute for Brain, Cognition,
    and Behaviour
Radboud University
Nijmegen, The Netherlands
Department of Psychology
Rutgers University
Camden, NJ

Athena Vouloumanos
Department of Psychology
New York University
New York, NY

Introduction
Herbert S. Terrace

METACOGNITION OF OUR own agency is as old as civilization in the sense that civilization could not exist if its members did not assume responsibility for their actions. Civilization could also not exist if we were unable to communicate with one another using language. As members of civilized societies, we learn to maintain our autonomous selves as agents, responsible for our own acts, while at the same time sharing mental states with other people, a capability that is essential for language. How this comes about is the topic of this book.

As we shall see, there is a constant tension between the need for the autonomy of self-knowing agents and the sharing of mental states needed to allow communication with others. These tensions are exemplified in research on *joint attention*, which requires the merging of two people's perception, and a metacognition of *agency*. That, in turn, requires the ability to separate one's own agency from another's.

During an infant's first year she engages in nonverbal mutual eye gaze with her mother while she is cradled in her mother's arms, a uniquely human practice. That experience provides the infant with many opportunities to differentiate herself from her mother, by noticing differences between hers and her mother's emotional state (chapter 5). From that differentiation there grows a more complex version of the "me" versus "you" concept (chapter 6) that is necessary for an infant to develop into an autonomous self-knowing agent. For attention to be joint, both the self and another have to be differentiated. But then those entities have to be merged to create the experience of a shared state of mind.

After learning about the origins of agency and joint attention, an uninitiated reader might well ask, What is the significance of studying infants to understand these concepts?

After all, couldn't we get much better evidence of those phenomena from older children or adults? Unfortunately, ignorance of the origins of these concepts makes it all the more difficult to understand them in their adult form.

Terrace's chapter (chapter 1) outlines two approaches to the evolution of language. One focuses on anatomical changes in the ancestors of *Homo sapiens* that caused human infants to require more maternal care than any other primate. The other is developmental and follows from the many species-specific opportunities a human infant has to engage her mother in face-to-face contact. Because a human infant's brain is only 25% of its adult size at birth, as compared with 40% to 45% in the case of other primates, a human infant requires more postnatal care than any other primate. That care also differs from that experienced by other primates because *Homo sapiens* lack fur. As a consequence, human infants have to be cradled by their mothers until they begin to crawl and walk.

Until a human infant develops autonomy from her mother, she has ample opportunities to engage her mother in mutual eye-gaze. During that period, the infant learns to differentiate herself from her mother by virtue of experiences in which the infant learns to recognize differences in hers and her mother's emotional state. One can also track the development of agency and joint attention in a human infant before she acquires language. Taken together, this approach provides both phylogenetic and ontogenetic accounts of the evolution of language. Terrace concludes that language could only develop in human infants because of their uniquely human experiences of mutual eye gaze with their mothers and the subsequent development of a uniquely human mechanism for nonverbal joint attention.

Joint attention can be defined as the shared focus of two individuals toward an object of mutual interest (chapters 2 and 3; Bruner, 1975, 1983). Indeed, joint attention provides evidence that an infant has a Theory of Mind (Premack & Woodruff, 1978) in the sense that an infant and her mother jointly share attention to the same object.

To digress for a moment, consider a basic question about language acquisition that was first articulated by Wittgenstein (1968) and elaborated by Quine (1980). Given the ever-shifting attention of an infant, how can she learn to associate objects and their names? What if an infant were looking at a cat when her mother tried to teach her the name for a table? As noted by Tomasello (1999), joint attention is an effective answer to this question because it ensures that an adult and an infant are attending the same object, in this case the table.

The observation that human infants can jointly attend an object prompts the question, are such exchanges observed in nonhuman primates? Although neither Carpenter and Call's nor Fletcher and Caruthers' chapters say much about mutual eye gaze, they both address the issue of a theory of mind, and ask if there was any psychological evidence of an ape's ability to differentiate itself psychologically from its mother.

Carpenter and Call and Penn and Povinelli (chapters 2 and 3) present two opposing views of the mental lives of animals and nonverbal human infants. After reviewing recent research on apes, Call and Carpenter conclude that, aside from sharing needs with their caretakers, apes lack the motivation for seeking social rewards. They also note that nonhuman caregivers do not return their infants' gaze or smile in response to their behavior. Even in the case of "encultured apes," there is a very low frequency of pointing, a response that human babies exhibit as early as 3 months. As for declarative statements, the only evidence that Carpenter and Call could find was an ape's ability to point to drawings after extensive training in that task. They conclude that whereas human infants engage in joint attention by the time they are 1 year old, there is little, if any, convincing evidence that chimpanzees and other apes do.

Based on their review of experiments on the mental life of a human infant's first year, Fletcher and Carruthers reach an opposite conclusion. They regard those experiments as evidence that favor a mindreading account, suggesting that simple forms of mentalizing are quite prevalent among highly social creatures outside of the *hominin* line.

The opposing positions of Carpenter and Call and Fletcher and Carruthers may turn out to be less than meets the eye. Carpenter and Call's focus is on experiments on apes. Most of the research that Fletcher and Caruthers review is on infant humans, in which they agree with most developmental psychologists that human infants have a theory of mind. They argue that the jury is still out about evidence that has been used to posit mental events in apes, and that more research, especially research that doesn't entail food rewards (e.g., grooming) might help to resolve this issue. Following Tomasello (2008), Fletcher and Caruthers argue that some nonhuman animals "understand some psychological states in others—the only question is which ones and to what extent."

Beebe et al. (chapter 5) provide evidence that infants have a concept of self at 4 months. In one experiment, they recorded, on separate videotapes using a 1-s time base, an infant's and her mother's facial/vocal affect, orientation, and touch. They then measured *self-contingency* and *stability* of each individual's behavior by analyzing time-synched videotapes of a mother and her infant playing together. Mothers responded with positive affect to changes in the infant's distress level within a quarter of a second of the time at which the infant displayed negative affect. Conversely, when the infant was distressed, she would just as quickly turn away from a mother who didn't perceive her distress. Beebe et al.'s (chapter 5) analysis of infant–mother interactions made it clear that an infant was able to detect changes in her mother's affect, however briefly that change occurred (cf. concept of "me" vs. "you;" Meltzoff & Brooks, chapter 6). That observation provided evidence of an infant's ability to distinguish between hers and her mother's emotional state, thereby creating a basis for a self–other concept. Although the infant's concept of self is very primitive, the mother's and infant's behavior provide a foundation for subsequent developments in agency (chapters 10–15).

Gergely's *Natural Pedagogy* is consistent with Beebe's view that humans have a natural species-specific communication system (chapter 7). Although humans acquire a sense of agency and the ability to engage in joint attention during their first year, it doesn't follow that they immediately acquired the ability to use language. Long before the appearance of language, our ancestors lived in what we might refer to as the Planet of Agents and Joint Attenders. As suggested by Terrace (chapter 1), they distinguished themselves from other primates by their ability to develop a sense of self and their openness in sharing attention to objects and events with their caretakers. This wasn't simply a matter of adding language to the intelligence of an ape. Instead, human infants were open to sharing their environments with adults for the sake of acquiring what Gergely refers to as "ostensive definitions": words whose meanings are learned when one person points to an object and says the name of the object. Such knowledge would be "opaque" without their caretaker's inclination to pass on their knowledge of ostensive names to the next generation and the human infant's disposition to learn them.

Developmental psychologists have argued about the cause of gaze following in infants for many years. Is it Theory of Mind? Is it imitation? Looking at an object to which an adult attends? Looking at particular features of that object? Meltzoff and Brooks (chapter 6) pursued these topics by performing experiments in which they fractionated questions about gaze following to allow for each possibility. These experiments were also tests of their "like-me" hypothesis, that infants will imitate adults so long as the infants themselves had experiences that were similar to the activity that the adult performed.

In one experiment, Meltzoff and Brooks compared head turning in groups of infants (12, 16, and 18 months old) who responded to a human adult turning toward target objects. In one condition, the adult's eyes were open; in the other, closed. Meltzoff found that babies looked significantly more frequently at the target when the adult's eyes were open than when they were closed. Moreover, those subjects looked at the target longer and vocalized and pointed while turning toward it. These results are consistent with the "like me" hypothesis because the infants themselves experienced the difference between having their eyes open and closed. In another experiment, on 18-month-old infants, Meltzoff and Brooks asked whether they would follow the gaze of a robot that was programmed to look left on some trials and right on others. They did not, presumably because the robot was not "like me." Interestingly, what did get the infants to turn their heads in response to the robot's turning its head was the experience of watching an adult and the robot engage in an imitation game. In this instance, the "like-me" hypothesis was supported because the visual game gave the infants a basis for understanding that the eyes of the robot functioned like their own.

By the end of an infant's first year, she has learned to engage another person's attention about objects in her immediate vicinity. Franco (chapter 8) provides an interesting analysis of communication between an infant and an adult as the infant begins to explore the world around her. To document those developments, Franco introduced two new concepts: *declarative* and *interrogative* pointing. During declarative pointing, the infant wants another person to look at some object that she sees; for example, an airplane flying in the sky. During interrogative pointing, the infant tries to draw attention to an object that she can't describe well herself, and seeks verbal instruction about the name of the object to which she is attending. In both declarative and interrogative pointing, the other person is not expected to do anything except to talk about the object that the infant is attending. These activities help the infant to free herself from the restrictions of her immediate environment.

Vouloumanos and Onishi (chapter 9) pursue the integration of joint attention into more complicated forms of communication during infancy and toddlerhood. Given the availability of language, verbal, written, and gestural, it is necessary to integrate those factors into analyses of a toddler's communicative skills. Vouloumanos' proposed four dimensions of a toddler's communicative skills to consider at this point. The first is *shared intentionality*, which implies that the toddler can recognize the degree of another person's agentive development and vice versa. The second is the *directional flow of the interaction* between the toddler and another person. The third is the degree to which communication takes place in *mutually readable formats*, and the fourth is *referential specificity*, the level of meaning that the toddler can understand.

In chapter 10, Gallese and Sinigaglia provide a magisterial account of the importance of mirror neurons in explanations of intentional actions of human and nonhuman animals. Mirror neurons are one of the major discoveries in the rapidly expanding field of neuroscience. Mirror neurons would also be high on any list of the most significant neuroscientific discoveries for psychology.

A major theme of Gallese and Sinigaglia's chapter is a discussion of evidence that shows that, motor neurons are more than "bare bones behavior." Instead, the motor system is organized in terms of motor goals and intentions rather than mere movements. Many so-called motor neurons take into account the physical dimensions of objects that one intends to grasp, for example, what type of object it is, its shape, and size.

An equally important property of motor neurons, which has been observed in experiments with monkeys, is that that they discharge both when the monkey performs a given motor act and also when it observes someone else performing the same or a similar motor act. These latter sensory-motor neurons are called "mirror neurons."

Gallese and Sinigaglia conclude that motor neurons take into account our rich and complex social life. The result is a rich social representation of the space that surrounds us: a space that is full of potential for own intentional behavior and how others might act in response to our own actions.

Because agency and joint attention involve at least two individuals, observation of both the initiator and the respondent are required to investigate the neural basis of joint attention and agency. Redcay and Saxe's chapter provides a well-organized review of recent research on the neurophysiological mechanisms that control agency and joint attention. Research on these topics, which is difficult enough to study at a psychological level, become inordinately more difficult when one attempts to understand their neurophysiology. In addition to functional magnetic resonance imaging (fMRI), they describe two newly adapted measures of neural activity that are especially important when working human infants: near-infrared spectroscopy (NIRS) and event-related potential (ERP). The images created by NIMS and ERP suggest that infants as young as 4 months old can engage in joint attention.

Redcay and Saxe's review is organized around three basic stages of joint attention: (1) detecting a shift in the partner's attention, (2) shifting one's attention to an object, and

(3) monitoring the relationship between one's own and another's attention. The dorsal medial prefrontal cortex (dMPFC) appears to be crucial for detecting a shift in attention of another individual. Activity of the dMPFC appears to respond when another person, the responder, is present as a social partner. Having detected the attention of the responder, the initiator must accurately represent that shift. To detect that this happens, the initiator must determine whether or not the attentional shift was intentional. They argue that the neuroscientific evidence, from both animal and human models, implicates the right posterior superior temporal sulcus (pSTS) in these calculations. The *sense that you are sharing intentionally with another person* is the key component in joint attention. Once the initiator is attending to the responder, the initiator shifts her attention to an object, the third member of a joint-attentional triad. Both the initiator and the responder must understand that the attentional shift was intentional.

Hoehl's chapter describes research on the development of social referencing, the tendency of an infant to seek information about the safety of novel and ambiguous stimuli. During an infant's first year, her response to novel stimuli depends on the facial expression of a trustworthy adult. In one experiment, the adult was represented in a cartoon that was presented directly in front of the infant. Hoehl reports that infants adjusted their behavior only toward target objects and not towards simultaneously presented distractors. Infants also pay attention to happy as opposed to neutral faces when they look directly at the infant. That difference disappears, however, when they are shown fearful as opposed to neutral faces. Infants are also sensitive to angry faces that gaze directly at them, as opposed to looking to a point on the side. By the time an infant is 9 months old, she pays more attention to fearful faces than neutral faces, regardless of whether she gazes directly at them or a novel object. More generally, by that age, she exerts more control over her attention and she becomes more amenable to the intentional and communicative stances of adults she trusts.

By maturity, people have become expert at joint attention, while at the same time consolidating their own sense of agency. In chapter 12, Böckler and Sebanz address three questions relating to joint attention: How are shared representations formed? How is temporal coordination between people accomplished? And, How do co-acting and co-attending individuals manage to keep self and other apart? Successful joint action requires that two individuals interact in a manner that allows them to predict and keep track of each other's actions and goals. They cite an example in which two people attempt to transport a piano down a flight of stairs. It is necessary for each actor to know how the other will perform his part of the joint task. Yet most people seem well equipped to rapidly and efficiently simulate and predict each other's behavior. Such coordination takes place despite the fact that the information available about self and other is quite different; for example, proprioception for the sender's behavior and vision in the case of the receiver's intentional state.

Metcalfe (chapter 15) isolates a number of cues that people use to evaluate whether they were, themselves, the agent responsible for a particular act. The judgment of agency is, of course, a judgment about the extent to which one's autonomous self was responsible for an action. Getting this right is necessary in any society, insofar as without it there is no basis for assigning credit and blame. This judgment should, in principle, be based on cues that provide an accurate differentiation of the self as cause from another as cause. But while these judgments *should* be heavily weighted toward distinguishing one's own separate causal affect from that others, this chapter illustrates that several of the cues that people actually use for making these judgments do nothing of the sort. Indeed, although several of the cues are simply noisy, nondiagnostic, or inaccurate, some of them actually treat others' actions and thoughts as if they were one's own. The thoughts and action of others are internalized—indistinguishable from one's own—and the individual takes responsibility for what others did.

The communal mental life that is characteristic of human beings is ever-present, and shows up even in a judgment that should be based exclusively on evidence of separateness and distinction. The tension between shared mental states needed for communication and the distinction between self and other that is needed to partial out the individual's responsibility for his or her own actions is particularly salient in these judgments of agency. But although this tension is apparent in everyone's judgments about their own agency, the complete breakdown of the separation between the self and the other and the ability to know whether the self or the other was the agent results in the kind of devastating pathology seen in schizophrenia.

Van der Wel and Knoblich (chapter 16) pursue a different approach than Metcalfe regarding factors that determine a sense of agency. Their point of departure is Wegner's (2002) theory of mental causation, in which one's sense of agency is based on mechanisms that trick humans into experiencing "the illusion of free will." Van der Wel and Knoblich focused on three aspects of Wegner's theory: *priority, consistency,* and *exclusivity*. Priority dictates that a thought needs to precede an action. Consistency dictates that thought needs to be consistent with the action that follows and exclusivity dictates that no alternative causes for the action are known. To the extent that these criteria are violated, one's sense of agency is reduced. A comprehensive theory of the experience of agency has two requirements. It has to explain why people make mistakes in their sense of agency and whether and how people use sensorimotor and perceptual information to determine whether they have control over their own actions and the external events that are caused by these actions.

Prinz, Diefenbach, and Springer's chapter attempts to integrate declarative and procedural descriptions of knowledge, two traditional cognitive approaches to agency that have created what many psychologists refer to as the "great divide." They argue that this duality is inherent in intentional movements

In an attempt to show how definitions of declarative and procedural knowledge have to include both terms, Prinz, Diefenbach, and Springer performed a series of experiments whose aim was to provide evidence of the so-called Action-Sentence Compatibility Effect (ACE). The ACE is meant to demonstrate online interactions between language comprehension and action selection, specifically how content-specific cross-talk between sentence comprehension and response selection support the notion that declarative knowledge is grounded in procedural processing and vice versa.

Prinz, Diefenbach, and Springer argue that declarative theories explain *what* people believe and think, whereas procedural theories explain *how* people perceive and act. Their experiments attempted to integrate these approaches in tests in which subjects were asked to interpret declarative statements, with respect to an implicit (nonverbal) interpretation that was either physically congruent or not, and vice versa.

Consider, for example, a paradigm that is based on a choice between two actions: "X is near" and "X is far." Subjects are asked to touch a central spot on a board on front of them in which X can be located at either end. After listening to the instruction, the subject is asked to carry out the command as quickly as possible. Reaction times to away-sentences were faster in the YES-IS-FAR condition than in the YES-IS-NEAR condition, whereas the reverse was true for toward-sentences. Those results suggest that words, the content of the sentence (away/toward), prime the selection of the response to that sentence. Prinz, Diefenbach, and Springer hypothesize that language comprehension is grounded in motor processes: One primes the other when both address a common spatial feature (away/toward). They postulate permanent cross-talk between the movements and meanings and that each and every entry in one domain is associated with mandatory entries in the other domain (cf. Morsella, Molapour, & Lynn, chapter 17).

In their review of agency, a topic that Morsella, Molapour, and Lynn assign to "volition" (similar in concept to free will), they argue for a functional approach. They argue that there is so little known about volition that we should approach that topic as "naïve naturalists."

Morsella, Molapour, and Lynn use three approaches for their analysis of voluntary action: phenomenology, ideomotor processing, and the skeletal output system. *Phenomenal states* provide the nervous system with a form of internal communication, "cross-talk," that integrates neural activities that would otherwise be independent and exist in a global workspace. They propose that phenomenal states are required to integrate information, *but* that only certain kinds of information can be integrated from specialized, high-level (and often multimodal) senses that influence action only through skeletal activity, the only type of activity about which we can be conscious.

Phenomenal states permit a form of cross-talk in the brain that is essential for *integrated action-goal selection*, a process that historically has been linked to the ventral processing stream of the brain. If the function of phenomenal states is to achieve integration among systems by broadcasting information, then we should expect that the nature of phenomenally accessible representations is to have a high *broadcast ability*, one that should be "understood" by the greatest number of action systems.

One of the basic truths of folk psychology is that one's intentions are a direct cause of the behavior that follows. Steele and Lau (chapter 18) argue that there is no direct scientific support for that conjecture and much evidence that motor programming of a particular event begins before we are conscious of our intentions.

Steele and Lau discuss a classic experiment by Libet (2004) in which subjects were asked to flex their wrists whenever they wished and to also observe a clock in their immediate view to estimate at which point they had a conscious urge to flex their wrist spontaneously. Libet also recorded the time at which the motor nerves began to generate activity of wrist muscles. The surprising result was that physiological recordings of motor plan activity related to the relevant wrist muscles occurred much earlier than a subject's reported awareness of the urge or intention to move his wrist. This result would seem to rule out the possibility that the awareness of intention may play a causal role in allowing us to select our actions.

The folk-psychology view that acts of volition are caused by conscious intention is a valid description of how we feel. What is less clear is whether the processes underlying the conscious experience are crucial for the execution of our actions. Although it is clear that many sophisticated functions can be performed on the basis of information that is perceived unconsciously, that should not imply that consciousness has no special function. It is likely that some psychological functions cannot be performed unconsciously, for example, pedagogy. The ability to form representations about intentional states may be linked with some of the basic features of humanity, such as Theory of Mind and linguistic abilities. But despite persistent difficulties in evaluating the specific causal role for conscious experiences, Steel and Lau remind us that we've made considerable progress in understanding the properties and limitations of experiences of agency.

Pacherie's chapter has two aims. The first is to draw a distinction between agentive experiences and agentive judgments that might help to resolve current disputes about the veridicality of our agency. The second is to discuss several criteria that could define the sense in which agentive experiences and judgments are metacognitive.

Pacherie begins her chapter by asking, What cues are needed to generate cues to agency? She describes one experiment that showed that self-recognition was more accurate when subjects initiated the action, even though visual and proprioceptive information was always the same. When the displacement of the participant's finger was externally generated, and when the subject only had afferent information, self-recognition performance dropped to near-chance levels. The authors of this experiment concluded that self-recognition of one's bodily movements was much more accurate when they are active, rather than passive, and that they made a crucial contribution to efferent signals for self-recognition.

The chapters discussed in this introduction were contributed in part by participants from a conference on Agency and Joint Attention that Janet Metcalfe and I organized to meet in June 2009 at Columbia University. We are grateful for the help of Ljubica Chatman and Karen Kelly. We would like to thank the authors for the outstanding scholarship they brought to bear in their chapters on the many areas of psychology that contribute to our understanding of agency and joint attention. We would also like to thank the University Seminars and the Department of Psychology for their generous financial contributions to cover the costs of housing and travel for each of the participants of this conference.

REFERENCES

Bruner, J. S. (1975). From communication to language: A psychological perspective. *Cognition*, *3*(3), 255–287.

Bruner, J. S. (1983). *Child's Talk: learning to Use Language*. New York: Norton.

Libet, B. (2004). *Mind Time: The Temporal Factor in Consciousness*. Cambridge, MA: Harvard University Press.

Premack, D., & Woodruff, G. (1978). Chimpanzee problem-solving: A test for comprehension. *Science, 202*, 532–535.

Quine, W. V. (1980). What is it all about? *American Scholar, 50*, 43–54.

Tomasello, M. (1999). The human adaptation for culture. *Annual Review of Anthropology, 28*, 509–529.

Tomasello, M. (2008). *Origins of Human Communication*. Cambridge, MA: MIT Press.

Wegner, D. M. (2002). *The Illusion of Conscious Will*. Cambridge, MA: MIT Press.

Wittgenstein, L. (1968). *Philosophical Investigations*. New York: Macmillian.

1 Becoming Human: Why Two Minds Are Better Than One
Herbert S. Terrace

LIKE WALKING, LANGUAGE is so natural and effortless that we seldom give it any thought. However, when viewed in a perspective that includes all animals, language and walking are exceptional. Only humans communicate with language and we are the only primate whose natural mode of locomotion is bipedal.

Language did not evolve until at least 6 million years after our ancestors became bipedal. Given that gap, it should be obvious that the juxtaposition of bipedalism and language is not intended to imply a causal relationship between those behaviors. But it is intended to contrast our knowledge of the evolution of those uniquely human abilities. The evolutionary history of bipedalism is pretty well understood; not so, language. Walking and talking seem similar in that, with virtually no systematic input, both activities seem to occur instinctively. But as we will later see, language requires too many social activities to assign it to a particular epoch of human development.

To see why, imagine the proverbial story of a newborn infant raised from birth on an island on which all of her basic needs were taken care of. Will she learn to walk? Of course! Now, imagine the same experiment and ask the question, would she learn to talk? Other than the reflexive cries one would expect from an infant in distress, I can't think of any reason to say yes.

Language, in the conversational sense, requires a speaker and a listener and the ability to reverse each role. Why would an individual speak about whatever interests her, be it a seashell, a tree, or a cat, without an audience? My point here is that language results from the interaction between two individuals, and to focus only on the learner is to miss the basic function of language. Indeed, how language develops from the unique social connection between an infant and her mother is the main topic of this chapter.

When our human ancestors and chimpanzees went their separate ways, the major distinction between those species was bipedal versus quadrupedal locomotion. Many so-called *Australopiths* were able to climb trees using four limbs but on the ground they walked bipedally. They differed from apes by their upright posture but their brains were not much larger.

Like walking, the only plausible explanation of the origins of language is the theory of evolution, a theory that has successfully accounted for the origins and characteristics of virtually all species of life on earth, both plant and animal. In recognition of its scope, Dobzhansky, an eminent 20th-century geneticist, observed that, "nothing in biology makes sense except in the light of evolution" (Dobzhansky, 1973). It is therefore distressing that language, a defining characteristic of the human species, has been the Achilles heel for the theory of evolution.

The basic problem is the inability of the theory of evolution to explain how language, a voluntary form of communication, could have been selected from the involuntary grunts and screams of chimpanzees, our closest living ancestors. Instead, I suggest that we focus on the development of language from the point at which direct ancestors of *Homo* appeared, that is, between 2 and 3 million years ago and the present.

Before I turn to that matter, it is important to correct a bias that many students of language still have. They regard human linguistic ability as the grandest achievement of evolution. They also believe that the process of evolution was designed to achieve that goal in a linear fashion (Fig. 1.1a). But the fact of the matter is that evolution does not produce species in a linear manner and it favors a particular species only *after* its members have adapted to a particular environment.

BACKGROUND

About 6 million years ago, the climate of east Africa underwent many changes. In some instances, the temperature was too low to support trees and various areas changed from forests to open grassland and back to forests within a few hundred years. In East Africa (mainly Kenya, Tanzania, and Uganda), tectonic forces created the Great Rift Valley, a steep ravine that stretches through East Africa. The Olduvai River, which runs along the base of the Great Rift Valley, is an important prehistoric site, sometimes called "the cradle of humankind." It earned that name because it contains stone tools, purportedly the first tools used by a member of the species, *Homo*. Figure 1.2 shows a map of the area in which these transitions took place.

A more apt metaphor of evolution is that is more like a bush with many branches, like those shown in Figures 1.1b. Each branch in Figure 1.1b has many sub-branches, all of which interact with the particular environments in which they live. A species is usually defined as the end point of a particular branch while others becomes extinct.

This area is also the site of Mt. Kilimanjaro and Mt. Kenya, the two tallest peaks in Africa. Those mountains, and some smaller ones, created a shadow that blocked the yearly

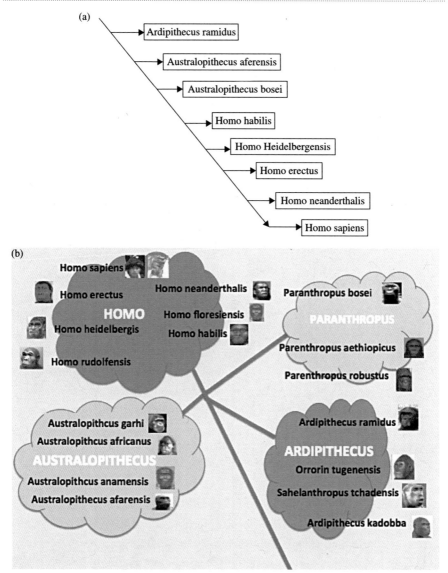

FIGURE 1.1 Linear vs. Bush Models of Evolution. (a) An oversimplified model of speciation that ignores intermediate species, many of which became extinct. (b) How some ancestors of Homo sapiens species survived while others became extinct. Notice the capricious paths leading from one species to another. Adapted from Smithsonian Museum of National History, Human Family Tree exhibition (2012).

monsoons that came from the west. As a result, the dwindling amount of forest cover on the eastern side created a new dry environment, in which the groups that remained gradually shifted from quadrupedal to bipedal locomotion (Ruff, 1991). At about the same time, our bipedal ancestors had to cope with rapidly changing temperature cycles in their new environment. Eventually, the brains of some *Australopiths* became larger and a new species emerged: *Homo habilis,* our oldest human ancestor.

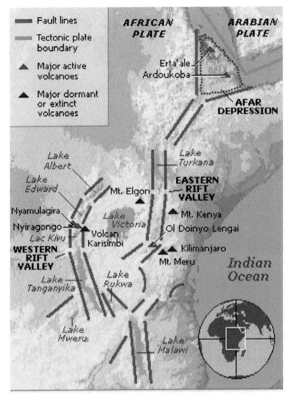

FIGURE 1.2 Some of the Main Areas of Eastern Africa That Have Yielded Fossils That Filled the Gap Between Chimpanzees and *Homo sapiens*. The Great Rift Valley varies in width from twenty to sixty miles and in depth from a few hundred to several thousand meters. The Rift Valley has been a rich source of fossils that allow study of human evolution. Richard Leakey has speculated that the diversity of environments resulting from the creation of the Rift Valley provided "an ideal setting for evolutionary change." The first members of the species Homo appeared about 2 mya and overlapped with Australopiths for roughly 1 million years.

During the transition from *Pan troglodytes* to the first appearance of *Homo*, our ancestors went through two distinct changes. First, *Australopiths* adapted a bipedal posture and then, approximately 2 million years later, their brains started to grow to complete the transition to *Homo*. A summary of the species that emerged after the split between *Pan troglodytes* and the hominids that gave rise to language is shown in Figure 1.3.

ANIMAL COMMUNICATION

As compared with language, all forms of animal communication are *innate, involuntary,* and *inflexible*. The exotic form of some instances of animal communication often creates an appearance of spontaneity. Foraging bees, for example, communicate the location and the quality of nearby food to their hive mates through elaborate dances. Those dances, however, are not learned and they are immutable. A bee cannot substitute a song or another dance to communicate about the source and quality of nearby nectar (Gould, 1982).

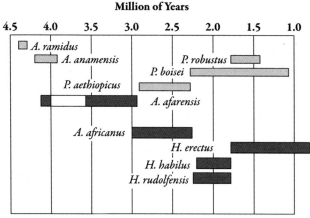

Million of Years

FIGURE 1.3 The main ancestors of *Homo* that lived after *Homo* split from the chimpanzee. The first members of the species *Homo* appeared about 2 million years ago and overlapped with *Australopithecus* for roughly 1 million years.

The same is true in the case of the distinctive alarm calls that vervet monkeys make when they perceive particular predators (Cheney & Seyfarth, 1986).[1]

A related limitation of animal communication is the *narrow scope of a signal's "meaning."* The only function of those signals is to convey information about basic needs; for example, alarm calls of a bird, signals that announce the discovery of food, an animal's intent to mate, a female's receptivity for mating, and so on.

Animal signals are also unidirectional in the sense that a speaker doesn't require a symbolic response from the listener. When, for example, an infant chimpanzee that cries because it is hungry, it expects a morsel of food rather than a symbolic statement from its mother. When a sequence of responses is necessary, as for example, in a mating sequence, each response is triggered by a signal from one mate to which the other must respond involuntarily.

The only reason to think of a direct jump from the natural forms of chimpanzee to language is that a chimpanzee is our closest living ancestor. When we discuss the possibility of *teaching* chimpanzees to use symbols, we will consider the findings of various projects devoted to that topic during the last 50 years and the limitations of their achievements. The best that we can say is that they've only succeeded in training a chimpanzee to use words of various artificial languages to request various basic rewards. Where they fall short is the absence of any two-way exchange of information in which the speaker and the listener alternate their roles.

But even if we agree that the communicative abilities of chimpanzees should not be our reference point for discussing the evolution of language, we are still faced with an equally difficult problem. All common definitions of language assume a sizeable vocabulary and a grammar that specifies how words can be combined to create particular meanings for young children. Where did they come from?

The major thrust of this chapter is to argue that an infant had to master various *nonver*bal skills during her first year of life before she can learn a spoken language. While considering those skills, it is important to realize that none of them were motivated by language. Beginning at the age of 4 months, and infant can nonverbally, distinguish her mother and other individuals when it comes to taking responsibility for some environmental event (Stern, Beebe, Jaffe, & Bennett, 1977; Trevarthen & Hubley, 1978). That process begins when the infant and her mother take turns in expressing emotions to one another. While the infant and her mother gaze into each other's eyes, they typically express delight with each other. There are times, however, when the infant's and the mother's expressions differ. This has been shown in pioneering experiments in which Beebe set up two cameras, one the focuses on the infant and another that focuses on the mother (see chapter 5). Both cameras were time-synched. What was evident during slow motion replays of those tapes were the immediate reactions of the mother and the infant that occurred a mere 25 msec after one party's affect changed. From that change the infant could learn that she and her mother could express themselves differently and that may be sufficient for the infant to notice the difference between a world centered around "me," as a first person, as opposed to one that is centered around her mother (you), a third person.

When an infant is about 12 months old, a shift takes place from dyadic to triadic communication that is referred to as *joint attention* (Tomasello, Hare, & Agnetta, 1999). Joint attention, which is not taught, is necessary for the child to learn vocabulary. After the infant goes through a few alternations between gazing at the object that has caught her attention and gazing at her mother, the mother turns to look at the same object that intrigued her daughter. At that point, the infant typically smiles, happy with the thought that she and her mother were sharing the same mental event.

Each of these nonverbal steps, all of which are uniquely human, is needed before an infant utters her first word. What's more, each of these steps is cumulative in the sense that they must occur in the order specified. One step does not guarantee the next. Consider, for example, mutual eye gaze between an infant and her mother. It would take hundreds, if not thousands, of generations to produce mother–offspring pairs that can maximize the time spent in direct mutual eye gaze. Because none of the intragenerational shifts needed for mutual eye gaze have anything to do with language, its only benefit would be sharper control by the mother of an infant, with whom she shared control, over a mother for whom that benefit didn't develop.

In hindsight, we can appreciate how the achievement of one step during the development of nonverbal language doesn't provide any guarantee the next "normal" step will actually occur. The retardation of language in autistic children (Mundy, Sigman, & Kasari, 1990; Ornitz, Guthrie, & Farley, 1977) and in children raised in orphanages (Hill, 2001; Windsor, Glaze, & Koga, 2007) are clear examples of how, for different reasons, the normal development of language can be thwarted. Likewise, there is no guarantee that I would be able to write these words or for you to understand them if the evolution of language stopped at the one-word stage. But even with a single word, there are substitutions that can convey a particular meaning. For example, the words *beware, caution, duck, hide, look out, peril, run* and *watch out can* among others, be used to convey *danger.* Unlike the calls used in animal communication, human vocabularies are not innate. Each word has to be learned individually.

But here we are, happy to communicate with each other in full language garb. This is a good point to shift from the topic of how animals communicate with each other to see what language adds to that mix.

WHAT HAS LANGUAGE ADDED TO COMMUNICATION?

Language is the only form of natural communication that is *voluntary.* Yet, all human languages use a grammar that is not taught. According to Chomsky (1955), young children use an innate *language acquisition device* (LAD) that compensates for their lack of particular knowledge by filling in blanks that were left out by the *poverty of the stimulus.* Chomsky applied the poverty of the stimulus argument to the absence of particular phrases that a child can produce without ever hearing them. But one could equally apply the same argument to social factors. Before the child utters her first word, she must acquire a dyadic sense of "me" and "other" her experiences of mutual eye gaze with her mother.

Language is used mainly for bi-directional communication. Conversations between human speakers and listeners are motivated by a desire to exchange information for its own sake rather than by basic needs for survival. Animal communication cannot because it lacks the arbitrary vocabularies and grammars that are characteristic of *all* human languages.

Different languages assign an arbitrary symbol to a particular object or event. Grammar allows humans to create particular meanings by combining two or more words to talk about the past, present, and future; state a negative; ask a question; and in general, to allow us to communicate ideas and feelings with remarkable precision. Language users can communicate about any imaginable topic; for example, politics, the fourth dimension, plans for the weekend, childhood memories, a recent novel, beauty, truth, or the latest gossip. There is no limit to the number of ways the words of a language can be combined to create a particular meaning.

TWO TYPES OF LANGUAGE USE

What refinements were added by language to create a totally new form of communication? Bates argued that there were *imperatives,* which I refer to as Language 1, and *declaratives,* which I refer to as Language 2 (Bates, 1976). Unfortunately, we are often stuck with *communication* and *language* as overlapping references to the same event and there is no convention that currently divides such utterances to fit each category. For example, does *signal,* meaning a cue, belong in Category 1; likewise, *communicate, attract, show fear*? Alternatively, *signal,* as used in Category 2, can refer to a traffic light.

One can hope that the meanings that are appropriate for each type of language can someday parse themselves into nonoverlapping words or phrases. Meanwhile, I will use Bates' strategy of distinguishing between Language 1 and Language 2. Language 1 consists of demands for primary rewards that can be observed in human and nonhuman primates. It is unidirectional, in the sense that, following a demand, the speaker does not expect a symbolic reply. Language 2 is the basis of any meaningful conversation and is obviously bi-directional. A speaker addresses a listener to convey some bit of information. The speaker is rewarded by the acknowledgment of the listener who then assumes the role of a speaker.

TWO APPROACHES TO UNRAVELING THE COMPLEXITIES OF LINGUISTIC STRUCTURES

Even Darwin, the quintessential gradualist, sometimes wavered in his faith in gradualism as a basic assumption of the theory of evolution. Consider his frustration when he tried to explain the evolution of the human eye. Like language, the human eye seemed too complicated to explain by the theory of evolution.

> *To suppose that the eye, with all its inimitable contrivances for adjusting the focus to different distances, for admitting different amounts of light, and for the correction of spherical and chromatic aberration, could have been formed by natural selection, seems, I freely confess, absurd in the highest possible degree.* (Darwin, 1872)

But upon reflection, Darwin formulated a strategy for unraveling that complexity.

> *...reason tells me, that if **numerous gradations** from a perfect and complex eye to one very imperfect and simple, each grade being useful to its possessor, can be shown to exist; if further, the eye does vary ever so slightly, and the variations be inherited, which is certainly the case; and if any variation or modification in the organ be ever useful to an animal under changing conditions of life, then the difficulty of believing that a perfect and complex eye could be formed by natural selection.* (Darwin, 1872, emphasis added)

Figure 1.4 shows how scientists that followed Darwin's strategy confirmed his hypothesis about the origins of the human eye.

In the case of cognitive skills, Darwin suggested a similar approach:

> *We must also admit that there is a much wider interval in mental power between one of the lowest fishes, as a lamprey or lancelet, and one of the higher apes, than between an ape and man; yet this interval is filled up by **numberless gradations**.* (Darwin, 1871, emphasis added)

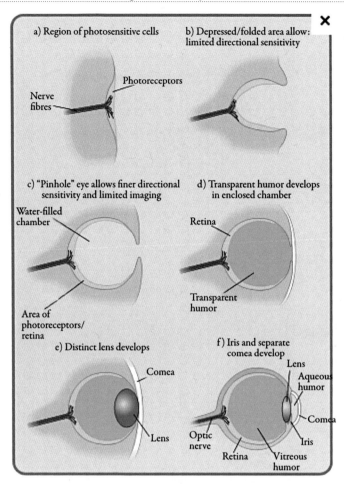

FIGURE I.4 The evolution of the eye has been a subject of significant study, as a distinctive example of a homologous organ present in a wide variety of taxa. Complex eyes appear to have first evolved within a few million years, in the rapid burst of evolution known as the Cambrian explosion. Eyes show a wide range of adaptations to meet the requirements of the organisms, which bear them. Eyes may vary in their acuity, the range of wavelengths they can detect, their sensitivity in low light levels, their ability to detect motion or resolve objects, and whether they can discriminate colors. This figure shows the growth of the human eye from a simple photosensitive cell to the modern eye, which has to bodies that contain the vitreous and the aqueous humors, a retina containing two types of photoreceptors, a lens that is mounted in an iris, and a cornea that contains the aqueous humor.

INITIAL APPROACHES TO THE EVOLUTION OF LANGUAGE

Following the publication of *The Origin of Species*, various members of the European intelligentsia (Darwin included) proposed what have been referred to as onomatopoetic theories of the evolution of language. These theories, which were referred to as the "bow wow," "pooh-pooh," "yo-he-ho," etc. theories (cf. Kenneally, 2007), assumed that our ancestors' first words were imitations of natural sounds. For example, the words, *moo, bark, hiss, meow,* and *quack-quack* referred, respectively, to cows, dogs, snakes, cats, and ducks. In this view, language was just another example of animal communication, albeit more complex. The obvious and fatal problem for all onomatopoetic theories is that, even if true, they could only account for a miniscule portion of the words of a basic vocabulary. They could not, for example, account for any of the words in this chapter.

In response to the onslaught of onomatopoetic and other uncritical theories of the evolution of language, the Linguistic Society of Paris issued an edict in 1866 that banned all further discussions of that topic. With minor exceptions, the ban was effective for almost a century.

MODERN THEORIES OF THE EVOLUTION OF LANGUAGE

During the second half of the 20th century, there's been a surge of renewed interest in the evolution of language, so much so that it is worth asking, What changed from a dormant period that lasted nearly 90 years? The answer is, quite a lot. The major developments were anatomical changes in hominids, behaviorism and its demise, the cognitive revolution (Chomsky's radically new approach to grammar in particular), various ape language projects, experiments on serial memory in monkeys, and new techniques for studying the nonverbal responses of human infants.

ANATOMICAL CHANGES IN HOMINIDS

An immediate consequence of bipedalism was a reduction in the weight that the pelvis had to bear. As a result, the pelvis shrank, and with it, the size of the birth canal. The main consequence of the latter change was a limit on the size of an infant's head at birth. At the time that we became bipedal (~6 million years ago), that limitation had no consequence. The approximate volume of the brains of *Australopthecus afarensis* was approximately 300 cc, as opposed to 1,350 to 1,400 cc for *Homo sapiens*. The size of the birth canal began to matter with the appearance of *Homo erectus*, whose brain volume was initially 900 cc, but during the course of a more than 1 million year interval, it grew to approximately 1,100 cc. Brains of that size could not pass through the birth canal.

Nature's solution to this problem was to limit the development of a fetus at birth to insure the safe passage of the fetus' brain. However, giving birth to a less developed infant meant that, at birth, her brain was approximately 20% to 25% of the size it would reach as an adult. By contrast, the size of a newborn chimpanzee is 40% to 50% of its adult size. Because movements are controlled by the motor cortex, a small brain size also meant that human infants were less agile at birth than their chimpanzee counterparts. Differences in the size of the pelvises of human and nonhuman primates are shown in Figure 1.5.

Two other major consequences of an upright posture were the shift in the concentration of the sun on the body and one's angle of view of the environment. As shown in Figure 1.6, the upper part of the body was less prone to the concentration of heat from the sun. Figure 1.7 shows why walking upright also provided a better view over the tall grass that accompanied bipedalism than the view that would be available to

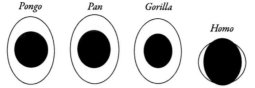

FIGURE 1.5 Human and Chimpanzee Pelvises The human pelvis limits the size of the brain that pass through it at birth to approximately 1,100 cc. Rosenberg KR, Trevathan WR. **Birth, obstetrics and human evolution.** *Br. J. Obstet. Gynaecol.* 2002;109:1199–1206.

a quadrupedal that would have to stretch into an unnatural position to obtain the same view.

About 1.5 million years ago, a major consequence of the diminutive size of a human infant's brain was its greater need for maternal care. Because human infants aren't able to crawl until they are approximately 8 months old, their mothers have to carry them for a much longer period than mothers of more developed primates. By itself, that increment in maternal investment wouldn't necessarily have altered the development of a human infant.

However, two other important physical changes also occurred during the era in which *Homo erectus* was the most prominent member of the *Homo* genus. One was the loss of bodily fur; the other, a whitening of the sclera of the human cornea.

The loss of bodily fur meant that an infant could no longer cling to her mother's hair. Instead, she had to be held in her mothers' arms, where she could now gaze directly into her mother's eyes. Finding her mother's eyes and gazing at them was facilitated by the high degree of contrast between the mother's white sclera and her dark iris. Given an approximately 8- to 9-month dependency period during which human infants were held by their mothers and the many opportunities she had for mutual gaze, these factors created a uniquely human dyad. Figure 1.8 illustrates the transition from the ape to the human eye with respect to the color of the sclera.

In sum, there are four reasons to look to our *Homo* heritage rather than to apes to understand the evolution of language: upright posture, a small birth canal, the loss of bodily fur, and a white as opposed to a dark sclera. It should be clear that none of these

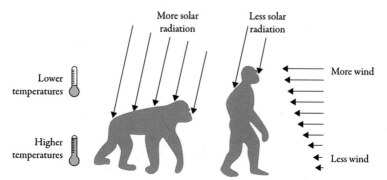

FIGURE 1.6 Differential Effects of the Sun on Quadrupedal and Bipedal Organisms.

FIGURE 1.7 Different Views of Bipedal (a) and Quadrupedal (b) Primates.

differences were selected to enhance linguistic ability. The most popular explanation of bipedalism is that it was an adaptation to changes in the environment that resulted from fewer trees and more open spaces. The loss of fur has been attributed to a warming of the environment. The loss of pigmentation in the cornea has been attributed to the need for closer interaction with the members of one's troop whose size resulted from a large increment in brain size during the period in which *Homo erectus* was the most dominant member of the Homo species.

BEHAVIORISM

In his *Principles of Psychology,* Herbert Spencer argued that, just as the theory of evolution was used to explain *anatomical* changes in different species over time, the

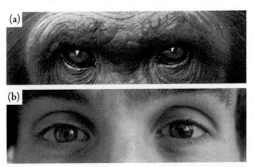

FIGURE 1.8 The Difference in the Color of the Pigment of the Sclera in Chimpanzees (a) and Humans (b) (see color insert).

logic of that theory applied with equal force to changes in animal behavior (Spencer, 1886). That idea fostered an interest in comparative psychology, a new discipline that studied differences and similarities in the behavior of various species. After a brief flirtation with anthropomorphic and cognitive interpretations of behavior (Romanes, 1884), most comparative psychologists adopted behaviorism as their guiding philosophy.

Even though association theory is too weak to explain the instances of animal cognition that I will discuss in this chapter, the law of parsimony requires a demonstration that the phenomena in question cannot be explained by association theory. Consider, for example, how a behaviorist would explain how you found your way back to your hotel in a strange town. By trial and error, you eventually learned which way to turn at, say, the following seven crucial choice points: left at the post office, right at the bank, right at the gas station, left after crossing a bridge, left at the playground, right at the library, and right after the high school. Your memory of which way to turn, at each physically distinct choice point, eventually gets you home. On this view, learning to find your hotel requires nothing more than the skills that a rat needs to navigate a seven-choice point maze.

As shown in Figure 1.9a, responding correctly at the first choice point ensures that you would next encounter the second choice point, and only that choice point; responding correctly at the second choice point ensures that you would next encounter the third choice point, and only that choice point, and so on, until you end up in front of your hotel. Learning theorists characterized what you learned while attempting to execute a sequence of S-R associations, in which S_n is a symbol for a particular choice point and R_n is a symbol for the correct response at that choice point. It is important to note that, with the exceptions of S_1 and S^R, each choice point functions as a secondary reward for the prior response and as a discriminative stimulus for the next one.

$$S_1{:}R_1 \rightarrow S_2{:}R_2 \rightarrow S_3{:}R_3 \rightarrow S_4{:}R_4 \rightarrow S_5{:}R_5 \rightarrow S_6{:}R_6 \rightarrow S_7{:}R_7 \rightarrow S^R$$
(Skinner, 1938).

Remarkably, Skinner's theory of grammatical sentences, which appeared in *Verbal Behavior* (1957), followed the same logic as that used to explain the behavior of a rat while learning a maze. According to Skinner, the first word of a sentence provided a cue for the second word, which in turn provided a cue for the third word, and so on.

In hindsight, Skinner's theory of sentence construction was embarrassingly simple. It should, however, be viewed in the context of an extraordinary string of successful experiments that demonstrated the ease with which the principles of instrumental conditioning could be applied to just about any behavior; for example, in such disparate areas as behavior therapy (Masters & Rimm, 1987) instruction by teaching machines (Skinner, 1959), explaining private events (Skinner, 1945), testing the effectiveness of particular

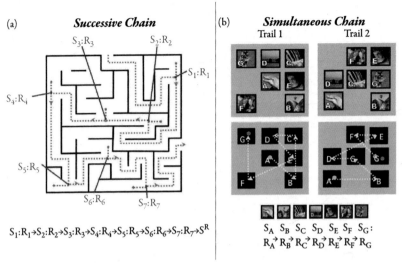

(a) *Successive Chain* (b) *Simultaneous Chain*

$S_1{:}R_1 \rightarrow S_2{:}R_2 \rightarrow S_3{:}R_3 \rightarrow S_4{:}R_4 \rightarrow S_5{:}R_5 \rightarrow S_6{:}R_6 \rightarrow S_7{:}R_7 \rightarrow S^R$

$S_A\ S_B\ S_C\ S_D\ S_E\ S_F\ S_G:$
$R_A^\rightarrow\ R_B^\rightarrow\ R_C^\rightarrow\ R_D^\rightarrow\ R_E^\rightarrow\ R_F^\rightarrow\ R_G$

FIGURE 1.9 (a) Basic plan of a traditional maze. Each choice point is separated, both spatially and temporally from the others. A run through the maze is characterized as a successive chain that is composed of a series of S-R associations. (b) Simultaneous chaining paradigm. Each panel depicts a trial during training on a simultaneous chain. The configuration of the items, typically photographs, varies randomly from trial to trial. The photographs at the bottom of the figure show, for the benefit of the reader, the correct order in which a subject must respond in order to obtain a reward. The bottom portion of each panel depicts the route that a subject must follow (*yellow arrows*) with respect to the items shown in the top panel in order to receive a reward. Barring a 1 in 5,040 guess, a simultaneous chain must be learned by trial and error. A reward is presented only after the subject has responded to each item in the correct order. An error at any point of the sequence ends the trial. See text for additional details. Terrace, H. S. (2005). The simultaneous chain: A new approach to serial learning. *Trends in Cognitive Science, 9,* 202–210.

drugs (Spiegel, 2003), and teaching pigeons to guide missiles and the match-to-sample paradigm (Skinner, 1960), to name but a few.

The success of this approach, in particular Skinner's imaginative applications of the principles of instrumental conditioning (Skinner, 1953) fostered a climate in which it seemed possible to teach an animal to master any skill, perhaps even language. It was therefore not surprising that Premack and Terrace, both Skinnerians, began independent programs whose goals were to obtain empirical evidence to support Skinner's theory of language.

THE EVOLUTION OF LANGUAGE ACCORDING TO CHOMSKY

Noam Chomsky, who is arguably the most brilliant theorist in the history of linguistics, espoused an *abrupt* strategy for explaining the origin of human language. He reasoned that human language should be attributed to a single mutation because the alternative, a *gradual* theory, would have to specify *what good is half a language?* Also, *which portion of language would constitute the first half?* To support his position, he asked the same question of other structures and their functions, e.g., *What good is half of a wing? What good is half of an eye?* and *What good is half of a grammar?*

I would argue that *half of a wing, half of an eye,* or *half of a grammar* are plenty good in the sense that they would be highly adaptive. Although a bird with half a wing wouldn't be able to fly as far or as rapidly as a bird with a full wing, it would still be able to escape predators more readily than a bird that had no wing or a quarter of a wing. Half an eye is highly adaptive because any light-sensitive organ would allow an organism to sense objects and navigate around them.

In the case of language, the ability to communicate with unconnected words, for which no grammatical rules exist, should improve communication profoundly. Indeed, as we shall later see, the use of words assumes a Theory of Mind and the ability to take turns in a conversation. It would therefore seem that different levels of human communication must have evolved before humans began to use the type of grammar with which we are now familiar and that they were sufficiently adaptive to justify the existence of fractions of language of the type that Chomsky appears to disdain.

These objections aside, Chomsky's arguments cannot overcome a basic empirical fact. The only type of evidence that could support an abrupt process is a mutation that would be orders of magnitude larger and more complex than any other mutation known to biologists, in short, a miracle. The second strategy, a *gradual* approach, recognized the evolution of different species during the long interval that followed the split between chimpanzees and our hominid ancestors. Although a gradualist approach eliminates the need for postulating a miraculous mutation, it replaces that problem with a new one, albeit one that is far less crucial. The gradualist position leaves room for discoveries of new and critical features of our ancestor's communicative repertoire whose features can always be interfaced between existing facets of gradualist knowledge.

CHOMSKY'S REVIEW OF VERBAL BEHAVIOR

One of Chomsky's main claims to fame was a highly influential review of *Verbal Behavior* (Chomsky, 1959) in which he exposed some fatal flaws in Skinner's theory of sentence construction. Consider, for example, an 8-year-old boy whose father told him that *Ted Williams, who spent a lot of time fishing with custom made fishing rods and who was also a famous pilot during World War II,* had the highest seasonal batting average in the records of baseball. Despite the gap of 22 words that separate the noun *Williams* and its predicate *had,* the boy would have no trouble understanding that sentence.

Chaining theory cannot explain an embedded sentence because each response can only take into account the step from one word to the next. It would therefore be unable to explain knowledge of relationships between nonadjacent words.

Chomsky also provided examples in which chaining theory could not even account for the meaning of adjacent words as, for example, in ambiguous sentences and phrases such as *they are visiting firemen* or *the shooting of hunters,* or in a nonsensical sentence, *green ideas sleep furiously,* which is meaningless but grammatically correct. Similarly, Skinner's theory of sentence construction cannot explain the sharp difference in meaning between such superficially similar sentences as *John is eager to please* and *John is easy to please.*

In his critique of *Verbal Behavior*, Chomsky explored grammars that were of greater complexity than the simple chains that Skinner espoused. He also devised grammars that could account for the effortless manner in which speakers of all languages were able to transform simple declarative sentences into other tenses; for example, *John throws the ball to Bill*, to its negative, interrogative, passive, and passive negative forms, respectively: *John is not throwing the ball to Bill, Did John throw the ball to Bill? John had thrown the ball to Bill*, and *John hadn't thrown the ball to Bill.*

Chomsky's paradigm for deriving grammar was to start with a rule of the simplest complexity that could account for a particular type of grammatical knowledge. If necessary, those rules would have to be modified to explain whatever the original grammar could not explain. We will not pursue more recent models of grammar that Chomsky and his students have proposed and, indeed are still proposing, because they are applicable to grammars that appeared long after language evolved.

More relevant are Chomsky's arguments that grammar is the distinguishing feature of language and that an innate language acquisition device (LAD) does the heavy lifting in learning language (Chomsky & Ronat, 1979). The LAD is an example of what cognitive psychologists refer to as a *module*; a functional portion of the brain that is dedicated to the control of a particular cognitive ability (e.g., perception, language, memory) (Cosmides & Tooby, 1992; Fodor, 1983).

In the case of language, the LAD has many functions that help to compensate for Chomsky's concept of the "impoverished stimulus." Chomsky argued that the verbal stimuli that a child experienced were too meager to explain her linguistic knowledge by any type of conditioning theory. Most words were learned after a single exposure to its referent, without any practice. Indeed, a mere 2 years after a child uttered her first word, her vocabulary increases dramatically to thousands of words, reaching a rate of acquiring new words that has been estimated to be as high as 1 word per hour. More impressive is a child's mastery of grammatical rules without any formal instruction. That led Chomsky to propose that the LAD allowed a child to effortlessly share the abstract rules of a universal grammar that the child never learned explicitly.

Chomsky and other linguists have asked, quite reasonably, how could so major a mechanism as an LAD have evolved by natural selection during the approximately 6 million years that have elapsed since humans and chimpanzees split from a common ancestor? To be sure, the point of Chomsky's question is not *whether* language evolved, but *how* natural selection could account for the sudden appearance (as measured in evolutionary time) of the most complex form of natural communication known to humans (Chomsky, 1986). Chomsky also asked, If there were such stages, what kind of grammars would they use?

Given the complexity of the LAD, Chomsky argued that it could not have evolved in what was the equivalent of an eye blink in evolutionary time. Instead, he suggested that the LAD took over a part of the brain that was used by some other function; say, navigation, by a process that is referred to as "exaptation" (Hauser, Chomsky, & Fitch, 2002). On this view, the LAD does not owe its existence to natural selection per se because it was already in place when the need to generate and comprehend grammatical utterances arose.

Some biologists, citing Darwin's concept of "pre-adaptation" (Gould, 1977; Gould & Vrba, 1982; Williams, 1966), have argued that many structures first appeared as exaptations. For example, wings were considered to be exaptations of structures whose original functions were predation and/or thermoregulation. It is important, however, to recognize that exapted structures are just as susceptible to the principle of natural selection as any other structures. As we saw earlier, partial functions can be useful. Primitive wings, for example, that could propel birds in flight for only a very short distance could be modified by natural selection for long distance flying. Similarly, a partial grammar that only provided rules for the present tense is more valuable than no grammar.

Ape Language Projects

Chomsky's controversial conclusion that only humans can use language didn't go unchallenged. Indeed, it provoked students of animal behavior to find evidence that he was wrong. They did so in experiments that sought to show that apes, chimpanzees in particular, could learn to use languages that required knowledge of sequences that followed particular rules.

There were many factors in the Zeitgeist of the 1960s and 1970s that contributed to the optimism that an ape could learn a grammatical language. As mentioned earlier, one was Skinner's renowned ability to train virtually any kind of behavior. Another was the discovery that the human and chimpanzee vocal apparatuses differed in ways that may have made it impossible for a chimpanzee to articulate human phones. Some investigators hypothesized that this difference could explain earlier failures to teach home-reared chimpanzees to speak English (Kellogg & Kellogg, 1933) or Russian (Kohts, 1935) and that a shift from an auditory to a visual language would be much more successful (Gardner, 1969).

The species that participated in these studies varied widely: parrots (Pepperberg, 1991), dolphins (Herman, Richards, & Wolz, 1984), orangutans (Miles, 1983), gorillas (Patterson, 1978), and chimpanzees, both *Pan troglodytes* (Gardner, 1969; Premack, 1971; Rumbaugh, Gill, & von Glasersfeld, 1973; Terrace, 1979a) and *Pan paniscus* (Savage-Rumbaugh, 1994).

Many of these projects presented data that purported to show that nonhuman animals could communicate by using language. If true, such claims would certainly question traditional criteria for distinguishing between humans and animals. A review of those claims, with which I strongly disagree, will also clarify why language remains a thorn in side of the theory of evolution. In the interest of brevity, I will focus on experiments that studied chimpanzees, the most popular subject of these projects. My conclusions, however, apply equally to any claims of language in other species.

During the mid-1960s, the Gardners began a project whose goal was to teach a chimpanzee to use American Sign Language (ASL), a natural gestural language used by thousands of deaf Americans (Bellugi & Siple, 1974; Lane, Boyes-Braem, & Bellugi, 1976; Stokoe, Casterline, & Croneberg, 1976). American Sign Language was the main medium of communication between Washoe (an infant female chimpanzee) and her caretakers and between the caretakers themselves while in Washoe's presence. At about the same time, Premack began a project in which he taught the principal subject of his study (a juvenile female chimpanzee named Sarah) to use an artificial visual language consisting of magnetized plastic shapes (Premack, 1971) of different colors, sizes, and shapes.

Sarah's education took place in a classroom in which combinations of various symbols were placed on a magnetic board. That set up allowed Premack to ask Sarah questions such as *Red = green?* If Sarah, who had access to the symbols for *yes* and *no,* replaced = with the symbol for *no,* her response was scored as correct. Unlike Washoe, who was raised with a family and a group of caretakers, Premack's paradigms allowed him to have strict control over Sarah's education. Rather than wait for language to emerge spontaneously, as one might with a child or Washoe, Premack devised specific training procedures for teaching Sarah various "atomic" components of language.

I need to digress for a moment to remind readers that grammar has two meanings: prescriptive and descriptive, and that our concern is only with descriptive grammars. Prescriptive grammar, which is what we learn in elementary school, states that the *correct* way to form sentences, e.g., *He went there*, rather than *He goed there; I'm not reading*, rather than *I ain't reading*, etc. Descriptive grammar consists of a set of rules that describe the formation of sentences, grammatically correct or not. For example, the sentence, *They are visiting firemen* can be generated by either of the following rules. The first meaning follows from a parsing of that sentence as a *noun phrase* (They) a *verb* (are) an *adverb* (visiting) and a *noun phrase* (firemen); the second, by parsing the same sentence as a *noun phrase* (They), an *auxiliary verb phrase* (are visiting) and a *noun phrase* (firemen).

Researchers studying ape language have, of course, focused on obtaining evidence of descriptive grammar. The have also accepted the widely held assumption that human language makes use of two levels of structure: the word and the sentence. In contrast to the fixed character of various forms of animal communication, the meaning of a word is arbitrary. One must keep in mind, however, that even though apes can learn substantial vocabularies of arbitrary symbols, there is no a priori reason to regard such accomplishments as evidence of human linguistic competence. Those accomplishments are examples of what Bates has referred to previously as Language 1. Their only function is to demand rewards. Dogs, rats, horses, pigeons, and other animals can also learn to produce arbitrary "words" to obtain specific rewards.

A second level of structure, Language 2, assumes the availability of an arbitrary vocabulary, a grammatical ability and the ability to converse. Sentences characteristically express propositions through words and phrases, each bearing particular grammatical relations to one another (actors, agents, objects, and so on). By following the rules of a grammar, a child can create an indefinitely large number of meaningful sentences from a finite number of words.

In an early diary report, the Gardners wrote, "Washoe used her signs in 29 different two sign combinations and four different combinations of three signs" (Brown, 1973). That report prompted Roger Brown to comment, "It was rather as if a seismometer left on the moon had started to tap out 'S-O-S'" (p. 211). Indeed, Brown, who was the most eminent psycholinguist of his time, compared Washoe's sequences of signs with the early sentences of a child and noted similarities in the structural meanings of Washoe and children's utterances (agent–action, agent–object, action–object, and so on).

Other projects reported similar combinations of two or more symbols. Sarah arranged plastic chips into strings (e.g., *Mary give Sarah apple*) (Premack, 1976). Lana, a juvenile female chimpanzee, was trained to use an artificial visual language of "lexigrams." Each lexigram, which was a combination of a specific geometric configuration and a specific colored background, was presented on the keys of a computer console or on a large visual display. After learning to use individual lexigrams, Lana learned to produce sequences of lexigrams (e.g., *Please machine give M&M*) (Rumbaugh et al., 1973). Because variations of these sequences occurred on the first occasion in which it was appropriate to use a particular lexigram, it was concluded that such sequences were actual sentences.

In a diary report, Roger Fouts, one of Washoe's main trainers, described what is arguably the most famous sequence of signs generated by a chimpanzee (Fouts, 1975). Washoe reportedly signed *water bird* after Fouts asked her, *What's that?* in the presence of a swan. What made this observation even more remarkable was the fact that Washoe did not have signs for specific water birds, swans in particular. It therefore seemed to Fouts that Washoe invented a way of conveying what she saw by a combination of signs.

Before we accept Fouts' rich interpretation of Washoe's sequence, it is necessary to rule out four simpler interpretations of *water bird*. (1) Washoe may have been prompted by Fouts to sign *water bird*. (2) Washoe may have signed *bird water*, but Fouts, out of habit, may have recorded Washoe's utterance in the order in which English-speaking people commonly combine adjectives and nouns. (3) Washoe may have signed *water* and *bird* as two separate utterances. (4) Fouts had previously trained Washoe to make the signs *water* and *bird* for food reward before the swan appeared and may have signed *water bird* for a food reward without any specific understanding of the meanings of those signs.

To eliminate such killjoy interpretations of these and other "sentences" that chimps were purported to have produced, I decided to start my own project whose goal was to obtain objective evidence of the grammatical ability of a chimpanzee (Terrace, 1979b). The subject was an infant chimpanzee, Nim Chimpsky, who was adopted by a family in New York when he was 2 weeks old. Nim was a young male chimpanzee that, like Washoe, had been reared by human surrogate parents in an environment in which ASL was the major medium of communication. Nim's trainers obtained evidence of his ability to use ASL by dictating the signs they observed him make, as well as their contexts, into miniature recorders and then transcribing their tapes immediately after each session.

Over the course of 2½ years, Nim's teachers recorded more than 20,000 combinations of two or more signs. Superficially, many of Nim's combinations appeared to be generated by simple finite-state grammatical rules (e.g., more + x; transitive verb + me or Nim). Indeed, many of Nim's multisign utterances resembled a child's initial multiword utterances (Braine, 1976; Bretherton & Bates, 1979; Nelson, 1981). All told, the corpus of Nim's utterances provided the strongest evidence to date of an ape's ability to create sentences.

Closer inspection showed otherwise. A frame-by-frame analysis of videotapes of Nim's signing revealed that his signs were nothing more than elaborate requests for rewards that he could not otherwise obtain and that there was no basis for interpreting the various sequences he produced as sentences (Terrace, 1979a,b).

The vast majority of Nim's signs, both in his single- and multi-sign utterances, occurred when his teachers withheld rewards until he signed. That ensured that Nim would sign as many multi-sign sequences that the teacher wanted before he received his reward. Nim's combinations were also full or partial imitations of signs that his teachers used as prompts. Thus, virtually none of Nim's sequences were spontaneous. When, for example, Nim wanted to play with a cat that his teacher brought to the classroom, he might sign *cat, Nim cat, me cat, hug cat, Nim hug cat* before his teacher handed him the cat. Even then, videotape analyses showed that the teacher prompted Nim continuously when by signing, *who that?* before removing the cat from its carrying case. Figure 1.10 shows Nim's trainer drilling him with the sign *cat* before the cat was released from her box at the beginning of this session. Figure 1.11 shows what appears to be a distinct three-item sequence, *me hug a cat.* However, closer inspection of Figure 1.12 reveals that they were triggered by the teacher's signs, whose names are printed at the bottom of the first three pictures.

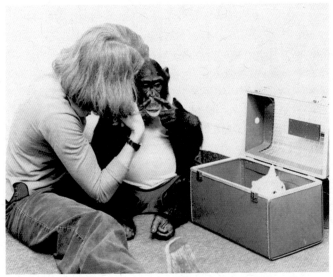

FIGURE 1.10 Nim Being Prompted to Sign "Cat" by His Teacher (Susan Quinby). Terrace, H.S. (1979) *Nim*, New York: Knopf.

FIGURE 1.11 Nim Signing the Combination *Me Hug Cat* to His Teacher (Susan Quinby). Terrace, H.S., Petitto, L.A., Sanders, R.J., & Bever, T.G. (1979). Can an Ape Create a Sentence. *Science, 206* (4421), 891–902.

FIGURE 1.12 Same as Figure 1.9 Except That Teacher's Signs Occurred Before Nim's Sign Had Been Added. Terrace, H.S., Petitto, L.A., Sanders, R.J., & Bever, T.G. (1979). Can an Ape Create a Sentence. *Science, 206* (4421), 891–902.

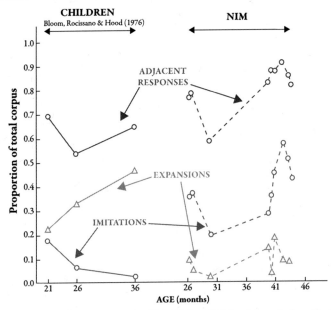

FIGURE 1.13 Proportion of utterances emitted by children (left-hand function) and by Nim (right-hand function) that are adjacent to, imitative of, or expansions of an adult's prior utterance. Terrace, H.S., Petitto, L.A., Sanders, R.J., & Bever, T.G. (1979). Can an Ape Create a Sentence. *Science*, 206 (4421), 891–902.

In hindsight, the meanings of Nim's signs were projections of his teachers, who directed all of their attention to his signing in the interest of obtaining objective records of each sign. So focused were they on Nim's signs that they were unaware of their nonspontaneous and imitative nature. It is, of course, true that young children imitate many of their parents' utterances. But, as shown in Figure 1.13, the relative frequency of utterances that a child imitates is substantially lower than that of a chimpanzee. Further, although the imitative phase in children is transitory, Nim never moved beyond that phase (Terrace, 1979a). Figure 1.14 shows that Nim's signing remained predominantly unspontaneous and imitative, unlike the highly accelerated growth of a child's vocabulary at the end of Stage I of language acquisition (Bloom, Rocissano, & Hood, 1976; Brown, 1973). Analyses of available films of other signing apes revealed similar patterns of unspontaneous and imitative discourse; for example, Washoe signing with the Gardners (Gardner & Gardner, 1973) and Koko signing with Patterson (Schroeder, 1977). Miles (1983) performed a discourse analysis of videotapes of the orangutan Chantek's signing with his teachers and reported that, "there is no evidence...that Chantek's multi-sign combinations...are sentences" (p. 53).

The conclusions of Project Nim were criticized on various methodological grounds by other investigators attempting to teach an ape to use sign language, for example, Gardner (1981) and Patterson (1981). However, these investigators have not revealed enough of their own procedures to show that they weren't immune to the same criticisms (Terrace, 1981, 1982). For example, while visiting the Washoe and Lana Projects, I noticed that the

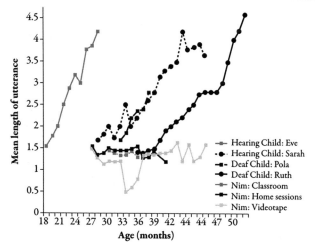

FIGURE 1.14 Mean length of signed utterances of Nim and three deaf children and mean length of spoken utterances of two hearing children. The functions showing Nim's MLU between January 1976 and August 1977 (age 26–45 months) is based upon video transcript data. Terrace, H.S., Petitto, L.A., Sanders, R.J., & Bever, T.G. (1979). Can an Ape Create a Sentence. *Science, 206* (4421), 891–902.

trainers on those projects regularly fed their chimpanzees with small pieces of food to motivate them to use the relevant "language." More importantly, I could have reached the same negative conclusion about Nim's signing just by looking at tapes of Nim, by looking at videotapes of other chimps using ASL or, for that matter, as an armchair psychologist who had no experience trying to teach an ape to use language. After all, anyone can invent a hypothesis. Until my hypothesis, whatever its origin, is refuted by contrary evidence, it provides the best explanation of an ape's signing.

All that would be needed to refute my hypotheses would be a single hour of *unedited* videotape of a chimpanzee that was purportedly signing with a human companion in which *both* parties were visible in each frame. That tape would reveal the extent to which the trainers prompted their chimps and whether the chimpanzee was given small rewards to keep it motivated to sign. During the 30 plus years that have elapsed since I published my conclusions, I have yet to see any evidence that challenged them.

ROTE SEQUENCES VERSUS SENTENCES

Different considerations led to a rejection of the claims that Sarah's and Lana's sequences were sentences. Thompson and Church (1980) analyzed a corpus of approximately 14,000 of Lana's combinations that were collected by a computer. They concluded that almost all of those combinations could be attributed to two nongrammatical processes: conditional discrimination and paired-associate learning. First, Lana learned paired associates, each consisting of a particular lexigram and a particular incentive (e.g., lexi-gram$_{apple}$ = apple). Lana then learned conditional discrimination rules that determined which of six stock sequences she should produce. For example, if the incentive was in view of the machine that dispensed rewards, the stock sequence would take the form, *Please machine give X, where X* refers to a symbolic version of that paired associate (e.g., the lexigrams *apple, M&M, banana,* and *chocolate*). If there were no incentive in view, the appropriate sequence would be, *Please put into machine X.* Typically, the paired-associate symbol was inserted into the last position of the stock sentence. Although Lana clearly understood the meanings of the paired-associates, in the sense that she could use them contrastively to make specific requests, there is no evidence that she understood the meanings of the other lexigrams. Similar arguments have been made about the plastic symbols that Sarah used to produce her sequences (Terrace, 1979).

THE COGNITIVE REVOLUTION

Behaviorists believed that mental processes, if they did indeed exist, took place in a "black box," which was not their concern. To address those processes they passed the buck to physiological psychologists whose job it was to find out how the black box worked. By contrast, the behaviorist's job was to describe the correlations between the inputs and the outputs of the black box, conditioned and unconditioned stimuli.

Computers, which began to be mass-produced during the 1950s, changed all that. Computer engineers used information theory, not only to predict output from input, but also to describe particular processes that intervened inside a computer in concrete and objective terms. Thus, mental processes could no longer be dismissed as a figment of the imagination. Of greater importance, models of cognitive events that were based on the architecture of a computer, and the software it ran, had greater predictive power than behavioral models that were based exclusively on observable input and output (Gardner, 1985). This was especially true of cognitive processes that required memory.

Without any means to describe memory, behaviorists had to rely on bizarre concepts to explain how a subject remembered stimuli; for example, the action of a stimulus over time, a process that has never been considered by any physicist. To the chagrin of many behaviorists, the memory component inside the black box allowed cognitive psychologists to increase its predictive value to a higher level than the behaviorists could achieve. Behaviorists could not ignore that fact because the ability to predict is a hallmark of "hard" sciences.

One unintended consequence of the cognitive revolution was the development of a parallel discipline, animal cognition. Although some behaviorists would regard animal cognition as an oxymoron, it is telling that most current investigators of animal cognition are former behaviorists. It would take us too far afield to review the impressive achievements of research in animal cognition. But it would be worthwhile to glance at some of those achievements, if for no other reason than to realize just how large a gap between animal communication and language remains even when these cognitive abilities were taken into account. Examples of animal cognition can be found in experiments on *concept formation* (Herrnstein, Loveland, & Cable, 1976; Wasserman & Bhatt, 1992), *delayed, symbolic and successive matching-to-sample* (Kendrick, Rilling, & Stonebraker, 1981; Wright, Santiago, Sands, & Urcuioli, 1984), *numerical ability* (Beran, Smith, Redford, & Washburn, 2006; Biro & Matsuzawa, 1999; Boysen & Capaldi, 1993; Brannon & Terrace, 1998; Cantlon & Brannon, 2006; Hauser, 1996), *serial learning* (Chen, Swartz, & Terrace, 1997; D'Amato & Colombo, 1988; Merritt, MacLean, Jaffe, & Brannon, 2007; Sands & Wright, 1980; Terrace, 1987; Terrace 2006; Terrace, Son, & Brannon, 2003), *metacognition* (Kornell, Son, & Terrace, 2007; Shields, Smith, & Washburn, 1997), *spatial learning* (Spetch & Kelly, 2006), *relational learning*, (Cook, Katz, & Cavoto, 1997; Young, Wasserman, & Dalrymple, 1997), *timing* (Breukelaar & Dalrymple-Alford, 1998; Gibbon, 1977; Meck & Church, 1983), and *transitive inference* (Treichler, Raghanti, & Van Tilburg, 2003), among others (see Zentall & Wasserman, 2012, for reviews of these and other recent experiments on animal cognition).

SERIAL LEARNING IN MONKEYS.

Further evidence of the nonsentential nature of Lana's (and Sarah's) sequences was provided by experiments that showed that monkeys could learn arbitrary sequences of photographs, such as a tree, a bird, a flower, and a person (Chen, Swartz, & Terrace, 1997). The lists on which the monkeys were trained differed radically from traditional tasks that have been used to train animals to learn an arbitrary sequence in a successive maze. Recall, for example, how a subject learns to navigate a maze by remembering how to respond at successive choice points (see Fig. 1.8a). Because those choice points are experienced in isolation from one another, there is no need to represent one's position in the sequence while navigating the maze. It was instead sufficient to recognize each choice point as an isolated stimulus of a *successive* chain and, to then respond appropriately.

Instead of training monkeys to learn successive chains, we trained them to learn *simultaneous* chains, a much more difficult task but one that was a closer approximation to a sentence than a successive chain. In contrast to a successive chain, all of the choice points that comprise a simultaneous chain were displayed at the same time (see Fig. 1.9b), typically on a touch-sensitive video monitor (Terrace, 1984).

Consider, for example, what you would have to do if you forgot the seven-digit personal identification number (PIN) that you need to operate your cash machine, say 9-2-1-5-8-4-7. On this machine the positions of the numbers were changed each time you tried to obtain cash. You could not enter your PIN by executing a sequence of distinctive motor movements, that is, by first touching the button in the lower right hand corner of the number pad to enter 9, then the button in the upper middle position to enter 2, and so on. Instead, you would have to search for each number and mentally keep track of your position in the sequence as you touched successive buttons.

As difficult as this task may seem, it would be far more difficult if you had to discover it by trial and error. Any error ended that trial and resulted in a new trial on which the digits were displayed in a different configuration. Thus, to determine your PIN, you would have to recall the consequences of any of the 21 types of logical errors you could make while attempting to produce the required sequence. Further, you would have to determine the first six digits without getting as much as a penny from the ATM. This is precisely the type of problem that monkeys had to solve at the start of training on each of four seven-item lists of photographs. Instead of cash, they were given banana pellets.

Figure 1.15 shows the items used to train monkeys to learn four simultaneous chains, each composed of new photographs. The monkey's task was to respond to each item in a particular order, regardless of its spatial position. To learn each list, subjects had to make logical errors while determining the ordinal position of each item at the start of training on a new list. A logical error is the first incorrect guess a subject makes to a particular item at a given position of the list; for example, responding to G on a seven-item list in the second position. Logical errors are made to obtain information by virtue of their consequences. Thus, G cannot be the second item because the trial was terminated. By definition, each type of *logical* error can occur only once. Although logical errors are necessary for discovering the ordinal position of an item, repetitions of the same error are not. *Repetitive* errors occur because the subject forgot the consequences of an earlier logical error.

Subjects acquired expertise at determining the ordinal position of each list item during the course of learning successive lists. The evidence was a steady decrease in the number of errors that occurred before satisfying the training criterion on successive lists. The likelihood of guessing the correct order in which to respond to the items of a novel seven-item

List One

List Two

List Three

List Four

FIGURE 1.15 Stimuli Used for Each of Four Seven-Item Lists That Were Trained by the Simultaneous Chaining Paradigm in Kornell, Son, and Terrace (2007). Terrace, H. S., Son, L. K., & Brannon, E. M. (2003). Serial expertise of Rhesus macaques. *Psychological Science, 14*, 66–73.

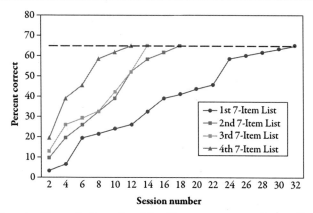

FIGURE I.16 Learning Curves for Seven-Item Lists. The mean accuracy of responding on each seven-item list during even-numbered sessions. The probability of executing a new seven-item list correctly by chance, assuming no backward errors, is 1/5,040 (1/7!). Note that the abscissa represents session (not list). Terrace, H. S., Son, L. K., & Brannon, E. M. (2003). Serial expertise of Rhesus macaques. *Psychological Science, 14*, 66–73.

list was less than one in 5,000. As can be seen in Figure 1.16, each monkey nevertheless needed progressively fewer sessions to satisfy the high accuracy criterion on these lists (criterion: 65% correctly completed trials in one session).

PROBLEM-SOLVING INTELLIGENCE

We have seen ample evidence that monkeys are surprisingly adept at memorizing long sequences and performing other serial tasks (Terrace, 2006). Monkeys, a species that has never been cited for its linguistic abilities, can learn rote sequences that are qualitatively similar to the sequences of signs, lexigrams, or plastic chips that chimpanzees were trained to produce by rote. Indeed, the number of items that constituted the sequences that monkeys learned to produce was nearly double the size of the sequences produced by apes in creating sentences. It appears therefore that the failure of various projects to train chimps to learn language and the ability of monkeys to learn long sequences constituted one of the two sides of the same coin. The sole function of the sequences that a chimpanzee acquired was to obtain various types of reward. In that sense, they are superficial examples of what linguists have referred to as *proto-imperatives;* verbal demands for a tangible reward (Bates, Camaioni, & Volterra, 1975).

I refer to those sequences as "superficial" proto-imperatives because the concept of a proto-imperative is only meaningful in the context of *proto-declaratives,* utterances that imply a speaker, a listener, and an exchange of information. It would, for example, be extravagant to claim that birdsong is an example of a proto-imperative because there is no expectation that birds could produce or understand proto-declaratives. As far as I'm aware, there is no evidence that a nonhuman animal can produce or understand proto-declaratives. Also, because proto-declaratives are spontaneous exchanges of new information expressed in an arbitrary manner, it is inconceivable that a paradigm could be devised to teach a nonhuman animal to use a proto-declarative.

SOCIAL INTELLIGENCE

At this point, it should be clear how to answer the question, What is missing in our account of the evolution of language? The answer is *social* intelligence. All of the experiments that we've considered thus far have been based on the assumption that once a nonhuman primate reaches a particular degree of *problem solving* intelligence, it would be ready to understand some of the complexities of language. In discussions of intelligence, in particular those that address animal intelligence, the emphasis has been on adopting items from tests of human intelligence that can be verbally translated into nonverbal behavior.

Although the use of touch-sensitive video screens has greatly facilitated this practice, virtually all of the problems used during the automatic administration of test items were inspired by examples of problem solving intelligence that were given to human subjects. In this connection, it is worth reminding the reader that Chomsky's concept of the "impoverished stimulus" during language training should include learning of social conventions that enable the use of conversational dialogue.

It appears that *conversation*, rather than grammar, defines the initial gap between animal communication and human language. There is nothing in animal communication that resembles the human ability to assume the roles of a speaker and a listener during a conversation. It is that ability that should be the primary concern of a theory of the evolution of language. A focus on conversation rather than a grammar would also reduce the gap between ape and human communication and render it into more manageable components because the step from animal communication to conversation is obviously smaller than a direct step from animal communication to a mechanism that has the complexity of a LAD.

Intersubjectivity

The mental life of an infant during her first year has become a new frontier in developmental psychology. For example, we now know that an infant a few hours old can imitate facial and manual gestures (Meltzoff & Moore, 1983), that a 4-month old infant can engage in spatial and numerical reasoning (Wang & Spelke, 2002; Lipton & Spelke, 2003), and that a 9-month old infant can direct the attention of others to inaccessible objects in her immediate environment (Bruner, 1977). These achievements are all the more impressive because they show that infants can think without language.

Investigators of animal cognition could reply that there is nothing special about an infant's mental life because birds, rats, monkeys, and chimpanzees also think without language. There is, however, one aspect of our mental life of that appears to be exclusively human. That is the concept of self. It goes without saying that the mere mention of self is likely to provoke controversy, if for no other reason than it lacks a simple definition. However, most psychologists find the concept of a "self" useful, especially when contrasted with "other," to refer to another person. We can also agree that without the concepts of the first and third person it would be meaningless to discuss language.

One compelling hypothesis about the origin of the concept of self is that it develops from intimate exchanges of mutual eye gaze between an infant and her mother soon after birth (Trevarthen, 1974). Those who argue for the continuity of cognitive events claim that the concept of self is innate on the grounds that it must derive from some cognitive antecedent and no such antecedents are available. I agree with that hypothesis in principle, but, given the state of the art, it would be helpful to have empirical data on infant-eye gaze interactions between non-human primate mothers and their offspring.

Psychologists often refer to the first year of an infant's life as *intersubjective*. Although the basis of that term may appear obvious, it is important to place it in a biological perspective. John Bowlby, a pioneer in the study of the emotional development of human infants, documented similarities in attachment behaviors in different primate species and human cultures (Bowlby, 1969). Bowlby viewed human attachment in the context of primate evolution, as did Harlow (Harlow, 1958; Harlow & Harlow, 1965) and Hinde (Hinde & Stevenson-Hinde, 1987). The significance of Bowlby's insights were highlighted by Winnicott (1986) and Klein and Riviere (1964) in object-relations theory, a psychoanalytic theory that describes the process of the developing mind in relation to others in the environment, in particular with an infant's mother.

Trevarthen (1974) and Stern (1977), both developmental psychologists, independently cited the importance of an infant's attachment to her mother and of the infant's ability to control communication between two individuals. Infants can control and predict the outcome of a moving object without any guidance from her mother. For example, she can predict what will happen when an object is dropped by virtue of her innate knowledge of physics (Spelke, Katz, Purcell, Ehrlich, & Breinlinger, 1994). However, an infant has to rely on her experience to control and predict the outcome of communication between herself and other individuals

By the age of 3 months, there is much evidence that an infant has begun to master each type of control. She looks at, listens to, and touches various inanimate objects but smiles, babbles, cries, coos, and laughs and points when she is in the presence of her mother. The mother's response is often predictable. She displays different facial expressions, engages in different displays of body language, talks in "motherese," sings, and so on Bruner (1983) presented a dramatic example of such interchanges while observing a 4-month-old infant playing peek-a-boo with her mother.

Most important is the time during which the infant and the mother gaze at each other. The outcome of those interactions can produce different emotional reactions in the infant and her mother. Those reactions are essential for the regulation of an infant's emotional state. For example, an infant's expression of fear can be quickly replaced by the mother's smile and her expression of contentment can be quickly replaced by the mother's frown or nonengagement. It is through these day-by-day interactions with her mother that the infant is said to develop a sense of other. The infant cannot always predict when her mother will smile or frown, but she can recognize when her mother's emotional state differs from hers.

As far as I'm aware, such intense interactions have not been observed in nonhuman primates. To be sure, there are examples of mutual eye gaze, laughter, and so on, but there is no evidence that they can be sustained with anything that approaches the intensity of the mother–infant relationship in humans. The most economical conclusion about the self–other distinction in nonhuman primates is that they rely on body language rather than another's mental state, to predict a conspecific's behavior. Indeed, there is virtually no evidence that a nonhuman primate entertains the possibility that their conspecifics have minds (Penn, Holyoak, & Povinelli, 2008).

JOINT ATTENTION

During the first 9 months of a human infant's life her interactions with her mother are dyadic; that is, they attend to each other rather than to objects in the environment (Bruner & Sherwood, 1976). That phase is often referred to as *primary intersubjectivity* in contrast to the next phase, *secondary intersubjectivity*, which normally begins at the age of 12 months. During secondary intersubjectivity, the infant and the mother begin to share attention to various objects in their environment; that is, they enter into *triadic* interactions or by the more transparent term *joint attention*. Discovered by Bruner (1975), and investigated by others (Tomasello, 1995), joint attention is regarded as foundational for establishing a declarative vocabulary. Once that process begins, the child is well on her way to learning language.

Joint attention requires mutual eye gaze between the infant and her mother to a particular object *and* the infant's acknowledgment that her mother is attending to that object. That acknowledgment, usually a smile, has been interpreted as evidence that the infant is sharing her perception with her mother's. Joint attention is often preceded by shifts in the infant's eye gaze from the object to her mother and from her mother to the object.

Joint attention is often regarded as the major cognitive achievement of infancy (Tomasello, 1999). Without joint attention, it is hard to imagine how vocabulary can be taught to an infant, or for that matter, how the infant can be taught to engage in any nonverbal activity (Premack, 1986). As (Tomasello, 1999) and (Hobson, 2002) have noted, there could be no sharing of cognitive events without joint attention, and that culture would not be possible.

The claim that joint attention is uniquely human has been questioned on the grounds that a similar phenomenon can be observed in nonhuman primates. To address those claims, it is important to distinguish between mutual eye gaze and what has erroneously been described as shared attention (Emery, Lorincz, Perrett, Oram, & Baker, 1997). Imagine two primates, each gazing in the direction of some object. This is not an example of joint attention because there is no coordination of their behavior when they gaze at the object and there is no evidence that one primate is aware of what the other primate sees.

As emphasized by Povinelli, there is a fundamental difference between gazing and specifically seeing an object (Povinelli & Vonk, 2003). Gazing describes a behavioral event; seeing a mental event. As in other instances of inferring mental events, the evidence is specific to particular forms of concomitant behavior. In the case of joint attention the infant's efforts to direct her mother's attention to an object by repetitively shifting her eye gaze between her mother and the object and by her smiles and coos when she achieves her goal, are behavioral markers of joint attention. As far as I'm aware, such behavior has not been observed in nonhuman primates.

CONCLUSIONS

1. Three anatomical changes that occurred after chimpanzees split off from our more immediate ancestors appear to have had a profound influence on the evolution of language. The first occurred when our ancestors shifted from quadrupedal to bipedal locomotion. That caused a reduction in the size of the pelvis and concomitantly the size of the birth canal. A second change was the loss of fur. That required a change in the way that mothers carried their newborn infants. Instead of hanging from her mother's hairs, infants born of mothers from the species *Homo erectus*, *Homo Neanderthal*, *Homo archaic sapiens*, and *Homo sapiens* had to cradle their infants in their arms.

2. At about the same time that our ancestors lost their fur, there was a shift in the color of the cornea from brown or black to white. That shift resulted in a sharply defined target for an infant to gaze at and vice versa.

3. Because the size of the human brain is larger than that of any other primate species, human infants were the least developed of any primate species at birth. As compared with chimpanzees, whose brains at birth are 40% to 50% the size of their adult brain, the size of a human infant's brain at birth is only 20% to 25% the size of an adult human's brain. An infant with a poorly developed brain, relatively plastic bones and poor coordination required more postnatal care than infants of any other nonhuman species.

4. Human infants have more extensive eye-to-eye contact with their mothers because their mothers cradle them much more than do mothers of nonhuman primates and because the most focused part of a newborn human infant's world is approximately 7.5 inches from her eyes. That is the natural distance between the eyes of a human infant and her mother.

5. During her first year, the infant experiences frequent mismatches between hers and her mother's emotional states; for example when the infant is happy, the mother may be sad, and vice versa. It has been suggested that those mismatches are responsible for the appearance of the concepts *self* and *other*. This is a crucial step in the development of an infant's theory of mind.

6. At the end of the first year, the infant enters into triadic relationships between herself, her mother, and environmental objects, a relationship that is often referred to as "joint attention." The infant's sense that her perception of an object matched her mother's, allowed them to refer to an object in the same manner. That foundation is essential for training vocabulary.

7. Concerted efforts to train chimpanzees to learn a language composed of arbitrary signs failed because the only function of the signs they learned was imperative.

8. Monkeys are able to learn long sequences of arbitrary items, an ability that Skinner and other behaviorists thought would be sufficient for creating sentences. They weren't because, in addition to intelligence for solving problems, language requires social intelligence.

9. During the recent resurgence of interest in the evolution of language, the predominant strategy was to equate language and grammar. That approach was heavily influenced by Chomsky, who wondered how language could have evolved from the involuntary, innate, and immutable grunts of chimpanzees, our nearest living ancestor. Indeed, Chomsky's skepticism about the relevance of evolution is understandable if the goal of a theory of the evolution of language is to explain the huge jump from chimpanzee communication to grammatical human languages. Chomsky argued that that jump had to occur full-blown, without any intervening steps.

10. Chomsky ruled out a gradual evolution of language because it didn't seem sensible to rely on fractions of a full-blown (modern) grammar. The goal of this chapter was to explain why, even before grammar became an issue, many uniquely human nonverbal skills had to evolve before any form of verbal communication could have evolved. The most important of these are joint attention and a theory of mind.

Note

1. It is important to distinguish between two types of communication: production and comprehension. Production is a more conservative test of communicative skills because it is much less susceptible to uncontrolled nonlinguistic cues (Bybee & Slobin, 1982).

REFERENCES

Bates, E. (1976). Sensorimotor performatives. In. In E. Bates (Ed.) *Language and Communication: The Acquisition of Pragmatics* (pp. 49–71). London: Academic Press.

Bates, E., Camaioni, L., & Volterra, V. (1975). The acquisition of performatives prior to speech. *Merill-Palmer Quarterly, 21*, 205–226.

Beran, M. J., Smith, J. D., Redford, J. S., & Washburn, D. A. (2006). Rhesus macaques monitor uncertainty during numerosity judgments. *Journal of Experimental Psychology: Animal Behavior Processes, 32*, 111.

Bellugi, U. & Siple, P. (1974). *Remembering with and without words; current problems in psycholinguistics*. Paris, France: Centre de National de la Recherche Scientifique.

Biro, D., & Matsuzawa, T. (1999). Numerical ordering in a chimpanzee (pan troglodytes): Planning, executing and monitoring. *Journal of Comparative Psychology, 113*, 178–185.

Bloom, L., Rocissano, L., & Hood, L. (1976). Adult-Child discourse: Developmental interaction between information processing and linguistic knowledge. *Cognitive Psychology, 8*, 521–552.

Bowlby, J. (1969). *Attachment and Loss: Separation: anxiety and anger*. New York: Basic Books.

Boysen, S. T., & Capaldi, E. J. (1993). *The Development of Numerical Competence: Animal and Human Models*. Hillsdale, NJ: Erlbaum.

Braine, M. D. S. (1976). Children's first word combinations. *Monographs of the Society for Research in Child Development, 41*, 1–96.

Brannon, E., & Terrace, H. (1998). Ordering of the numerosities 1–9 by monkeys. *Science, 282*, 746–749.

Bretherton, I., & Bates, E. (1979). The emergence of intentional communication. *New Directions for Child Development, 4*, 81–100.

Breukelaar, J. W. C., & Dalrymple-Alford, J. C. (1998). Timing ability and numerical competence in rats. *Journal of Experimental Psychology: Animal Behavior Processes, 24*, and 84.

Brown, R. (1973). *A First Language: The Early Stage*. Cambridge, MA: Harvard University Press.

Bruner, J. S. (1975). From communication to language: A psychological perspective. *Cognition, 3*, 255–287.

Bruner, J. S. (1975). The ontogenesis of speech acts. *Journal of Child Language, 2*, 1–19.

Bruner, J. S. (1977). Early social interaction and language acquisition. In H. R. Schaffer (Ed.), *Studies in Mother-Infant Interaction* (pp. 271–289). London: Academic Press.

Bruner, J. S. (1983). *Child's Talk: Learning to Use Language*. New York: Norton.

Bruner, J. S., & Sherwood, V. (1976). Peekaboo and the learning of rule structures. In J. S. Bruner, A. Jolly, & K. Sylva (Eds.), *Play: Its Role in Development and Evolution* (pp. 277–287). Harmondsworth, UK: Penguin.

Bybee, J., & Slobin, D. (1982). Rules and schemas in the development and use of the english past tense. *Language, 58*, 265–289.

Cantlon, J., & Brannon, E. (2006). Shared system for ordering small and large numbers in monkeys and humans. *Psychological Science, 17*, 401–406.

Chen, S., Swartz, K., & Terrace, H. (1997). Knowledge of the ordinal position of list items in rhesus monkeys. *Psychological Science, 8*, 80–86.

Cheney, D. L., & Seyfarth, R. M. (1986). The recognition of social alliances by vervet monkeys. *Animal Behavior, 34*, 1722–1731.

Chomsky, N. (1955). *The logical structure of linguistic theory*. New York: Plenum. Published in 1975.

Chomsky, N. (1959). A review of skinner's verbal behavior. *Language, 35*, 26–58.

Chomsky, N., & Ronat, M. (1977). *On Language*. New York, NY: Flammarion.

Chomsky, N. (1986). *Knowledge of Language*. Westport, CT: Praeger.

Cook, R., Katz, J., & Cavoto, B. (1997). Pigeon same-different concept learning with multiple stimulus classes. *Journal of Experimental Psychology: Animal Behavior Processes, 23*, 417–433.

Cosmides, L., & Tooby, J. (1992). Cognitive adaptations for social exchange. In C. T. Barkow (Ed.), *The Adapted Mind: Evolutionary Psychology and the Generation of Culture*. New York: Oxford University Press.

D'Amato, M. R., & Colombo, M. (1988). Representation of serial order in monkeys (*Cebus apella*). *Journal of Experimental Psychology: Animal Behavior Processes, 14*, 131–139.

Darwin, C. (1871). *The Descent of Man and Selection in Relation to Sex*. Princeton, NJ: Princeton University Press.

Darwin, C. (1872). *The Expression of Emotions in Man and Animals*. London: J. Murray.

Dawkins, R. (1996). *The Blind Watchmaker: Why the Evidence of Evolution Reveals a Universe without Design*. New York, NY: W. W. Norton.

Dobzhansky, T. (1973). Nothing makes sense in biology except in the light of evolution. *American Biology Teacher, 35*, 125–129.

Emery, N. J., Lorincz, E. N., Perrett, D. I., Oram, M. W., & Baker, C. I. (1997). Gaze following and joint attention in rhesus monkeys (macaca mulatta). *Journal of Comparative Psychology, 111*, 286–293.

Fodor, J. (1983). *Modularity of Mind*. Cambridge, MA: MIT Press.

Fouts, R. S. (1975). Capacity for language in great apes. In R. Tuttle (Ed.), *Socioecology and Psychology of Primates* (pp. 371–390). Chicago: Mouton Publishers.

Gardner, B. T. (1981). Project Nim: Who taught whom? *Contemporary Psychology, 26*, 425–426.

Gardner, H. (1985). *The Minds New Science: A History of the Cognitive Revolution*. New York: Basic Books.

Gardner, R. A., & Gardner, B. T. (1973). *Teaching Sign Language to the Chimpanzee: Washoe* [Motion Picture]. University Park, PA: Psychological Cinema Register.

Gardner, W. M. (1969). Auto shaping in bobwhite quail. *Journal of Experimental Analysis of Behavior, 12*, 279–281.

Gibbon, J. (1977). Scalar expectancy theory and weber's law in animal timing. *Psychological Review, 84*, 279–325.

Gould, S. J. (1977). *Ontogeny and Phylogeny*. Cambridge, MA: Harvard University Press.

Gould, J. (1982) Ethology: The mechanisms and evolution of behavior. New York W.W. Norton

Gould, S. J., & Vrba, E. S. (1982). Exaptation: A missing term in the science of form. *Paleobiology, 8*, 4–15.

Harlow, H. F. (1958). *The Nature of Love*. New York: American Psychological Association.

Harlow, H. F., & Harlow, M. K. (1965). The affectional systems. *Behavior of Nonhuman Primates, 2*, 287–334.

Hauser, M., Chomsky, N., & Fitch, W. T. (2002). The faculty of language: What is it, who has it, and how did it evolve? *Science, 298,* 1569–1579.

Hauser, M. D.,. M. P. &. W. M. (1996). Numerical representations in primates. *Proceedings of the National Academy of Sciences, 93,* 1514–1517.

Herman, L. M., Richards, D. G., & Wolz, J. P. (1984). Comprehension of sentences by bottle-nosed dolphins. *Cognition, 16,* 129–219.

Herrnstein, R. J., Loveland, D. H., & Cable, C. (1976). Natural concepts in pigeons. *Journal of Experimental Psychology: Animal Behavior Processes, 2,* 285–302.

Hill, E. L. (2001). Non-Specific nature of specific language impairment: A review of the literature with regard to concomitant motor impairments. *International Journal of Language & Communication Disorders, 36,* 149–171.

Hinde, R. A., & Stevenson-Hinde, J. (1987). Interpersonal relationships and child development* 1. *Developmental Review, 7,* 1–21.

Hobson, P. (2002). *The Cradle of Thought: The Origins of Thinking.* London, Macmillan.

Kellogg, L. A., & Kellogg, W. N. (1933). *The Ape and the Child: A Study of ENVIRONMENTAL influence and Its Behavior.* New York, NY: McGraw-Hill.

Kendrick, D., Rilling, M., & Stonebraker, T. (1981). Stimulus control of delayed matching in pigeons: Directed forgetting. *Journal of the Experimental Analysis of Behavior, 36,* 241–251.

Kenneally, C. (2007). *The First Word: The Search for the Origins of Language.* New York: Viking.

Klein, M., & Riviere, J. (1964). *Love, Hate and Reparation.* New York, NY: W. W. Norton.

Kohts, N. (1935). *Infant Ape and Human Child.* Moscow: Museum Darwinianum.

Kornell, N., Son, L., & Terrace, H. (2007). Are monkeys metacognitive? *Psychological Science, 18,* 64–71.

Lane, H. (1976). *The Wild Boy of Aveyron.* Cambridge, MA: Harvard University Press.

Lane, H., Boyes-Braem, P., & Bellugi, U. (1976). Preliminaries to a distinctive feature analysis of American Sign Language. *Cognitive Psychology, 8,* 262–289.

Lipton, J., & Spelke, E. (2003). Origins of number sense: Large number discrimination in human infants. *Psychological Science, 14,* 396–401.

Masters, J. C., & Rimm, D. C. (1987). *Behavior Therapy: Techniques and Empirical Findings.* San Diego: Harcourt Brace Jovanovich.

Meck, W. H., & Church, R. M. (1983). A mode control model of counting and timing processes. *Journal of Experimental Psychology: Animal Behavior Processes, 9,* 320–334.

Meltzoff, A. N., & Moore, M. (1983). Newborn infants imitate adult facial gestures. *Child Development, 54,* 702–709.

Merritt, D., MacLean, E., Jaffe, S., & Brannon, E. (2007). A comparative analysis of serial ordering in ring-tailed lemurs (lemur catta). *Journal of Comparative Psychology, 121,* 363–371.

Miles, H. L. (1983). Apes and language: The search for communicative competence. In J. de Luce & H. T. Wilder (Eds.), *Language in Primates: Perspectives and Implications* (pp. 43–61). New York: Springer-Verlag.

Mundy, P., Sigman, M., & Kasari, C. (1990). A longitudinal study of joint attention and language development in autistic children. *Journal of Autism and Developmental Disorders, 20,* 115–128.

Nelson, K. (1981). Individual differences in language development: Implications for development and language. *Development of Psychology, 17,* 170–187.

Ornitz, E. M., Guthrie, D., & Farley, A. H. (1977). The early development of autistic children. *Journal of Autism and Childhood Schizophrenia, 7,* 207–229.

Patterson, F. G. (1978). The gestures of a gorilla: Language acquisition by another pongid. *Brain and Language, 12,* 72–97.

Patterson, F. G. (1981). Ape language. *Science, 211,* 86–87.

Penn, D. C., Holyoak, K. J., & Povinelli, D. J. (2008). Darwin's mistake: Explaining the discontinuity between human and nonhuman minds. *Behavioral and Brain Sciences, 31,* 109–129.

Pepperberg, I. (1991). Language acquisition and form in a bilingual environment: A framework for studying birdsong in zones of sympatry. *Ethology, 89,* 1–26.

Povinelli, D., & Vonk, J. (2003). Chimpanzee minds: suspiciously human? *Trends in Cognitive Science, 7,* 157–160.

Premack, D. (1971). Language in a chimpanzee? *Science, 172,* 808–822.

Premack, D. (1976). *Intelligence in Ape and Man.* Hillsdale, NJ: Erlbaum.

Premack, D. (1986). *Gavagai.* Cambridge, MA: The MIT Press.

Romanes, G. (1884). *Mental Evolution in Animals.* New York: AMS Press.

Ruff, C. B. (1991). Climate and body shape in hominid evolution. *Journal of Human Evolution, 21,* 81–105.

Rumbaugh, D. M., Gill, T. V., & von Glasersfeld, E. C. (1973). Reading and sentence completion by a chimpanzee. *Science, 182,* 731–733.

Sands, S. F., & Wright, A. A. (1980). Primate memory: Retention of serial list items by a rhesus monkey. *Science, 209,* 938.

Savage-Rumbaugh, E. S. (1994). *Kanzi: The Ape at the Brink of the Human Mind.* New York: Wiley.

Schroeder, B. (1977). *Koko: The Talking Gorilla* [Motion Picture]. Home Vision.

Shields, W. E., Smith, J. D., & Washburn, D. A. (1997). Uncertain responses by humans and rhesus monkeys (*macaca mulatta*) in a psychophysical same-different task. *Journal of Experimental Psychology: General, 126,* 147–164.

Skinner, B. F. (1938). *The behavior of organisms.* New York, NY: Appleton-Century-Crofts.

Skinner, B. F. (1945). The operational analysis of psychological terms. *Psychological Review, 52,* 270–277.

Skinner, B. F. (1953). *Science and Human Behavior.* New York: Macmillan.

Skinner, B. F. (1957). The experimental analysis of behavior. *American Scientist, 45,* 343–371.

Skinner, B. F. (1959). *Cumulative Record* (pp. 158–182). New York: Appleton-Century-Crofts.

Skinner, B. F. (1960). Pigeons in a pelican. *American Psychologist, 15,* 28–37. doi:10.1037/h0045345

Spelke, E., Katz, G., Purcell, S., S., Ehrlich, S. M., & Breinlinger, K. (1994). Early knowledge of object motion: continuity and inertia. *Cognition, 51,* 131–176.

Spencer, H. (1886). *The Principles of Psychology.* New York: Appleton.

Spetch, M. L., & Kelly, D. M. (2006). Comparative spatial cognition: Processes in landmark-and surface-based place finding. In E. A. Wasserman & T. R. Zentall (Eds.), *Comparative Cognition: Experimental Explorations of Animal Intelligence* (pp. 210–228), New York, NY: Oxford University Press.

Spiegel, R. (2003). *Psychopharmacology: An Introduction.* Chichester, UK: John Wiley & Sons.

Stern, D. N. (1977). *The First Relationship: Infant and Mother.* Cambridge, MA: Harvard University Press.

Stern, D. N., Beebe, B., Jaffe, J., & Bennett, S. L. (1977). The infant's stimulus world during social interaction: A study of caregiver behaviours with particular reference to repetition and timing. In H. R. Schaffer (Ed.), *Studies in Mother-Infant Interaction* (pp. 177–202). London: Academic Press.

Stokoe, W. C., Casterline, D. C., & Croneberg, C. G. (1976). *A Dictionary of American Sign Language on Linguistic Principles.* Silver Spring, MA: National Association of the Deaf.

Terrace, H. (1979a). How Nim Chimpsky changed my mind. *Psychology Today, 13,* 65–76.

Terrace, H. (1979b). Is problem solving language? A review of Premack's intelligence in apes and man. *Journal of the Experimental Analysis of Behavior, 31,* 161–175.

Terrace, H. (1981). Reply to Bindra and Patterson. *Science, 211,* 87–88.

Terrace, H. (1982). Why Koko can't talk. *The Sciences, 22,* 8–10.

Terrace, H. (1984). Simultaneous chaining: The problem it poses for traditional chaining theory. In M. Commons, R. Herrnstein, & A. Wagner (Eds.), *Quantitative Analyses of Behavior: Discrimination Processes* (pp. 115–138). Cambridge, MA: Ballinger.

Terrace, H. S. (2006). The simultaneous chain: A new look at serially organized behavior. In E. A. Wasserman & T. R. Zentall (Eds.), *Comparative Cognition: Experimental Explorations of Animal Intelligence* (pp. 481–514). New York: Oxford University Press.

Terrace, H. (1987). Chunking by a pigeon in a serial learning task. *Nature, 325,* 149–151.

Terrace, H., Son, L., & Brannon, E. (2003). Serial expertise of rhesus macaques. *Psychological Sciences, 14,* 66–73.

Terrace, H. S. (1979). *Nim.* New York: A. Knopf.

Thompson, C. R., & Church, R. M. (1980). An explanation of the language of a chimpanzee. *Science, 208,* 313–314.

Tomasello, M. (1995). Language is not an instinct. *Cognitive Development, 10,* 131–156.

Tomasello, M. (1999). Having intentions, understanding intentions, and understanding communicative intentions. In J. W. Astington, D. R. Olson, & P. D. Zelazo (Eds.), *Developing Theories of Intention: Social Understanding and Self-Control* (pp. 63–76). Mahwah, NJ: Erlbaum.

Tomasello, M., Hare, B., & Agnetta, B. (1999). Chimpanzees, pan troglodytes, follow gaze direction geometrically. *Animal Behaviour, 58,* 769–777.

Treichler, F. R., Raghanti, M. A., & Van Tilburg, D. N. (2003). Linking of serially ordered lists by macaque monkeys: List position influences. *Journal of Experimental Psychology: Animal Behavior Processes, 29,* 211. doi:10.1037/0097-7403.29.3.211

Trevarthen, C. (1974). The psychobiology of speech development. *Language and Brain: Developmental Aspects. Neurosciences Research Program Bulletin, 12,* 570–585.

Trevarthen, C., & Hubley, P. (1978). Secondary intersubjectivity: Confidence, confiding, and acts of meaning in the first year. In A. Lock (Ed.), *Action, Gesture, and Symbol: The Emergence of Language.* New York: Cambridge University Press.

Wang, R. F., & Spelke, E. S. (2002). Human spatial representation: Insights from animals. *Trends in Cognitive Sciences, 6,* 376–382.

Wasserman, E., & Bhatt, A. (1992). Conceptualization of natural and artificial stimuli by pigeons. In W. Honig, & K. Fetterman (Eds.), *Cognitive Aspects of Stimulus Control* (pp. 203–223). Hillsdale, NJ: Erlbaum.

Williams, G. C. (1966). *Adaptation and Natural Selection.* Princeton, NJ: Princeton University Press.

Windsor, J., Glaze, L., Koga, S. (2007). Language acquisition with limited input: Romanian institution and foster care. *Journal of Speech, Language, and Hearing Research, 50,* 1365–1381.

Winnicott, D. W. (1986). The newborn and his mother. In C. Winnicott. et al. (Eds.), *Babies and Their Mothers* (pp. 35–49). Reading, MA: Addison-Wesley.

Wright, A., Santiago, H., Sands, S., & Urcuioli, P. (1984). *Animal Cognition: Pigeon and Monkey Serial Probe Recognition: Acquisition, Strategies, and Serial Position Effects.* Hillsdale, NJ: Erlbaum.

Young, M. E., Wasserman, E. A., & Dalrymple, R. M. (1997). Memory-Basedsame-Different conceptualization by pigeons. *Psychonomic Bulletin & Review, 4,* 552–558.

Zentall, T., & Wasserman, E. (Eds.). (2012). *The Oxford Handbook of Comparative Cognition.* New York, NY: Oxford University Press.

FIGURE 1.8 The Difference in the Color of the Pigment of the Sclera in Chimpanzees (a) and Humans (b).

2 How Joint Is the Joint Attention of Apes and Human Infants?

Malinda Carpenter and Josep Call

RECENTLY THERE HAS been much debate about whether chimpanzees and other apes engage in joint attention: Some researchers (e.g., Leavens & Racine, 2009; Tanner & Byrne, 2010) argue that they do, whereas others (e.g., Tomasello, Carpenter, Call, Behne, & Moll, 2005) argue that they do not. A similar debate is emerging in developmental psychology, as some researchers argue that joint attention emerges ontogenetically around 9 to 12 months of age (e.g., Tomasello, 1995), whereas others argue that it emerges much earlier (e.g., Grossmann & Johnson, 2010; Striano & Bertin, 2005). However, different participants in these debates often use different definitions of joint attention, a problem that likely is responsible for much of the disagreement in both areas. Thus, in the hopes of eventually clearing up some of these disagreements, in this chapter we first argue for the adoption of a relatively conservative definition of joint attention—one that requires the coordination of attention in joint attention to be truly *joint*. Then we examine the empirical evidence relevant for determining whether apes—and when human infants—engage in joint attention under this definition. We conclude that whereas human infants engage in truly joint joint attention by 1 year of age, there is so far little if any convincing evidence that chimpanzees and other apes do. We end by discussing possible reasons for differences between humans and apes in joint attention and other related abilities such as joint action.

What Makes Joint Attention Joint?

The classic definition of joint attention involves a triadic interaction in which two individuals coordinate attention to an object of mutual interest (e.g., Bakeman & Adamson, 1984). Across time, this definition has been pulled in different directions by different researchers. Some focus more on the "triadicness" and the fact that the two individuals are looking at the same thing, whereas others focus more on the coordination aspect of it and the active *sharing* of attention. For example, in the former group, Leavens and Racine (2009, p. 241) define joint attention as "the intentional co-orientation of two or more organisms to the same locus," with "at least one of the organisms" doing something intentionally so as to end up focusing on the same thing as the other. They take a variety of triadic behaviors as evidence of joint attention; for example, gaze following, gesturing about objects (including requests), and social referencing. In contrast, the latter group of researchers (including the authors) argue that attending to the same thing that one's partner is attending to is not enough for joint attention: In addition, it is crucial that both partners *know together* that they are attending to the same thing (see, e.g., Tomasello, 1995). In this view, both partners are (at least eventually) equally involved, *actively sharing* attention *about* the thing. This is what makes joint attention joint, rather than just parallel attention to the same object.

To help see the difference between these two approaches, imagine a gaze following situation in which one individual sees another turn to look at something, and then turns to look at it himself. Both individuals are now simultaneously attending to the same thing. But where is the jointness here? They may be looking at the same thing but they are not necessarily doing so *together*. Gaze following can be done in a unilateral, even exploitative manner, and the looker need not even know that the follower is present, much less sharing attention (note that some other triadic behaviors such as social referencing can work in this unilateral, exploitative way as well). Similarly, imagine a situation in which one individual uses a gesture like a reach or point to direct another individual's attention to an object. Again, they may end up looking at the same object simultaneously but where is the jointness here? The gesturer could simply want the recipient to see the object individually; for example, so that the recipient gives it to him or is informed about it. Thus, many triadic behaviors can involve parallel, rather than joint or shared attention.

Let us be clear that we are not claiming that behaviors such as gaze following and attention-directing gestures are not joint attention, just that they are not *necessarily* joint attention. There are clearly cases in which these behaviors can involve participants knowing together that they are sharing attention. The challenge for researchers who claim that chimpanzees or very young infants engage in joint attention is thus to provide evidence of this knowing together—the third leg of the "joint attentional triangle" (see Fig. 2.1).

The most commonly used evidence of this knowing together or sharing of attention is gaze alternation between the object of interest and the eyes/face of the partner. However, gaze alternation alone is not enough to prove the existence of joint attention because

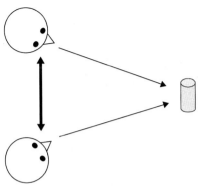

FIGURE 2.1 The joint attention triangle. The double, bold arrow represents the crucial "knowing together" or sharing component of joint attention.

there are many situations in which one might look back and forth between an object and a social partner without coordinating attention with that individual. Gaze alternation can be a sign of alternating or checking attention, rather than of coordinated attention (Tomasello, 1995).

If it is so difficult to know whether two individuals are engaging in joint attention, then how do we know that human infants (at any age) do it? One approach is to look for interactions in which the sole purpose is to share attention about objects or events: joint attentional engagement and declarative gestures (in other words, participants' production of joint attention behaviors). Another approach is to conduct experiments aimed at determining whether participants recognize whether they have shared attention with others about something (i.e., participants' comprehension of whether they have been in joint attentional engagement with someone). We turn to both of these types of evidence now, focusing (very briefly) on the few studies that have addressed this question directly.

Evidence for Joint Attentional Engagement, Declarative Gestures, and "Knowing Together" in Human Infants

By 9 months of age, most typically developing human infants have started participating in interactions thought to involve joint attentional engagement (e.g., Carpenter, Nagell, & Tomasello, 1998). The classical operational definition of (coordinated) joint engagement involves a look to a caregiver's face/eyes about an object or event in the infant's and caregiver's mutual focus of attention (i.e., an object that they both have just been looking at, and will turn back to again afterward) (e.g., Bakeman & Adamson, 1984). However, we think it likely that this type of operational definition may sometimes result in false positives, and thus that coding schemes that capture the quality of the looks to the social partner, like the one Hobson and Hobson (2007) used with much older children to distinguish "sharing" from "checking" and "orienting" looks, would be more useful in identifying true joint attentional engagement. When infants' looks to the adult in these

FIGURE 2.2 Sequential frames from a video of a 9-month-old initiating joint attention with his mother. (a) He watches as his mother makes a rubber duck they are both looking at squeak. (b) He looks to his mother's face with a smile to share attention and interest with her.

interactions are true sharing looks (e.g., see Fig. 2.2b), we think previous researchers are justified in describing these interactions as a "meeting of minds" (e.g., Bruner, 1995).

Luckily, at around the same age as they begin initiating mutual gaze about objects, infants begin to produce so-called declarative gestures,[1] and this makes the diagnosis of joint attention much more straightforward. Infants' first declarative gestures are usually shows (i.e., holding up an object toward an adult's face with a look and smile to the adult); then around age 12 months infants start pointing to more distal objects (again with an accompanying look and smile to the adult) to share attention and interest about the objects with the adult (e.g., Carpenter et al., 1998; for more on declarative pointing, see chapter 8).

The theory is that with both joint attention looks and declarative gestures, sharing attention with the other person is an end in itself (e.g., Gómez, Sarriá, & Tamarit, 1993). However, there are other plausible interpretations of these behaviors, so it is important to test empirically what infants are attempting to do when they perform them. One way to test this is to experimentally manipulate the adult's reaction to infants' looks or gestures, in order to rule out possible lower-level explanations. Most work in this area has been done on declarative pointing because it is so easy to elicit and code in infants. For example, following Perucchini and Camaioni (1993), one way to know whether infants are pointing simply because they want to obtain the object they are pointing to, instead of to share attention, is to have the adult respond to the infants' points with just a comment and smile ("Oh, that's nice!"). If infants are satisfied with this reaction, then that is apparently all they wanted from her, whereas if they keep pointing, then they probably want to obtain the object. Using this method, Carpenter et al. (1998) found that declarative pointing emerged at 12 months, on average, in their longitudinal sample. Similarly, we have tested whether infants are pointing simply to gain rewarding positive emotions to the self (Bates et al., 1975; Moore & D'Entremont, 2001) or just so that the adult sees the object for herself, rather than to share attention about the object. We found that if an adult responds to 12-month-olds' points by speaking enthusiastically with positive emotion only to infants (ignoring the object), infants are apparently unsatisfied and repeat their pointing. They show the same response if the adult just looks at the object silently. However, if the adult responds with joint attention (alternating gaze between the infant and the object while speaking with positive emotion), infants are satisfied with her reaction and do not repeat their point (Liszkowski, Carpenter, Henning, Striano, & Tomasello, 2004).

Further studies show that 12-month-olds repair adult misunderstandings about the precise referent of their declarative points (Liszkowski, Carpenter, & Tomasello, 2007b), so their points are clearly *about* something specific. Twelve-month-olds can even point declaratively about absent referents—objects that were previously present but that have now been taken away (Liszkowski, Carpenter, & Tomasello, 2007a)—showing that the sharing of attention and interest takes place on a mental level (and is not simply about having the adult physically turn and look at something). Finally, by 18 months of age, infants point selectively to referents that are relevant to their previously shared experiences with the particular person for whom they are pointing (Liebal, Carpenter, & Tomasello, 2010). Thus, 1-year-old infants show great flexibility and complexity in their declarative pointing, inviting others to share attention with them to specific, relevant, and even currently perceptually absent things.

But what evidence is there that infants at this age understand that they and the adult know together that they are sharing attention? The most direct evidence of this comes from a study by Moll, Richter, Carpenter, and Tomasello (2008). They had 14-month-olds share (i.e., interact excitedly about) three objects with an adult in sequence, one of them in a special way (they encountered it several times on the way to the testing room). When later the adult gestured excitedly toward the three objects together on a tray and ambiguously requested, "Wow, look, can you give it to me please?" infants gave her the object they had shared in a special way. To test the possibility that infants simply gave the adult that object because it was special for them, individually (not because it was the one they had shared together), Moll and colleagues included a control condition in which infants shared the three objects with the adult exactly as before, one in a special way, but then a *different* adult ambiguously requested one of the objects in exactly the same manner. If infants were just choosing the special object because it was most interesting to them, they should have chosen it in this condition too, but they did not—they chose that object at chance levels. To test the possibility that infants gave the adult the special object because it was the object that was apparently special for *her*, in another control condition infants watched as the adult experienced the objects individually (again, one in a special way) and then requested one of the objects from them ambiguously. Again, in this condition infants chose the special object at chance levels. In summary, infants responded not based on what they themselves knew about the objects, nor based on what the adult knew individually, but instead based on what they knew together with the adult. By 14 months, infants thus know what "we" know together (see also, e.g., Liebal, Behne, Carpenter, & Tomasello, 2009; Liebal et al., 2010; Saylor & Ganea, 2007; for further evidence of this).

YOUNGER INFANTS

There are now a number of studies that have looked for production and comprehension of joint attention in infants younger than 9 months of age. To take just two examples, Striano and Bertin (2005) found evidence of gaze alternation between objects and adults as young as 5 and 7 months of age, and Grossmann and Johnson (2010) showed that 5-month-olds are sensitive to whether interactions are triadic or not (see chapter 13 for a more in-depth review). And of course, infants from very early on are able to follow others' gaze, at least to nearby objects (e.g., D'Entremont, Hains, & Muir, 1997). However, we know of no evidence that infants this young know together with others that they are sharing attention; so far the best evidence we have of this begins at 12–14 months (see the preceding section). Future research is clearly needed on this topic.

Chimpanzees and Other Apes

Chimpanzees follow others' gaze, and can do so in quite sophisticated ways (see Call & Santos, 2012; Call & Tomasello, 2008 for reviews). For example, they can follow gaze to locations behind themselves and behind barriers (e.g., Povinelli & Eddy, 1996; Tomasello, Call, & Hare, 1998), and they only follow gaze through barriers that the looker can see through (Okamoto-Barth, Call, & Tomasello, 2007). They can follow both head and eye direction (Tomasello, Hare, Lehmann, & Call, 2007), and when they follow gaze and do not see anything interesting, they look back to double check the looker's line of regard (Bräuer, Call, & Tomasello, 2005; Call, Hare, & Tomasello, 1998). Thus, chimpanzees have quite highly developed skills of gaze following, and are apparently motivated to attend to the same things to which others are attending.

Chimpanzees also direct others' attention to things to which they themselves are attending. They routinely gesture toward objects for human caregivers in order to get them to attend to the objects and act on them (see Call & Tomasello, 2007, for an overview of ape gestures). These attention-directing gestures are quite sophisticated too. They are intentional (e.g., Gómez, 1996; Leavens, Russell & Hopkins, 2005; Tomasello, Call, Nagell, Olguin, & Carpenter, 1994) and referential (e.g., Leavens, Hopkins, & Thomas, 2004; Menzel, 1999). In addition, chimpanzees often alternate gaze between the object and the recipient while communicating (Leavens et al., 2004) and they choose different gestures depending on the attentional state of the recipient, using visual gestures for recipients who are looking at them but auditory or tactile gestures more often for recipients who are not already looking at them (Tomasello et al., 1994, 1997). Chimpanzees are thus clearly both able and motivated to direct others' attention in sophisticated ways to objects they are attending to in their environment.

As we have already explained, however, gaze following and attention-directing gestures can involve individual, parallel attention to an object, rather than *joint* attention. We thus need to look for additional evidence, again, of (1) a motivation to share attention and interest with others with no other more instrumental goals, and (2) both individuals knowing together that they are sharing attention. For the first point, researchers from several different labs have concluded that apes do not appear to share attention and interest with others either in joint attentional engagement (e.g., Bard & Vauclair, 1984; Tomasello & Carpenter, 2005; Tomonaga et al., 2004) or by using declarative gestures such as shows and declarative points (e.g., Gómez et al., 1993; Tomasello & Carpenter, 2005; Tomonaga et al., 2004). There are a few papers that report evidence of joint attention and declarative gestures, however. Next we detail what that evidence consists of—and why we find it unconvincing.

With regard to joint attentional engagement, one of us has reported that chimpanzees and bonobos spend less time in joint attentional episodes than 18-month-old infants, but the apes were still credited with some joint attention in that study (Carpenter, Tomasello, & Savage-Rumbaugh, 1995). However, for practical reasons, in that study we simply coded looks to the experimenter's face and the objects present, and it was our impression at the time that the rather sterile nature of the coding—which did not consider *why* participants looked to the experimenter's face, just whether and when they did—almost certainly led to many false positives in terms of truly joint attention with sharing looks. Tanner and Byrne (2010) report triadic social play in gorillas, with joint attention and invitations to share interest in and attention to objects. However, although these interactions are clearly very social and do involve objects, we see little indication in the video clips of these interactions (available on Joanne Tanner's web page: http://www.gorillagestures.info/CH_TRIADIC_PLAY_INTRO.htm) that the gorillas are sharing attention to the objects as an end in itself, the way human infants do. Instead, the objects seem mainly to be an incidental part of a basically dyadic, rough-and-tumble social interaction (similar in some ways to Bates and colleagues', 1975, original characterization of the use of an object to get the partner's attention to the self). Gómez (2010) also reports many observations of triadic social play between a young gorilla and her human caregivers, but notes that there was one main difference in the gorilla's looks to the humans, compared with the looks of human infants to their caregiver: Whereas human infants often look and smile to their caregiver after something interesting happens (as if to comment on it, we would argue—see Carpenter & Liebal, 2011), this gorilla did not do this. Instead her looks to the humans occurred in the midst of social interactions like taking turns throwing things at each other. Thus, the message conveyed by the looks of the gorillas in both these studies seems to be something like, "Come on, let's play!" or "Do it again!" instead of something like, "Wow, wasn't that [object/event] interesting?" a typical joint attention response.

With regard to declarative gestures, Carpenter et al. (1995) reported two instances of possible declarative gestures by a human-reared bonobo, but both were extremely questionable in terms of the ape's intentions (again the coding was done based on superficial behavior, e.g., stretching out the leg with an object on it in the direction of the experimenter, and the coder was not convinced that the ape really was attempting to share attention). Leavens and colleagues (e.g., Leavens, 2004; Leavens & Racine, 2009; Leavens, Racine, & Hopkins, 2009) list numerous reports of what they say appear to be declarative points by apes. For example, gestures used to inform a human about the location of a tool that is needed to get a reward are considered declaratives, as are warning points, and trained responses to requests for information (e.g., a language-trained chimpanzee touching her nose after being asked to "show me your nose")—all apparently simply because they are not imperatives. There is also a single report of a single wild bonobo pointing (Veà & Sabater-Pi, 1998), which several authors have taken as evidence of declarative pointing in wild apes (although Veà & Sabater-Pi themselves do not claim that it is declarative pointing). However, in these reports we see no evidence of declarative gestures in the sense that this term is used with human infants: gestures performed with the motivation to share attention with others simply for the sake of sharing attention, nothing more (in the Veà & Sabater-Pi observation it appears to us to be a point to inform/warn others about the presence of humans hiding in a bush). Finally, Lyn, Greenfield, Savage-Rumbaugh, Gillespie-Lynch, and Hopkins (2011) report an example of an enculturated chimpanzee pointing to a plane for an experimenter. It is simply not clear from the written record whether this was to inform the experimenter of the plane or to share attention with him or her to it.

Greenfield and Savage-Rumbaugh (1991) and Lyn et al. (2011) have also suggested that enculturated apes use lexigrams declaratively. In their studies, chimpanzees and bonobos used lexigrams not only to request food and activities, but also to respond to questions and announce what they were going to do next. These last two behaviors were considered declaratives because they provide information to the recipient and do not involve a request. However, these responses were often explicitly trained, not spontaneous, and anyway again this is not the typical use of the term declarative, as it is used with human infants (i.e., simply to share attention to objects). It is important to keep in mind the distinction between informative gestures/utterances, which can be achieved with parallel attention, and declarative gestures/utterances, which require joint attention. In fact, other research shows that enculturated and human-reared apes left to their own devices produce very few gestures or lexigram "utterances" that would be classified as declaratives—in any use of the term (e.g., Gómez, 2010; Gómez et al., 1993; Hayes, 1951; Rivas, 2005; Tomonaga et al., 2004; see chapter 1). Thus, overall, even when using a very lenient and overly inclusive definition of declarative gestures, they are rare at best in nonhuman apes.

With regard to evidence of "knowing together" or comprehension of what has been shared with others, few relevant studies have been conducted with apes. There is some evidence suggesting that apes know what others know, in the sense of what others have seen in the immediate past (e.g., Hare, Call, & Tomasello, 2001; Kaminski, Call, & Tomasello, 2008; see also chapters 3 and 4), and there is even some evidence suggesting that they know what they themselves know in this sense (Call, 2010; Call & Carpenter, 2001). However, we are unaware of any studies that show that apes know what they know together with others. Future studies similar to those conducted with human infants are needed to investigate this (see, e.g., the Moll et al., 2008 study discussed previously).

SUMMARY

Whereas there is plenty of evidence (from both observational and experimental studies) that 1-year-old human infants engage in truly joint joint attention, there is little if any convincing evidence that chimpanzees and other apes do. Unlike humans, apes do not appear to participate in interactions involving joint attentional engagement, they do not produce declarative gestures serving to share attention with others, and there is so far no evidence of comprehension of having been in joint attentional engagement (although more work needs to be done to address this latter point in particular). When they follow others' gaze, there is no indication that they know together or actively share the fact with the other individual that they are looking at the same thing (in contrast to human 1-year-olds, who do sometimes show this evidence, for example when they follow an adult's gaze and then point to the target object themselves with a look and smile to the adult, as if to comment on it or confirm with her that they have seen it too; Brooks & Meltzoff, 2002; Carpenter et al., 1998). Likewise, when apes gesture for others, there is no unequivocal evidence that they do so with the sole (and spontaneous) goal of sharing attention and interest with others about something, or with any consideration of what they have shared with others in the past. Even those researchers who claim to have found evidence of "triadic" interactions or declarative gestures admit that they are rare (e.g., Leavens & Racine, 2009; Lyn et al., 2011; Tanner & Byrne, 2010), whereas in infants much more convincing behaviors are extremely frequent. Still, not much work has been done on joint attention in apes with the more conservative definition of joint attention we advocate in mind, so the challenge to ape joint attention researchers is to provide this evidence if it can be found.

Why Don't Nonhuman Apes Engage in Joint Attention?

If apes do not engage in joint attention, why not? They have most of the prerequisites needed, both in terms of social-cognitive understanding and the physical behaviors involved: They are sensitive to what others see, know, and intend (e.g., Call & Tomasello, 2008), and they communicate with superficially identical gestures in other, imperative contexts (e.g., Call, 2009; Gómez et al., 1993). Leavens et al. (2009) have proposed that nonenculturated apes may not point declaratively because of the impoverished relationships they have with their human caregivers, but this cannot be the full story because mother-reared apes (even those in the wild) do not point declaratively for their conspecifics either. Besides, the idea that only a proper human upbringing will enable apes to develop declarative pointing is not supported by the data (in that enculturated apes still do not spontaneously communicate declaratively to share attention with others as an end in itself)—and also clearly begs the question of why only humans provide this type of environment.

We think the answer to this question is that only humans have evolved the basic motivation to share psychological states with others. We think that apes not engaging in joint attention is part of a broader pattern involving also not participating in joint action (i.e., collaboration; Tomasello & Carpenter, 2007; Tomasello et al., 2005) and certain types of social imitation (Carpenter & Call, 2009). What all of these abilities have in common is the motivation to share or align psychological states with others. The parallels to joint action are particularly strong, and thus similar sorts of challenges apply for researchers claiming to have found joint action in apes (e.g., Boesch, 2005; Pika & Zuberbühler, 2008): Is there evidence of a shared goal—that apes know together with the other individual(s) that they are participating in a joint action, rather than simply engaging in parallel activity or using the other as a social tool? We are not erecting an insurmountable wall: These are questions that can be brought under empirical scrutiny, as the research done on human infants has shown. Here we simply hope to highlight the most important aspect of joint attention—its jointness—and recommend that it be an integral part of both its theoretical and operational definitions. This will help us determine whether apes and very young human infants engage in joint attention.

NOTE

1. Note that although Bates, Camaioni, and Volterra (1975) coined the term proto-declarative gestures, the term is typically now used in a different, social-cognitively richer way than in their original account: as gestures used to direct others' attention to objects for the purpose of sharing attention and interest to them.

REFERENCES

Bakeman, R., & Adamson, L. B. (1984). Coordinating attention to people and objects in mother-infant and peer-infant interaction. *Child Development, 55*, 1278–1289.

Bard, K. A., & Vauclair, J. (1984). The communicative context of object manipulation in ape and human adult-infant pairs. *Journal of Human Evolution, 13*, 181–190.

Bates, E., Camaioni, L., & Volterra, V. (1975). The acquisition of performatives prior to speech. *Merrill-Palmer Quarterly, 21*, 205–224.

Boesch, C. (2005). Joint cooperative hunting among wild chimpanzees: Taking natural observations seriously. *Behavioral and Brain Sciences, 28*, 692–693.

Bräuer, J., Call, J., & Tomasello, M. (2005). All great ape species follow gaze to distant locations and around barriers. *Journal of Comparative Psychology, 119*, 145–154.

Brooks, R., & Meltzoff, A. N. (2002). The importance of eyes: How infants interpret adult looking behavior. *Developmental Psychology, 38*, 958–966.

Bruner, J. (1995). From joint attention to the meeting of minds: An introduction. In C. Moore & P. J. Dunham (Eds.), *Joint Attention: Its Origins and Role in Development* (pp. 1–14). Hillsdale, NJ: Lawrence Erlbaum Associates.

Call, J. (2009). Contrasting the social cognition of humans and nonhuman apes: The shared intentionality hypothesis. *Topics in Cognitive Science, 1*, 368–379.

Call, J. (2010). Do apes know that they can be wrong? *Animal Cognition, 13*, 689–700.

Call, J. & Carpenter, M. (2001). Do chimpanzees and children know what they have seen? *Animal Cognition, 4*, 207–220.

Call, J., Hare, B. H., & Tomasello, M., (1998). Chimpanzee gaze following in an object-choice task. *Animal Cognition, 1*, 89–99.

Call, J. & Santos, L. (2012). Understanding other minds. In J. Mitani, J. Call, P. Kappeler, R. Palombit & J. Silk (Eds.). *The Evolution of Primate Societies* (pp. 664–681). Chicago: University of Chicago Press.

Call, J., & Tomasello, M. (2007). *The Gestural Communication of Apes and Monkeys*. Mahwah, NJ: Lawrence Erlbaum Associates.

Call, J., & Tomasello, M. (2008). Does the chimpanzee have a theory of mind? 30 years later. *Trends in Cognitive Sciences, 12*, 187–192.

Carpenter, M., & Call, J. (2009). Comparing the imitative skills of children and nonhuman apes. *Revue de primatologie* [online], 1 | 2009. URL: http://primatologie.revues.org/263.

Carpenter, M., & Liebal, K. (2011). Joint attention, communication, and knowing together in infancy. In A. Seemann (Ed.), *Joint Attention: New Developments in Psychology, Philosophy of Mind, and Social Neuroscience* (pp. 159–181). Cambridge, MA: MIT Press.

Carpenter, M., Nagell, K., & Tomasello, M. (1998). Social cognition, joint attention, and communicative competence from 9 to 15 months of age. *Monographs of the Society for Research in Child Development, 63* (4, Serial No. 255).

Carpenter, M., Tomasello, M., & Savage-Rumbaugh, S. (1995). Joint attention and imitative learning in children, chimpanzees, and enculturated chimpanzees. *Social Development, 4*, 217–237.

D'Entremont, B., Hains, S. M. J., & Muir, D. W. (1997). A demonstration of gaze following in 3- to 6-month-olds. *Infant Behavior and Development, 20*, 569–572.

Gómez, J.C. (1996). Non-human primate theories of (non-human primate) minds: some issues concerning the origins of mind-reading. In P Carruthers, & P. K. Smith (Eds.), *Theories of Theories of Mind* (pp. 330–343). New York: Cambridge University Press.

Gómez, J. C. (2010). The ontogeny of triadic cooperative interactions with humans in an infant gorilla. *Interaction Studies, 11*, 353–379.

Gómez, J.C., Sarriá, E., & Tamarit, J. (1993). The comparative study of early communication and theories of mind: Ontogeny, phylogeny, and pathology. In S. Baron-Cohen, H. Tager-Flusberg, & D. J. Cohen (Eds.). *Understanding Other Minds. Perspectives from Autism* (pp. 397–426). New York: Oxford University Press.

Greenfield, P. M., & Savage-Rumbaugh, E. S. (1991). Imitation, grammatical development, and the invention of protogrammar by an ape. In N. A. Krasnegor, D. M. Rumbaugh, R. L. Schiefelbusch, & M. Studdert-Kennedy (Eds.), *Biological and Behavioral Determinants of Language Development* (pp. 235–258). Hillsdale, NJ: Lawrence Earlbaum Associates.

Grossmann, T., & Johnson, M. H. (2010). Selective prefrontal cortex responses to joint attention in infancy. *Biology Letters, 6*, 540–543.

Hare, B., Call, J., & Tomasello, M., (2001). Do chimpanzees know what conspecifics know and do not know? *Animal Behaviour, 61*, 139–151.

Hayes, C. (1951). *The Ape in Our House*. New York: Harper.

Hobson, J. A., & Hobson, R. P. (2007). Identification: The missing link between joint attention and imitation? *Development and Psychopathology, 19*, 411–431.

Kaminski, J., Call, J., & Tomasello, M. (2008). Chimpanzees know what others know but not what they believe. *Cognition, 109*, 224–234.

Leavens, D. A. (2004). Manual deixis in apes and humans. *Interaction Studies, 5*, 387–408.

Leavens, D. A., Hopkins, W. D., & Thomas, R. K. (2004). Referential communication by chimpanzees (*Pan troglodytes*). *Journal of Comparative Psychology, 118*, 48–57.

Leavens, D. A., & Racine, T. P. (2009). Joint attention in apes and humans. Are humans unique? *Journal of Consciousness Studies, 16*, 240–267.

Leavens, D. A., Racine, T. P., & Hopkins, W. D. (2009). The ontogeny and phylogeny of non-verbal deixis. In R. Botha, & C. Knight (Eds.), *The Prehistory of Language* (pp. 142–165). Oxford, UK: Oxford University Press.

Leavens, D. A., Russell, J. L., & Hopkins, W. D. (2005). Intentionality as measured in the persistence and elaboration of communication by chimpanzees (*Pan troglodytes*). *Child Development, 76*, 291–306.

Liebal, K., Behne, T., Carpenter, M., & Tomasello, M. (2009). Infants use shared experience to interpret pointing gestures. *Developmental Science, 12*, 264–271.

Liebal, K., Carpenter, M., & Tomasello, M. (2010). Infants' use of shared experience in declarative pointing. *Infancy, 15*, 545–556.

Liszkowski, U., Carpenter, M., Henning, A., Striano, T., & Tomasello, M. (2004). Twelve-month-olds point to share attention and interest. *Developmental Science, 7*, 297–307.

Liszkowski, U., Carpenter, M., & Tomasello, M. (2007a). Pointing out new news, old news, and absent referents at 12 months of age. *Developmental Science, 10*, F1–F7.

Liszkowski, U., Carpenter, M., & Tomasello, M. (2007b). Reference and attitude in infant pointing. *Journal of Child Language, 34*, 1–20.

Lyn, H., Greenfield, P. M., Savage-Rumbaugh, S., Gillespie-Lynch, K., & Hopkins, W. D. (2011). Nonhuman primates do declare! A comparison of declarative symbol and gesture use in two children, two bonobos, and a chimpanzee. *Language & Communication, 31*, 63–74.

Menzel, C. R. (1999). Unprompted recall and reporting of hidden objects by a chimpanzee (*Pan troglodytes*) after extended delays. *Journal of Comparative Psychology, 113*, 426–434.

Moll, H., Richter, N., Carpenter, M., & Tomasello, M. (2008). Fourteen-month-olds know what "we" have shared in a special way. *Infancy, 13*, 90–101.

Moore, C., & D'Entremont, B. (2001). Developmental changes in pointing as a function of attentional focus. *Journal of Cognition and Development, 2*, 109–129.

Okamoto-Barth, J., Call, J., & Tomasello, M. (2007). Great apes' understanding of others' line of sight. *Psychological Science, 18*, 462–468.

Perucchini, P., & Camaioni, L. (1993, September). *When intentional communication emerges? Developmental dissociations between declarative and imperative functions of the pointing gesture.* Paper presented at the Developmental Conference of the British Psychological Society, Birmingham, UK.

Pika, S., & Zuberbühler, K. (2008). Social games between bonobos and humans: Evidence for shared intentionality? *American Journal of Primatology, 70*, 207–210.

Povinelli, D. J., & Eddy, T. J. (1996). Chimpanzees: Joint visual attention. *Psychological Science, 7*, 129–135.

Rivas, E. (2005). Recent use of signs by chimpanzees (*Pan troglodytes*) in interactions with humans. *Journal of Comparative Psychology, 119,* 404–417.

Saylor, M. M., & Ganea, P. (2007). Infants interpret ambiguous requests for absent objects. *Developmental Psychology, 43,* 696–704.

Striano, T., & Bertin, E. (2005). Coordinated affect with mothers and strangers: A longitudinal analysis of joint engagement between 5 and 9 months of age. *Cognition & Emotion, 19,* 781–790.

Tanner, J. E., & Byrne, R. W. (2010). Triadic and collaborative play by gorillas in social games with objects. *Animal Cognition, 13,* 591–607.

Tomasello, M. (1995). Joint attention as social cognition. In C. Moore, & P. J. Dunham (Eds.), *Joint Attention: Its Origins and Role in Development* (pp. 103–130). Hillsdale, NJ: Lawrence Erlbaum Associates.

Tomasello, M., Call, J., & Hare, B. H. (1998). Five primate species follow the visual gaze of conspecifics. *Animal Behaviour, 55,* 1063–1069.

Tomasello, M., Call, J., Nagell, K., Olguin, R., & Carpenter, M. (1994). The learning and use of gestural signals by young chimpanzees: A trans-generational study. *Primates, 35,* 137–154.

Tomasello, M., Call, J., Warren, J., Frost, G. T., Carpenter, M., & Nagell, K. (1997). The ontogeny of chimpanzee gestural signals: A comparison across groups and generations. *Evolution of Communication, 1,* 223–259.

Tomasello, M., & Carpenter, M. (2005). The emergence of social cognition in three young chimpanzees. *Monographs of the Society for Research in Child Development, 70* (1, Serial No. 279).

Tomasello, M., & Carpenter M. (2007). Shared intentionality. *Developmental Science, 10,* 121–125.

Tomasello, M., Carpenter, M., Call, J., Behne, T., & Moll, H. (2005). Understanding and sharing intentions: The origins of cultural cognition. *Behavioral and Brain Sciences, 28,* 1–17.

Tomasello, M., Hare, B., Lehmann, H., & Call, J. (2007). Reliance on head versus eyes in the gaze following of great apes and human infants: The cooperative eye hypothesis. *Journal of Human Evolution, 52,* 314–320.

Tomonaga, M., Tanaka, M., Matsuzawa, T., Myowa-Yamakoshi, M., Kosugi, D., Mizuno, Y., et al. (2004). Development of social cognition in infant chimpanzees (Pan troglodytes): Face recognition, smiling, gaze, and the lack of triadic interactions. *Japanese Psychological Research, 46,* 227–235.

Veà, J. J., & Sabater-Pi, J. (1998). Spontaneous pointing behavior in the wild pygmy chimpanzee (*Pan paniscus*). *Folia Primatologica, 69,* 289.

3 The Comparative Delusion: The "Behavioristic/Mentalistic" Dichotomy in Comparative Theory of Mind Research

Derek C. Penn and Daniel J. Povinelli

IT IS NO secret that research on the Theory of Mind (ToM) abilities of nonhuman animals has been "fraught with controversy" (Shettleworth, 1998). "Low-level," "behavioristic" hypotheses purportedly claim that nonhuman animals learn about the statistical regularities in others' observable behaviors using low-level mechanisms akin to Pavlovian conditioning without any ability to reason about the causal relation between those behaviors in an abstract or inferentially coherent fashion. "High-level," "mentalistic" hypotheses, on the other hand, propose that nonhuman subjects attribute (at least some) mental states to others and reason about the causal role played by those mental states in a fashion roughly analogous to the way that we (the folk) do. The debate between these two dichotomous alternatives dominated comparative ToM research for the first two decades after Premack and Woodruff's (1978) original paper (see Heyes, 1998; Tomasello & Call, 1997; for reviews) and continues unabated to this day (see, for example, Emery & Clayton, 2008; Santos et al., 2006; Suddendorf & Whiten, 2003; Tomasello & Call, 2006; Tomasello et al., 2003a, 2003b; Wood et al., 2007).

To be sure, the debate has become an exercise in shadow boxing. The overwhelming consensus among comparative psychologists today is that a mentalistic explanation of some kind is warranted for at least certain species and certain tasks (e.g., Emery & Clayton, 2008; Santos et al., in press; Suddendorf & Whiten, 2001; Tomasello & Call, 2006; Tomasello et al., 2003a; Wood et al., 2007). Few experimentally-minded comparative researchers claim that nonhuman animals have a ToM equivalent to that of a normal adult human. But most would probably now agree with Tomasello et al. (2003a) when they conclude that nonhuman animals "understand some psychological states in others—the only question is which ones and to what extent."

Notwithstanding the eminent consensus arrayed against us, we do not believe that a mentalistic explanation for nonhuman social cognition is warranted. But not because we believe that the behavioristic alternative is any more compelling. In our opinion, both alternatives are equally implausible and the entire dichotomy is specious—or, as Heyes and Papineau (2006) aptly put it, "just Descartes dressed up in modern garb." In the present chapter we attempt to argue for a more empirically grounded and theoretically cogent middle way.

Admittedly, Povinelli and colleagues have long argued that comparative researchers should explore the possibility that nonhuman animals may be able to reason about the world in a representationally rich and inferentially coherent fashion without necessarily being able to reason about unobservable, hypothetical entities such as mental states and causal forces (Penn & Povinelli, 2007a, 2007b; Povinelli, 2000; Povinelli & Eddy, 1996; Povinelli & Vonk,2003, 2004; Povinelli et al., 2000; Vonk & Povinelli, 2006). But unfortunately, Povinelli's "Reinterpretation" hypothesis has been persistently misinterpreted as a kind of "derived behaviorism" or "sophisticated behavior-reading" and widely criticized as "unfalsifiable" and "unparsimonious" (see, for example, Andrews, 2005; Suddendorf & Whiten, 2003; Tomasello et al., 2003b; Tomasello & Call, 2006; Emery & Clayton, 2008; Santos et al., in press). So in this chapter, we try a very different tack.

We start by reviewing why a "behavioristic" account of nonhuman social cognition is, indeed, entirely implausible. We then show why the mentalistic consensus that dominates comparative research today is nevertheless unwarranted. And we finish by arguing that comparative researchers have failed to critique the most obvious limitation in Povinelli's "Reinterpretation" hypothesis: to wit, Povinelli's original hypothesis significantly *overes-timated* the cognitive abilities of nonhuman animals. We propose a new version of the Reinterpretation hypothesis that corrects this error.

Flogging the Behavioristic Straw Man

The terms "behaviorist" and "behavior reader" have played a crucial role in the comparative ToM debate: typically as pejorative labels for an implausible null hypothesis (for recent examples, see Emery & Clayton, 2008; Hare et al., 2006; Santos et al., in press; Tomasello & Call, 2006; Tomasello et al., 2003b). To be sure, it is often not clear that any real-life researcher has ever held the views attributed to this straw man.

Krebs and Dawkins (1984), for example, famously hypothesized that the "mindread-ing" ability of nonhuman animals was due to their ability to keep track of the "statisti-cal rules" that govern "sequences of behavior." But it is hard to see how even Krebs and Dawkins' low-level model could be implemented using purely Pavlovian learning or non-representational processes. Heyes (1998) roundly criticized the evidence for ToM-like abilities in nonhuman primates but explicitly acknowledged the importance of "inferences based on nonmental categories" in addition to purely associative learning processes. And Povinelli and colleagues suggested that chimpanzees might not actually cognize the referential or goal-directed nature of others' looking behavior in mentalistic terms but were always very clear that chimpanzees were fully cognitive creatures with a rich suite of representations at their disposal (e.g., Povinelli, 2000; Povinelli & Eddy, 1996; Povinelli et al., 2000).

In any case, the evidence that has accumulated over the past 10 years has thoroughly eliminated any doubt that a behavioristic explanation of nonhuman cognition is untenable. In particular, we know that nonhuman animals form highly structured representations about the past as well as the occurrent behavior of other agents. They are not limited to learning about statistical contingencies between behavioral cues in an ad hoc or bottom-up fashion. They often do represent the special causal structure among behavioral cues, particularly the goal-directed relation between other agents' perceptual acts and how those agents are likely to behave. And they are able to generalize this top-down causal knowledge in an inferentially flexible and ecologically rational (i.e., adaptive) fashion. Perhaps most importantly, we now know beyond a shadow of a doubt that all of these sophisticated social-cognitive abilities are not limited to primates or even to mammals.

ANIMALS FORM ABSTRACT, STRUCTURED REPRESENTATIONS ABOUT OTHERS' PAST AS WELL AS OCCURRENT BEHAVIORS

On one particularly implausible interpretation of the behavior-reading hypothesis, nonhuman subjects are only able to respond to occurrent stimuli in the immediate environment and are incapable of using representations of past events or states of affairs in order to infer how to behave in novel situations. We are not aware of any contemporary comparative researcher who has actually advocated a stimulus-bound version of behavior-reading in print—certainly not Povinelli and colleagues, who have always emphasized the importance of abstract off-line representations in nonhuman social cognition (Povinelli & Vonk, 2003, 2004; Povinelli et al., 2000). But just in case there is an advocate of stimulus-bound behavior-reading lurking silently in the bushes, it is worth noting, for the record, that any nonrepresentational account of nonhuman social cognition has been dead in the water for quite some time. Indeed, thanks to the research of Emery, Clayton, and colleagues (see Emery & Clayton, 2008, for a review), we now know that sophisticated representations of both past and present states of affairs are not limited to primates or mammals alone.

Dally et al. (2006) for example, had scrub-jays cache food successively in two trays, each in view of a different observer. At recovery, the original storers recached significantly more food caches when they retrieved their caches in the presence of a previous observer than when they retrieved their caches in private. Furthermore, if a previous observer was present, storers tended to recache from the tray that the previous observer had actually observed. A stimulus-bound explanation of these results might postulate that the storers were simply responding to intimidating perceptual cues being emitted by the observers—what Tomasello et al. (2003a) call the "evil eye" hypothesis. But Dally et al. (2006) designed a control experiment in which the trays were removed from the original storer and another bird was allowed to cache food in both trays in the presence of an additional "control" observer. If storers based their recaching decisions solely on the occurrent behavior of the observer bird, they should have recached items in the presence of the control bird just as often as they did in the presence of the actual observers because the control bird had witnessed caching in both trays (although by a different storer) and was presumably emitting the same intimidating cues. In fact, the original storers exhibited very little recaching in the presence of the control bird (see discussion by Emery & Clayton, 2008).

Results such as these rule out any explanation in terms of occurrent behavioral cues alone. Clearly, scrub jays are able to keep track of "who" was present for "what" events in the past; and they use this information in an adaptive fashion to protect their cache sites from potential pilferers. Moreover, these birds are keeping track of the relation between numerous cache sites and various potential pilferers in a combinatorial and productive fashion. The ability to represent the combinatorial relation between numerous cache sites and competitors would be literally unthinkable (i.e., computationally infeasible) without some mechanism for encoding the compositional relation between particular constituents of a representation such that when different constituents have the same relation to each other, the fact that it is the same *relation* in each case is somehow manifest in the structural similarity between the representations. Horgan and Tienson (1996) argue that this is all it should take in order for a representational system to qualify as "syntactically structured"; and we agree (see Penn et al., 2007 for a more extensive discussion of this point).

In our view, it is indisputable that scrub jays form syntactically structured representations about the "what," "when," "where," and "who" properties associated with concrete events in the past as well as about the abstract statistical regularities that have held across a number of similar situations. Furthermore, they can combine these concrete and abstract representations in order to respond in a rational (i.e., adaptive) fashion to the relation between a particular competitor and a particular cache site. Presumably these representational and inferential abilities are not limited to corvids.

ANIMALS POSSESS QUITE A LOT OF CAUSAL KNOWLEDGE ABOUT THE PERCEPTUAL BEHAVIOR OF OTHER INTENTIONAL AGENTS

It has been well known for quite some time that nonhuman apes spontaneously follow the gaze of other anthropoid subjects and will track another subject's gaze to areas outside of their own immediate visual field (Povinelli & Eddy, 1996; Povinelli et al., 2000; Tomasello et al., 1998; Tomasello et al., 1999). On a behavioristic explanation of this phenomenon, apes follow the gaze of other apes because they have learned that when they do so, they often see interesting events or objects in the world: the gaze of another anthropoid agent is simply a statistically reliable cue of something interesting to look at and the nonhuman ape has no real understanding of the special epistemic relation between the other agent's gaze and the state of affairs being observed. A considerable number of experiments have demonstrated that this behavioristic account of gaze-following is untenable.

There is now compelling evidence that chimpanzees and other primates are sensitive to many (though not all) of the observable factors determining other agents' line of sight and "what" other agents are looking at (Barth et al., 2005; Brauer et al., 2007; Call et al., 1998, 2000; Flombaum & Santos, 2005; Hare et al., 2000; Hare et al., 2001; Kaminski et al., 2004; Okamoto-Barth et al., 2007; Povinelli et al., 2003). For example, chimpanzees tend to "check back" if another agent's gaze does not seem to lead to anything interesting; and they will move around barriers in order to see what other individuals are looking at. Chimpanzees treat transparent barriers differently from opaque ones when approaching food that a competitor might be able to see (Hare et al., 2000, 2006) or when inferring the external target of another agent's line of sight (Okamoto-Barth et al., 2007). And in certain circumstances, they will even use a human experimenter's gaze as a cue to the location of food (Barth et al., 2005). Many of these abilities are not limited to apes or even to mammals. Flombaum and Santos (2005), for example, showed that rhesus monkeys prefer to steal food from human competitors who are looking away or whose eyes are covered rather than from human competitors who are looking in their direction. And Dally et al. (2004, 2005) have shown that western scrub-jays prefer to hide food in dimly lit and/or more distant sites when being observed by potential pilferers and take into account whether a competitor has an unobstructed line of sight to a given location when making their caching and recaching decisions.

None of this evidence suggests that nonhuman animals cognize "seeing" as an epistemic act or are reasoning in terms of other agents' mental experience (we will critique these mentalistic claims below). But the animals' behaviors are clearly too flexible to be explained in terms of innate orienting reflexes alone. And it would be equally implausible to suggest that nonhuman animals acquire all of these sophisticated gaze-relevant behaviors through general purpose, bottom-up statistical learning alone. As Santos et al. (in press) point out, without some additional top-down structure or knowledge, the statistical regularities causally relevant to tracking another agent's gaze to its real-world target would be swamped among a practically infinite number of equally salient but spurious correlations. Moreover, unstructured statistical models cannot explain how nonhuman animals are able to infer what another agent is looking at even when they are confronted by novel combinations and configurations of cues (e.g., Brauer et al., 2007; Hare et al., 2000, 2006).

To be sure, the limitations of uninformed, unstructured statistical learning are hardly news (Clark & Thornton, 1997). As far as we can see, uninformed, bottom-up, unstructured statistical learning models are all but extinct among computational and cognitive researchers (see Chater et al., 2006 for a recent introduction). It is widely agreed that even basic object perception requires a sophisticated interplay between top-down and bottom-up statistical processes (Kersten et al., 2004). The same is true for computational models of gaze-following (see, for example, Breazeal & Scassellati, 2001; Hoffman et al., 2006).

At the very least, then, gaze-following in primates requires quite sophisticated, flexible, embodied, representational mechanisms for inferring the external target of another agent's looking behavior from unique combinations of contextual and behavioral cues, using prior knowledge about the physical factors relevant to determining other agents' line of sight. Thus, inferring the external target of another agent's "looking" behavior clearly requires cognitive mechanisms that go far beyond the limitations of uninformed statistical behavior-reading or associative learning. And there is now compelling evidence that nonhuman animals' understanding of others' looking behavior goes a good deal farther than just looking where others are looking (see also Povinelli et al., 2002).

ANIMALS UNDERSTAND SOME ASPECTS OF THE GOAL-DIRECTED RELATION BETWEEN AGENTS' PERCEPTUAL ACTS AND THE WORLD

It is increasingly clear that nonhuman animals do, in fact, recognize some aspects of the special, goal-directed relation between intentional agents' perceptual acts and the world. For example, Hare et al. (2001) put two chimpanzees, one dominant to the other, on opposite sides of a middle chamber. The experimenters hid a piece of food in one of two containers in the middle of this chamber. In the *informed* condition, both the subordinate and the dominant chimpanzees were able to observe where the food was hidden. In the *uninformed* condition, the dominant's door was shut and only the subordinate subject was able to see where the food was placed. When released into the middle chamber, subordinates tended to approach the food reward more frequently in the uninformed than in the informed condition even when they were given a slight headstart and were provided no occurrent cues as to the competitor's intentions.

This seminal experiment does not warrant the high-level mentalistic interpretation it is routinely given (e.g., Hare et al., 2001; Santos et al., in press; Suddendorf & Whiten, 2003; Tomasello et al., 2003a; Tomasello & Call, 2006). As Povinelli and Vonk (2003, 2004) point out, it is likely that the subordinate chimpanzees simply realized that they should avoid competing for desirable and monopolizable resources with dominants who have had an unobstructed line of sight to the resource in the recent past. It was not necessary for subordinates to reflect on the visual perspective of the dominant as a distinctively *mental* experience nor was it necessary for subordinates to reason about what the dominant had seen in terms of an unobservable epistemic mental state. Thus, the additional claim that the subordinates behaved the way they did because they knew that *the dominant had seen the food and therefore knows where it is* may satisfy our all-too-human need to posit a conscious (i.e., folk psychological) reason for the subordinates' behavior, but it is not warranted by the evidence.

This said, even Povinelli and Vonk's nonmentalistic account of the chimpanzees' behavior implies that the subordinates understood quite a lot about the causal relation between the competitor's line of sight, the nature of the object being observed, and how the competitor was likely to behave in the near future. As Tomasello and Call (2006) point out, the subordinates would not have made the same inference if the dominant had been oriented toward a rock and subordinates did, in fact, make the same inference regardless of whether the food was an apple or a banana (see also Brauer et al., 2007; Hare et al., 2000). Thus, chimpanzees—and perhaps other animals as well—use some of the characteristics of the object located at the endpoint of a competitor's line of sight in order to infer how that competitor is likely to act in the near future. This relational inference does not require mentalistic reasoning; but it is certainly no mean cognitive feat.

Picking out causally relevant *relations* in the world amid all the salient but spurious correlations presents uninformed statistical learning mechanisms with a computational quagmire. Yet, as Clark and Thornton (1997) point out, life is rife with problems that require relational solutions; and, at least outside the laboratory, animals routinely solve these problems, typically quite well. This implies that both human and nonhuman animals are eminently *relational* reasoners; not just uninformed statistical learners. Clark and Thornton (1997) suggest that biological cognizers circumvent the limitations of uninformed statistical learning by employing a range of top-down heuristics, ploys, and biases to recognize and reason about the relations that matter. And we agree. The comparative evidence strongly suggests that nonhuman animals possess a variety of top-down heuristics, ploys, and biases for picking out the causal features of other agents' occurrent behaviors and for reasoning about other agents' future behavior in terms of their goal-directed relation to the world.

We hasten to add that the ability to reason in terms of the goal-directed relation between an intentional agent and a particular state of affairs in the world does not necessarily entail, *in addition*, the ability to cognize others as intentional agents with their own distinct and unobservable psychological states. This latter ability, we will argue below, is of a different kind altogether.

On the Lack of Evidence for Anything Even Remotely Resembling a Theory of Mind among Nonhuman Animals

Faced by the sophistication of nonhuman animals' social behaviors and the manifest failure of low-level behavioristic models to account for these impressive cognitive abilities, many comparative researchers have come to the intuitively appealing conclusion that nonhuman animals must reason about other minds in largely the same way that we (the folk) do. Santos et al. (in press) put it bluntly: "we would like to propose that, in fact, primates do reason about unobservable mental states, and that they do so with the same basic cognitive systems that we humans use to reason about mental states." Generous mentalistic claims such as these are no longer limited to primates or mammals. Emery and Clayton (2008), for example, argue that there is now "good evidence" for Theory of Mind in scrub-jays as well.

We disagree. As we argue below, not only is there a lack of compelling evidence for anything remotely resembling a ToM among nonhuman animals, there is consistent evidence of an absence (see also Penn & Povinelli, 2007b; Povinelli & Vonk, 2003, 2004; Povinelli et al., 2000).

THERE IS NO EVIDENCE THAT NONHUMAN ANIMALS REPRESENT OR REASON ABOUT OTHER AGENTS' EPISTEMIC MENTAL STATES

Following Premack and Woodruff's (1978) seminal paper, many philosophers and psychologists argued that the acid test of a representational ToM is whether a given subject can reason about the causal implications of another agent's *false* beliefs (Bennett, 1978; Dennett, 1978; Harman, 1978; Wimmer & Perner, 1983). Certainly, reasoning about false-beliefs is not the only distinctive component of a ToM or the only valid test of a ToM (see Bloom & German, 2000). But it is exceedingly hard to claim that a nonverbal subject understands another agent's true beliefs as epistemic mental states if the subject is not capable of reasoning about the causal consequences of that agent's false beliefs as well.

To date, nonhuman primates have failed every well-controlled test of their ability to reason about the epistemic contents of another agent's counterfactual representations (e.g., Call & Tomasello, 1999). As Tomasello et al. (2003a) frankly acknowledge, "there is no evidence anywhere that chimpanzees understand the beliefs of others" (see also Tomasello et al., 2005). Worse, all of the experiments to date that purport to show that nonhuman animals can reason about "false beliefs" lack the power, even in principle, of showing that subjects are reasoning about the epistemic contents of others' mental states as distinct from observable behavioral cues (e.g., Bugnyar & Heinrich, 2005; Hare et al., 2001, 2006; Povinelli et al., 1990; Santos et al., 2006). The difference is crucial and persistently overlooked.

For example, Hare et al. (2001) tested whether or not subordinate chimpanzees would distinguish between trials in which the food had been moved and rehidden while the dominant was not looking ("misinformed" condition) and trials in which the dominant competitor had witnessed the correct placement of the food ("informed" condition). As it turned out, the subordinates did not approach the food significantly more frequently in the misinformed condition than in the informed condition. But even if they had, this would not have warranted a mentalistic explanation. To pass this test, it suffices to recognize that a potential competitor is less likely to compete for food if the food was last hidden when that competitor was not present. In other words, the subordinates only had to reason in terms of the competitor's propensity to try and retrieve the food, not about *what* the competitor (falsely) believed was located beneath each occluder. Thus, for the same reasons that Dennett (1978) and many others pointed out 30 years ago, Hare et al.'s (2001) protocol lacks the power, even in principle, of demonstrating that chimpanzees know what other chimpanzees do and do not know (for examples of the kind of protocols that could, at least in principle, provide such evidence, see Penn & Povinelli, 2007b).

The same deflationary analysis applies, mutatis mutandis, to the more recent (and more impressive) performance of corvids (cf. Emery & Clayton, 2008). In every experiment reported to date, it suffices for the scrub-jays to keep track of *who* was present for which caching event without, *in addition*, keeping track of the distinct counterfactual representations being maintained by each individual competitor. Indeed, Dally et al. (2006 p. 1665) themselves acknowledge that scrub jays' ability to keep track of which competitors have observed which cache sites "need not require a human-like 'theory of mind' in terms of unobservable mental states, but […] may result from behavioral predispositions in combination with specific learning algorithms or from reasoning about future risk."

NONHUMAN ANIMALS DO NOT APPEAR TO REASON ABOUT "GOALS" AS INTERNAL REPRESENTATIONAL STATES

As we argued previously, at least some nonhuman animals recognize the perceptual relations causally relevant to predicting an intentional agent's goal-directed behaviors. Indeed, there is even evidence that nonhuman apes understand some of the perceptual cues causally relevant to discriminating between "intentional" and "accidental" behaviors in other anthropoid agents (see Call & Tomasello, 1998; Call et al., 2004). But this evidence does not suggest that nonhuman animals reason about other agents' goals as mental representations. As Tomasello et al. (2005) point out, the psychological literature has been plagued by a pervasive ambiguity in the way that the term, "goal," is used:

> "The word *goal* contains a systematic ambiguity that has contributed to much confusion…When it is said that a person wants a box open, for example, we may distinguish the external goal—a certain state of the environment such as an open box—and the internal goal—an internal entity that guides the person's behavior (e.g., a mental representation of a desired state such as an open box)." (Tomasello et al., 2005 p. 676)

When hypothesizing about how cognizers understand the goal-directed behavior of other agents, it is crucial, Tomasello et al. (2005) argue, to distinguish between *external goals* (i.e., the external state of affairs used as a reference point by the other agent's cognitive process) and *internal goals* (i.e., the internal representation of that external goal). We agree. Reasoning about the relation between an external goal and a given agent's behavior is not the same thing as reasoning about the relation between an internal goal and an agent's behavior: Only in the latter case do unobservable mental states play a distinctive causal role.

Numerous comparative researchers have claimed that nonhuman animals do, in fact, reason about other agents' internal goals (Flombaum & Santos, 2005; Hare et al., 2000, 2001, 2006; Santos et al., 2006; Santos et al., in press; Tomasello et al., 2003a; Wood et al., 2007). Indeed, Tomasello et al. (2005) themselves claim that nonhuman animals reason about internal goals.[1] But all of the evidence to date is consistent with the more modest hypothesis that nonhuman animals reason solely about an agent's relation to external goals. As Tomasello et al. (2005) point out, the defining feature of being a goal-directed subject is that one is sensitive to the current value of one's internal goals and the dynamic, causal relation between one's own actions and the desired outcome. There is extensive evidence that animals as humble as laboratory rats are, indeed, goal-directed subjects in this sense (see, for example, Dickinson & Balleine, 2000). But there is no evidence that any nonhuman animal recognizes that another agent's goal-directed behaviors are sensitive to *that* agent's representation of the current value of the goal and to *that* agent's representation of the instrumental efficacy of a given action as distinct from the subject's own representations of the goal's value and the instrumental efficacy of a given action. Indeed, there is not simply an absence of evidence that nonhuman animals reason about other agents' goals in this mentalistic manner, there is consistent evidence of an absence.

The crux of Tomasello et al.'s (2005) hypothesis is that human children undergo a qualitative change in their social–cognitive abilities at around 12 to 15 months of age: specifically they start to engage in triadic interactions with other individuals involving shared goals and socially coordinated action plans. These collaborative interactions show that children in their second year of life start to recognize that different agents may have different internal goals and different representations of the instrumental efficacy of various possible actions. Tomasello et al. (2005) argue, rightly we believe, that "shared intentionality" is a uniquely human capability. As they point out (pp. 685–686), nonhuman animals do not naturally point, show, or even actively offer things to conspecifics. There is no convincing evidence for instructional teaching among any nonhuman species. And there is no evidence for anything remotely resembling the extensive collaborative interactions among humans. As Tomasello et al. (2005 p. 685) put it, "it is almost unimaginable that two chimpanzees might spontaneously do something as simple as carry something together or help each other make a tool."

In short, nonhuman primates lack precisely those social–cognitive behaviors that require an ability to reason about others' goals as internal representational states—susceptible to revaluation and collaborative alignment—and manifest only those behaviors that are possible when reasoning about other agents' goal-directed behavior in terms of those agents' relation to external states of affairs. Although nonhuman primates clearly understand and reason about others' *external* goals, the ability to reason about *internal* goals appears to be a uniquely human specialization.

NONHUMAN ANIMALS DO NOT APPEAR TO POSSESS ANYTHING REMOTELY
RESEMBLING A MENTALISTIC UNDERSTANDING OF OTHERS'
PERCEPTUAL ACTS

The comparative evidence firmly demonstrates that at least some nonhuman animals recognize how particular combinations of contextual and behavioral cues can be used to
infer what another agent is "looking at." But contrary to the general consensus, we do
not believe that this finely tuned inferential ability—as sophisticated as it may be—is
functionally or representationally equivalent to reasoning about another agent's "visual
perspective" (cf. Brauer et al., 2007; Hare et al., 2000, 2006; Okamoto-Barth et al.,
2007; Emery & Clayton, 2008). Comparative researchers often seem to believe that
there is nothing more to claiming that a nonhuman animal attributes a visual epistemic
perspective to others' perceptual acts than that the subject engages in behaviors that are
interpretable as attributing a visual epistemic perspective to others' perceptual acts.[2] In
other words, comparative researchers rarely differentiate between subjects who have an
implicit understanding of another agent's perceptual mental state (i.e., one that is implied
by the subject's behavior and imputed by a human observer but not necessarily tokened
or predicated by the subject's own cognitive system) and subjects who have an *explicit*
understanding of another agent's perceptual mental state (i.e., one in which the subject's
cognitive system has predicated the causal relation between the other agent's internal,
unobservable mental state and the other agent's external, observable perceptual behavior). One notable exception is Whiten (1996), who proposed an elegant specification of
what it means to say that a nonverbal creature possesses an explicit concept of another
agent's mental state.

To make a credible distinction between implicit and explicit mental state concepts,
Whiten (1996) suggested that researchers look for the ability to recognize the relational
similarity between perceptually disparate behavioral patterns in terms of the common
causal role play by some unobservable mental state. For example, a chimpanzee that
encodes the observable patterns, "*X saw Y put food in bin A*," "*X hid food in bin A*," and "*X
sees Y glancing at bin A*" as members of the same abstract equivalence class with analogous
causal consequences could be said, on Whiten's account, to recognize that "X *knows* food
is in bin A" and thus possess an "explicit" concept of "knowing" as a mental state.

Whiten's definition may very well qualify as the minimal reasonable criterion for claiming that a nonverbal animal possesses an explicit concept of a mental state. His definition
does not require a subject to possess metarepresentational mental states, a theory-like
understanding of the mind, or the ability to reason about counterfactual mental representations. Indeed, a subject might possess an explicit mental state concept of "seeing"
or "hearing" sensu Whiten without any inkling that other animals have mental states "in
their heads." Nevertheless, not only is there a striking absence of evidence for anything
remotely resembling an explicit concept of perceptual mental states sensu Whiten in any
nonhuman species, there is converging and growing evidence of an absence.

As Whiten (1996) points out, demonstrating that a nonverbal subject possesses an explicit mental state concept requires "triangulating" across disparate protocols and showing that the subject cognizes the common causal role play be a given mental state across perceptually disparate task contexts (see also Heyes, 1998). But in the last 10 years, a growing body of evidence suggests that nonhuman animals do not, in fact, recognize the mental states relations that are common across disparate task contexts. The lack of an overarching "theory of mind" is particularly striking when comparing the behavior of nonhuman primates on "competitive" and "cooperative" protocols.

With respect to "seeing," for example, nonhuman primates appear to be highly sensitive to the disposition of an anthropoid competitor's eyes when attempting to steal food from them (e.g., Brauer et al., 2007; Flombaum & Santos, 2005) but are relatively insensitive to the disposition of another agent's eyes in cooperative–communicative tasks (Barth et al., 2005; Call et al., 1998; Call et al., 2000; Kaminski et al., 2004; Povinelli & Eddy, 1996). In other words, at least for nonhuman primates, the disposition of the eyes in the context of stealing food apparently does not belong to the same abstract mental state equivalence class as the disposition of the eyes in the context of begging for food.

With respect to "hearing," Call (2004) showed that nonhuman apes are able to use the noise of food being shaken in a container to determine in which container the food is hidden. And Santos et al. (2006) showed that rhesus monkeys try to avoid making unexpected noises when stealing food from a competitor who is not already looking in their direction. But Brauer et al. (2008) has shown that, if someone else makes the noise, chimpanzees do not realize that their competitors can use the noise of food being hidden to locate the food. To put these contradictory results in Whiten's terms, nonhuman primates apparently do not classify the observable patterns "*The container makes noise when I try to steal food from A*" and "*X makes noise hiding food in the presence of A*" as indicative of the same mental state relation, "*A hears where the food is located.*"

Many comparative researchers have interpreted the discrepancy between nonhuman primates' behavior on competitive and cooperative tasks as evidence that nonhuman primates are employing two different cognitive systems: a behavioristic system in cooperative situations and a mentalistic system in competitive ones (e.g., Hare, 2001; Santos et al., in press; Tomasello et al., 2003a). Certainly, the discrepancy between nonhuman primates' behavior on competitive and cooperative tasks suggests that they are employing cognitive mechanisms that are tuned to the ecologically relevant features of each task. But possessing cognitive mechanisms finely tuned to particular social tasks is not the "essence" of a ToM system (cf. Santos et al., in press). The essence of an ToM—in both the theory-like sense defined by Premack and Woodruff (1978) as well as the minimalist sense set forth by Whiten (1996)—is the ability to explicitly represent (i.e., predicate) and reason about the causal role played by a given mental state across disparate behavioral contexts. This ability, Whiten (1996) argues convincingly, should allow a mentalistic subject to draw inferences about the causal consequences of a given mental state—e.g., "seeing," "hearing"—in *novel* behavioral contexts. But the evidence to date suggests that this is precisely the ability that nonhuman animals lack—and Whiten's analysis suggests why.

Whiten's example of "explicit" mindreading is a textbook example of analogical reasoning: Whiten's hypothetical chimpanzee must infer a systematic relational correspondence among perceptually disparate behavioral patterns that have nothing in common other than a common but unobservable causal mechanism (i.e., what X "knows"). If this is an "intervening variable," it is an intervening variable that requires reasoning about the analogical similarity between disparate causal relations in order to be tokened. But apart from the remarkable and unreplicated feats of a single highly enculturated chimpanzee (i.e., Gillan et al., 1981), there is no evidence that nonhuman animals are able to reason by analogy and considerable evidence that they are not (see Penn et al., 2007). Ex hypothesi, the reason why only human subjects possess explicit mental state concepts is because only humans have the representational architecture necessary to reason by analogy.

Povinelli's Hypothesis Revisited

If a low-level behavioristic hypothesis was the only alternative to a high-level mentalistic hypothesis, then the current mentalistic consensus might be justified on the grounds that it is less implausible than the alternative. But Povinelli and colleagues have long pointed out that there is a vast and largely unexplored middle ground between construing animals as nothing more than operant learners and claiming that they have a mentalistic appreciation of other minds (Povinelli, 2000; Povinelli & Bering, 2002; Povinelli & Eddy, 1996; Povinelli & Giambrone, 1999; Povinelli & Prince, 1998; Povinelli & Vonk, 2003, 2004; Povinelli et al., 2000; Vonk & Povinelli, 2006).

THE ORIGINAL REINTERPRETATION HYPOTHESIS

For many years now, Povinelli and colleagues have argued that chimpanzees and other animals are fully "cognitive creatures" endowed with mental representations and inferential abilities similar to those of humans but that nonhuman animals' representational capabilities might not encompass *all* the same semantic possibilities as human subjects. In particular, given the lack of compelling evidence for mentalistic representations and abstract causal reasoning among chimpanzees, Povinelli hypothesized that chimpanzees are unable to reason about unobservable entities such as mental states and causal mechanisms (see, in particular, Povinelli, 2000; Povinelli et al., 2000).

To explain both the profound similarities and dissimilarities between human and nonhuman cognition, Povinelli proposed that chimpanzees and humans share a suite of representationally sophisticated systems for coping with the social and physical worlds. In addition to these shared mechanisms, humans possess a unique representational system that allows us, and us alone, to interpret the outputs from these ancestral systems in a novel, and quite peculiar, manner—namely, to interpret the behavior of the self and others as being strongly influenced by unobservable entities known as "mental states." According to the "Reinterpretation" hypothesis, this uniquely human system for representing mental states did not replace the ancestral systems we share with other primates. Rather, the human mind is still composed of both kind of systems and both are inextricably intertwined with each other. Indeed, the original Reinterpretation hypothesis proposed that most of the social–cognitive mechanisms currently employed by normal humans are largely shared with other primates and were in full operation long before humans acquired the means for reinterpreting others' behaviors in terms of unobservable mental states.

The original Reinterpretation hypothesis has much to recommend it. It was developed primarily in response to the inherent logical weaknesses in the then (and now once again) current claims that chimpanzees and other animals possess a ToM. And the fundamental philosophical and methodological challenge thrown out by the Reinterpretation hypothesis has never been acknowledged or refuted by those advocating a mentalistic explanation of nonhuman cognition: to wit, comparative researchers have consistently failed to specify what *unique causal work* is being performed by nonhuman subjects' ToM system that could not have been performed by a sophisticated cognitive system representing and reasoning about observable behaviors alone (see also Penn & Povinelli, 2007b; Povinelli & Vonk, 2003, 2004).

In hindsight, however, the original Reinterpretation hypothesis has a glaring limitation: Because of its myopic focus on exposing the weakness of existing claims for mentalistic and abstract causal reasoning in nonhuman animals, the Reinterpretation hypothesis seriously *over*estimated the cognitive abilities of nonhuman animals and the degree of similarity between the mental systems of chimpanzees and humans. Indeed, the original Reinterpretation hypothesis never proposed any limitation on the inferential abilities of nonhuman animals other than an inability to reason about unobservable entities such as causal mechanisms and mental states (see, for example, Vonk & Povinelli, 2006). Even though it suggested some general parameters, Povinelli's original Reinterpretation hypothesis never offered a detailed account of the differences between the representational architectures of human and nonhuman minds. We now believe that the discontinuity between human and nonhuman cognition is much broader and deeper than an inability to reason about unobservable entities alone.

THE RELATIONAL REINTERPRETATION HYPOTHESIS

Penn, Holyoak, and Povinelli (2007) have recently proposed a revision to Povinelli's original Reinterpretation hypothesis that provides a preliminary specification of the kind of representational-level changes necessary to account for the discontinuity between human and nonhuman cognition. Like the original Reinterpretation hypothesis, the "Relational Reinterpretation" hypothesis proposes that both human and nonhuman animals possess a rich suite of heuristics, biases, top-down knowledge, and inferential mechanisms that allow them to pick out the causally relevant relations in the world amid all the salient but spurious correlations and to form syntactically structured mental representations about these relations that can be used in a flexible, reliable and ecologically rational (i.e., adaptive) fashion. Unlike the original Reinterpretation hypothesis, however, our new hypothesis argues that only human animals possess a cognitive architecture capable of systematically reinterpreting perceptual, embodied relations in terms of the kind of higher-order, role-governed relational representations found in a physical symbol system (Newell, 1980; Newell & Simon, 1976)—or, to be more precise, only human subjects possess a cognitive architecture capable of *approximating* these higher-order features of a physical symbol system, subject to the evolved, content-specific biases and processing capacity limitations of the human brain. Indeed, after reviewing the comparative evidence from numerous domains of research, Penn, Holyoak, and Povinelli (2007) argue that almost all of the salient functional discontinuities between human and nonhuman minds—including our species' unique linguistic, mentalistic, cultural, logical, and causal reasoning abilities—result in large part from the substantial difference in degree to which the human and nonhuman cognitive architectures are able to approximate the higher-order, systematic, relational capabilities of a physical symbol system.

With respect to social interactions, for example, we believe that both human and nonhuman animals possess a variety of mechanisms for recognizing those relations that are causally relevant to predicting the goal-directed behavior of other intentional agents. These heuristics enable both human and nonhuman animals to pick out the causally relevant relation between "what" an agent is "looking" at and how that agent is likely to behave in the near future without computing massive correlations among all possible statistical regularities. However, only humans cognize the higher-order analogical similarities between perceptually disparate behaviors and thus only humans possess the ability to reinterpret other agents' goal-directed relations in terms of abstract mental state relations disembodied from any particular task context.

Importantly, we are not claiming that our higher-order relational capabilities are sufficient to explain all of our species' unique ToM abilities. It is clear that human culture (Tomasello et al., 2005), specialized neural systems (Saxe, 2006), and language (de Villiers, 2000)—to name only the most obvious factors—all play crucial roles in subserving the unique features of human social cognition. Much like Whiten (1996), we are simply suggesting that the ability to recognize and reason about higher-order analogical similarities between perceptually disparate behaviors is a necessary—but not sufficient—condition for enabling our human ToM.

The suggestion that mentalistic explanations are more "parsimonious" than nonmentalistic explanations is a constant refrain in the comparative literature (e.g., Emery & Clayton, 2008; Tomasello & Call, 2006; Whiten, 1997; Whiten & Byrne, 1991). Our new Relational Reinterpretation hypothesis provides a representational-level explanation for why the putative "parsimony" of mentalistic explanations is illusory. If the last few decades of computational cognitive research have taught us anything, it is that higher-order relational reasoning and analogical inferences are not particularly easy to implement in a biologically plausible neural network: indeed, they require an enormous degree of representational complexity above and beyond the functionality necessary to reason about first-order perceptual relations alone (Gentner et al,. 2001; Holyoak & Hummel, 2000). Positing that nonhuman animals are limited to reasoning about first-order relations between observable states of affairs is thus both more consistent with the comparative evidence and more parsimonious from a computational and representational point of view (see Penn et al., 2007 for a more extended version of this argument).

Notwithstanding the monumental impact our uniquely human system for reasoning about higher-order relations and analogical inferences has had on human cognition, we suspect that humans nevertheless *overestimate* the importance and cognitive efficacy of our symbolic-relational abilities. As Povinelli's original Reinterpretation hypothesis first suggested, the vast majority of humans' everyday social interactions do *not* engage our uniquely human ToM system (see also Bermudez, 2003). The role of explicit mentalistic theorizing in human affairs is more post-hoc than we folk would like to admit—and often misguided to boot. Indeed, our species' cognitive system for reasoning about higher-order symbolic relations does not merely subserve our unique linguistic, logical, causal reasoning and mentalistic abilities. It also subserves our inveterate predilection to reinterpret the behavior of heterospecifics in mentalistic terms…and many other uniquely human delusions.

NOTES

1. To be clear, Tomasello et al. (2005 p. 676) stipulate that they will "reserve the term goal for the internal goal, and for the external goal we will use such expressions as 'the desired result.'" They then go on to claim that "apes understand that others have goals" (p. 685).

2. If comparative psychologists mean the term "visual perspective" to be taken in a "non-epistemic" sense (e.g., Dretske, 1969), this is certainly in need of explication. It is not clear how understanding another agent's visual perspective in a nonepistemic fashion would warrant the kind of mentalistic claims being routinely made (e.g., Hare et al., 2000).

REFERENCES

Andrews, K. (2005). Chimpanzee theory of mind: Looking in all the wrong places? *Mind and Language, 20*, 521–536.

Barth, J., Reaux, J. E., & Povinelli, D. J. (2005). Chimpanzees' (pan troglodytes) use of gaze cues in object-choice tasks: Different methods yield different results. *Animal Cognition, 8*, 84–92.

Bennett, J. (1978). Some remarks about concepts. *Behavioral and Brain Sciences, 1*, 557–560.

Bermudez, J. L. (2003). The domain of folk psychology. In A. O'Hear (Ed.), *Mind and Persons* (pp. 25–48). Cambridge, UK: Cambridge University Press.

Bloom, P., & German, T. P. (2000). Two reasons to abandon the false belief task as a test of theory of mind. *Cognition, 77*, B25–B31.

Brauer, J., Call, J., & Tomasello, M. (2008). Chimpanzees do not take into account what others can hear in a competitive situation. *Animal Cognition, 11*, 175–178.

Brauer, J., Call, J., & Tomasello, M. (2007). Chimpanzees really know what others can see in a competitive situation. *Animal Cognition, 10*, 439–448.

Breazeal, C., & Scassellati, B. (2001). Challenges in building roobts that imitate people. In K. Dautenhahn, & C. Nehaniv (Eds.), *Imitation in Animals and Artifacts* (pp. 363–390). Cambridge, MA: MIT Press.

Bugnyar, T., & Heinrich, B. (2005). Ravens, Corvus corax, differentiate between knowledgeable and ignorant competitors. *Proceedings of the Royal Society, London B., Biological Sciences, 272*, 1641–1646.

Call, J. (2004). Inferences about the location of food in the great apes (pan paniscus, pan troglodytes, gorilla gorilla, and pongo pygmaeus). *Journal of Comparative Psychology, 118*, 232–241.

Call, J. (2006). Descartes' two errors: Reason and reflection in the great apes. In S. Hurley, & M. Nudds (Eds.), *Rational Animals?* (pp. 219–234). Oxford: Oxford University Press.

Call, J., Agnetta, B., & Tomasello, M. (2000). Cues that chimpanzees do and do not use to find hidden objects. *Animal Cognition, 3*, 23–34.

Call, J., Hare, B., Carpenter, M., & Tomasello, M. (2004). 'Unwilling' versus 'unable': Chimpanzees' understanding of human intentional action. *Developmental Science, 7*, 488–498.

Call, J., Hare, B., & Tomasello, M. (1998). Chimpanzee gaze following in an object-choice task. *Animal Cognition, 3*, 23–34.

Call, J., & Tomasello, M. (1998). Distinguishing intentional from accidental actions in orangutans (pongo pygmaeus), chimpanzees (pan troglodytes), and human children (Homo sapiens). *Journal of Comparative Psychology, 112*, 192–206.

Call, J., & Tomasello, M. (1999). A nonverbal false belief task: The performance of children and great apes. *Child Development, 70*, 381–395.

Chater, N., Tenenbaum, J. B., & Yuille, A. (2006). Probabilistic models of cognition: Conceptual foundations. *Trends in Cognitive Sciences, 10*, 287–292.

Clark, A., & Thornton, C. (1997). Trading spaces: Computation, representation, and the limits of uninformed learning. *Behavioral and Brain Sciences, 20*, 57–90.

Dally, J. M., Emery, N. J., & Clayton, N. S. (2004). Cache protection strategies by western scrub-jays (aphelocoma californica): Hiding food in the shade. *Proceedings, Biological Sciences/ The Royal Socieety, 271* Suppl 6, S387–390.

Dally, J. M., Emery, N. J., & Clayton, N. S. (2005). Cache protection strategies by western scrub-jays (aphelocoma californica): Implications for social cognition. *Animal Behaviour, 70*, 1251–1263.

Dally, J. M., Emery, N. J., & Clayton, N. S. (2006). Food-caching western scrub-jays keep track of who was watching when. *Science, 312*, 1662–1665.

de Villiers, J. (2000). Language and theory of mind: What is the developmental relationship? In S. Baron-Cohen, H. Tager-Flusberg, & D. J. Cohen (Eds.), *Understanding Other Minds: Perspectives from Autism and Developmental Cognitive Neuroscience* (pp. 83–123). Cambridge University Press.

Dennett, D. (1978). Beliefs about beliefs. *Behavioral and Brain Sciences, 4*, 568–570.

Dickinson, A., & Balleine, B. (2000). Causal cognition and goal-directed action. In C. M. Heyes, & L. Huber (Eds.) *The Evolution of Cognition* (pp. 185–204). Cambridge: MIT Press.

Dretske, F. I. (1969). *Seeing and knowing.* Chicago: University of Chicago Press.

Emery, N. J., & Clayton, N. S. (2008). How to build a scrub-jay that reads minds. In S. Itakura, & K. Fujita (Eds.), *Origins of the Social Mind: Evolutionary and Developmental Views* (pp. 65–98). Tokyo: Springer Japan.

Flombaum, J. I., & Santos, L. R. (2005). Rhesus monkeys attribute perceptions to others. *Current Biology, 15*, 447–452.

Gentner, D., Holyoak, K. J., & Kokinov, B. N. (Eds.). (2001). *The Analogical Mind: Perspectives from Cognitive Science.* Cambridge, MA: MIT Press.

Gillan, D. J., Premack, D., & Woodruff, G. (1981). Reasoning in the chimpanzee: I. Analogical reasoning. *Journal of Experimental Psychology: Animal Behavior Processes, 7*, 1–17.

Hare, B. (2001). Can competitive paradigms increase the validity of experiments on primate social cognition? *Animal Cognition, 4*, 269–280.

Hare, B., Call, J., Agnetta, B., & Tomasello, M. (2000). Chimpanzees know what conspecifics do and do not see. *Animal Behaviour, 59*, 771–785.

Hare, B., Call, J., & Tomasello, M. (2001). Do chimpanzees know what conspecifics know? *Animal Behaviour, 61*, 771–785.

Hare, B., Call, J., & Tomasello, M. (2006). Chimpanzees deceive a human competitor by hiding. *Cognition, 101*, 495–514.

Harman, G. (1978). Studying the chimpanzee's theory of mind. *Behavioral and Brain Sciences, 4*, 576–577.

Heyes, C. M. (1998). Theory of mind in nonhuman primates. *Behavioral and Brain Sciences, 21*, 101–114; discussion 115–148.

Heyes, C. M., & Papineau, D. (2006). Rational or associative? Imitation in Japanese quail. In M. Nudds, & S. Hurley (Eds.), *Rational Animals?* (pp. 187–196). Oxford: Oxford University Press.

Hoffman, M. W., Grimes, D. B., Shon, A. P., & Rao, R. P. (2006). A probabilistic model of gaze imitation and shared attention. *Neural Networks, 19*, 299–310.

Holyoak, K. J., & Hummel, J. E. (2000). The proper treatment of symbols in a connectionist architecture. In E. Dietrich, & A. B. Markman (Eds.), *Cognitive Dynamics: Conceptual Change in Humans and Machines* (pp. 229–263). Mahwah, NJ: Erlbaum.

Horgan, T., & Tienson, J. (1996). *Connectionism and the Philosophy of Psychology.* Cambridge, MA: The MIT Press.

Kaminski, J., Call, J., & Tomasello, M. (2004). Body orientation and face orientation: Two factors controlling apes' behavior from humans. *Animal Cognition, 7*, 216–223.

Kersten, D., Mamassian, P., & Yuille, A. (2004). Object perception as Bayesian inference. *Annual Review of Psychology, 55*, 271–304.

Krebs, J. R., & Dawkins, R. (1984). Animal signals: Mind reading and manipulation. In J. R. Krebs, & N. B. Davies (Eds.), *Behavioural Ecology: An Evolutionary Approach* (pp. xi, 493). Sunderland, MA: Sinauer Associates.

Newell, A. (1980). Physical symbol systems. *Cognitive Science, 4*, 135–183.

Newell, A., & Simon, H. A. (1976). Computer science as empirical inquiry: Symbols and search. *Communications of the ACM, 19*, 113–126.

Okamoto-Barth, S., Call, J., & Tomasello, M. (2007). Great apes' understanding of other individuals' line of sight. *Psychological Science, 18*, 462–468.

Penn, D. C., Holyoak, K. J., & Povinelli, D. J. (2007). Darwin's mistake: Explaining the discontinuity between human and nonhuman minds. *Behavioral and Brain Sciences, 30*, 109–130.

Penn, D. C., & Povinelli, D. J. (2007a). Causal cognition in human and nonhuman animals: A comparative, critical review. *Annual Review of Psychology, 58,* 97–118.

Penn, D. C., & Povinelli, D. J. (2007b). On the lack of evidence that non-human animals possess anything remotely resembling a 'theory of mind'. *Philosophical Transactions of the Royal Society B, 362,* 731–744.

Povinelli, D. J. (2000). *Folk Physics for Apes: The Chimpanzee's Theory of How the World Works.* Oxford: Oxford University Press.

Povinelli, D. J., & Bering, J. M. (2002). The mentality of apes revisited. *Current Directions in Psychological Science, 11,* 115–119.

Povinelli, D. J., Bering, J. M., & Giambrone, S. (2000). Toward a science of other minds: Escaping the argument by analogy. *Cognitive Science, 24,* 509–541.

Povinelli, D. J., Dunphy-Lelii, S., Reaux, J. E., & Mazza, M. P. (2002). Psychological diversity in chimpanzees and humans: New longitudinal assessments of chimpanzees' understanding of attention. *Brain, Behavior and Evolution, 59,* 33–53.

Povinelli, D. J., & Eddy, T. J. (1996). What young chimpanzees know about seeing. *Monographs of the Society for Research in Child Development, 61,* i–vi, 1–152; discussion 153–191.

Povinelli, D. J., & Giambrone, S. (1999). Inferring other minds: Flaws in the argument by analogy. *Philosophical Topics, 27,* 167–201.

Povinelli, D. J., Nelson, K. E., & Boysen, S. T. (1990). Inferences about guessing and knowing by chimpanzees (pan troglodytes). *Journal of Comparative Psychology, 104,* 203–210.

Povinelli, D. J., & Prince, C. G. (1998). When self met other. In M. Ferrari, & R. J. Sternberg (Eds.), *Self-Awareness: Its Nature and Development* (pp. 37–107). New York: Guilford.

Povinelli, D. J., Theall, L., A., Reaux, J. E., & Dunphy-Lelii, S. (2003). Chimpanzees spontaneously alter the location of their gestures to match the attentional orientation of others. *Animal Behaviour, 66,* 71–79.

Povinelli, D. J., & Vonk, J. (2003). Chimpanzee minds: Suspiciously human? *Trends in Cognitive Sciences, 7,* 157–160.

Povinelli, D. J., & Vonk, J. (2004). We don't need a microscope to explore the chimpanzee's mind. *Mind and Language, 19,* 1–28.

Premack, D., & Woodruff, G. (1978). Does the chimpanzee have a theory of mind? *Behavioral and Brain Sciences, 4,* 515–526.

Santos, L. R., Flombaum, J. I., & Phillips, W. (2006). The evolution of human mindreading: How non-human primates can inform social cognitive neuroscience. In S. Platek, J. P. Keenan, & T. K. Shackelford (Eds.), *Evolutionary Cognitive Neuroscience* (pp. 433–456). Cambridge, MA: MIT Press.

Santos, L. R., Nissen, A. G., & Ferrugia, J. A. (2006). Rhesus monkeys, macaca mulatta, know what others can and cannot hear. *Animal Behaviour, 71,* 1175–1181.

Saxe, R. (2006). Uniquely human social cognition. *Current Opinion in Neurobiology, 16,* 235–239.

Shettleworth, S. J. (1998). *Cognition, Evolution and Behavior.* New York: Oxford University Press.

Suddendorf, T., & Whiten, A. (2001). Mental evolution and development: Evidence for secondary representation in children, great apes and other animals. *Psychological Bulletin, 127,* 629–650.

Suddendorf, T., & Whiten, A. (2003). Reinterpreting the mentality of apes. In J. Fitness, & K. Sterelny (Eds.), *From Mating to Mentality: Evaluating Evolutionary Psychology* (pp. 173–196). New York: Psychology Press.

Tomasello, M., & Call, J. (1997). *Primate Cognition.* New York: Oxford University Press.

Tomasello, M., & Call, J. (2006). Do chimpanzees know what others see—or only what they are looking at? In S. Hurley, & M. Nudds (Eds.), *Rational Animals?* (pp. 371–384) Oxford: Oxford University Press.

Tomasello, M., Call, J., & Hare, B. (1998). Five primate species follow the visual gaze of conspecifics. *Animal Behaviour, 55,* 1063–1069.

Tomasello, M., Call, J. & Hare, B. (2003a). Chimpanzees understand psychological states—the question is which ones and to what extent. *Trends in Cognitive Sciences, 7,* 153–156.

Tomasello, M., Call, J., & Hare, B. (2003b). Chimpanzees versus humans: It's not that simple. *Trends in Cognitive Sciences, 7,* 239–240.

Tomasello, M., Carpenter, M., Call, J., Behne, T., & Moll, H. (2005). Understanding and sharing intentions: The origins of cultural cognition. *Behavioral and Brain Sciences, 28,* 675–691.

Tomasello, M., Hare, B., & Agnetta, B. (1999). Chimpanzees, pan troglodytes, follow gaze direction geometrically. *Animal Behaviour, 58,* 769–777.

Vonk, J., & Povinelli, D. J. (2006). Similarity and difference in the conceptual systems of primates: The unobservability hypothesis. In T. Zentall, & E. A. Wasserman (Eds.), *Comparative Cognition: Experimental Explorations of Animal Intelligence* (pp. 363–387). Oxford: Oxford University Press.

Whiten, A. (1996). When does behaviour-reading become mind-reading. In P. Carruthers, & P. K. Smith (Eds.), *Theories of Theory of Mind* (pp. 277–292). New York: Cambridge University Press.

Whiten, A. (1997). The Machiavellian mindreader. In A. Whiten, & R. W. Byrne (Eds.), *Machiavellian Intelligence II: Extensions and Evaluations* (pp. 240–263) Cambridge: Cambridge University Press.

Whiten, A., & Byrne, R. W. (1991). The emergence of metarepresentation in human ontogeny and primate phylogeny. In A. Whiten (Ed.), *Natural Theories of Mind* (pp. 267–281). Oxford: Basil Blackwell.

Wimmer, H., & Perner, J. (1983). Beliefs about beliefs: Representation and constraining function of wrong beliefs in young children's understanding of deception. *Cognition, 13,* 103–128.

Wood, J. N., Glynn, D. D., Phillips, B. C., & Hauser, M. D. (2007). The perception of rational, goal-directed action in nonhuman primates. *Science, 317,* 1402–1405.

4 Behavior-Reading versus Mentalizing in Animals
Logan Fletcher and Peter Carruthers

WE BEGIN WITH some comments on the manner in which Penn and Povinelli (chapter 3) frame the debate about primate mindreading. Thereafter, in the sections that follow, we will consider some of their arguments, as well as the related arguments of Perner (2010). We will suggest that this debate should not be considered in isolation, but must be taken along with an evaluation of recent evidence of mindreading abilities in very young human infants.

Penn and Povinelli protest that their critics are misguided to charge them with being behaviorists. They say they want to insist, on the contrary, that many animal species possess high-level forms of cognition, and are capable of nonassociative forms of learning. But this is not what the debate is about. The question is not whether we, as theorists, should be behaviorists in our interpretation of the behavior of other primates. The question is rather whether the animals themselves are behaviorists. Do these animals, in their social interactions with others, understand those others in terms of some set of behavior-rules, as Penn and Povinelli maintain? (An example of such a rule might be: "A dominant will approach food to which it has had uninterrupted line of sight in the recent past"; Povinelli & Vonk, 2003.) Or do the animals comprehend those behaviors in terms of some set of underlying mental states (including desires, percepts, and knowledge), as many of Povinelli and colleagues' critics claim?

So although Penn and Povinelli (chapter 3) embark on an extended demonstration that primates bring to bear an impressive set of cognitive and inferential resources in navigating their social worlds, this is really a red herring. Although we (and most others in the field) fully accept the conclusion, this is not what is at issue. What is really at stake (to repeat) is whether or not the animals in question represent and reason about some of the mental states of other agents. Penn and Povinelli maintain that they do not, and propose a behavior-rule account instead, whereas many others claim that they do (Buttelmann et al., 2007; Call et al., 2006; Call & Tomasello, 2008; Hare et al., 2000, 2001; Hare et al., 2006; Kaminski et al., 2008; Melis et al., 2006).

Penn and Povinelli also protest against the charge that their behavior-rule hypothesis is unfalsifiable and unparsimonious, seemingly believing that these criticisms are somehow linked to the allegation that they are behaviorists. But of course there is no such link, because there is no such allegation. And the behavior-rule hypothesis is, indeed, unfalsifiable in a quite straightforward way. (The issue of parsimony is more complex. We will return to it later.) For it is too underspecified to make determinate predictions, hence there is no risk of it turning out to be wrong. Claiming only that primates employ *some* set of behavior rules provides us with no clues as to how the animals might be expected to react in particular circumstances and suggests no potential lines of experimentation. Moreover, in respect of any new item of behavioral evidence, an explanation in terms of the animals' deployment of some or other behavior rule can always be constructed after the fact. And this is very much the way in which Povinelli and colleagues have employed the behavior-rule hypothesis. When some new item of evidence that is claimed to support a mentalizing interpretation of primate behavior is described, Povinelli and colleagues set out to show that there is a behavior rule that can accommodate the evidence equally well. Hence they are always playing "catch up," and are forced to postulate behavior rules ad hoc to accommodate the data.

Of course, the hypothesis that the animals make use of all and only members of some determinate set of (specified) behavior rules *does* make predictions and *is* liable to falsification. But no such determinate set has ever been put forward. And although specific behavior rules have been proposed (like the one about recent line of sight to food, noted in the preceding), it is plain that the previous proposals are by no means complete because there are now a number of experiments demonstrating that additional behavior rules would need to be postulated to explain the animals' behavior, as we will see later in this chapter.

The mentalizing hypothesis, in contrast, although admitting of various strengths (depending on the range of mental states that are thought to be understood by the animals in question), provides a clear framework for generating novel predictions. And this is just the way in which it has been employed by Povinelli's opponents, in many cases issuing in positive results. In particular, there have been positive results generated by the claim that primates attribute desires, percepts, and knowledge or ignorance to other agents (Buttelmann et al., 2007; Call et al., 2004; Call & Tomasello, 2008; Hare et al., 2000, 2001, 2006; Kaminski et al., 2008; Melis et al., 2006). But all recent experimental tests of the claim that these animals attribute false beliefs to others have been negative (Call & Tomasello, 1999; Hare et al., 2001; Kaminski et al., 2008; Krachun et al., 2009; O'Connell & Dunbar, 2003). This has led to the hypothesis that the animals possess

"Stage 1" mindreading abilities, of the sort that are thought to emerge in human infancy before the capacity to understand false beliefs (Kaminski et al., 2008; Krachun et al., 2009).

What Povinelli and colleagues have ranged against them, therefore, is a regular scientific research program of good standing that generates determinate predictions capable of falsification when combined with auxiliary assumptions (e.g., concerning the animals' other forms of knowledge). Moreover, it is a progressing research program, issuing in a stream of positive results and increasingly precise theories. The behavior-rule hypothesis, in contrast, is too indeterminate and ad hoc to qualify as a scientific research program at all. This isn't to say that it can't be true, of course, and we don't really want to fight over the applicability of the phrase "scientific theory." But it does mean that the behavior-rule idea hasn't yet entered into serious scientific competition with the mentalizing hypothesis. That said, the remainder of this chapter is devoted to comparing additional strengths and weaknesses of the two approaches.

General-Purpose versus Domain-Specific Learning Mechanisms

Penn and Povinelli (chapter 3) argue that we should not expect to find mentalizing abilities of any sort in nonhuman primates because these animals seem to lack the capacity to reason about similarities and analogies (or "relations between relations"; Penn et al., 2008). The rationale is that only by noticing the similarity between different items of behavior in various contexts can a creature learn that it is guided by a single underlying variable (a desire for food, say). And Penn et al. (2008) amass a considerable body of evidence to show that nonhuman primates are incapable of reasoning analogically. What this argument betrays, however, is Penn and Povinelli's tacit empiricism.

The capacity to reason analogically is only relevant to the possession of mentalizing abilities if the latter need to be *learned*, and learned on the basis of hypothesis formation and testing, at that. Although something like this has been proposed as the means by which human children acquire a "Theory of Mind" (Gopnik & Meltzoff, 1997), this is by no means endorsed by all developmental psychologists. On the contrary, there are significant numbers of "modularists" who think that core mentalizing abilities result from the maturation of an innately channeled module, or at least from the operations of a domain-specific learning mechanism of some sort (Baron-Cohen, 1995; Leslie, 1994; Song & Baillargeon, 2008; note that the notion of "module" in play here can be quite weak; see Barrett & Kurzban, 2006; Carruthers, 2006). Indeed, the burgeoning evidence of very early mindreading abilities in infants (discussed later) suggests that a broadly modularist position is now pretty much mandatory, at least in the human case. Moreover, comparative psychologists who attribute mentalizing abilities to animals certainly don't think that those abilities result from general-purpose reasoning about relations between relations. Indeed, the entire tradition of thinking about the evolution of mindreading capacities, from "Machiavellian intelligence" (Byrne & Whiten, 1988, 1997) onward, has presumed that they are an innately channeled adaptation of some sort. So Penn and Povinelli's argument is question begging.

By appealing to the possibility of an innately channeled mindreading module we can also reply to another of Penn and Povinelli's arguments. This is grounded in the well-known finding that primates make little or no use of their alleged mindreading capacities in cooperative contexts, but only in competitive ones. This finding is said to be problematic for the claim that they possess such capacities at all. But it only raises a difficulty for the mentalizing hypothesis on the assumption that mindreading would involve some sort of general-purpose theory embedded in a general-purpose mind. If that were the case, then it really would be puzzling that an animal might draw on a set of beliefs about the mind in the service of one sort of goal but not another. For surely, one might think, if these animals are rational agents, capable of surveying the entire set of their beliefs to figure out how to satisfy their desires, then they ought to realize that their beliefs about another agent's mental states are relevant to successful begging behavior (for example). But if one holds even a weakly modular conception of the architecture of animal minds, then the puzzle disappears because in that case certain types of goal might have proprietary links to certain informational modules, while ignoring the output from other such modules.

It is important to realize that, from a modularist perspective, this proposal is by no means arbitrary because nonhuman primates are not naturally cooperative in their normal lives in the wild, except in highly restricted contexts (such as cooperative hunting and border patrolling by male chimpanzees). They are, however, intensely competitive, with continual jostling and conflict over access to food, mates, and other resources. It makes good sense, then, that an evolved mindreading system might be linked specifically to the goals that are operative in such contexts.

Is it really plausible to claim that animal minds are so different from our own, however? Can it really be the case that the minds of other primates have a modular architecture, whereas their close relatives (humans) are general-purpose reasoners? Indeed, this would not be plausible. But the claim that humans have a general-purpose cognitive architecture is itself highly controversial. Indeed, the best account of the differences among primate species is that all share essentially the same architecture of modules arranged as consumers for the "global broadcast" of attended perceptual information, but that humans possess a much more highly developed ability to maintain, rehearse, and manipulate globally broadcast representations (including so-called "inner speech") in working memory (Carruthers, 2006, 2011; Shanahan, 2010; Shanahan & Baars, 2005). This enables us to utilize reflective "System 2" forms of reasoning, thus approximating general-purpose reasoners in some contexts and for some purposes, despite an underlying modular architecture (Carruthers, 2009).

Stage 1 versus Stage 2 Mindreading

We now turn to a finding that is problematic for the behavior-rule approach, which is that although primates act in such a way as to suggest that they understand the desires, perceptions, and knowledge or ignorance of other agents, they fail otherwise parallel tests of false belief understanding. The mentalizing account can give a principled explanation of this divergence, drawing on the distinction between Stage 1 and Stage 2 mindreading adopted by most developmental psychologists. Indeed, there is remarkable agreement among developmentalists that desire/perception/knowledge–ignorance psychology is earlier to emerge in childhood than false-belief psychology, no matter whether the theorists in question are general-learning theorists (Gopnik & Meltzoff, 1997; Wellman, 1990) or modularists (Baron-Cohen, 1995; Leslie, 1994; Song & Baillargeon, 2008). It makes good sense then (especially from a modularist perspective) that nonhuman primates might have only Stage 1 of this two-stage structure.

These divergent findings are much more difficult for a behavior-rule theorist to explain. For as Penn and Povinelli themselves point out, there would have been no difficulty finding a behavior-rule to explain the animals' behavior if it had turned out that they could pass a standard false-belief task. The rule could have been, for example, "A potential competitor will approach the previous location of food if the competitor was absent when the food was moved to its present location." This rule doesn't seem any more complex, nor any more difficult to learn or evolve, than the corresponding behavior-rule for an ignorance task, namely, "A potential competitor won't compete for food that isn't and wasn't recently in its line of sight." Why is it, then, that the animals seemingly know the latter rule but not the former?

Penn and Povinelli might try to argue that the behavior-rule needed in conditions of false belief is actually more complex than the ignorance-rule. This is because it requires the animal to keep in mind two distinct locations—the place where the competitor saw the food, and the place where the food is now. The ignorance-rule, in contrast, mentions only a single location (the current position of the food). There is a simpler version of the false-belief behavior rule, however, which doesn't suffer from this problem. For the animals could have utilized the rule, "A competitor that has, or has recently had, line of sight to the location of some food will go to that location if it can." This can predict that the competitor will approach the previous location in a case in which the food has been moved during the competitor's absence, without the animals needing to represent where the food is now in order to make the prediction.

Penn and Povinelli might also try to argue that behavior-rules for dealing with false-belief situations are absent from the primate rule-kit because they are significantly less *useful* in competitive situations, not because they are significantly more difficult than their ignorance-task counterparts. To a primate competing for food, it is highly relevant whether or not one's conspecifics are as knowledgeable as oneself regarding the food's location. Therefore upon seeing it being moved from one place to another when one's competitors are absent, it pays off to register that they are now *ignorant* of its present location. (Or rather, in the context of the present debate, it is important to know a rule that can predict that they aren't likely to approach the food at its present location.) This is because one can then know that it is safe to approach it oneself. But beyond that, it is unclear why it should be useful to know where in particular one's competitors will now (falsely) *think* the food is hidden, or where they will now go given their previous history of line-of-sight to food, so long as this is distinct from the food's actual location. Or at least, so Penn and Povinelli might try to argue.

These considerations are insufficient by themselves to explain the absence in other primates of behavior-rules covering false-belief situations because it frequently *does* matter quite a lot to a primate where a competitor is likely to be when the primate is retrieving some food (or doing anything else over which there might be competition, such as mating). For if the competitor will be in a place that has line of sight to the competed-over resource, then that is likely to lead to conflict and loss of an opportunity to eat (or mate). So a behavior-rule that tells one where a competitor is likely to go, given its previous perceptual access to the location of some food, would surely be advantageous. It might perhaps be claimed that such situations are less frequent in natural circumstances than are situations in which an ignorance-based behavior-rule would apply. But this remains to be demonstrated. And even if demonstrated, it would still need to be shown that the benefits of employing a behavior-rule covering false-belief situations would be minimal enough for us to predict the absence of such rules among primates. So it remains as a challenge for Penn and Povinelli to explain why ignorance-based behavior rules should be used by nonhuman primates, whereas false-belief-based rules are not.

Of course, given that the set of behavior-rules is heterogeneous and potentially infinite in extent, it is perhaps not surprising that animals should happen to have evolved some but not other equally-easy-to-evolve rules from this set. Nor should it be surprising that there might be quirks of their evolved learning systems that enable them to acquire some but not others of the set, although the latter look to us humans to be equally easy to learn. But these hypotheses are unprincipled, and appeal to accident or coincidence. They therefore fail to provide us with an *explanation* of the phenomenon. In contrast, the competing mentalizing explanation can make good sense of these findings, as noted. This gives us reasons to prefer the latter. For theories that can explain the data are generally better than theories that can't.

Explanatory Virtues

Penn and Povinelli (chapter 3) complain that the mentalizing account of primate behavior has failed to demonstrate that mindreading is *necessary* to produce some of the behavior we observe, or that the same behavior *could not* have been produced by a set of behavior rules. But this is too strong a demand to place on any theory. No theory, in any domain of science, can ever show that the data *cannot* be explained in any other way. Despite popular-science mythology to the contrary, there are no such things as decisive experiments in science. Any set of results can always be accommodated by means of suitable theoretical adjustments, or by altering some of the auxiliary assumptions that are always needed for a theory to make determinate predictions. As has long been known by philosophers of science (Kuhn, 1962; Lakatos, 1970; Newton-Smith, 1981), and is understood tacitly by most working scientists, theory choice is never a matter of proof, but of judgment—incorporating such factors as simplicity, predictive accuracy, explanatory scope, coherence with surrounding theories, and scientific fruitfulness.

Consider how the two approaches stack up along these dimensions. The question of simplicity is discussed later. But we have already seen that the mentalizing account is significantly stronger in terms of predictive accuracy, especially because the behavior-rule account is only capable of "predicting" new findings after they are discovered, postulating a novel behavior-rule for the purpose. The mentalizing theory also does better in terms of explanatory scope because although both accounts are equally capable of explaining why mindreading-like behavior is only found in competitive contexts, the mentalizing account can explain why the animals should pass tests of Stage 1 mindreading while failing tests of false-belief understanding, whereas the behavior-rule account seemingly cannot. Likewise, the mentalizing theory is much more scientifically fruitful, issuing in novel tests and positive results, whereas the behavior-rule approach is entirely defensive, explaining away positive results as they are discovered. In addition, the mentalizing account coheres better with surrounding theories in cognitive science, especially the existence of both Stage 1 and Stage 2 mindreading in human infants. (This point is elaborated later.)

It appears, then, that when compared along most of the normal dimensions governing theory choice in science, the mentalizing hypothesis is significantly preferable to the behavior-rule one. But the comparative simplicity of the two theories has yet to be considered, and the claimed greater coherence of the mindreading hypothesis with surrounding theories has yet to be established. To these tasks we now turn.

Comparative Simplicity

This section takes up the vexed question of the comparative simplicity of the two types of hypothesis. On the face of it, simplicity favors a mentalizing account. For the behavior-rule theory is forced to postulate a multitude of distinct rules, whereas the mentalizing theory postulates a single mindreading faculty. Perner (2010), however, argues that the alleged simplicity of the mindreading hypothesis is illusory, and depends upon treating the hypothesized system as a "black box." In fact, it must have significant internal complexity, including rules for inferring goals from behavioral cues, as well as rules for judging perceptual access and for inferring knowledge or ignorance. Indeed, in cases in which just a single goal (like getting food) is in play, Perner claims that for every rule postulated by a behavior-rule theorist (such as, "A competitor will move to secure food at a location that was recently in its line of sight"), a mentalizing theorist will need to postulate two (in this case, "A competitor that has seen the location of food knows the location of food" and, "A competitor that knows the location of food will move to secure it"). So the behavior-rule hypothesis is the simpler of the two.

These claims hold good, however, only if the number of behavior-rules at stake is quite small. The advantage of mindreading is that distinct cues can indicate the presence of the same goal (such as moving toward it as well as begging for it) and distinct cues can indicate the presence of knowledge of something (including both seeing and hearing). Moreover, different goals can interact with different items of knowledge to issue in novel forms of pairing between the initial cues and subsequent behavior. On the mindreading account, one needs to posit as many rules as the total number of different indicator-cues of knowledge and indicator-cues of goals, combined additively. On the behavior-rule account, in contrast, these numbers combine multiplicatively to give the total number of rules required because every possible combination of knowledge plus goal that issues in behavior requires its own rule. Moreover, on a mindreading account much of the required complexity can be "farmed out" to other faculties of the mind. Almost all theorists in the field accept that mindreading operates in part by *simulation* of the minds of others, enabling the mindreading system to rely on beliefs that are produced by other mental faculties when generating predictions of a target agent's behavior. So when the number of goals and items of knowledge tracked by an animal become sufficiently large (either explicitly, using mental state attributions, or implicitly, using a set of behavior rules), then a mindreading account of the animal's behavior will utilize far fewer rules.

It has to be admitted that in this respect the data do not yet provide much direct support for a mentalizing account, however, because all of the mindreading tasks employed to date have involved competition over food. Since all involve the same presumed goal, this means that the number of behavior-rules that are needed to explain the data are also quite limited. Indeed, as discussed later, all of the data to date can be explained using just a handful of behavior-rules, whereas a mentalizing account needs to postulate roughly the same number of rules governing the assignment of mental states. So it might seem that the data at this point provide support for neither side (along the simplicity-dimension of evaluation, at any rate).

It is possible to push back against Perner's (2010) "black box" argument, however, because it presupposes a narrow theoretical focus, aimed only at explaining the behavior of nonhuman primates. But what matters for science is not the relative simplicity of narrowly framed theories, considered discretely. Rather, it is the total set of mechanisms and processes that our theories require us to accept. Therefore, if a local theory can import some complex structure from another related domain that we already have reason to believe in, then the presence of that complexity does *not* render the resulting theory equally complex. This is because the structure in question already formed part of our theoretical ontology. Hence importing it into the new theory can be considered just a single addition to the complexity of the latter, rather than many. In fact there are numerous circumstances in which "black boxing" a complex structure for purposes of judging comparative simplicity is perfectly legitimate. And we believe that this is so here.

We argue later that the data from human infants warrant us in claiming that both Stage 1 and Stage 2 mindreading are present and operating at very early ages (before the end of the first year of life for the former, and by the age of 18 months for the latter). If so, then it seems almost certain that both are heavily innately channeled in their development. This means, then, that we should be committed to the existence of an evolved and weakly modular Stage 1 mindreading system. The cost of importing such a system into the explanation of nonhuman primate behavior then merely entails supposing that it evolved earlier than one might otherwise have thought (in the lineage of the last common ancestor of all of the primate species in question, instead of only among hominins).

Note that, given the construal of the infancy data, a behavior-rule theorist must be committed to three distinct kinds of structure underlying primate social competence. There is an innately channeled set of behavior-rules that operate among nonhuman primates, on the one hand, whereas there is a mindreading faculty in humans that consists of both Stage 1 and Stage 2 components. In contrast, the mentalizing theorist is only committed to the existence of two of these structures—a Stage 1 mindreading system that is possessed by a number of primate species in addition to humans, and a Stage 2 system that is unique to humans. This means that the mentalizing hypothesis comes out simpler overall, despite the extra complexity that is postulated to exist in the minds of nonhuman primates through their possession of a complexly structured Stage 1 mindreading system.

Penn and Povinelli might attempt to reply by claiming that Stage 1 mindreading isn't needed. Perhaps the same set of behavior rules that is (they claim) operative in nonhuman primates is also at work early in infancy, before the capacity to pass nonverbal false-belief tasks. But there are two reasons why this won't work. First, although later we focus mostly on nonverbal evidence of false-belief understanding, many of the same sorts of points could be made in respect of the evidence of Stage 1 mindreading in infants. Second, the false-belief data make no sense in the absence of a capacity to attribute goals, perceptions, and knowledge to other agents because the experiments are all designed around just such an assumption, and no one has any idea how a set of behavior-rules could fit together with belief understanding to issue in the patterns of behavior we observe.

Indeed, the mentalizing account of nonhuman primate capacities provides a more coherent evolutionary theory of primate social behavior overall. Everyone agrees that the evolutionary pressure toward mindreading derives from the exigencies of life in complex social groups, and although the sociality of humans is no doubt extreme, many other primates also live in such groups. One might predict, then, that simpler forms of mindreading would be found in such creatures. The behavior-rule hypothesis, in contrast, must postulate that the entire evolutionary history of mindreading took place in the hominin line. Although this is possible, of course, it does place the onus on behavior-rule theorists to specify what it was about early forms of hominin social life that resulted initially in the emergence of Stage 1 mindreading, and why it is that social living among nonhuman primates should have resulted in a set of behavior-rules instead. Indeed, it is especially puzzling how Stage 1 mindreading abilities could have evolved among hominins on a behavior-rule account. For there would already have been behavior-rules in place sufficient to underwrite something functionally equivalent to competence at passing Stage 1 mindreading tasks. So what would a genuinely mentalistic Stage 1 mindreading system have evolved *for*?

We conclude, therefore, that on the simplicity-dimension of theoretical evaluation, just as with the other factors considered previously, the mentalizing hypothesis comes out ahead of the behavior-rule one. But this argument has been premised on an assumption of innately channeled mindreading capacities in human infants. This is where we go next; discussing the nature and strength of the existing data. We then make some comparisons with the data from nonhuman primates. This enables us to provide a few suggestions for future experimental work with primates that would make the case for a mentalizing account even more powerful.

Mindreading Data from Infants

Beginning with Woodward (1998), there are now numerous nonverbal looking-time studies demonstrating that human infants can attribute goals and intentions to others within the first year of life (Csibra et al., 2003; Csibra, 2008; Johnson, 2000; Luo & Baillargeon, 2005). There are also a number of experiments showing that infants are sensitive to the difference between knowledge and ignorance in others (Liszkowski et al., 2006, 2007; Luo & Baillargeon, 2007; Luo & Johnson, 2009). Moreover, following the ground-breaking work of Onishi & Baillargeon (2005), there has been a rapidly expanding body of data suggesting that human infants can understand false beliefs and can make behavioral predictions accordingly by around the age of 18 months (Buttelmann et al., 2009b; Scott & Baillareon, 2009; Scott et al., 2011; Song et al., 2008; Southgate et al., 2007, 2010; Surian et al., 2007). These studies have come out of a number of different labs, using a variety of distinct measures, including not only expectancy-violation looking time, but also anticipatory looking time, as well as behavior intended to help another person or comply with a request.

As with the primate data, alternative behavior-rule explanations have been proposed (Perner, 2010; Perner & Ruffman, 2005). In particular, it has been suggested that the data collected by Onishi and Baillargeon (2005), as well as at least some of the data collected since, might be explained by assuming that infants know and apply the rule, "People will search for a desired object where they last saw it" or, "Ignorance leads to error." Notice, to begin with, that these are not pure behavioral rules, but rather presuppose the existence in infants of Stage 1 mindreading. Although making a rule-based account somewhat more plausible, this isn't absolutely essential. The search-rule might instead be formulated as a pure behavior-rule by substituting in place of an ascription of desire what-ever behavioral cues would enable Stage 1 mindreaders to ascribe a desire (and likewise for the ignorance-rule). Moreover, the "ignorance leads to error" rule has been directly tested and found not to be operative (Baillargeon et al., 2013; Scott & Baillargeon, 2009; Southgate et al., 2007).

The data are now so voluminous and varied, however, that behavior-rule explanations have become unsustainable. This claim is defended in some detail in Carruthers (2011). Here we simply sketch some of the main points. One factor is that a variety of goals to be attributed to the target agent have been employed across experiments, in addition to that of finding a desired object. These include the goal of *pretending* that something is the case (Onishi et al., 2007), the goal of *referring* to one thing rather than another (Southgate et al., 2010), and the goal of making a rattling noise happen (Scott et al., 2011). With four distinct goals in play, then, as well as a number of different kinds of belief (each of which is caused in a distinct way), it is easy to see that the total number of behavior-rules that would be needed to accommodate the data are multiplying rapidly (although admittedly, not all of the studies needed to fill in each of the cells in this potential matrix have yet been completed). It is already more parsimonious to assume that infants are capable of mindreading (utilizing a set of principles for ascribing beliefs and desires) than to claim that they deploy a large and varied set of behavior-rules.

Moreover, some of the behavior-rules that would be required to explain specific pieces of experimental data are quite strange and elaborate. There seems very little chance that they could be innate, and it is exceedingly hard to see how the infants would have had sufficient opportunity to learn them. For example, the behavior-rule needed to explain the data from Scott and Baillargeon (2009) would be this: "People who want to obtain the divisible one of two otherwise-similar objects will reach for the location of the unseen member of the pair when the other of the two is visible in its joined state, provided that the construction of that object out of its parts didn't take place within the person's line of sight." And the behavior-rule needed to explain the data from Baillargeon et al. (2013) would be this: "People who desire a rigid-seeming object, who have not observed that the object can be collapsed to make it small, will search for the object in a large container rather than a small one when presented with the two options."

In addition, the methodology employed in devising these studies is particularly reveal-ing. By assuming that infants are capable of ascribing simple goals, perceptions, and beliefs, the experimenters make predictions about the behavior that we should then observe (while also including various controls to rule out other possibilities). The result has been an extensive set of positive results, which a behavior-rule theorist would have had no reason to predict. Applying normal scientific standards, then, these results pro-vide powerful confirmation of the initial theoretical assumptions.

Even more impressive, a number of studies have capitalized on beliefs about the world that we have independent reason to think that infants possess. Experiments have then been designed by assuming that infants will attribute these same beliefs to the target agents in the experiments (using the same "default attribution" heuristic that adults, too, employ; see Nichols & Stich, 2003). Baillargeon et al. (2013), for example, make use of an earlier finding that infants understand that a large object cannot be contained within a small one (Hespos & Baillargeon, 2006). They use this to predict that the infants should be surprised when the agent who hasn't seen the collapsible nature of a desired toy reaches for the small container (even though that is where the toy really is). Likewise Scott et al. (2011) capitalize on the fact that 18-month-old infants as well as older children expect objects that are more similar in their surface properties to resemble one another in non-obvious properties as well. This enables them to set up a scenario involving three cups, two of which are similar in appearance but the third of which is quite different. They then predict that infants should be surprised when the agent, who hasn't seen that it is the dissimilar cup that also makes a rattling sound, reaches for that cup when another agent exhibits one of the two similar cups, rattles it, and asks (while continuing to hold onto the demonstrated cup), "Can you make it happen too?" Again, normal scientific standards should lead us to see the positive results obtained in these experiments as powerful confirmation of the mindreading hypothesis.

In fact one of the strengths of the mindreading account is that it is, in a certain sense, generalizable. For it can be combined with other theories of the belief-forming competence of human infants to generate indefinitely many novel hypotheses about what infants should or should not expect a target agent to do. The result has been a rapidly expanding set of confirmed predictions that would never have been made in advance by a behavior-rule theorist. There should be no dispute that this provides powerful confirmation of the mindreading hypothesis.

Our view, then, is that it is now reasonable to believe that human infants possess innately channeled mechanisms underlying both Stage 1 and Stage 2 mindreading capacities. (In addition, Carruthers, 2011, argues that these mechanisms are significantly modular in character.) Given that this is so, such a result should now have a powerful impact on the debate over Stage 1 mindreading in nonhuman primates, as we argued earlier. In particular, it means that the hypothesis of Stage 1 mindreading in nonhuman primates both coheres better with surrounding scientific theories than does a behavior-rule account, and is also genuinely simpler than the latter (enabling us to "black box" the internal complexity of a Stage 1 mindreading mechanism for purposes of judging comparative simplicity).

Mindreading Data from Animals

This section briefly reviews the data on Stage 1 mindreading in nonhuman primates, comparing them with the infancy data, and using this to motivate some tentative suggestions for future research. To this end we discuss the data on their own merits, using a narrow theoretical focus of the sort adopted by Perner (2010), but rejected by us earlier.

From our review of the existing data we believe that as few as nine separate behavior-rules might be sufficient to explain them (setting aside the point that because the behavior-rule hypothesis wouldn't have predicted the data, it can't really explain those data either—except ad hoc, and after the fact). The rules are as follows.

1. "A competitor will move to secure food that is in its line of sight" (see Hare et al., 2000).

2. "A competitor will move to secure food that was recently in its line of sight" (see Hare et al., 2001). So far as we can see, the same rule can also be used to explain the data from Call et al. (2004). We also think it can explain the results obtained by Kaminski et al. (2008). Although the authors of the latter say that their experiment rules out a behavior-rule interpretation (see p. 227), we don't see how it does. All it excludes is an "evil eye" form of behavior rule.

3. "A competitor with food within reach will move to secure the food if another agent approaches within line of sight" (see Hare et al., 2006). It is possible, however, that this rule may need to be made more complex, conditionalizing on circumstances in which the competitor cannot issue an effective threat to protect the food, because of the presence of Plexiglas. A probabilistic application of this rule might also be sufficient to explain the data from Melis et al. (2006). In a condition in which the competitor was not visible within the booth, and the line of sight was not known, the apes preferred to reach for the food through an opaque tube rather than a transparent one.

4. "A competitor with food within reach will move to secure the food if another agent approaches noisily" (see another of the conditions in Melis et al., 2006). Alternatively, one could use #3 together with: "A competitor with food within reach will orient toward a nearby noise."

5. "A compliant agent with food is more likely to provide some if one begs within their line of sight" (see Liebal et al., 2004). Note that knowledge of a behavior-rule for distinguishing between competitive and compliant agents will also need to be postulated.

6. "A human who makes an accidental-dropping when reaching food to one is more likely to provide food later than a human who makes an intentional-dropping" (see Call et al., 2004). The hyphenated phrases are intended to be stand-ins for nonmentalistic behavior descriptions. We return to raise some doubts about the adequacy of this rule shortly.

7. "A competitor who makes a pleased-face to one item of food and a disgust-face to another is more likely to eat the former" (see Buttelmann et al., 2009a). Again, the hyphenated phrases are intended to be stand-ins for purely behavioral descriptions.

8. "When humans use an unusual body part to bring about an effect in circumstances where they could have used their hands, then the use of that body part

is likely to be necessary to achieve the effect; but when humans use an unusual body part to bring about an effect where their hands are occupied, then the use of that body part is unlikely to be necessary to achieve the effect" (see Buttelmann et al., 2007). We will shortly return to comment on this rule, too.

9. "A competitor who has line of sight to two objects, one of which is in a physical arrangement that suggests the presence of food while the other does not, will select the former" (see Schmelz et al., 2011). The plausibility of this rule will shortly be discussed alongside rule #8.

Overall this is not an especially large number of behavior-rules. For the mindreading approach will need to postulate in place of #1 that line of sight leads to seeing, and in place of #2 that seeing leads to knowing, as well as that competitors generally want to secure available food. These should then be sufficient when combined to replace #3, although to replace #4 we will need to add the rule that hearing leads to knowing. They are also sufficient to replace #5 when combined with a rule for identifying a compliant agent. In place of #6 the mindreading hypothesis will need rules for recognizing the presence of a desire to help (in cases of accidental dropping), as well as a desire to tease or annoy (in cases of intentional dropping). Instead of #7, there will need to be rules for recognizing from facial expressions desires to eat or not eat a given food item. And to replace #8 one will need a rule to the effect that when someone performs a movement that has an interesting effect, they probably intended that effect. In contrast, one may not need any additional rule to replace #9, if the behavior can be explained by *simulation* of the reasoning of the competitor. This seemingly adds up to slightly more mindreading rules (10). But given that behavior-rules #5 and #6 are arguably each a conjunction of two distinct rules, and that a behavior-rule theorist also needs to appeal to a rule for identifying compliant or helpful agents, the total count for behavior-rules should probably be slightly larger (12).

It seems to us that three of the behavior-rules #1 through #9 are intrinsically problematic, however. One is #6, which is inadequate to explain the totality of the data obtained in the experiment. For although one finding was that the apes left the testing area more quickly in the intentional-dropping condition than in the accidental-dropping condition (suggesting that they might be reasoning in accord with #6), another finding was that they also exhibited more attention-grabbing and coercive forms of behavior in the intentional-dropping condition. This is the opposite of what would be predicted by rule #6 because if there is no point waiting around, one might think that there would be no point begging or banging on the cage either. On the contrary, the data are suggestive of anger or irritation. And this only seems to make sense if the animals have recognized that the human in the intentional-dropping condition is teasing them.

The other problematic behavior-rules seem to us to be #8 and #9. This isn't because they can't handle the data, but rather because it seems quite unlikely that the animals would have had sufficient opportunity to learn such rules. (We assume that it is extremely unlikely that these rules would be innate.) How often would they have observed a human using an unusual body part to bring about some physical effect while their hands are unoccupied, or a competitor choosing between two covers, one of which is partially supported by an item of hidden food and the other of which is not? And notice that although they might sometimes have seen a human whose hands are occupied with a load nudge open a door with his elbow or backside, for example, this isn't sufficient basis for learning rule #8. In contrast, a Stage 1 mindreader can make the appropriate inferences, provided that the mindreading system can co-opt the resources of the mindreader's own planning abilities when generating predictions about the likely behavior of other agents (Nichols & Stich, 2003).

Therefore, although the number of rules that need to be postulated by behavior-rule and mindreading accounts are presently more or less equivalent, there is some reason to think that the behavior-rule account has significant problems in explaining the totality of the existing data—even after the fact. But we think that the evidential base for attributing Stage 1 mindreading to nonhuman primates would be strengthened if future experiments were to mimic some of the impressive features of the recent infancy data reviewed previously. In particular, it would be helpful if experiments could be devised that would test for understanding of other goals in addition to eating. Of course, we understand that there may be severe practical limitations in devising experiments that would test for primates' understanding of the desire to mate, for example. But it should be easy enough to set up conditions in which primates would compete for grooming opportunities, say, rather than for food. This would at least be a start in the right direction.

Moreover, it would be helpful if additional experiments could be devised that would capitalize on forms of physical understanding that we already have reason to think the animals possess, in the way that the experiments conducted by Schmelz et al. (2011) do. Some of the most impressive data with human infants capitalize on their belief that a large object cannot fit into a small container, or that objects that are similar on the surface are likely to share other properties as well. In addition, more experiments need to be devised that can explicitly exclude rule #2 from the mix.

Conclusion

Although the data are by no means probative, we believe that there is currently a strong case for saying that some nonhuman animals are capable of at least Stage 1 mindreading. This is partly because the mindreading hypothesis predicted the existing positive data, and can therefore genuinely explain it; whereas the behavior-rule hypothesis is entirely reactive, attempting to explain the data on a piecemeal basis after the fact. But it is also because the behavior-rule account has no explanation of the failures of these animals to exhibit competence with Stage 2 mindreading tasks, whereas the mindreading account can provide a principled explanation of the finding. Moreover, although considered narrowly both the behavior-rule and mindreading accounts are about equivalent in terms of their complexity, the latter provides a simpler and more coherent account of the overall evolution of mindreading capacities in the primate line. None of this is to say, however, that no further experiments need to be conducted. On the contrary, we have tentatively indicated some directions in which future inquiries might go.

Acknowledgments

We are grateful to Josep Call and Josef Perner for comments on an earlier draft of this chapter. This research was supported by NSF award number 0924523.

REFERENCES

Baillargeon, R., He, Z., Setoh, P., Scott, R., Sloane, S., & Yang, D. (2013). The development of false-belief understanding and why it matters: the social-acting hypothesis. In M. Banaji, & S. Gelman (Eds.), *Navigating the Social World: What Infants, Children, and Other Species Can Teach Us*. New York: Oxford University Press.

Baron-Cohen, S. (1995). *Mindblindness*. Cambridge, MA: MIT Press.

Barrett, H., & Kurzban, R. (2006). Modularity in cognition. *Psychological Review*, *113*, 628–647.

Buttelmann, D., Carpenter, M., Call, J., & Tomasello, M. (2007). Enculturated chimpanzees imitate rationally. *Developmental Science*, *10*, F31–F38.

Buttelmann, D., Call, J., & Tomasello, M. (2009a). Do great apes use emotional expressions to infer desires? *Developmental Science*, *12*, 688–698.

Buttelmann, D., Carpenter, M., & Tomasello, M. (2009b). Eighteen-month-old infants show false belief understanding in an active helping paradigm. *Cognition*, *112*, 337–342.

Byrne, R., & Whiten, A., eds. (1988). *Machiavellian Intelligence*. New York: Oxford University Press.

Byrne, R., & Whiten, A., eds. (1997). *Machiavellian Intelligence II*. New York: Cambridge University Press.

Call, J., & Tomasello, M. (1999). A nonverbal false belief task: The performance of children and great apes. *Child Development*, *70*, 381–395.

Call, J., & Tomasello, M. (2008). Does the chimpanzee have a theory of mind? 30 years later. *Trends in Cognitive Sciences*, *12*, 187–192.

Call, J., Hare, B., Carpenter, M., & Tomasello, M. (2004). "Unwilling" versus "unable": Chimpanzees' understanding of human intentional action. *Developmental Science*, *7*, 488–489.

Carruthers, P. (2006). *The Architecture of the Mind*. New York: Oxford University Press.

Carruthers, P. (2009). An architecture for dual reasoning. In J. Evans, & K. Frankish (Eds.), *In Two Minds*. New York: Oxford University Press.

Carruthers, P. (2011). *The Opacity of Mind: An Integrative Theory of Self-Knowledge*. New York: Oxford University Press.

Csibra, G. (2008). Goal attribution to inanimate agents by 6.5-month-old infants. *Cognition*, *107*, 705–717.

Csibra, G., Bíró, S., Koós, O., & Gergely, G. (2003). One-year-old infants use teleological representations of actions productively. *Cognitive Science*, *27*, 111–133.

Gopnik, A., & Meltzoff, A. (1997). *Words, Thoughts, and Theories*. Cambridge, MA: MIT Press.

Hare, B., Call, J., Agnetta, B., & Tomasello, M. (2000). Chimpanzees know what conspecifics do and do not see. *Animal Behavior, 59*, 771–785.

Hare, B., Call, J., & Tomasello, M. (2001). Do chimpanzees know what conspecifics know? *Animal Behavior, 61*, 139–151.

Hare, B., Call, J., & Tomasello, M. (2006). Chimpanzees deceive a human competitor by hiding. *Cognition, 101*, 495–514.

Hespos, S., & Baillargeon, R. (2006). Décalage in infants' knowledge about occlusion and containment events: Converging evidence from action tasks. *Cognition, 99*, B31–B41.

Johnson, S. (2000). The recognition of mentalistic agency in infancy. *Trends in Cognitive Sciences, 4*, 22–28.

Kaminski, J., Call, J., & Tomasello, M. (2008). Chimpanzees know what others know, but not what they believe. *Cognition, 109*, 224–234.

Krachun, C., Carpenter, M., Call, J., & Tomasello, M. (2009). A competitive nonverbal false belief task for children and apes. *Developmental Science, 12*, 521–535.

Kuhn, T. (1962). *The Structure of Scientific Revolutions*. Chicago: University of Chicago Press.

Lakatos, I. (1970). The methodology of scientific research programs. In I. Lakatos, & A. Musgrave (Eds.), *Criticism and the Growth of Knowledge* (pp. 91–196). New York:, Cambridge University Press.

Leslie, A. (1994). ToMM, ToBy, and Agency: Core architecture and domain specificity. In L. Hirchfeld & S. Gelman (Eds.), *Mapping the Mind*. New York: Cambridge University Press, pp. 119–148.

Liebal, K., Pika, S., Call, J., & Tomasello, M. (2004). To move or not to move: How apes adjust to the attentional state of others. *Interaction Studies, 5*, 199–219.

Liszkowski, U., Carpenter, M., Striano, T., & Tomasello, M. (2006). 12- and 18-month-olds point to provide information for others. *Journal of Cognition and Development, 7*, 173–187.

Liszkowski, U., Carpenter, M., & Tomasello, M. (2007). Pointing out new news, old news, and absent referents at 12 months of age. *Developmental Science, 10*, F1–F7.

Luo, Y., & Baillargeon, R. (2005). Can a self-propelled box have a goal? Psychological reasoning in 5-month-old infants. *Psychological Science, 16*, 601–608.

Luo, Y., & Baillargeon, R. (2007). Do 12.5-month-old infants consider what objects others can see when interpreting their actions? *Cognition, 105*, 489–512.

Luo, Y., & Johnson, S. (2009). Recognizing the role of perception in action at 6 months. *Developmental Science, 12*, 142–149.

Melis, A., Call, J., & Tomasello, M. (2006). Chimpanzees (Pan troglodytes) conceal visual and auditory information from others. *Journal of Comparative Psychology, 120*, 154–162.

Newton-Smith, W. (1981). *The Rationality of Science*. New York: Routledge.

Nichols, S., & Stich, S. (2003). *Mindreading*. New York: Oxford University Press.

O'Connell, S., & Dunbar, R. (2003). A test for comprehension of false belief in chimpanzees. *Evolution and Cognition, 9*, 131–140.

Onishi, K., & Baillargeon, R. (2005). Do 15-month-olds understand false beliefs? *Science, 308*, 255–258.

Onishi, K., Baillargeon, R., & Leslie, A. (2007). 15-month-old infants detect violations in pretend scenarios. *Acta Psychologica, 124*, 106–128.

Penn, D., Holyoak, K., & Povinelli, D. (2008). Darwin's mistake: Explaining the discontinuity between human and nonhuman minds. *Behavioral and Brain Sciences, 30*, 109–178.

Perner, J. (2010). Who took the cog out of cognitive science? Mentalism in an era of anti-cognitivism. In P. Frensch, & R. Schwarzer (Eds.), *Cognition and Neuropsychology: International Perspectives on Psychological Science: Volume 1.* (pp. 241–262) *New York:* Psychology Press.

Perner, J., & Ruffman, T. (2005). Infants' insight into the mind: How deep? *Science, 308*, 214–216.

Povinelli, D., & Vonk, J. (2003). Chimpanzee minds: Suspiciously human? *Trends in Cognitive Sciences, 7*, 157–160.

Scott, R., & Baillargeon, R. (2009). Which penguin is this? Attributing false beliefs about object identity at 18 months. *Child Development, 80*, 1172–1196.

Scott, R., Baillargeon, R., Song, H., & Leslie, A. (2011). Attributing false beliefs about non-obvious properties at 18 months. *Cognitive Psychology, 61*, 366–395.

Shanahan, M. (2010). *Embodiment and the Inner Life.* New York: Oxford University Press.

Shanahan, M., & Baars, B. (2005). Applying global workspace theory to the frame problem. *Cognition, 98*, 157–176.

Schmelz, M., Call, J., & Tomasello, M. (2011). Chimpanzees know that others make inferences. *Proceedings of the National Academy of Sciences, 108*, 3077–3079.

Song, H., & Baillargeon, R. (2008). Infants' reasoning about others' false perceptions. *Developmental Psychology, 44*, 1789–1795.

Song, H., Onishi, K., Baillargeon, R., & Fisher, C. (2008). Can an actor's false belief be corrected by an appropriate communication? Psychological reasoning in 18.5-month-old infants. *Cognition, 109*, 295–315.

Southgate, V., Senju, A., & Csibra, G. (2007). Action anticipation through attribution of false belief by 2-year-olds. *Psychological Science, 18*, 587–592.

Southgate, V., Chevallier, C., & Csibra, G. (2010). Seventeen-month-olds appeal to false beliefs to interpret others' referential communication. *Developmental Science, 13*, 907–912.

Surian, L., Caldi, S., & Sperber, D. (2007). Attribution of beliefs by 13-month-old infants. *Psychological Science, 18*, 580–586.

Wellman, H. (1990). *The Child's Theory of Mind.* Cambridge, MA: MIT Press.

Woodward, A. (1998). Infants selectively encode the goal object of an actor's reach. *Cognition, 69*, 1–34.

5   On Knowing and Being Known in the 4-Month Origins of Disorganized Attachment: An Emerging Presymbolic Theory of Mind

Beatrice Beebe, Sara Markese, Lorraine Bahrick, Frank Lachmann, Karen Buck, Henian Chen, Patricia Cohen, Howard Andrews, and Joseph Jaffe

THIS CHAPTER ADDRESSES the infant's experiences of knowing, and being known by, the mind of the mother, during a face-to-face encounter. "Knowing and being known" is construed from the point of view of the infant as expectancies of procedurally organized action sequences. We compared the 4-month mother–infant interactions of infants who were classified at 1 year as secure (B) versus disorganized (D) attachment (Beebe, Jaffe, Markese, Buck, Chen, Cohen, et al., 2010). We will argue that the future D infant has difficulty feeling known by his mother, has difficulty knowing his mother, and has difficulty knowing himself, especially at moments of distress.

We first review the literature documenting that infants generate procedurally organized expectancies, which constitute "schemas" or "models" of features of stimuli, events, and contingent action sequences. These models allow infants to recognize what is new, and to compare it with the familiar. Such model formations provide an index of fundamental representational processes. Using these capacities, infants generate expectancies and procedural representations or models of recurrent and characteristic interaction patterns. These models include expectancies of knowing, and being known by, their partners, and of knowing themselves.

We then summarize the findings of specific 4-month mother–infant interaction patterns of attention, affect, orientation, and touch that predicted 12-month D versus B attachment. We use these findings to infer experiences of knowing, and being known by mother, in future D versus B infants. We refer to 4-month infants who will be classified as disorganized (D) attachment at 12 months as "future" D infants; to those who will be classified as secure at 12 months as "future" B infants. Finally, we relate these experiences of knowing and being known to a presymbolic "Theory of Mind" at 4 months.

Knowing and Being Known: Procedural Expectancies of Contingent Relations and Behavioral Correspondences

Infant procedural representational capacities in the first 3 to 4 months are extensive (for reviews see Beebe & Lachmann, 2002; Bornstein, 1985; Goodman, 1988; Haith, Hazan, & Shields & Rovee-Collier, 1992; Lewis & Goldberg, 1969; Lewkowicz, 2000; Mandler, 1988; Singer & Fagen, 1992; Stern, 1985). Infants perceive time, and can estimate durations of events lasting seconds or fractions of seconds. They detect features of stimuli, such as facial shapes, temporal patterns, and spatial trajectories. They translate cross-modally, for example between visual and auditory channels, facilitating abstraction of pattern from different modalities. Infants can determine whether behavior patterns are similar or different, and can recognize recurrence, determining whether an event is likely to recur after seeing it only twice, generating rules that govern their expectancies. Infants remember the details of stimuli in learning experiments across days and weeks. These generalized expectancies are based on the serial pattern in which events occur (Fagen, Morrongiello, Rovee-Collier, & Gekoski, 1984; Shields & Rovee-Collier, 1992). Serial pattern information is continuously available in social interactions, on the basis of which infants detect the presence and degree of the partner's contingency.

Haith, Hazan, & Goodman (1988, p. 477) showed that 3- to 4-month infants develop visual expectations rapidly and tend to organize their behavior on the basis of these expectations, arguing that "as early as 3.5 months of age, the baby can create an action-based perceptual model of the situation he or she confronts, can generate short-term expectations from this model and can support action…This modeling, expectation and action sequence serves to maintain continuity in an ever-changing perceptual world."

These processes can be described as "schema" or "model" formation, the generation of procedural models of features of stimuli, events, and contingent action sequences, allowing the infant to recognize what is new, and to compare it with the familiar. Such model formation is an index of fundamental representational processes (Bornstein, 1985). Using these capacities, infants generate expectancies, procedural representations, of recurrent and characteristic interaction patterns.

Self- and Interactive Contingencies

The infant is a "contingency detector" from birth (DeCasper & Carstens, 1980; Papousek, 1992), detecting predictable consequences of his own actions. For an event to be perceived as contingent by the infant, it must occur rapidly, within 1 to 2 seconds (Watson, 1985), and it must be predictable, occurring with greater than chance probability following the infant's behavior.

Infants at 4 months are highly sensitive to the consequences of their behavior (DeCasper & Carstens, 1980; Haith et al., 1988; Jaffe, Beebe, Feldstein, Crown & Jasnow, 2001; Millar, 1988; Murray & Trevarthen, 1985; Stern, 1971, 1985; Tarabulsy, Tessier & Kappas, 1996; Watson, 1985). The partner's contingent behavior is the central cue of the partner's intentionality for the infant (Muir & Hains, 1993). Gergely and Watson (1996) suggested that the infant's capacity to interpret stimulation as contingent (or not) may well be the most fundamental of the infant's capacities for interpreting sensory information.

The Role of Self-Contingency

Self-regulation remains curiously separate from interactive regulation in much research on face-to-face interaction (but see Gianino & Tronick, 1988; Weinberg, Tronick, Cohn & Olson, 1999 as exceptions). We adopt the terms self- and interactive contingency to avoid confusion over the many different meanings of the term "regulation." We nevertheless construe our self- and interactive contingency measures as *forms* of self- and interactive regulation.

A theory of interaction must address how each person is affected by his own behavior, as well as by that of the partner (Beebe et al, 1992; Beebe & Lachmann, 1998, 2002; Gianino & Tronick, 1988; Sander, 1977; Thomas & Martin 1976). The rhythms of behavior, as well as states of activation/arousal, are simultaneously regulated within the organism, as well as through interaction with the partner (Feldman, 2006). Furthermore, the nature of self- and interactive contingencies continuously affect one other (Gianino & Tronick, 1988). How infants sense the state of the partner, a key question of research on knowing and being known, will of necessity be influenced by how infants sense and regulate their own states, as well as how they perceive and align with the state of the partner.

DEFINITIONS OF SELF- AND INTERACTIVE CONTINGENCY

"Contingency" is a neutral term that is defined as a temporal relation between the occurrence of two events (Tarabulsy et al., 1996).

It acquires meaning only in relation to some other outcome, such as attachment security/insecurity. *Interactive contingency* is defined as adjustments of one individual's behavior that are correlated with the partner's prior behavior. *Self-contingency* is defined as adjustments of an individual's behavior that are correlated with his or her own prior behavior (in the context of a particular partner). It refers to the degree of predictability (in a range from stability to lability) within an individual's own rhythms of activity.

Self-contingency provides the individual with continuous procedural information about the likelihood of staying in the same state.

The perception of contingent relations allows infants to develop ongoing expectancies of sequences of events, within the self, within the partner, and between the two. This procedural form of representation is based on the "if-then" predictability of events and the perception of degree of contingent control over events (Beebe & Lachmann, 1988, 2002; Jaffe et al., 2001; Stern, 1985; Tarabulsy et al., 1996). The infant's experience of interactive agency can be found in these if-then sequences, a form of causal understanding (Gopnik, 2008, 2009; Saffran, Aslin, & Newport, 1996). For example, predictable effects of the infant's own action on the partner are referred to as the infant's "interactive contingency:" metaphorically, expectancies of "how I affect you." Similarly, predictable effects of the partner's actions on the infant can be metaphorically construed as expectancies of "how you affect me." The infant's expectation that he can affect, and be affected by, the partner is one crucial origin of the experience of effectance (White, 1959) or agency (see Sander, 1977).

We argue that high interactive contingency is not necessarily better. Both high and low degrees of contingency were shown to be related to insecure outcomes in our work on vocal rhythm, whereas midrange degrees were related to secure outcomes (Jaffe et al., 2001). Interactive contingency can be both heightened, and lowered, as a function of distress in either partner. Social experiences that force the infant to pay too much attention to the partner, *heightened contingent coordination,* or to pay too little attention, *lowered contingent coordination,* interfere with the infant's developing ability to attend to the environment, disturbing social and cognitive development (Hay, 1997). Likewise, both high and low self-contingency has been associated with maternal distress in our prior work, although low self-contingency is more prevalent as a risk index (Beebe, Jaffe, Buck, Chen, Cohen, Blatt, et al, 2007; Beebe, Jaffe, Buck, Chen, Cohen, Feldstein, et al, 2008; Beebe, Steele, Jaffe, Buck, Chen, Cohen, et al., 2011).

Behavioral Correspondences and Shared States

Infants also develop expectancies of patterns of correspondence/difference between their own behaviors and those of the partner. The concepts of correspondence and contingency are differentiated: correspondence per se does not imply contingency. For example, each partner might look away at the same time, without being a recurrent and predictable pattern. Likewise, contingency can occur without correspondence: my frown can be contingent on your smile.

Infants apprehend correspondences between body transformations they see (e.g., mouth opening) and their own body transformations that they do not see. Using imitation experiments in the first weeks of life, Meltzoff argues that infants are biologically prepared to perceive cross-modal correspondences of form, between what they see on the face of the partner and what they sense proprioceptively on their own faces (Meltzoff, 1985; Meltzoff & Moore, 1998).

In Meltzoff's (1985, 2007) view, the infant's perception of these correspondences provides the infant with a fundamental relatedness between self and other. Moreover, infants represent these actions, not merely as a visual image or iconic copy, but rather as a non–modality-specific description of the event, utilizing visual, auditory, and motor information. The representation constitutes a model against which the infant can match his own performance and guide his behavior. Through the perception of cross-modal correspondences, both infant and partner sense the state of the other, and sense whether the state is shared. In essence, the infant can determine whether that (perceived in the other) looks like this feels (perceived in the self) (Meltzoff, 2007). Meltzoff argues that the perception and production of correspondence has a privileged position in the experience and representation of relatedness. Thus infants create procedural representational models of behavioral correspondences as well as contingencies.

Stern (1985, 1995) and Trevarthen (1977, 1998) argue that infants are sensitive to correspondences not only of form, but also of time and intensity, across modalities. Stern describes correspondence as a reciprocal dyadic process across time: each changes with the other. Trevarthen describes mother and infant behaviors as contingently coupled in time, imitated in form, and brought into register in intensity range. This intercoordination enables each to resonate with or reflect the other. The particular temporal-spatial-intensity patterns formed by the dyad will guide action, learning, and memory. Meltzoff, Trevarthen, and Stern agree that infant capacity to recognize cross-modal correspondences is the central mechanism allowing infants to capture the quality of another's inner feeling state (Beebe, Knoblauch, Rustin, & Sorter, 2005).

Meltzoff, Trevarthen and Stern all conceptualize the origins of a Theory of Mind in infancy, a mind that begins as shared mind. Whereas Meltzoff (1985, 2007) argues that the origin of mind begins with the perception, "you are like me," Stern (1985, 1995) and Trevarthen (1977, 1998), by contrast, see the origin of mind in the interactive process itself. For Meltzoff, the key mechanism is the perception and production of behavioral correspondence. The sense of self derives from one's own movements as seen in the actions of the other, and actions of the other experienced proprioceptively as similar to one's own movements. The partner may have states similar to one's own. For Trevarthen, patterns of movement, transferred from subject to subject via form, timing, and intensity, permit the intercoordination of inner psychological states; the key mechanism is the rhythmic coupling or contingent coordination of these patterns of movement (Beebe et al, 2005).

A further concept elaborating of the meaning of correspondences is Sander's (1977, 1995) "matched specificities," defined as a "sort of resonance between two systems attuned to each other by corresponding properties" (Weiss, 1970, p. 62). An example might be similar vocal rhythms in mother and infant. The presence of matched specificities yields awareness in each partner of the state of the other, a view similar to that of Meltzoff. This concept underlies Sander's "moment of meeting," a match between two partners such that the way one is known by oneself is matched by the way one is known by the other. This match facilitates the development of agency, identity, and coherence in the child's experience of inner and outer (Sander, 1995).

Our position is that both behavioral correspondences (and differences), as well as interpersonal contingencies of behavior (and degrees of contingency), are critical components in the infant's developing construction of expectancies of knowing and being known by the partner. Sensing that one impacts the partner in ongoing predictable ways, and that the partner has a reciprocal impact on oneself, are just as important in the origins of knowing and being known as the perception of correspondence (and difference) itself. Interpersonal contingencies have to do with the *process* of dyadic patterns of relatedness across time; correspondences have to do with whether the partner is similar or different at a particular *moment*.

Thus we suggest that infant procedural expectancies of face-to-face social interaction are organized by (a) contingent relations between the self and the partner (interactive contingency), metaphorically, how I affect you and how you affect me; (b) contingent relations within the self (self-contingency), metaphorically, the stability/lability of the rhythms of behavior within the self (while in a dyadic relation); (c) correspondences/differences in behavior patterns between the self and the partner, such as a correspondence pattern of "I smile as you smile;" or a difference pattern such as "I whimper as you smile;" and (d) specific behavioral qualities (features) in the self or the partner, such as infant facial/vocal distress, or maternal "looming" movements into the infant's face.

Interaction Patterns of Infant Procedural Expectancies

To describe further the organization of these procedural expectancies of how face-to-face social interactions unfold, both correspondences and contingencies will operate in the dimensions of time, space, affect, and arousal: (1) In time, infants will store models of the rate, rhythm, sequence, and tightness of contingency of the behaviors. (2) In space, infants will store patterns of mutual approach-approach or approach-avoid. (3) In affect, infants will store the positive and negative tones of faces and voices, their patterns of moving in the same affective direction or not, and whether these are shared. (4) In arousal, infants will store an associated arousal pattern, and a proprioceptive experience of their movements over time (see Beebe & Lachmann, 1988, 1994, 2002; Beebe, Lachmann, & Jaffe, 1997; Beebe & Stern, 1977).

Based on these dimensions of time, space, affect, and arousal, Beebe and Lachmann (1988, 1994, 2002; Beebe et al., 1997) described salient interaction patterns of infant procedural social representations, which may be organized by contingencies, correspondences, or both: (1) facial/vocal mirroring, the expectation of matching and being matched in the direction of affective change, providing each partner with a behavioral basis for entering into the other's feeling state and generating experiences that contribute to feeling "known," attuned to, or "on the same wave length;" (2) state transforming, the expectation of being able to transform an arousal state through the contribution of the partner (see Stern, 1985); (3) disruption and repair, the expectation of interactive repair following facial-visual mismatches (see Tronick, 1989); (4) "chase and dodge," the expectation of misregulation of spatial-orientation patterns, without repair, such that "As you move in, I move away; as I move away, you move in" (Beebe & Lachmann, 1988, p. 114); and (5) interpersonal timing, the expectation of degree of contingency in the self and the partner, generating expectancies of the degree of stability in the self's own behavioral rhythms, and the degree to which the partner responds to the self, and the self responds to the partner (see Jaffe et al, 2001). We will use these interaction patterns to guide our description of the origins of secure versus disorganized attachment.

Lyons-Ruth (1999, 2008) argues the organization of intimate relating is at stake as the infant develops early procedural social representations. Intimate relating entails the fundamental issue of how the infant comes to know, and be known by, another's mind. Similarly, Stern argues that processes of affect attunement are so powerful because the individual learns that some subjective states are shareable, and some are not. This learning then powerfully affects attachment security and the capacity for intimacy. Learning which states are shareable, and which are not, defines the arenas in which one can, and cannot, know and be known by another's mind.

Lyons-Ruth (1999, 2008) proposes that the outcome of this process of coming to know and be known by another's mind is dependent on whether the partner is capable of a *collaborative dialogue*. Collaborative dialogue involves close attention to the other's initiatives; openness to the other's state across the entire range of positive to negative emotions; attempts to comprehend the state or subjective reality of the other; the attempt to respond in a way that acknowledges or elaborates on that state; ability to negotiate similarity and difference; and efforts to repair disruptions. Collaborative dialogues generate procedural expectancies or models in which both partners are represented as open to the experience of the other; each can know and be known by the partner's mind. Lyons-Ruth's position is similar to that of Meltzoff, Trevarthen, and Stern.

Lyons-Ruth (1999) suggests that incoherent or contradictory dialogues involve a collapse of intersubjective space in which only one person's subjective reality is recognized. The partner's initiatives are ignored, overridden, or not acknowledged. Lyons-Ruth (1999, 2008) argues that such failures of collaborative dialogue generate contradictory procedural models, in which the partner represents both roles: "I should accept your control; I should attempt to control you." Lyons-Ruth's description is consistent with our position that procedural representations are a mutually organized and mutually understood code in which any role implies its reciprocal.

To understand contradictory dialogues, Lyons-Ruth (1999) builds on the models of Case (1991) and Fischer (1980) describing how complex "control systems" for skilled actions, such as communicating, are developed by coordinating single relational procedures, such as facial affect, with other procedures, such as vocal affect, from second to second. Flexible integration of these procedures is essential to higher-order coordinations. However, when procedures conflict, such as simultaneous positive facial affect but negative vocal affect (as we will see in our results following), the lack of integration can disturb the development of flexible control systems. This description of conflicting or unintegrated domains of knowledge is consistent with the concept of intermodal discordances, in which contradictory procedures are organized in different communication modalities at the same time. Discordant information is difficult to integrate into a coherent percept, and may remain unintegrated (Bahrick & Lickliter, 2002; Shackman & Pollak, 2005).

In summary, the following concepts guide our understanding of variations in procedural expectancies of 4-month infants who will be classified as secure versus disorganized at 12 months. (1) In the social sphere, procedural, presymbolic expectancies or representational models are being organized, formed in the interactive process of self-in-relation-to-other, and thus inherently dyadic. (2) Through the perception of correspondences and contingencies between one's own behavior and that of the partner, which are organized via form, time, and intensity across modalities, both infant and partner can sense the state of the other, and can sense whether the state is shared or not. (3) Infant procedural expectancies or models of face-to-face interactions include a variety of patterns, such as (a) state-transforming; (b) facial mirroring; (c) disruption and repair; (d) mutual approach or approach/avoid spatial orientation, including spatial patterns of intrusion; and (e) degrees of self- and interactive contingency. (4) When contradictory procedures are organized in different communication modalities, unintegrated, conflicting procedural representations are likely to develop. (5) Collaborative versus contradictory dialogues generate coherent versus unintegrated infant expectancies or models of relatedness. (7) What is at stake in these procedural expectancies is the organization of intimate relating, which entails the fundamental issue of how the infant comes to know, and to be known by, another's mind.

Using this approach, we discuss a portion of the findings of a large study that predicted 12-month disorganized (vs. secure) attachment from 4-month self- and interactive contingency, as well as from 4-month qualitative features of behaviors (Beebe et al., 2010). The contingency analyses predicted disorganized (vs. secure) attachment by evaluating (1) which partner (mother or infant) may show altered 4-month degree of contingency; (2) whether contingency was increased, or decreased, relative to secure dyads; (3) the type of contingency that was altered, self- or interactive; and (4) the modality of contingency that was altered.

Our central hypothesis is that disorganized attachment biases the system toward contingencies that are *both heightened and lowered,* compared with those of secure dyads. This hypothesis stands in contrast to the usual position of the infant literature, which postulates that "more" contingency is "better" (see for example Van Egeren, Barratt & Roach, 2001, but see Cohn & Elmore, 1988; Jaffe et al, 2001 for critiques). This hypothesis is based on prior findings that interactive contingency of vocal rhythms in insecure dyads was both heightened and lowered compared with secure dyads, which were midrange

(Leyendecker, Lamb, Fracasso, Scholmerich, & Larson, 1997; Jaffe, et al., 2001). Thus, as a function of partner (mother/infant) and communication modality (attention, affect, spatial orientation, and touch), we hypothesize that values of self- and interactive contingency will be both heightened (in some modalities) and lowered (in others), in insecure (vs. secure) dyads, consistent with Jaffe et al.'s (2001) "optimum midrange model." Regarding correspondences, we hypothesize that disorganized attachment biases the system toward difference, discrepancy, and failures of correspondence.

In our study, mothers were recruited from a large urban hospital for a study of "infant social development" within 24 hours of delivering a healthy firstborn infant. The subjects ($N = 84$) completed two lab visits: a 4-month videotaping of mother–infant face-to-face interaction and a 12-month videotaping of a separation–reunion paradigm, the "strange situation" (Ainsworth, Blehar, Waters, & Wall, 1978). The subjects were a low-risk, ethnically diverse community group of primiparous women delivering full-term, singleton infants without major complications. The mothers turned out to be highly educated. In this study we compare 17 4-month dyads in which infants were classified disorganized (D) at 12 months, with 47 4-month dyads in which infants were classified secure (B) at 12 months. For details of method, see Beebe et al. (2010).

At 4 months, mothers were instructed to play with their infants as they would at home, but without the use of toys, for approximately 10 minutes. Mothers were seated opposite the infant who sat in an infant seat on a table. Two video cameras generated a split-screen view of the interaction. At 12 months, consistent with our prior procedure (Jaffe et al., 2001), following a face-to-face interaction, a break and a snack, mothers and infants participated in the Ainsworth "strange situation."

The first 2½ uninterrupted continuous minutes of videotaped 4-month mother–infant interaction were coded on a 1s time base, by coders blind to attachment status. Ambady and Rosenthal (1992) showed that accuracy in predicting interpersonal consequences did not differ among observations varying from 30 seconds to 5 minutes. Samples of face-to-face interaction of 2 to 3 minutes are stable, generating robust session-to-session reliability (Cohn & Tronick, 1989; Moore, Cohn & Cambell, 1997; Weinberg & Tronick, 1991). For coding details see Beebe et al. (2010).

We examined *separate* modalities of communication, *attention, affect, spatial orientation, and touch,* as well as a composite measure of facial-visual engagement. For each modality, we created an ordinalized behavioral scale as required by time-series methods, with the exception of *gaze*, which was coded on-off partner's face. *Mother facial affect* was ordinalized from a high of "mock surprise" to a low of "negative face"; *infant facial affect* was ordinalized from a high of "high/ medium positive" to a low of "negative"; *infant vocal affect* was ordinalized from "positive/neutral" to "angry protest/cry"; *mother spatial orientation* was ordinalized as "sitting upright," "leaning forward," and "looming in"; *infant head orientation* was ordinalized from "en face" to "arch"; *mother touch* was ordinalized from a high of "affectionate" to a low of "high intensity/intrusive"; and *infant-initiated touch* (touch self [own skin], object [clothing/strap], mother) was ordinalized as two or more touch behaviors, one, or none. We also created ordinalized facial-visual "engagement" scales for mother and for infant, which capture a more holistic gestalt than single modalities. In addition we examined two dyadic codes, "mother chase and infant dodge," and "mother positive while infant distressed."

SELF AND INTERACTIVE CONTINGENCY

Each person's behavior is affected both by one's own prior behavior (self-contingency) and by that of the partner (interactive contingency) (Thomas & Malone, 1979; Thomas & Martin, 1976). Time-series methods are designed to partition these two sources of variance. Because any behavior pattern in a face-to-face encounter may participate simultaneously in self- *and* interactive contingency functions, every behavior must be assessed for both functions. *Self- and interactive contingency* are defined, using lag correlations, as predictability within (autocorrelation) and between (lagged cross-correlation) two partners' behavioral streams over time. The SAS PROC MIXED program (Littell, Miliken, Stoup, & Wolfinger, 1996; McArdle & Bell, 2000; Singer, 1998) was used to estimate random (individual differences) and fixed (common model) effects on patterns of self- and interactive behavior over 15s. In addition, the SAS GLIMMIX program (Cohen, Chen, Hamgiami, Gordon, & McArdle, 2000; Littell et al., 1996) was used to analyze mother gaze—infant gaze (on/off gaze), in which the dependent variable is dichotomous. Modeling the complexity of real-time interactions remains difficult. Whereas time-series analysis has been considered state-of-the-art, the multilevel time-series models used in this study have many advantages. They are designed to address patterns over time, translated here into the course of behavior second-by-second, either within the individual (self-contingency), or between two individuals (interactive contingency) (see Chen & Cohen, 2006, for details of multi-level time-series modeling). Figure 5.1 illustrates our approach.

CODING OF SECURE AND DISORGANIZED ATTACHMENT

In the reunion episodes following brief separations from mother in a laboratory setting, 12-month infants who are classified as secure attachment immediately greet the mother, and are able to be easily comforted and to return to play, showing a balance of secure-base behavior and exploration of the environment. In contrast, in the reunion episodes, disorganized attachment infants show fearful, odd, and conflicted behaviors. The core definition of disorganized attachment is a breakdown of an organized strategy for dealing with distress, leading to fear, apprehension, and confusion. The core coding criterion is simultaneous display of approach and avoidance behaviors. Infants may also show sequential displays of contradictory behavior; undirected, misdirected, interrupted behavior; asymmetrical, mistimed, or anomalous behaviors; freezing, stilling, and slowed movements; or apprehension regarding the parent. In addition to the categories of secure

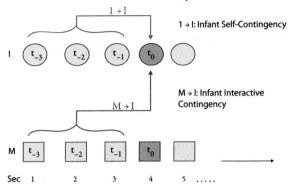

Infant Self- and Interactive Contingency Defined by
Time Series Analysis

FIGURE 5.1 Illustration of Self- and Interactive Contingency by Time-Series Methods. To calculate infant self-contingency, second 4 in the infant's stream of behavior identifies t_0, the predicted second. A weighted average of seconds t_{-1}, t_{-2}, and t_{-3} in the infant's behavioral stream identify the "weighted lag," which is used to predict t_0. To calculate infant interactive contingency, a weighted average of seconds t_{-1}, t_{-2}, and t_{-3} in the mother's behavioral stream is used to predict t_0 in the infant's behavioral stream. For both self- and interactive contingency, this is an iterative process in which second 5 will then identify the new t_0, and seconds 2, 3, and 4 will identify the new "weighted lag." A parallel diagram would depict mother self- and interactive contingency.

versus disorganized attachment, we also classified infants by the 7-point "degree of disorganization" scale (Lyons-Ruth et al, 1999).

Future Disorganized (vs. Secure) Dyads

In this section we describe how 4-month interactions of future D (vs. B) dyads differ. We organize the results by the domains of attention, affect, spatial orientation, and touch, examining differences in both behavioral qualities and degrees of self- and interactive contingency. All results described have been shown to be statistically significant (for details see Beebe et al., 2010). Although there were no associations of maternal ethnicity, age or education with future D versus B infants, male infants were overrepresented in D infants. It is important to note that mothers of future D infants have their own difficult attachment histories (i.e., fears regarding intimate attachments that may involve unresolved loss or abuse), and difficulties managing their own distress (Main & Hesse, 1990).

ATTENTION DYSREGULATION IN FUTURE D DYADS

Those mothers who gazed away from the infant's face "excessively" (30 seconds or more across the 2½ minutes coded) were more likely to have infants with greater "degree" of disorganization at 12 months. These mothers also looked and looked away in a less predictable fashion, a lowered self-contingency of gaze, indicating a lowered stability of the rhythms of mothers' gaze behavior. Extensive looking away, in a less predictable fashion, disturbs the "attentional frame" of the face-to-face encounter.

AFFECT DYSREGULATION IN FUTURE D DYADS: INFANTS

Future D (vs. B) infants showed complex patterns of greater distress: more (1) vocal distress, (2) combined facial and/or vocal distress, and (3) discrepant affect (simultaneous positive and negative facial and vocal behavior within the same second). Discrepant affect was likely to be vocal distress, such as whimper, while simultaneously facially positive (smiling). Future D (vs. B) infants also showed lowered self-contingency in the composite variable of facial-visual engagement. We infer that it is harder for future D (vs. B) infants to sense their own next engagement "move," as well as harder for future D (vs. B) mothers to anticipate infant engagement changes. Because future D infants lowered their engagement self-predictability in the context of lowered maternal engagement coordination (discussed below) this infant finding may be a compensatory adjustment. That is, infant engagement "self-destabilization" may occur in relation to maternal failure to adequately coordinate with infant engagement (or vice-versa). This is an infant intrapersonal dysregulation linked to a maternal interpersonal dysregulation.

AFFECT DYSREGULATION IN FUTURE D DYADS: MOTHERS

Affect dysregulation was seen in three maternal findings. The first was a *lowered maternal contingent engagement* coordination with infant engagement. This finding indicates a lowered maternal ability to emotionally "enter" and "go with" the infants' facial and vocal distress, as well as positive moments. Thus these mothers were less likely to follow infant direction of gaze (on and away from mother's face); less likely to become facially positive as their infants became facially/vocally positive; and less likely to dampen their faces toward interest, neutral, or "woe face" as their infants became more facially/vocally distressed. Lowered maternal contingent coordination lowers the infant's contingent "control," compromising infant agency. It is harder for these infants to anticipate the maternal behavior that is likely to follow their own previous behavior, and thus harder for them to come to expect that their own behavior affects that of the mother.

In the second finding of maternal affect dysregulation, future D (vs. B) mothers heightened their facial self-contingency, remaining overly facially stable. An overly stable face is a way of "closing up" one's face. It may operate as a way to avoid facial involvement. Mothers may look almost blank, as their faces stay relatively neutral and stable over several seconds, similar to mothers who are instructed to keep a "still-face" (Tronick, 1989). In the third finding of maternal affect dysregulation, mothers who were more likely to show positive expressiveness or surprise while infants were facially/vocally distressed were more likely to have infants with greater degree of disorganization at 12 months. This finding is consistent with Goldberg, Benoit, Blokland, and Madigan (2003), Lyons-Ruth et al. (1999), and Madigan et al. (2006), in studies of disorganized attachment at 12 months.

SPATIAL DYSREGULATION IN FUTURE D DYADS

Future D mothers showed more "loom": movements of the head close in toward the infant's face. Loom behavior is one postulated as frightening by Main and Hesse (1990). Maternal loom was accompanied by lowered maternal self-contingency of spatial orientation, from sitting upright, to leaning forward, to loom. Thus future D mothers not only loomed, but they did so in a less predictable way. Both may be threatening to infants and might exacerbate the infant's difficulty in decoding and predicting these maternal behaviors. More maternal looming, in a less predictable fashion, disturbs the "spatial frame" of the interaction.

TOUCH DYSREGULATION IN FUTURE D DYADS

Future D infants spent less time in touch of any kind (touching own skin, an object, the mother, or none), and less time specifically touching their own skin, indicating a lowered access to self-soothing through touch. In addition, they showed a heightened self-contingency of touch, specifically a higher probability of staying in the state of "no touch." Metaphorically they became "stuck" in states of not touching. These findings suggest a lowered infant access to her own touch for self-soothing. Moreover mothers of future D infants lowered their touch coordination with their infants' touch. Compared with future secure dyads, mothers of future D infants were less likely to use increases in infant touch behavior as a signal for more affectionate touching (and vice-versa). This lowered maternal touch contingency, interpreted as a maternal "withdrawal" from coordination, disturbs infant interactive efficacy in the tactile modality. We construe these findings as a reciprocal mother and infant tactile dysregulation.

GENDER DIFFERENCES IN FUTURE D INFANTS

Male infants were over-represented in future D infants, consistent with the literature. Boys, as opposed to girls, are more likely to develop insecure attachments (Murray, Fiori-Cowley, Hooper, & Cooper, 1996). Moreover, male infants are more emotionally reactive than females (Weinberg et al., 1999), so they may be more vulnerable to disorganized insecurity.

CENTRAL INTERACTION PATTERNS OF FUTURE DISORGANIZED ATTACHMENT INFANTS

All central interaction patterns showed disturbance in future D dyads: maternal affective correspondence, infant state transforming, maternal spatial intrusion, and maternal lowered interactive contingency, which disturbs infant interactive efficacy.

Future D dyads had difficulty in maternal facial mirroring and the more general arena of maternal affective correspondence, such as maternal smile/surprise expressions to infant distress, and not following the infant's direction affective/attentional change as he became more and less engaged. Thus future D mothers showed difficulty in sharing the affect state of the infant, particularly distress, through disturbances in both behavioral correspondence and interactive contingency. Future D dyads showed difficulties with infant and dyadic state transforming, and the maternal loom pattern of spatial intrusion. In patterns of temporal contingency, future D dyads showed difficulties in mother and infant self-contingency, but only *mothers* showed difficulties in interactive contingency, that is, contingent coordination with infants.

A number of new interaction pattern disturbances were also identified in future D dyads: (1) a disturbance in the predictability of the maternal "spatial frame" and "attentional frame" (see Downing, 2004), (2) destabilized infant engagement self-contingency, (3) infant lowered access to touch/touch own skin, (4) infant simultaneous discrepant affect, (5) maternal "closing up the face," and (6) maternal extensive looking away. Disturbances in the spatial and attentional frame disrupt the very foundation of the face-to-face exchange. Extensive maternal looking away and closing up her face, which create further distance from the infant, are interpreted as maternal methods of managing her own state.

INTRAPERSONAL AND INTERPERSONAL CONFLICT: AN INTERPRETATION OF THE RESULTS

There are many forms of intrapersonal and interpersonal conflict, intermodal discordance, or contradiction in our findings. We use an ethological definition of conflict, in which behavior is organized simultaneously in opposing directions. We describe the representational models of future D infants as characterized by expectancies of emotional distress and emotional incoherence, difficulty predicting what will happen both in oneself and in one's partner, disturbance in experiences of recognition, and difficulty in obtaining comfort.

Future D infants showed more vocal and combined facial/vocal distress. Moreover they showed more discrepant positive and negative affect in the same second, especially positive affect such as smile, with negative affect such as whimper. The infant pattern of simultaneous positive and negative affect fits an ethological definition of an infant in conflict.

Not only the infant, but also the dyad, is in affective conflict. Mothers of future D (vs. B) infants are likely to show smiles or surprise faces specifically during infant facial and vocal distress moments: an emotional "denial" of infant distress. Thus mothers show the affective discrepancy interpersonally; infants show the affective discrepancy intrapersonally. The infant's expectation of affective correspondence, which ordinarily lays the groundwork for feeling "known" or "on the same wavelength," is disturbed. We infer that it is extremely difficult for infants to feel that their mothers sense and acknowledge their distress. Infants instead come to *expect* that they cannot count on their mothers to empathically share their distress.

A second form of dyadic conflict is seen in the finding that, despite the greater facial/vocal distress of future D infants, their mothers showed excessive looking away from infants' faces. Not only did these mothers gaze away extensively, but they also lowered their gaze "self-contingency," that is, they lowered the predictability/stability of their gaze rhythms of looking at and away from the infant's face. We infer that future D infants have difficulty coming to rely on predictable patterns of maternal visual attention, the "attentional frame," which may exacerbate infant distress, and may lead to feelings of not being "seen." These infants are too visually "separate" from their mothers and may become confused about mother's visual presence and availability.

Moreover mothers of future D infants themselves exhibited a conflict or intermodal discordance between attention, where mothers gazed away extensively, and thus were "too far away;" and spatial orientation, where mothers loomed "too close in." For example, in one sequence involving maternal loom, the infant puts his hands up in front of his face (a defensive gesture available from the beginning of life) as mother looms; as mother looms in further, the infant raises his hands still more. In another loom sequence, the infant looks at mother with his bottom lip pulled in (a gesture of "uh-oh") as mother looms in, smiling. Then, as mother looms in closer, the infant closes his eyes and pulls his lips into a full "compressed lips" expression. As mother looms in still closer with a bigger smile, the infant dips his head down, with a slightly negative expression. Finally, the infant shows an unhappy grimace; only now does mother's partial surprise face show that she senses something is wrong. At each point the infant signals discomfort, but mother overrides that signal until the final infant grimace-face.

A third form of dyadic conflict can be seen in the following: despite the greater distress of future D infants, their mothers lowered facial-visual engagement coordination with infant facial-visual engagement. This pattern is a maternal emotional/attentional withdrawal from contingently coordinating with infant emotional/attentional "ups and downs," difficulty coordinating with infant positive moments as well as distress moments. They did not join the infant's attentional/affective direction, disturbing affective correspondence over time. We found no difference in the prevalence of positive or negative faces in future D (vs. B) mothers. Instead, the difference was found in the ways that mothers *contingently coordinated* their facial-visual behavior with those of the infants. Thus it was the maternal *process* of relating rather than the maternal affective content of behavior that distinguished future D (vs. B) mothers here. This maternal emotional/attentional withdrawal makes it difficult for future D (vs. B) infants to come to expect that their emotional/attentional states can influence their mothers to coordinate with them. Infants will have difficulty coming to expect that their mothers will join both their distressed and positive states. Infants are thus relatively helpless to affect their mothers through their facial/visual behavior, disturbing the infant's sense of interactive efficacy.

Lowered maternal facial/visual engagement coordination was accompanied by heightened maternal facial self-contingency. This finding indicates that mothers of future D infants inhibited the variability of facial changes and remained overly facially stable or too "steady-state," like a momentary "still-face" (see Tronick, 1989). We interpret this finding as mothers "closing up their faces," another way of not being available to the "play of faces," another way of saying "you can't affect me." In one example of mother "closing up" her face, across a 4-second sequence, as the distressed infant opens his eyes, mother's closed-up face, with a blank look, remains stabilized although her head angle shifts; as infant distress increases, mother's facial affect remains stabilized.

We conjecture that infants may experience the combination of maternal withdrawal of engagement coordination, and "too-steady" faces, as a kind of affective "wall." Maternal positive faces, specifically at moments of infant distress, further connote a "stone-walling" of infant distress. This active maternal emotional refusal to "go with" the infant, a refusal to join infant distress, disturbs the infant's ability to feel sensed. We infer that future D infants come to expect that their mothers will not "join" their distress with acknowledgments such as maternal "woe face," an empathic form of maternal facial mirroring. Instead infants may come to expect that their mothers seem happy, surprised, or "closed up" when they are distressed.

In the context of lowered maternal engagement coordination, future D infants themselves showed lowered engagement self-predictability, a lowered stability of the infant's own rhythms of facial-visual behavior. The infant's ability to anticipate his or her own moment-to-moment action tendencies is lowered, generating a decreased sense of self-familiarity and coherence over time, metaphorically "destabilized." Infant engagement destabilization is interpreted as an adjustment to maternal failure to adequately coordinate with infant engagement (or vice-versa).

Mothers of future D infants not only lowered their contingent engagement coordination with infant engagement, but they also lowered contingent touch coordination with infant touch. These maternal patterns disturb infant interactive efficacy in the engagement and touch realms. Compared with mothers of future B infants, mothers of future D infants did not acknowledge increasing infant touch as a cue for more affectionate, tender maternal touch. We infer that future D infants come to expect that their mothers will be unavailable to help modulate states of affective distress through touch coordination with their own touch behaviors. Infants are left too alone, too separate, in the realm of touch.

Simultaneously future D infants themselves showed a touch dysregulation: (1) less touch across all codes (touching object, mother or own skin); (b) specifically less touching of their own skin; and (c) greater likelihood of continuing in states of "no touch," metaphorically "getting stuck in 'no touch.'" This configuration depicts an infant intrapersonal dysregulation linked to a maternal interpersonal dysregulation, which we term a dyadic touch dysregulation. Future D (vs. B) infants cannot rely on mothers to help in the touch domain, nor can they rely on themselves to provide self-comfort and modulation of vocal distress through touch. These interpersonal and intrapersonal forms of touch dysregulation compromise infant interactive efficacy and self-agency, in the capacity to self-soothe through touch.

Together, future D infants and their mothers showed a dyadic touch dysregulation, illustrating a disturbance in the interaction pattern of "dyadic state transforming," the expectation of being able to transform an arousal state through the contribution of the partner (Beebe et al, 1997; Stern, 1985). In addition, the infant findings (less touch, less touching one's own skin, in the context of greater vocal distress) illustrate a disturbance in an *infant* "intrapersonal state transforming," the expectation of being able to help one-self transform arousal states. Future D infants thus come to expect that they are relatively helpless to affect mothers, in the realms of facial-visual engagement and touch. They also come to expect that they are relatively helpless to help themselves, by providing touch self-comfort and touch modulation of vocal distress.

If their procedural experience could be put into words, using all the findings, we imagine D infants might experience, "I'm so upset and you're not helping me. I'm smil-ing at you and whimpering; don't you see I want you to love me? When I'm upset, you smile, or close up your face, or look away. You make me feel worse. I feel confused about what I feel and about what you feel. I can't predict you. I don't know what is going on. What am I supposed to do? I feel helpless to affect you. I feel helpless to help myself. I feel frantic."

If the procedural experience of the mother of the future D infant could be put into words, we imagine that she might feel, "I can't let myself be too affected by you. I'm not going to let myself be controlled by you and dragged down by your bad moods (Karlen Lyons-Ruth, October 17, 2008). I refuse to be helpless. I'm going to be upbeat and laugh off your silly fussing." She might feel, "I can't bear to know about your distress. Don't be like that. Come on, no fussing. I just need you to love me. I won't hear of anything else. You should be very happy." And she might feel, "Your distress frightens me. I feel that I am a bad mother when you cry" (Estelle Shane, personal communication, November 12, 2006). Or she might feel, "Your distress threatens me. I resent it. I just have to shut down" (Mary Sue Moore, personal communication, July 2, 2007).

Thus the central feature of future D dyads is intrapersonal and interpersonal conflict in the context of infants who are intensely emotionally distressed. *Maternal withdrawal from distressed infants* compromises infant interactive agency and emotional coherence in future D (vs. B) infants. These infants are "frantic," not sensed or "known" in their distress, and relatively helpless to influence mothers with their distress. Infant attempts to manage distress become hierarchically organizing (Werner, 1948) for the future D infant. We interpret the maternal withdrawal from distressed infants as the future D mother's difficulty with her own unresolved loss, mourning, or abuse, and presumably an inability to bear her own distress, as well as that of her infant. We understand these mothers to be preoccupied with regulating their own state (by looking way or closing up their faces).

On Knowing and Being Known in the Origins of Disorganized Attachment

We now return to the proposal that the organization of intimate relating is at stake in these early expectancies or internal working models (Lyons-Ruth, 1999, 2008). Intimate relating entails the fundamental issue of how the infant comes to know, and be known by, another's mind. We construe "mind" here from the point of view of the infant, that is, expectancies of procedurally-organized action sequences.

A number of authors (see Lyons-Ruth, 2008; Meltzoff, 1985; Meltzoff & Moore, 1998; Sander, 1977, 1995; Stern, 1985, 1998; Trevarthen, 1998; Tronick, 1989) have argued for several decades that the infant's perception of correspondences and contingency (in time, form and intensity) between his own behavior and that of the partner provides the infant with a means of sensing the state of the partner, and of sensing whether the state is shared, or not. These correspondences and contingency patterns have been variously described as "changing with" and "affect attunement" (Stern, 1985), a resonance based on "matched specificities" (Sander, 1977), being "on the same wavelength" (Beebe & Lachmann, 1988), "a fundamental relatedness between self and other" (Meltzoff, 1985), "mutually sensitive minds," (Trevarthen, 1998). These patterns of correspondence and contingency facilitate the development of infant agency, coherence, and identity (Sander, 1995; Stern, 1985; Trevarthen, 1998).

These patterns of correspondence and contingency are disturbed in future D versus B infants, generating difficulties in knowing, and being known by, the mother's mind, as well as in knowing his own mind. Our findings allow us to describe *how* these difficulties are organized.

We propose that the future D infant will have difficulty *feeling known* by his mother (1) in moments when he is distressed, and she shows smile or surprise expressions: a failure of Meltzoff's "you are like me," and an illustration of Stern's (1985) moments in which the infant learns that his distress states are not shareable, which may accrue to later experiences of "not-me"; (2) in moments when the mother looks away repeatedly and unpredictably, so that he does not feel *seen*; (3) as mother does not coordinate her facial-visual engagement with his facial-visual engagement, thus not able to coordinate with the overall "gestalt" of her infant; (4) as mother does not coordinate her affectionate-to-intrusive touch patterns with his frequency of touch; generating infant expectations that mother does not *change with* him, and that she does not match his direction of change, in the arenas of facial-visual engagement and touch; and (5) by clinical observation, as mother does not seem curious about, and makes no efforts to repair powerful disruptions. This observation suggests that these mothers have difficulty thinking about the infant's mind and motivation (Fonagy, Gergely, Jurist, & Target, 2002).

We propose that the future D infant will have difficulty *knowing* his mother's mind (1) because he has difficulty integrating mother's discrepant smile/surprise face to his distress into a coherent percept; (2) because he has difficulty predicting whether mother will look or look away, and for how long; (3) because he has difficulty predicting whether she will sit upright, lean forward, or loom in; (4) because she "closes up" her face and becomes inscrutable; (5) because mother's lowered contingent engagement coordination makes it difficult for the infant to "influence" mother with his facial-visual engagement, to use his own state to anticipate where she is going next, leading to the infant's expectation that mother does not join his direction of attentional/affective change; and (6) because mother's lowered contingent touch coordination makes it difficult for the infant to "influence" mother with the frequency of his touch behaviors, to anticipate the nature of her touch based on his own just prior touch behavior, leading to the infant's expectation that mother does not "follow" his touch behaviors by touching him more affectionately as he touches more (and vice-versa).

We propose that the future D infant will have difficulty *knowing himself* (1) in his moments of discrepant affect, for example as he smiles and whimpers in the same second; (2) as his own engagement self-contingency is lowered, making it more difficult to sense his own facial-visual action tendencies from moment-to-moment, more difficult to develop a coherent expectation of his own body; and (3) as he has difficulty touching (self, object, mother), and specifically difficulty touching his own skin, and as he gets "stuck" in states of "no touch," all of which disturb his visceral feedback through touch, and disturb his own agency in regulating distress through touch. As Sander (1977, 1995) notes, infant inner experience is organized in the interactive context. Sander argues that the infant–caretaker system may both facilitate, and constrain, the infant's access to and awareness of his own states and his ability to use his states in organizing his behavior. We propose that the future D infant experiences a disturbance in the experience of agency with regard to his own states.

One important aspect of these difficulties of the future D infant's ability to know, and be known by, another's mind, as well as to know his own mind, are identified through disturbances in maternal affective correspondence and state-sharing (Meltzoff, 2007; Sander, 1977; Stern, 1985; Trevarthen, 1998). However, many other aspects of these difficulties are identified through dysregulated contingencies. Moreover, not only affect, but also tactile, spatial, and attentional realms were dysregulated, an important addition.

As we noted, Lyons-Ruth (1999, 2008) proposed that the outcome of the process of coming to know and be known by another's mind is dependent on whether the partner is capable of a *collaborative dialogue*. Overall, the mother of the future D infant does not generate collaborative dialogues. Her infant will be unlikely to be able to generate procedural models in which both partners are represented as open to the full range of experiences of the other. Lyons-Ruth (1999, 2008) also suggested that failures of collaborative dialogue generate contradictory procedural models. An example in our data are moments when infants whimper and smile in the same second, possibly generating an infant procedural model such as, "I smile to find your smile, while I whimper to protest your uncomfortable touch." Another example of contradictory procedures are moments where infants are distressed but mothers smile or look surprised, possibly generating procedural models of, "While I am upset, you are happy." Contradictory procedures, intrapersonal or dyadic, disturb the ability to know and be known by the partner, and to know the self. They also disturb the higher-order coordinations essential to social and cognitive development (Lyons-Ruth, 1999). Moreover, they set the stage for dissociative defenses in which contradictory arenas of knowledge are entertained.

In summary, the future D infant represents *not being sensed and known* by the mother, particularly in states of distress: "you are not on my wavelength"; he represents *not knowing the mother*: "I can't read you, influence you, or count on you, especially when I am upset"; and he represents *confusion in sensing and knowing himself*, especially at moments of distress; "I can't tell what I feel, I can't sense my self, I can't help myself." Thus the emerging procedural model of future D infants represents confusion about their own basic emotional organization, about their mothers' emotional organization, and about their mothers' response to their distress, setting a trajectory in development that may disturb the fundamental integration of the person.

IMPLICATIONS FOR THE ORIGINS OF A PRESYMBOLIC THEORY OF MIND

This study documented many differences in patterns of correspondence and self- and interactive contingency in mother–infant interactions at 4 months, which predicted those infants who were classified as disorganized versus secure attachment at 12 months. Procedural expectancies of these contingent interaction patterns, and of patterns of behavioral correspondence, between self and mother, provide 4-month infants with complex presymbolic representational models of "how interactions go." We argued that these models have implications for how infants may know and feel known by the mother's mind, as well as how infants may know their own minds.

We suggest that these presymbolic procedural expectancies constitute an essential bedrock of the infant's emerging ability to know other minds and to be known by them, prior to the emergence of a symbolic mind. There is considerable precedent for the position that infants know other minds and are known by them, via procedural action sequences. Gopnik (2008, 2009) argues that infants do know something about minds, which they find out by making inferences from their own experiences and their experience of others. Meltzoff (1985, 2007) argues that, from birth, infants link aspects of their own mind and emotions with those of their partners via action correspondences.

The nature of these infant procedural expectancies predicted infant attachment classifications 8 months later. We argue that these procedural expectancies will bias the course of the infant's developing "Theory of Mind" of interpersonal relations as symbolic functioning emerges. Thus infants make sense of actions of self and other by reference to presymbolic procedural expectancies, based on the history of correspondences and contingent action sequences of self and other. Procedural expectancies are precursors of making sense of actions of self and other by reference to symbolized mental states (desires, thoughts, memories, feelings) of self and other. These procedural models enable the 4-month infant to anticipate what will happen next, both in his own behavior and in that of the partner; based on correspondences as well as contingencies. These models enable the infant to predict the actions of self and other, to predict how one's own behavior influences the other, and how the other will likely influence him. Thus infants generate models (expectancies) of knowing and being known, as well as of knowing oneself. These are important dimensions of an emerging presymbolic Theory of Mind.

REFERENCES

Ainsworth, M., Blehar, M., Waters, E., & Wall, S. (1978). *Patterns of Attachment: A Psychological Study of the Strange Situation.* Hillsdale, NJ: Erlbaum.

Ambady, N., & Rosenthal, R. (1992). Thin slices of expressive behavior as predictors of interpersonal consequences: A meta-analysis. *Psychological Bulletin, 2,* 256–274.

Bahrick, L., & Lickliter, R. (2002). Intersensory redundancy guides early perceptual and cognitive development. *Advances in Child Development and Behavior, 30,* 153–187.

Beebe, B. (2005). Mother-infant research informs mother-infant treatment. *Psychoanalytic Study of the Child, 60,* 7–46.

Beebe, B., Jaffe, J., Buck, K., Chen, H., Cohen, P., Blatt, S., et al. (2007). Six-week postpartum maternal self-criticism and dependency and 4-month mother-infant self- and interactive contingency. *Developmental Psychology, 4,* 1360–1376.

Beebe, B., Jaffe, J., Buck, K., Chen, H., Cohen, P., Feldstein, S., et al. (2008). Maternal depressive symptoms at 6 weeks predict mother-infant -month self- and interactive contingency. *Infant Mental Health Journal, 29,* 1–29.

Beebe, B., Jaffe, J., & Lachmann, F. (1992). A dyadic systems view of communication. In N. Skolnick, & S. Warshaw (Eds.), *Relational Perspectives in Psychoanalysis* (pp. 61–81). Hillsdale, NJ: Analytic Press.

Beebe, B., Jaffe, J., Markese, S., Buck, K., Chen, H., Cohen, P., et al. (2010). The origins of 12-month attachment: A microanalysis of 4-month mother-infant interaction. *Attachment & Human Development, 12,* 3–141.

Beebe, B., Knoblauch, S., Rustin, J., & Sorter, D. (2005). *Forms of Intersubjectivity in Infant Research and Adult Treatment.* NY: Other Press.

Beebe, B., & Lachmann, F. (1988). The contribution of mother-infant mutual influence to the origins of self- and object representations. *Psychoanalytic Psychology, 5,* 305–337.

Beebe, B., & Lachmann, F. (1994). Representation and internalization in infancy: Three principles of salience. *Psychoanalytic Psychology, 11,* 127–165.

Beebe, B., & Lachmann, F. (2002). *Infant Research and Adult Treatment: Co-Constructing Interactions.* Hillsdale, NJ: The Analytic Press.

Beebe, B., Lachmann, F., & Jaffe, J. (1997). Mother-infant interaction structures and presymbolic self- and object representations. *Psychoanalytic Dialogues, 7,* 133–182.

Beebe, B., & Stern, D. (1977). Engagement-disengagement and early object experiences. In N. Freedman, & S. Grand (Eds.), *Communicative Structures and Psychic Structures* (pp. 35–55). New York: Plenum Press.

Beebe, B., Steele, M., Jaffe, J., Buck, K.A., Chen, H., Cohen, P., et al. (2011). Maternal anxiety symptoms and mother-infant self- and interactive contingency. *Infant Mental Health Journal, 32,* 174–206.

Bornstein, M. (1985). Infant into adult: Unity to diversity in the development of visual categorization. In J. Mehler, & R. Fox (Eds.), *Neonate Cognition* (pp. 115–138). Hillsdale, NJ: Erlbaum.

Case, R. (1991). *The Mind's Staircase*. Hillsdale, NJ: Lawrence.

Chen, H., & Cohen, P. (2006). Using individual growth model to analyze the change in quality of life from adolescence to adulthood. *Health and Quality of Life Outcomes, 4*, 1–7.

Cohen, P., Chen, H., Hamgiami, F., Gordon, K., & McArdle, J. (2000). Multilevel analyses for predicting sequence effects of financial and employment problems on the probability of arrest. *Journal of Quantitative Criminology, 16*, 223–235.

Cohn, J., & Elmore, M. (1988). Effect of contingent changes in mothers' affective expression on the organization of behavior in 3-month-old infants. *Infant Behavior and Development, 11*, 493–505.

Cohn, J., & Tronick, E. (1989). Mother–infant face-to-face interaction: The sequence of dyadic states at 3, 6, 9 months. *Developmental Psychology, 23*, 68–77.

DeCasper, A., & Carstens, A. (1980). Contingencies of stimulation: Effects on learning and emotion in neonates. *Infant Behavior and Development, 9*, 19–36.

Downing, G. (2004). Emotion, body and parent-infant interaction. In J. Nadel, & D. Muir (Eds.), *Emotional Development: Recent Research Advances* (pp. 429–449). Oxford: Oxford University Press.

Fagen, J., Morrongiello, B., Rovee-Collier, C., & Gekoski, M. (1984). Expectancies and memory retrieval in three-month-old infants. *Child Development, 55*, 936–943.

Feldman, R. (2006). From biological rhythms to social rhythms: Physiological precursors of mother-infant synchrony. *Developmental Psychology, 42*, 175–188.

Fischer, K. (1980). A theory of cognitive development: The control and construction of hierarchies of skills. *Psychological Bulletin, 87*, 77–531.

Fonagy, P., Gergely, G., Jurist, E., & Target, M. (2002). *Affect Regulation, Mentalization and the Development of the Self.* New York: Other Press.

Gergely, G., & Watson, J. (1996). The social biofeedback model of parental affect-mirroring. *International Journal of Psycho-Analysis, 11*, 1181–1212.

Gianino, A., & Tronick, E. (1988). The mutual regulation model: The infant's self and interactive regulation coping and defense. In T. Field, P. McCabe, & N. Schneiderman (Eds.), *Stress and Coping* (pp. 47–68). Hillsdale, NJ: Erlbaum.

Goldberg, S., Benoit, D., Blokland, K., & Madigan, S. (2003). Typical maternal behavior, maternal representations and infant disorganized attachment. *Development and Psychopathology, 15*, 239–257.

Gopnik, A. (2010). How babies think. *Scientific American, 303*, 76–81.

Haith, M., Hazan, C., & Goodman, G. (1988). Expectation and anticipation of dynamic visual events by 3.5 month old babies. *Child Development, 59*, 467–479.

Hay, D. (1997). Postpartum depression and cognitive development. In L. Murray, & P. Cooper (Eds.), *Postpartum Depression and Child Development* (pp. 85–110). New York: Guilford Press.

Jaffe, J., Beebe, B., Feldstein, S., Crown, C., & Jasnow, M. (2001). Rhythms of dialogue in infancy. *Monographs of the Society for Research in Child Development, 66* (2, Serial No. 264), 1–132.

Lewis, M., & Goldberg, S. (1969). Perceptual-cognitive development in infancy: A generalized expectancy model as a function of the mother-infant interaction. *Merrill Palmer Quarterly, 15*, 81–100.

Lewkowicz, D. (2000). The development of intersensory temporal perception: An epigenetic systems/limitations view. *Psychological Bulletin, 126*, 281–308.

Leyendecker, B., Lamb, M., Fracasso, M., Scholmerich, A., & Larson, D. (1997). Playful inter-action and the antecedents of attachment: A longitudinal study of Central American and Euro-American mothers and infants. *Merrill Palmer Quarterly, 43*, 24–47.

Littell, R., Miliken, G., Stoup, W., & Wolfinger, R. (1996). *SAS System for Mixed Models.* Cary, NC: SAS Institute.

Lyons-Ruth, K. (1999). The two-person unconscious: Intersubjective dialogue, enactive relational representation, and the emergence of new forms of relational organization. *Psychoanalytic Inquiry, 19*, 576–617.

Lyons-Ruth, K. (2008). Contributions of the mother-infant relationship to dissociative, borderline, and conduct symptoms in young adulthood. *Infant Mental Health Journal, 29*, 203–218.

Lyons-Ruth, K., Bronfman, E., & Parsons, E. (1999). Maternal disrupted affective communica-tion, maternal frightened or frightening behavior, and disorganized infant attachment strate-gies. *Monographs of the Society for Research in Child Development, 64* (3, Serial No. 258).

Madigan, S., Bakermans-Kranenburg, M., Van IJzendoorn, M., Moran, G., Pederson, D., & Benoit, D. (2006). Unresolved states of mind anomalous parental behavior, and disorga-nized attachment: A review and meta-analysis of a transmission gap. *Attachment & Human Development, 8*, 89–111.

Main, M., & Hesse, E. (1990). Parents' unresolved traumatic experiences are related to infant disorganized attachment status: Is frightened and/or frightening parental behavior the link-ing mechanism? In M. Greenberg, D. Cicchetti, & E. Cummings (Eds.), *Attachment in the Preschool Years: Theory, Research, and Intervention* (pp. 161–182). Chicago: University of Chicago Press.

Mandler, J. (1988). How to build a baby: On the development of an accessible representation system. *Cognitive Development, 3*, 113–136.

McArdle, J., & Bell, R. (2000). An introduction to latent growth models for developmental data analysis. In T. D. Little, K. L. Schnabel, & J. Baumert (Eds.), *Modeling Longitudinal and Multilevel Data: Practical Issues, Applied Approaches, and Specific Examples* (pp. 69–107). Mahwah, NJ: Erlbaum.

Meltzoff, A. (1985). The roots of social and cognitive development: Models of man's original nature. In T. Field, and N. Fox (Eds.), *Social Perception in Infants* (pp. 1–30). Norwood, NJ: Ablex.

Meltzoff, A. (2007). Like me: A foundation for social cognition. *Developmental Science, 10*, 126–134.

Meltzoff, A., & Moore, M. (1998). Infant intersubjectivity: Broadening the dialogue to include imitation, identity and intention. In S. Braten (Ed.), *Intersubjective Communication and Emotion in Early Ontogeny* (pp. 47–62). Cambridge: Cambridge University Press.

Millar, W. (1988). Smiling, vocal and attentive behavior during social contingency learning in seven and ten month old infants. *Merrill Palmer Quarterly, 34*, 301–325.

Moore, G., Cohn, J., & Campbell, S. (1997). Mother's affective behavior with infant siblings: Stability and change. *Developmental Psychology, 33*, 856–860.

Muir, D., & Hains, S. (1993). Infantile sensitivity to perturbations in adult facial, vocal, tac-tile, and contingent stimulation during face-to-face interaction. In B. DeBoysson-Bardies, S. DeSchonen, P. Jusczyk, P. McNeilage, and J. Morton (Eds), *Developmental Neurocognition: Speech and Face Processing in the First Year of Life* (pp. 171–185). Netherlands: Kluwer.

Murray, L., Fiori-Cowley, A., Hooper, R., & Cooper, P. (1996). The role of postnatal depression and associated adversity on early mother-infant interactions and later infant outcome. *Child Development, 67*, 2512–2526

Murray, L., & Trevarthen, C. (1985). Emotional regulation of interactions between two-month-olds and their mothers. In T. Field, & N. Fox (Eds.), *Social Perception in Infants* (pp. 177–197). Norwood, NJ: Ablex.

Papousek, M. (1992). Early ontogeny of vocal communication in parent-infant interaction. In H. Papousek, U. Juergens, & M. Papousek (Eds.), *Nonverbal Vocal Communication* (pp. 230–261). New York: Cambridge University Press.

Saffran, J., Aslin, R., & Newport, E. (1996). Statistical learning by 8-month-old infants. *Science, 274*, 1926–1928.

Sander, L. (1977). The regulation of exchange in the infant-caretaker system and some aspects of the context-content relationship. In M. Lewis, & L. Rosenblum (Eds.), *Interaction, Conversation, and the Development of Language* (pp. 133–156). New York: Wiley.

Sander, L. (1995). Identity and the experience of specificity in a process of recognition. *Psychoanalitic Dialogues, 5*, 579–593.

Shackman, J., & Pollak, S. (2005). Experiential influences on multimodal perception of emotion. *Child Development, 76*, 1116–1126.

Shields, P., & Rovee-Collier, C. (1992). Long-term memory for context-specific category information at six months. *Child Development, 63*, 245–259.

Singer, J. (1998). Using SAS PROC MIXED to fit multilevel models, hierarchical models, and individual growth models. *Journal of Educational and Behavioral Statistics, 24*, 323–355.

Singer, J., & Fagen, J. (1992). Negative affect, emotional expression, and forgetting in young infants. *Developmental Psychology, 28*, 48–57.

Singer, J., & Willett, J. (2003). *Applied Longitudinal Data Analysis*. New York: Oxford University Press.

Stern, D. (1971). A microanalysis of the mother-infant interaction. *Journal of the American Academy of Child Psychiatry, 10*, 501–507.

Stern, D. (1985). *The Interpersonal World of the Infant*. New York: Basic Books.

Stern, D. (1995). *The Motherhood Constellation*. New York: Basic Books.

Stern, D. (1998). The process of therapeutic change involving implicit knowledge: Some implications of developmental observations for adult psychotherapy. *Infant Mental Health Journal, 19*, 300–308.

Tarabulsy, G., Tessier, R., & Kappas, A. (1996). Contingency detection and the contingent organization of behavior interactions: Implications for socioemotional development in infancy. *Psychological Bulletin, 120*, 25–41.

Thomas, E., & Malone, T. (1979). On the dynamics of two-person interactions. *Psychological Review, 86*, 331–360.

Thomas, E., & Martin, J. (1976). Analyses of parent-infant interaction. *Psychological Review, 83*, 141–155.

Trevarthen, C. (1977). Descriptive analyses of infant communicative. In H. Schaffer (Ed.), *Studies in Mother-Infant Interaction*, (pp. 227–270). London, Academic Press.

Trevarthen, C. (1998). The concept and foundations of infant intersubjectivity. In S. Braten (Ed.), *Intersubjective Communication and Emotion in Early Ontogeny* (pp. 15–46). Cambridge, MA: Cambridge University Press.

Tronick, E. (1989). Emotions and emotional communication in infants. *American Psychologist,* *44,* 112–119.

Van Egeren, L., Barratt, M., & Roach, M. (2001). Mother-infant responsiveness: Timing, mutual regulation, and interactional context. *Developmental Psychology, 37,* 684–697.

Watson, J. (1985). Contingency perception in early social development. In T. Field, & N. Fox (Eds.), *Social Perception in Infants* (pp. 157–176). Norwood, NJ: Ablex.

Weinberg, K., Tronick, E. (1991). *Stability of infant social and coping behaviors and affective displays between 6 and 15 months: Age-appropriate tasks and stress bring out stability.* Paper presented at the Society for Research in Child Development, Seattle, WA.

Weinberg, M., Tronick, E., Cohn, J., & Olson, K. (1999). Gender differences in emotional expressivity and self-regulation during early infancy. *Developmental Psychology, 35,* 175–188.

Weiss P. (1970). Whither life or science? *American Scientist, 8,* 156–163.

Werner, H. (1948). *The Comparative Psychology of Mental Development.* New York: International Universities Press.

6 Gaze Following and Agency in Human Infancy
Andrew N. Meltzoff and Rechele Brooks

IF A PERSON looks through a hole in a fence, onlookers are also induced to look. We do so because we want to see what the person is looking at. We could ask them to linguistically describe what they see, or we could look for ourselves. Both inform us about what the gazer is looking at.

There is a debate about whether human infants are trying to see what others are looking at. Some propose that gaze following is innate and reflexive: The visual pattern of averted eyes compels one's eyes to move in the same direction. Others maintain that it is a conditioned response: The gaze follower has been conditioned to turn to the side upon seeing a conspecific's head turn (reinforced by interesting sights).

From one perspective, these views are contradictory. The former argues that gaze following is triggered by a narrowly tuned evolutionary stimulus: A red light would not trigger the inbuilt system. The latter view argues that the stimulus is arbitrary: Infants would be equally likely to learn to turn left upon seeing a red light as a left-turning human head—it all depends on learned contingencies. From another perspective, the views are similar. They are ways of getting the infant's eyes to turn without the infant attributing mental states to the gazer. They are "simple mechanisms."

This presents a developmental problem, however. If infants start off simply responding to innate or conditioned directional cues, when do they get past this? Through what mechanism do they come to appreciate the other person as having visual experiences like their own? Unless one thinks that adults do not do this, we have to explain how and when this attribution to others arises.

Here we argue that the crucial ingredients of human gaze following are not conditioning or innate eyespot following. The ontogenesis of infant gaze following depends on experience but not of the Skinnerian type. We argue that infants use their own visual experiences to help them interpret the visual experiences of others. We draw on the "like-me" framework, a view that has been successfully applied to other aspects of social–cognitive development such as imitation and in-group preferences (Meltzoff, 2007, 2013). We lay out the case for "like-me" understanding as an essential component of gaze following in human infancy. (Gaze following in other species may or may not rely on this mechanism; most of the details about human gaze following enumerated in this chapter have yet to be tested in nonhuman species.)

This chapter brings together several converging lines of work. In one set of studies, we manipulate the effective stimulus for gaze following in human infants. In another, we directly test the role of self-experience in changing infants' understanding of others' vision. In a third, we test the conditions under which infants attribute mental states to artificial agents (robots). We conclude by sketching a theory about how infant gaze following and infant notions of agency (both of their own agency and that of others) mutually interact to generate the behavior we observe as "gaze following."

Conceptual and Methodological Issues

"Gaze following" seems so simple as to not require a definition. We believe, however, that it is important for theory to distinguish gaze following from other related behavior involving: (1) attention to eyes, (2) cued looking to the periphery, and (3) visual habituation, violation of expectancy.

DEFINITIONAL MATTERS

The most interesting cases of gaze following occur when: (1) the follower *looks at* the object or event that the gazer is looking at, (2) the looking behavior of the gazer is the *external stimulus* causing the gaze-follower's response, and (3) the gaze follower *seeks to see what the gazer has looked at*.

Criterion 1 excludes giving infants credit for gaze following if they simply look to a hemifield in space (they must look at the target). Complete accuracy is not called for, but experiments should attempt to show that infants are looking at the target specified by the adult's gaze to credit them with gaze following to the object.

Criterion 2 eliminates infants turning by chance in synchrony with an adult (the observed gaze must be the "cause"). If there are dynamically changing objects in the field, infants may spot them independent of the adult's act. A salient visual object or sound could catch both the adult's and infant's attention. Synchronous looking because of a common third cause is not gaze following, although both parties end up looking at the same object. Also, if the infant generates the first look to the object, and the caretaker follows, the causal arrow runs in the wrong direction. It is not infant gaze following, although the adult and infant both end up fixating the same thing.

Criterion 3 is the Holy Grail. It involves an effort to see what the other sees and implies that infants process the perceptual states of others. The other's look is interpreted to be "about" something, and infants seek to look at that something. Often the best evidence for the third criterion comes from converging measures that provide clues to infants' interpretation and motivation for looking at the target indicated by the adult's look. Infant points, vocalizations, and checking back to the gazer provide such converging information.

DIFFERENTIATING GAZE FOLLOWING FROM OTHER EYE-RELATED PHENOMENA

We can now differentiate several eye-related phenomena.

Eye Preference

One set of studies concerns young infants' sensitivity to human eyes and preferences for facelike patterns containing eyespots (e.g., Baron-Cohen, 1995; Farroni, Csibra, Simion, & Johnson, 2002). This could be the "front end" of a gaze-following mechanism, but clearly, such perceptual biases and preferences are not evidence of gaze following per se.

Cued-Looking to Periphery

Another literature concerns cued looking to peripheral targets (e.g., Farroni, Johnson, Brockbank, & Simion, 2000; Frischen, Bayliss, & Tipper, 2007; Hood, Willen, Driver, 1998; Johnson, Grossmann, & Farroni, 2008; Senju, Johnson, & Csibra, 2006). The classic stimulus used in this paradigm is a digitized face with eyes that shift to one side before a target appears on that side or the other side (arrows are sometimes used instead of eyes). In this procedure, *the pointer stimulus disappears before the peripheral probes appear.* Adults and infants look with shorter latencies to the cued side. Critically, the pointer stimulus and the visual targets are *only a few inches away* from one another, so there is little or no projection out into distal space. Although there is a shorter latency to notice the peripheral target, this is not necessarily gaze following (criteria 2 and 3 are not satisfied).

Gaze following in the real world differs markedly from this cued-looking setup. First, when a mother looks at an object, her face does not extinguish (but in most cued-looking studies the pointer disappears to "free up" infants' attentional resources). Second, in real-world gaze following, the peripheral targets do not pop into existence to attract attention immediately after the pointer has extinguished (as is commonly done in the cued-looking paradigm). Third and most importantly, in the cuing paradigm, infants need only make a minimal gaze shift to targets that are a few inches from the pointer. If the pointer's movement provides a directional bias, infants can succeed. The cued-looking paradigm simply seeks cues to bias the child to the left or right side, rather than requiring infants to project their looks into space to find what the gaze is "about." There are many ways to produce side biases without infants gaze following. Infants' directional cueing may be a primitive precursor to genuine gaze following (an empirical question), but the two phenomena are not identical. The factors controlling the two are not the same (e.g., arrows may be effective for cued responses but not for gaze following), and the developmental sequella are not identical (e.g., early gaze following predicts accelerated word learning in human infants, Brooks & Meltzoff, 2008, but such longitudinal predictions have not been shown for infant cued-looking).

Visual Habituation: Violation of Expectancy Measures

A third body of work that is often cited relies on habituation studies (e.g., Luo & Baillargeon, 2007; Woodward, 2003). This literature suggests that infants encode the relationship between the looker and the object, and that they dishabituate when the link is broken. The data document infants' recognition of looking, but the paradigm does not require that infants *produce* a gaze-following act. They needn't take action and gaze follow at all. The dishabituation effects are important, but for the purposes of this chapter, we distinguish them from data showing that infants take spatially directed action and turn to look where the adult is looking.

Gaze Following With and Without Occluders

Experimental techniques assess whether infants engage in genuine gaze following. In the Eyes Open/Closed test, two identical objects are placed across the room from the infant and the adult's eyes are the key factor manipulated (Brooks & Meltzoff, 2002). The spatial placement of the targets requires that successful gaze following entails a large head turn *away* from the salient, adult face and toward the distal object. In the 2002 study, infants were randomly assigned to two groups. For one, the adult turned to the target object with eyes open; for the other, the adult turned with eyes closed. If infants relied solely on head movements as a pointer, they should turn in both cases. If, however, infants understand that the eyes are relevant for psychologically connecting the agent and object, they should differentiate the conditions and turn to look at the target object in one case only.

We assessed 12-, 14-, and 18-month-old infants. Importantly, infants were scored as gaze following only if they looked directly at the distal target, not if they simply looked to the same side in space indicated by the adult's movement. Infants at all ages looked significantly more often at the target when the adult turned with open rather than closed eyes. We also scored infants' average duration of correct looking—how long the infant stayed looking at a target once they gaze followed. This key measure (not used in other paradigms cited earlier) revealed that infants inspected the target longer when the adult turned to it with open versus closed eyes (as would be predicted if infants were fulfilling criterion 3). Also, more infants vocalized and pointed when turning to the correct target in the open-eyes versus the closed-eyes condition (suggesting communicating with the gazer). This is again in line with criterion 3, suggesting more ostensive pointing when the adult can see the infant's act (e.g., Franco, Perucchini, & March 2009; Liszkowski, Carpenter, Henning, Striano, & Tomasello, 2004).

MECHANISM

The most conservative interpretation of previous infant work is that a visible movement simply drags infants' attention to a hemifield of space in which they (by chance) see an interesting object (e.g., Moore, 1999). This cannot explain the 2002 results, because head movement was controlled. Moreover, infants marshal other target-directed acts, such as pointing and vocalizing toward the object when the adult can see the target. Infants are generating ostensive acts that the adult did not produce.

Finally, the duration measure, indicates that the object takes on special valence when it is looked at by another person. It is as if having the adult shine her psychological spotlight on an inanimate object leaves a trace on that object. Infants are curious about the object and linger longer in their inspection of it (criterion 3). This creates a temporal window for parental verbal labeling, providing a basis by which gaze following and language may be related (see Carpenter, Nagell, & Tomasello, 1998 and Brooks & Meltzoff, 2008).

GAZE FOLLOWING DEVELOPS

When does such gaze following begin? Brooks and Meltzoff (2005) evaluated infants within a tightly controlled age window. We assessed infants within one week of their 9, 10, and 11 month old birthdays to focus on the suspected developmental change.

We discovered that 9-month-olds did not discriminate between the open- versus closed-eyes conditions. They turned equally often in *both* cases. However, there was a developmental shift. For the 10- and 11-month-olds, the looking scores in the open-eyes condition were significantly greater than in the closed-eyes condition.

The 9-month-olds do not fail to follow the adult's turn. Quite the contrary, they follow too much; they turn even when the adult turns with closed eyes. This is essential for theory because it makes sense of the literature claiming that gaze following starts as early as 3 or 4 months old (e.g., Butterworth & Jarrett, 1991; Hoehl & Striano, 2010; Scaife & Bruner, 1975). We believe that infants do turn to follow the direction of head movements, postural changes, and other attention-getting shifts at 9 months and younger. But they do not selectively gaze follow. Nine-month-olds turn even if the adult cannot possibly be looking at the target, and so they are not truly *gaze* following.

Our theoretical position is that 9-month-olds understand others as "body orienters" and are sensitive to the postural/physical changes with respect to objects, but that older infants understand agents as visually connected to the external world and turn to follow their gaze (see Meltzoff & Brooks, 2007, pp. 232–238). This is an important step in understanding the other as an intentional agent (a gazer or perceiver). This interpretation of others helps infants narrow down the referent of a verbal label uttered by an interacting adult (Baldwin, 1995; Carpenter et al., 1998). The age change we found also fits well with reports using visual habituation techniques, which also highlight 9 to 12 months as a time of change (Johnson, Ok, & Luo, 2007; Woodward, 2003).

Using Self-Experience to Interpret the Gaze of Others

So far we have discussed one type of visual occlusion—eye closure. Infants might have a different understanding of how animate versus inanimate occluders effect vision. To test this, we used a blindfold to block the adult's view. This seemed like a minor variation, but the results were surprisingly different.

The 12-month-olds mistakenly followed the adult when she wore the blindfold (Brooks & Meltzoff, 2002, Experiment 2). Yet we had already shown that 12-month-olds did not follow the adult's turn when the adult's view is blocked by eye closure. It seems that 1-year-olds know that eye closure blocks the adult's vision, but not that an inanimate occluder does so. Why?

Our idea is that infants are *using their own agentive experience to give special meaning to the eye closures of others*. Infants have control over opening and closing of their eyes. When they don't want to see something they close their eyes. We believe that they are using their own phenomenological experience to give meaning to the matching acts of others. Perhaps providing infants with first-person experience that blindfolds block their own vision would change their interpretation of how blindfolds affect others.

Meltzoff and Brooks (2008) ran the relevant experiment with 12-month-olds. Infants sat at a table, which had an interesting object on it. When they turned to look at the object, the experimenter raised a blindfold to block their vision (Fig. 6.1). The blindfold was subsequently lowered and infants were allowed to play with the object. Then another interesting object was put on the table, the infants looked, and the process was repeated for about 7 minutes. The training *was restricted to infants' own vision* rather than anyone else wearing blindfolds. Then, for the first time, the adult wore the blindfold and the standard gaze-following test was administered.

The experience changed infants' interpretation of the adult. Now infants did not follow the blindfolded adult's "gaze" to the object (Meltzoff & Brooks, 2008). Infants generalized from their own experience to that of another person.

In the natural course of development, infants change their understanding of visual perception. By 14 to 18 months of age, infants refrain from following the adult's look if an opaque barrier, blindfold, or wall blocks the adult's view (e.g., Brooks & Meltzoff, 2002; Butler, Caron, & Brooks, 2000; Dunphy-Lelii & Wellman, 2004).

FIGURE 6.1 12-month-old infants were given self-experience with a blindfold (Meltzoff & Brooks, 2008). Infants looked at an interesting object (*left*). The blindfold blocked their view (*right*). Subsequently, infants used this self-experience to make inferences about how blindfolds influence others' vision in a gaze-following test.

Meltzoff and Brooks (2008, Experiment 2) provided 18-month-olds with novel experience that countered this expectation about opaque occluders. We designed a trick blindfold that looked opaque from the outside but was made of special material that could be seen through when held close to the eyes. Infants were randomly assigned to one of three groups: (1) experience with this trick blindfold, (2) experience with the opaque blindfold, and (3) baseline control (familiarity with the blindfold laying flat on the table). After training, the adult wore the blindfold for the standard gaze-following test.

Infants who were randomly assigned experience with the trick see-through blindfold followed the adult's head turns significantly more than did infants in the two other groups. This countered all of their previous conditioning experiences about people (people with opaque occluders are not good predictors of interesting sights), and it contradicted any biological–maturational view about occluded eyes. The infants with the relevant self-experience treated the adult with occluded eyes as if she could see.

These training effects showcase the power of the "like-me" developmental framework and the unique predictions it makes beyond conditioning and innate eyespot sensitivity. The information infants learned through self-experience is immediately applied to others. As infants gain self-experience they transform their understanding of others: "If I can (or cannot) see in this situation, then another person in the same situation will have the same perceptual experiences."

Gaze Following of Robots: What Is a Social Agent to an Infant?

Infants don't gaze follow in response to every physical movement they see. If the door opens, they are unlikely to "gaze follow" the doorknob. We used a programmable robot to investigate what sorts of entities infants would follow (Meltzoff, Brooks, Shon, & Rao, 2010; for related work see also Johnson, Slaughter, & Carey, 1998; Movellan & Watson, 1987; and the Meltzoff et al. paper for detailed comparisons among these studies).

  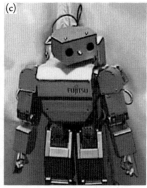

FIGURE 6.2 Robot used in the gaze-following test (Meltzoff, Brooks, Shon, & Rao, 2010). After watching this robot interact socially (reciprocal imitation) with an adult, infants readily followed the robot's gaze to distal targets.

In the Meltzoff et al study, an 18-month-old sat face to face with a hunk of metal, a robot (Fig. 6.2), and we systematically manipulated how the robot acted. Without prior training, when the robot moved its rectangular head (complete with eyespots) to the side, infants did not gaze follow. They tracked the motion but did not *project out into space* and seek what the robot was seeing. Occasionally, after tracking the motion to the left or the right side, they caught sight of the target object, but it was apparent that they were simply tracking the physical movement and catching sight of the object in their peripheral view by accident.

We tried many manipulations to endow the robot with sentience, using gaze following as our measure. The one that worked most readily was to have the infant watch as the adult and robot engaged in a social interchange, including reciprocal imitation of each other's actions. The adult performed an action and the robot would imitate, and reciprocally the robot would initiate a novel action that the adult would imitate. The infant him- or herself never had any contingent interaction with the robot. Nor did the robot have any contingent interaction with the target. The infant simply watched as a bystander, eavesdropping on the "social" adult–robot interaction.

After infants watched this adult–robot interaction, the robot turned to face a distal object. Infants readily gaze followed. This did not occur in control groups where the robot exhibited identical motions but not as part of a reciprocal social interaction. In fact we used three controls—control 1: the robot made the same movements but the human did not respond; control 2: the human made the same movements and the robot did not respond; control 3: both generated their same movements patterns, but did so out of synch with one another (Meltzoff et al., 2010).

Several alternative accounts of these findings can be rejected. First, the dependent measure was whether infants shifted their visual gaze outward in space to the target. It is not just that infants treated the robot's movement as a salient event to be tracked; they directed their gaze away from the robot and to the target, which was more than a meter away from the robotic movement.

Second, the robot had humanoid physical features, but this alone did not drive the results. It is not sufficient that infants treat the robot's black disks as "eyes" and then generalize from human experience based on physical features alone. The robot was morphologically identical in all groups, yet infants' responses significantly varied.

Third, the robot appeared to be a self-actuated agent (moved by itself), but this cannot account for the results across the groups. The robot in three groups performed identical movements via computer playback, but the infants' responses significantly varied across these groups This suggests that it is not solely the robots actions, but the nature of the *interaction* that carries weight.

What essential aspects of the interaction made a difference? Who (or what) is worthy of driving your own visual system so that it aligns with this other entity? The current experiment did not independently manipulate all possible factors, but we speculate that reciprocal imitation acts as a strong cue to psychological agency and communication in human infants (Meltzoff, 2007). An entity that imitates is one whose "gaze" should be followed. Future work will need to determine through systematic study the weights given to multiple factors—imitation, contingent turn taking, responsivity to language (Gergely, 2011; Johnson et al., 1998; Meltzoff, 2013; Movellan & Watson, 1987)—and how they influence infants' gaze following of the entity that exhibits them.

Social–Cognitive Developmental Theory

Gaze following is a powerful mechanism for learning in preverbal infants (Meltzoff, Kuhl, Movellan, & Sejnowski, 2009). Information is not equally distributed in the world. Specific people, places, things, and events are informationally rich—information "hot spots." It would be adaptive to draw the learner's attention to them. Before the use of language, three Ss are available for directing infant attention: salience, shoving, or showing.

Salience demands that the information hotspot has telltale physical attention-getting properties, such as brightness, size, or movement. This is not always the case. Shoving is even less reliable. One uses manual force to turn a child's head in the right direction, with dubious results. Evolution has hit upon an unlikely trick to get infants to the information hotspots—showing.

Adults turn to look at the information hotspot, not necessarily because of physical salience, but because they are interested in it, want to label it, or have an emotional reaction to it. The object/event is meaningful to the perceiver. Gaze following draws infants to the same object. The adult and infant share the perception. Empirical research shows that infants who are good at gaze following learn language more quickly, possibly in part because they are put in a position for pairing the parental labels with their referents (Baldwin, 1995; Brooks & Meltzoff, 2008; Bruner, 1983; Carpenter et al., 1998; Mundy et al., 2007; Sage & Baldwin, 2010)—although Quine (1960) and Markman

(1989) importantly show that solving the puzzle of reference certainly entails additional mechanisms.

The potential value of gaze following for learning is clear, but there is disagreement concerning how infants come to follow another's gaze in the first place and whether mental state attribution enters into the equation. One conservative interpretation is that infants—until they are approximately 18 months of age—do not actually follow the gaze of others. They simply visually track the movement of a salient object in the field (the head), and get to the correct hemifield in space, where they catch sight of interesting objects by chance. Although younger infants may rely on head tracking, 10- to 12-month-olds grant special status to human eyes. By this age, infants treat the adult looking behavior as object-directed, singling out a referent in the surroundings. Gaze following of this type is the entrée into a psychological world in which objects gain importance not because of their physical properties or the child's own preferences, *but because they are referred to by others.*

WHAT'S AGENCY GOT TO DO WITH IT?

We have argued that infant gaze following and understanding of social agents—themselves and others—are intimately linked. We conjectured that infants capitalize on self-generated experience of themselves as a looker/perceiver to understand the perceptions of others—the "like-me" hypothesis (Meltzoff, 2007, 2013).

But how does this work? We can flesh it out in more detail. Infants in the first year of life can imitate head turning and eye blinking (Meltzoff, 1988; Meltzoff & Moore, 1989; Piaget, 1962). This suggests that infants can map between others' head movements and their own, and between others' eyelid closures and their own. Infants' subjective experiences gained from "turning their head in order to see" could be used to make sense of the head movements of others. More subtly, infants experience that eye closure cuts off their own perceptual access. If an infant can map the eye closures of others onto his own eye closures, these mappings can provide data for developing inferences about visual perception in others.

This makes sense of the fact that young infants have more advanced understanding of eye closure than inanimate barriers to vision. Certainly, 1-year-olds have had months of first-person experience with voluntary looking away and eye closing to cut off unwanted stimuli. This bodily act is well understood and under their own agentive control. In contrast, it is only at 12- to 14-months-old that infants begin actively experimenting with hiding, finding, and re-hiding objects from themselves behind inanimate barriers (Gopnik & Meltzoff, 1997; Moore & Meltzoff, 1999, 2004). Our prediction was that an intervention with inanimate occluders blocking *their own view* could accelerate infants' understanding of the effects of blindfolds *on other people's vision.* This was indeed documented in the Meltzoff and Brooks (2008) intervention study. We believe that infants imbue the behaviors of others with new meaning based on their own experience.

SOCIAL-COGNITIVE CONSEQUENCES OF PERCEIVING OTHERS AS "LIKE ME"

This "like-me" projection opens a way of thinking about infant's understanding of mental states, beyond visual perception. Take the case of reading intentionality into others' manual acts. It has been shown that infants can infer the simple intentions of other people. In one study, an adult tried to pull apart a barbell-shaped toy, but his hands slipped off and the goal was not achieved (Meltzoff, 1995). He tried again in a new way and was also not successful. The infant only saw the efforts but not the successful act. Nonetheless, when infants were given the object they carefully wrapped their hands around the ends of the object and firmly pulled it apart (and did not do so in control groups). Preverbal infants understand our goals and re-enact what we intend to do, not what we did do.

One reason infants can make sense of the purposeful behavioral of others is that they have goals and intentions themselves. They have tried unsuccessfully to pull apart objects. Others who act "like me" have similar mental states like me. I infuse the behavior of other agents with my own phenomenological experience. When this is applied to visual perception, it provides a first step toward understanding perspective taking (see Moll & Meltzoff, 2011a and 2011b for arguments about how infant gaze following gives rise to childhood perspective-taking; and see Carey, 2009; Gergely, 2011; and Johnson, 2003 for related theoretical discussions about agency and gaze).

So far we have highlighted the role of self-experience in infants learning about other agents. But it is fundamental to the "like-me" framework that infants can also learn from observing the structured behavior of others—not exclusively or uniquely through their own first-person experience (Meltzoff, 2013; Meltzoff, Waismeyer, & Gopnik, 2012). This was underscored in this chapter by the study using social robots. The infant simply observed the robot-adult interaction as a bystander. The robot did not act contingently on the child's actions, nor did it react contingently with the target object. Instead, the robot engaged in reciprocal imitation with the other social agent in the room, the adult. Observing this social interaction transformed infants' attributions toward the robot. The swiveling cuboid atop of the metallic entity was no longer interpreted as a physical movement, but as a meaningful perceptual act directed to the distant target. Infants turned and gaze followed.

Young infants' understanding of social agency and their gaze following are inextricably linked. On the one hand, what infants learn about visual perception from their own agentive experience is projected to others. On the other hand, when they observe an entity acting as a social agent, infants make attributions to this entity beyond the observed movements themselves. The hunk of metal transforms from something that simply moves, to an agent who sees.

Acknowledgments

Supported by a grant from NSF (SMA-0835854) to ANM, and the University of Washington Royalty Research Fund to RB.

REFERENCES

Baldwin, D. A. (1995). Understanding the link between joint attention and language. In C. Moore, & P. J. Dunham (Eds.), *Joint Attention: Its Origins and Role in Development* (pp. 131–158). Hillsdale, NJ: Erlbaum.

Baron-Cohen, S. (1995). *Mindblindness: An Essay on Autism and Theory of Mind.* Cambridge, MA: MIT Press.

Brooks, R., & Meltzoff, A. N. (2002). The importance of eyes: How infants interpret adult looking behavior. *Developmental Psychology, 38,* 958–966. doi:10.1037//0012-1649.38.6.958

Brooks, R., & Meltzoff, A. N. (2005). The development of gaze following and its relation to language. *Developmental Science, 8,* 535–543. doi:10.1111/j.1467-7687.2005.00445.x

Brooks, R., & Meltzoff, A. N. (2008). Infant gaze following and pointing predict accelerated vocabulary growth through two years of age: A longitudinal, growth curve modeling study. *Journal of Child Language, 35,* 207–220. doi:10.1017/S030500090700829x

Bruner, J. (1983). *Child's Talk: Learning to Use Language.* New York, NY: Norton.

Butler, S. C., Caron, A. J., & Brooks, R. (2000). Infant understanding of the referential nature of looking. *Journal of Cognition and Development, 1,* 359–377. doi: 10.1207/S15327647JCD0104_01

Butterworth, G., & Jarrett, N. (1991). What minds have in common is space: Spatial mechanisms serving joint visual attention in infancy. *British Journal of Developmental Psychology, 9,* 55–72. doi: 10.1111/j.2044-835X.1991.tb00862.x

Carey, S. (2009). *The Origins of Concepts.* Oxford, UK: Oxford University Press.

Carpenter, M., Nagell, K., & Tomasello, M. (1998). Social cognition, joint attention, and communicative competence from 9 to 15 months of age. *Monographs of the Society for Research in Child Development, 63*(4, Serial No. 255).

Dunphy-Lelii, S., & Wellman, H. M. (2004). Infants' understanding of occlusion of others' line-of-sight: Implications for an emerging theory of mind. *European Journal of Developmental Psychology, 1,* 49–66. doi:10.1080/17405620444000049

Farroni, T., Csibra, G., Simion, F., & Johnson, M. H. (2002). Eye contact detection in humans from birth. *Proceedings of the National Academy of Sciences, 99,* 9602–9605. doi:10.1073/Pnas.152159999

Farroni, T., Johnson, M. H., Brockbank, M., & Simion, F. (2000). Infants' use of gaze direction to cue attention: The importance of perceived motion. *Visual Cognition, 7,* 705–718. doi: 10.1080/13506280050144399

Franco, F., Perucchini, P., & March, B. (2009). Is infant initiation of joint attention by pointing affected by type of interaction? *Social Development, 18,* 51–76. doi:10.1111/j.1467-9507.2008.00464.x

Frischen, A., Bayliss, A. P., & Tipper, S. P. (2007). Gaze cueing of attention: Visual attention, social cognition, and individual differences. *Psychological Bulletin, 133,* 694–724. doi:10.1037/0033-2909.133.4.694

Gergely, G. (2011). Kinds of agents: The origins of understanding instrumental and communicative agency. In U. Goswami (Ed.), *The Wiley-Blackwell Handbook of Childhood Cognitive Development* (2nd ed., pp. 76–105). Malden, MA: Wiley-Blackwell.

Gopnik, A., & Meltzoff, A. N. (1997). *Words, Thoughts, and Theories.* Cambridge, MA: MIT Press.

Hoehl, S., & Striano, T. (2010). The development of emotional face and eye gaze processing. *Developmental Science, 13,* 813–825. doi:10.1111/j.1467-7687.2009.00944.x

Hood, B. M., Willen, J. D., & Driver, J. (1998). Adult's eyes trigger shifts of visual attention in human infants. *Psychological Science, 9*, 131–134. doi: 10.1111/1467-9280.00024

Johnson, M. H., Grossmann, T., & Farroni, T. (2008). The social cognitive neuroscience of infancy: Illuminating the early development of social brain functions. In R. V. Kail (Ed.), *Advances in Child Development and Behavior* (Vol. 36, pp. 331–372). San Diego, CA: Elsevier.

Johnson, S. C. (2003). Detecting agents. *Philosophical Transactions of the Royal Society of London. Series B, Biological Sciences, 358*, 549–559. doi: 10.1098/rstb.2002.1237

Johnson, S. C., Ok, S.-J., & Luo, Y. (2007). The attribution of attention: 9-month-olds' interpretation of gaze as goal-directed action. *Developmental Science, 10*, 530–537. doi:10.1111/J.1467-7687.2007.00606.X

Johnson, S. C., Slaughter, V., & Carey, S. (1998). Whose gaze will infants follow? The elicitation of gaze-following in 12-month-olds. *Developmental Science, 1*, 233–238. doi:10.1111/1467-7687.00036

Liszkowski, U., Carpenter, M., Henning, A., Striano, T., & Tomasello, M. (2004). Twelve-month-olds point to share attention and interest. *Developmental Science, 7*, 297–307. doi: 10.1111/j.1467-7687.2004.00349.x

Luo, Y., & Baillargeon, R. (2007). Do 12.5-month-old infants consider what objects others can see when interpreting their actions? *Cognition, 105*, 489–512. doi: 10.1016/j.cognition.2006.10.007

Markman, E. M. (1989). *Categorization and naming in children: Problems of induction.* Cambridge, MA: MIT Press.

Meltzoff, A. N. (1988). Infant imitation after a 1-week delay: Long-term memory for novel acts and multiple stimuli. *Developmental Psychology, 24*, 470–476. doi:10.1037/0012-1649.24.4.470

Meltzoff, A. N. (1995). Understanding the intentions of others: Re-enactment of intended acts by 18-month-old children. *Developmental Psychology, 31*, 838–850. doi:10.1037/0012-1649.31.5.838

Meltzoff, A. N. (2007). The "like me" framework for recognizing and becoming an intentional agent. *Acta Psychologica, 124*, 26–43. doi:10.1016/j.actpsy.2006.09.005

Meltzoff, A. N. (2013). Origins of social cognition: Bidirectional self-other mapping and the "Like-Me" hypothesis. M. Banaji & S. Gelman (Eds.), *Navigating the Social World: What Infants, Children, and Other Species Can Teach Us* (pp. 139–144). New York: Oxford University Press.

Meltzoff, A. N., & Brooks, R. (2007). Eyes wide shut: The importance of eyes in infant gaze following and understanding other minds. In R. Flom, K. Lee, & D. Muir (Eds.), *Gaze-Following: Its Development and Significance* (pp. 217–241). Mahwah, NJ: Erlbaum.

Meltzoff, A. N., & Brooks, R. (2008). Self-experience as a mechanism for learning about others: A training study in social cognition. *Developmental Psychology, 44*, 1257–1265. doi:10.1037/a0012888

Meltzoff, A. N., Brooks, R., Shon, A. P., & Rao, R. P. N. (2010). "Social" robots are psychological agents for infants: A test of gaze following. *Neural Networks, 23*, 966–972. doi:10.1016/j.neunet.2010.09.005

Meltzoff, A. N., Kuhl, P. K., Movellan, J., & Sejnowski, T. J. (2009). Foundations for a new science of learning. *Science, 325*, 284–288. doi:10.1126/science.1175626

Meltzoff, A. N., & Moore, M. K. (1989). Imitation in newborn infants: Exploring the range of gestures imitated and the underlying mechanisms. *Developmental Psychology, 25*, 954–962. doi: 10.1037/0012-1649.25.6.954

Meltzoff, A.N., Waismeyer, A., & Gopnik, A. (2012). Learning about causes from people: Observational causal learning in 24-month-old infants. *Developmental Psychology, 48,* 1215–1228. doi: 10.1037/a0027440

Moll, H., & Meltzoff, A. N. (2011a). How does it look? Level 2 perspective-taking at 36 months of age. *Child Development, 82,* 661–673. doi:10.1111/j.1467-8624.2010.01571.x

Moll, H., & Meltzoff, A. N. (2011b). Joint attention as the fundamental basis of understanding perspectives. In A. Seemann (Ed.), *Joint Attention: New Developments in Psychology, Philosophy of Mind, and Social Neuroscience* (pp. 393–314). Cambridge, MA: MIT Press.

Moore, C. (1999). Gaze following and the control of attention. In P. Rochat (Ed.), *Early Social Cognition: Understanding Others in the First Months of Life* (pp. 241–256). Mahwah, NJ: Erlbaum.

Moore, M. K., & Meltzoff, A. N. (1999). New findings on object permanence: A developmental difference between two types of occlusion. *British Journal of Developmental Psychology, 17,* 623–644. doi: 10.1348/026151099165410

Moore, M. K., & Meltzoff, A. N. (2004). Object permanence after a 24-hr delay and leaving the locale of disappearance: The role of memory, space, and identity. *Developmental Psychology, 40,* 606–620. doi:10.1037/0012-1649.40.4.606

Movellan, J. R., & Watson, J. S. (1987). *Perception of directional attention.* Infant Behavior & Development, Abstracts of the 6th International Conference on Infant Studies. Norwood, NJ: Ablex.

Mundy, P., Block, J., Van Hecke, A. V., Delgado, C., Venezia Parlade, M., & Pomares, Y. (2007). Individual differences and the development of joint attention in infancy. *Child Development, 78,* 938–954. doi:10.1111/j.1467-8624.2007.01042.x

Piaget, J. (1962). *Play, dreams and imitation in childhood* (C. Attegno & F. M. Hodgson, Trans.). New York, NY: Norton.

Quine, W. V. O. (1960). *Word and Object.* Cambridge, MA: MIT Press.

Sage, K. D., & Baldwin, D. (2010). Social gating and pedagogy: Mechanisms for learning and implications for robotics. *Neural Networks, 23,* 1091–1098. doi:10.1016/j.neunet.2010.09.004

Scaife, M., & Bruner, J. S. (1975). The capacity for joint visual attention in the infant. *Nature, 253,* 265–266. doi: 10.1038/253265a0

Senju, A., Johnson, M. H., & Csibra, G. (2006). The development and neural basis of referential gaze perception. *Social Neuroscience, 1,* 220–234. doi:10.1080/17470910600989797

Woodward, A. L. (2003). Infants' developing understanding of the link between looker and object. *Developmental Science, 6,* 297–311. doi: 10.1111/1467-7687.00286

7 Ostensive Communication and Cultural Learning: The Natural Pedagogy Hypothesis

György Gergely

HUMAN COMMUNICATION IS a species-unique social cognitive adaptation that subserves different forms of epistemic cooperation (as well as competition) among conspecifics (Csibra & Gergely, 2009, 2011; Sperber & Wilson, 1995; Tomasello, 2008). For example, people communicate about episodic facts to help each other in achieving their goals (even as early as 18 months of age, Warneken & Tomasello, 2006), they monitor and modify each other's beliefs by providing relevant episodic information that they need to share in order to accomplish joint action plans in the pursuit of common goals during cooperative activities (Sebanz, Bekkering, & Knoblich, 2006; Tomasello, Carpenter, Call, Behne, & Moll, 2005), they manipulate and deceive each other in competitive situations by misinforming the other about a relevant episodic state of affairs (Mascaro & Sperber, 2009; Sperber, 2006), and they gossip conveying (true or false) episodic information about other people's life events that are not directly accessible to the recipients of the communication (Dunbar, 1997). In fact, most evolutionary accounts of the origins of human communication make reference to one or more of these social epistemic functions as providing an adaptive advantage that may have contributed to the selection of the human cognitive capacity to communicate.

Ostensive Referential Communication of Episodic Versus Generic Information

A common feature of the various types of epistemic functions of communication mentioned above is that they all involve the transfer of relevant *episodic information* to others. Importantly, however, the kinds of epistemic cooperation that human communication can support are not restricted to the exchange of episodic knowledge only. Referential communication is also a primary vehicle for the manifestation and transmission of different types of cultural information that are *generalizable* beyond the particular referents and situational contexts of the communicative acts through which they are conveyed (Csibra & Gergely, 2009; Gergely, 2010). Ostensive referential communication functions as an important and early source of social information to enable the fast and efficient intergenerational transfer of culturally *shared functional knowledge* about artifact kinds as well as *generalizable practical knowledge* about stereotypic manners of tool use or tool manufacturing procedures (Casler & Kelemen, 2005; Csibra & Gergely, 2006, 2009; Futó, Téglás, Csibra, & Gergely, 2010; Gergely & Csibra, 2005, 2006). Through ostensive communications about particular referents, adults can convey to young children *generic information* about kind-relevant referent properties that specify sortal kinds and that are readily generalized to other referents belonging to the same kind (Cimpian & Markman, 2008; Csibra & Gergely, 2009, 2011; Gelman, 2003; Leslie, 2008). The ostensively demonstrated practical cultural knowledge about nonobvious technological skills and procedural know-how embedded in stereotypic manner of application of means-action routines are acquired and interpreted early on as generalizable beyond the particular referential context of the communication. Ostensive cuing therefore induce the cultural acquisition of demonstrated technological procedures or manner of artifact use even when these cultural skills are *cognitively opaque* to the naïve learner (Csibra & Gergely, 2006, 2007; Gergely, Bekkering, & Király, 2002; Gergely & Csibra, 2006; Király, Csibra, & Gergely, in press). Similarly, communication serves as an important vehicle for the transmission of *arbitrary and conventional forms of shared cultural knowledge* such as referential symbols, social behavioral traditions, or normative conventions (Rakoczy, Warneken, & Tomasello, 2008; Tomasello, 2008). Communicative demonstrations of such conventional forms of knowledge have been shown to be interpreted from very early on by infants and young children as generalizable across relevant situational contexts and as representing common knowledge that is assumed to be shared by and accessible to all members of the cultural community (Csibra & Gergely, 2009; Egyed, Király, & Gergely, in press; Gergely, Király, & Egyed, 2007). Similarly to cultural knowledge of practical skills and functional knowledge about tool use and artifact kinds, communicatively conveyed *conventional and/or normative cultural knowledge* (including traditions, behavioral conventions, representational devices, normative rules, etc.) also tends to be partially or fully *cognitively opaque* to the naïve learner when first acquired from demonstrative communicative acts of others (Gergely, 2007; 2010).

It has been argued (see Sperber, 1997) that the uniquely human cognitive ability to acquire, entertain, and transmit *cultural beliefs with opaque or only partially understood contents* (what Sperber calls "reflective beliefs with semipropositional contents") such as religious dogmas, is inherently related to social communication as the primary source of origin of such culturally shared but cognitively opaque epistemic constructs. Humans' metarepresentational cognitive attitude toward the opaque contents of such cultural beliefs involves justificatory deference to and basic epistemic trust in the authority of their communicative source, which therefore contributes significantly to their maintenance, spread, and stabilization within the culture (Sperber, 2000).

This raises important questions concerning the relationship between our evolved capacity to communicate on the one hand, and our uniquely human ability for the cultural transmission of generic, conventional, and cognitively opaque cultural knowledge on the other. Has the design structure of the human cognitive adaptation for communication evolved in the first place to support the transmission of relevant episodic information only in order to support the coordination of collaborative joint actions between individuals to achieve socially shared joint goals? Does communication about generic cultural knowledge depend on the availability (and acquisition) of specialized linguistic devises (such as universal quantifiers and specific linguistic markers) that encode and referentially disambiguate generic interpretations of ostensive referential communicative acts from episodic interpretations?

Or alternatively, could it be the case that the presumption of genericity of referential content has evolved as a primary interpretive strategy or default bias of referential interpretation that is triggered by ostensive signals of communication even when it is referentially ambiguous or underdetermined by the context? Such a built-in sensitivity to ostensive signals and their specialized constraining effects on referential interpretation would arguably subserve the crucial social epistemic function of ensuring the efficient social transmission of generalizable and shared cultural knowledge about generic dispositional properties of the conceptual kinds of different domains of knowledge that human social groups share. Does this evolved functional property of ostensive signals form part of the basic design structure of our evolved communicative system from the beginning? In particular, are the evolved structural features of our adaptation for referential communication especially suited to allow for the efficient transmission of generic, shared, conventional, and cognitively opaque knowledge even in cases of nonverbal (and possibly preverbal) ostensive referential communicative acts that are necessarily restricted to the deictic identification of particular referents only?

In this chapter I shall briefly summarize a new theoretical approach to the evolutionary origins of the specialized cognitive mechanisms dedicated to human cultural learning and their hypothesized evolutionary link to the human adaptation for ostensive communication. According to this view (that we call the theory of "natural pedagogy," see Csibra, 2010; Csibra & Gergely, 2006, 2009, 2011; Gergely, 2010; Gergely & Csibra, 2005, 2006; Gergely et al., 2007) a central evolutionary function for which the social cognitive adaptation for ostensive communication has been selected during hominin evolution was to enable the efficient intergenerational transmission of newly emerging uniquely human forms of cultural skills and knowledge that (1) were *cognitively opaque* to the naïve learner, (2) represent *generic information* about referent properties that are generalizable to kinds, and (3) convey *shared or common cultural knowledge* that is assumed to be available to all members of the cultural community.

Cognitive Opacity and Natural Pedagogy: Relevance-Guided Cultural Learning through Ostensive Communication

As argued in more detail elsewhere (Csibra & Gergely, 2006; Gergely, 2007; Gergely & Csibra, 2006), the early emergence of relatively complex technological skills and stone tools during hominin evolution (as evidenced by the available archeological record, see Mithen, 2002; Moore, 2010; Schick and Toth, 1993; Semaw, 2000; Stout, 2005, 2010; Tehrani & Riede, 2008) involved aspects of tool use, tool manufacturing procedures, and the recursive functional application of tools (using tools to make other tools) that were *cognitively opaque* for the naïve observational learner. This therefore represented a new kind of learnability problem that endangered the successful intergenerational transmission, spread, and stabilization of these highly useful new forms of cultural knowledge. The lack of cognitive transparency of the relevant teleological and/or causal properties of such cultural inventions (Csibra & Gergely, 2006, 2007; Gergely & Csibra, 2006) rendered it difficult (or impossible) for the naïve juvenile learner to acquire them by relying solely on the types of purely observational learning mechanisms that are available to our closest nonhuman primate relatives (such as statistical and associative learning, trial-and-error emulation, and maybe "blind" automatic imitative motor copying). Lacking cognitive insight into the opaque aspects of the means-end structure or hidden causal properties that such cultural skills involved, the naïve observational learner faced a *problem of relevance-selection*: without the appropriate informational basis it was difficult to identify which aspects of the observed—but cognitively opaque—skill should be retained as relevant and which should be omitted as nonrelevant or incidental.

We hypothesized (Csibra & Gergely, 2006; Gergely & Csibra, 2006) that the ensuing need for a viable relevance-sensitive learning mechanism to allow for the efficient intergenerational transmission and stabilization of such highly useful, but cognitively opaque, cultural forms of knowledge led to the selection of a new kind of social communicative system of information transfer of mutual design. The system involved: (1) active relevance-guidance of the learner's attention by means of ostensive referential demonstrations provided by knowledgeable others, (2) special receptivity on the part of the naïve learner to the ostensive and referential communicative signals addressed to them, and (3) built-in interpretive biases to constrain and disambiguate the referential scope of such ostensive demonstrative knowledge manifestations by the naïve learner to whom such pedagogical demonstrations were directed. The hypothesized cognitive adaptation for "natural pedagogy" refers to the consequently evolved species-unique communicative learning mechanism of mutual design that is dedicated to the fast and efficient intergenerational transfer of cultural knowledge in humans.

However, the proposal that human communication may have evolved in part to facilitate the efficient intergenerational transfer of cultural knowledge is contradicted by the fact that there are population-specific socially transmitted cultural traditions in nonhuman primates as well (Perry, 2011; Tomasello & Call, 1997; Whiten, 2000; Whiten & van Schaik, 2006). The existence of nonhuman primate cultures indicate that at least certain types of cultural skills and behavioral traditions can be acquired from social models by mechanisms of observational learning (such as trial-and-error emulation or imitative motor copying) that do not involve or presuppose relevance-guided communication (see Heyes, Huber, Gergely, and Brass, 2009; Whiten & Custance, 1996; Whiten, McGuigan, Marshall-Pescini, & Hopper, 2009).

Nevertheless, it remains a noteworthy human-specific feature of our social cultural environment (Gergely, 2007; Gergely & Unoka, 2008) that, unlike other primates, humans routinely observe others' intentional actions in two qualitatively different input contexts: either in *non-communicative observation contexts* (where the child witnesses another agent functionally performing a novel instrumental action such as "eating soup with a spoon"), or in *communicative demonstration contexts* (as when mother demonstrates "for" the infant *"how to* eat soup with a spoon"). It seems that humans are naturally inclined to introduce and mark the latter kind of communicative displays of novel intentional actions by *ostensive behavioral signals* that are directed to the addressee (Csibra, 2010; Sperber & Wilson, 1995). These ostensive cues function to indicate that the agent has a *communicative intention* to manifest relevant and new information about a referent (the *informative intention*) "for" the addressee to selectively attend to and learn about (Csibra & Gergely, 2006, 2009).

In fact, there is a growing body of converging evidence indicating that human infants show species-unique innate sensitivity and preference for specific ostensive behavioral signals such as direct eye contact, eyebrow raising, contingent reactivity, or being addressed by infant-directed speech ("motherese") (Csibra, 2010; Deligianni, Senju, Gergely, & Csibra, 2011; Farroni, Csibra, Simion, & Johnson, 2002; Grossmann, Johnson, Lloyd-Fox, Blasi, Deligianni, Elwell, et al., 2008; Senju & Csibra, 2008; see Csibra & Gergely, 2006, 2009, 2011, for recent reviews).

In communicative contexts, ostensive cues are followed by deictic *referential gestures* (such as gaze-shift, head-turn, or pointing) designed to help the addressee to identify the referent about which new and relevant knowledge is about to be manifested (Csibra, 2003; Csibra and Gergely, 2006, 2009). Although primates also follow gaze, it turns out to be a uniquely human adaptation that spontaneous gaze-following in infants takes place *only if* the deictic referential cues were preceded and/or accompanied by one or more of the innate ostensive communicative framing cues (for direct eye-contact: Farroni et al.,

2002; Senju & Csibra, 2008; for motherese, Senju & Csibra, 2008; for contingent reactivity: Deligianni et al., 2011; Johnson, Slaughter, & Carey, 1998; Movellan & Watson, 2002). Human communicative interactions also involve species-unique attention monitoring and visual checking-back behaviors to establish, direct, and maintain joint triadic attention between the communicating agent, the infant, and the referent (Tomasello et al., 2005; Tomasello, 2008).

Another species-unique feature of communicative action manifestations is that they involve salient *motor transformations* of the primary functional execution pattern of motor action schemes (Gergely, 2007; Gergely & Unoka, 2008). Humans seem naturally inclined to produce such *"ostensive marking"* of communicatively demonstrated motor actions by transforming the manner of motor execution of novel cultural skills when they are demonstrated to a naïve conspecific learner. Parents spontaneously modify their actions when they ostensively demonstrate them to infants (Brand, Baldwin, & Ashburn, 2002) and infants prefer these "motionese" versions over adult-directed action demonstrations (Brand & Shallcross, 2008). Such "manifestatively" transformed communicative action demonstrations involve schematized, partial, slowed down, repeated, or selectively exaggerated production of certain aspects of the primary motor routine. These transformations not only "mark" the action performance as a communicatively intended ostensive demonstration (rather than primary functional use), but they are also actively used for *relevance-guidance* of the naïve learner. They background nonrelevant and foreground relevant parts of the manifested skill in order to lead the pupil's attention to selectively identify and extract the relevant new information to be learned and retained (Gergely et al., 2002; Gergely, 2007, 2010; Király, 2009).

In contrast, the comparable input conditions available to primate learners of cultural skills are severely limited. When adult primates perform a socially transmitted cultural skill (such as nut cracking) in front of on-looking naïve juveniles, they do not produce ostensive and referential signals to capture and direct the attention of the other to relevant aspects of the skill and do not (and possibly cannot) modify the primary functional pattern of efficient execution of their motor action scheme for purposes of demonstration and relevance-guidance (Gergely, 2010; Gergely & Csibra, 2006; Gergely & Unoka, 2008).

The juvenile primate learner must acquire its cultural skills from conspecific users through un-guided passive observation of their standard functional use and unguided attempts at their reproduction. Cultural learning in nonhuman primates must, therefore, exclusively rely on individual observational learning mechanisms (such as associative learning, stimulus and response enhancement, emulation, and—possibly though controversially—rudimentary skills of "blind" imitation, Gergely & Csibra, 2006). Arguably, the fact that population-specific cultural routines in nonhuman primates tend to be few in number, and are restricted to the slow acquisition of only cognitively transparent behavioral skills is a causal consequence of the restricted range of purely observational learning mechanisms available to primate learners and the lack of ostensive demonstrations and active relevance-guidance by the social models from whom the cultural skills are learned.

Evidence for Natural Pedagogy in Human Infants: The Interpretation-Modulating Role of Ostensive Communicative Signals

Concerning the hypothesis that natural pedagogy is an evolved mechanism for relevance-guided cultural learning, the most informative type of evidence comes from recent infant studies that have systematically manipulated whether the same novel intentional action is presented to infants in an *ostensive communicative demonstration context* (involving ostensive signals such as eye-contact, eyebrow raising, contingent reactivity, smiling, and being addressed by own name in infant-directed speech) or in a *noncommunicative, purely observational context* (wherein infants simply witness the purposeful functional performance of the target action by the model, who exhibits no communicative signals). We have applied this general paradigm in a variety of knowledge domains to test the central hypothesis of natural pedagogy theory that ostensive communicative signals activate built-in interpretive constraints and biases in the infant learner, leading to differential encoding of the demonstrated event in terms of its presumed relevance, genericity of referential scope, and assumed availability of its manifested content across other individuals in the culture.

The Presumption of Relevance: Selective Learning of Cognitively Opaque Novel Actions in Ostensive Communicative Contexts

According to natural pedagogy theory ostensive signals trigger a *presumption of relevance* in infants leading them to infer from the manifested demonstration what is new and relevant for them to learn. Therefore, it is predicted that infants will be ready to acquire even *cognitively opaque contents* if these are ostensively manifested for them. For example, since Gergely et al.'s (2002) original selective imitation study, a series of experiments demonstrated infants' tendency to selectively retain and re-enact even apparently nonrational or inefficient goal-directed actions (such as lighting up a touch-lamp by contacting it with one's head) as long as these target actions are demonstrated to them in ostensive-communicative contexts. Several studies included control conditions in which the same subefficient or unnecessary—and therefore cognitively opaque—actions were also presented in a noncommunicative observation context to a different group of infants. The findings converge to indicate that without the presence of social communicative cues, the nonefficient opaque target actions were either not reproduced at all or were significantly less frequently re-enacted than in the ostensive demonstration conditions by infants even as young as 14-months of age (Brugger, Lariviere, Mumme, & Bushnell, 2007; Gergely, 2007; Király, 2008, 2009; Király, Csibra, & Gergely, in press; Király & Gergely, 2010; Nielsen, 2006).

The Assumption of Genericity: Extracting Generic Information about Kind-Relevant Properties of Referents in Ostensive Communicative Contexts

The "generic interpretation bias" hypothesis (Csibra & Gergely, 2009) proposes that ostensive signals trigger in infants a *default setting of the referential scope* of the communicative act which is assumed to manifest relevant information about *generic properties of the referent kind* that the deictically indicated referent belongs to. We have recently tested this hypothesis in the domain of learning about artifact functions in 10-month-olds (Futó et al., 2010) by applying the object individuation paradigm (Xu & Carey, 1996). Two different novel artifacts were sequentially brought out at either one or the other side of an occluder by a hand that performed a different action on each, resulting in the consequent display of a different sensory effect. When a female voice greeted the infant in motherese before the artifacts emerged (ostensive function demonstration condition), infants interpreted the two different functional uses as providing generic information specifying two different artifact kinds to which the particular artifacts were represented to belong. As a result, infants inferred that there must be *two* objects behind the occluder, showing increased looking times when only one was revealed during the test phase. In contrast, in the nonostensive cueing condition (wherein instead of motherese, a synthesized mechanical nonspeech sound transform was presented) the 10-month-olds showed no object individuation (i. e., they did not expect two objects behind the screen). This suggests that they interpreted the two manual actions as different episodic functional uses of the *same* object. Furthermore, in another version of the ostensive cuing condition, we found that the sequential demonstration of the two different functions on a *single* artifact emerging at one or the other side of the occluder generated the illusion of the presence of *two* objects behind the screen. These results indicate that ostensively presented information on artifact function was used by 10-month-olds as an indicator of kind membership, and infants expected one specific function to define one specific artifact kind.

In another series of experiments, we could demonstrate that the robust perseverative search error in the classical A-not-B object search task in 10-month-olds (Piaget, 1954) is dependent on the ostensive communicative context in which the object hiding actions are typically performed in this paradigm (Topál, Gergely, Miklósi, Erdőhegyi, & Csibra, 2008, Topál, Gergely, Erdőhegyi, Csibra, & Miklósi, 2009). In the standard object search task, infants repeatedly succeed in retrieving an object that they observe being placed by a demonstrator under one of two containers (A trials). During subsequent B trials, however, when they observe the experimenter hiding the object in the other container, infants continue to perseveratively (and erroneously) search at its previous hiding location (under the—now empty—A container). The perseverative error, however, was found to be drastically reduced when the hiding actions were not accompanied by ostensive signals (Topál et al., 2008, 2009), suggesting that the phenomenon is in fact largely caused by the interpretation modulating influence of the communicative cuing context. It seems that the demonstrator's ostensive signals induce a pragmatic misinterpretation ("the illusion of being taught") of this essentially episodic hide-and-search game, which is (mis)construed as a "teaching demonstration" to manifest new and relevant knowledge about some enduring functional property of the objects involved. This may have led infants to infer (and learn) from the A hiding trials that "the object 'belongs to'—not just being presently hidden in—container A." This resulted in continued search for the object in container A (where it "ought to be") even during subsequent B trials.

In the domain of object processing, Yoon, Johnson, & Csibra (2008) demonstrated that ostensive referential gestures toward an object result in differentially inhibiting the processing of spatial information while resulting in better encoding of featural information in a change detection violation-of-expectation looking time task. The opposite pattern was found, however, when the agent performed a goal-directed manual reach toward the object (as if attempting to grasp it) but did so without any ostensive communicative signals being presented. Note that featural information (such as shape) is likely to be relevant for identifying kind-generalizable object properties, whereas spatial location is clearly irrelevant for that purpose. Therefore the asymmetric pattern of processing may reflect a strategy to optimize the extraction of kind-relevant generic information about the referent kind that the object belongs to that is induced by the ostensively triggered generic interpretation bias of natural pedagogy.

The Shared Knowledge Assumption: Generalization of Ostensively Demonstrated Cultural Knowledge about Referent Properties to Other Individuals

Finally, it is hypothesized that ostensive communicative signals trigger a *shared knowledge assumption* of natural pedagogy (Csibra & Gergely, 2011; Egyed et al., in press) whereby infants expect ostensively manifested referential information to represent common cultural knowledge that is shared by and accessible to other individuals as well and not only to the communicating person demonstrating it. We tested this assumption in the domain of understanding object-directed emotion expressions of others during social referencing situations in 14- and 18-month-old infants (Gergely et al., 2007; Egyed et al., in press).

Others' object-directed emotion expressions can provide two types of information. On the one hand, they can express episodic information about the individual's current emotional reaction and person-specific subjective disposition toward the referent object (such as "Mom is afraid of the snake in the corner"). On the other hand, when adults use ostensive-communicative signals to address their referential emotion display to infants they often do so to communicate relevant knowledge about the referent that is (1) *generalizable* beyond the situation and (2) represents *shared knowledge* that is available to others as well (e.g., that "Snakes are dangerous"). In a violation-of-expectation looking time study Gergely et al., (2007) found that when 14-month-olds observed others' ostensively cued object referential emotion displays, they tended to interpret these emotion gestures as conveying valence information about the properties of the object ("object-centered interpretation") rather than expressing the person-specific subjective attitude of the communicator toward the referent ("person-centered interpretation"). More recently, Egyed et al. (in press) used an object-request paradigm with different groups of 18-month-olds in which infants first observed an experimenter presenting a positive emotion display toward one unfamiliar object and a negative emotion toward another either in an ostensive-communicative or in a non-communicative observation context. During the test phase either a different person or the demonstrator herself requested from the infants to give them one of the two target objects. Egyed et al. (in press) found that the 18-month-olds could flexibly assign either a person-centered or an object-centered interpretation to the demonstrator's referential emotion displays as a function of the presence or absence of ostensive communicative signals. In the ostensive cuing context, infants generalized their object-centered interpretation of the demonstrator's emotion expression to a different requester person (giving her the object toward which the demonstrator expressed a positive emotion), whereas in the noncommunicative context they attributed a person-specific emotional disposition to the demonstrator without generalizing this attribution to others. This finding indicates that—as proposed by natural pedagogy theory (Csibra & Gergely, 2011)—infants are prepared to learn about shared cultural knowledge through ostensive-communicative demonstrations at a remarkably early age even without the involvement of linguistic communication.

Conclusion

Although social learning and communication are both widespread in nonhuman animals, social learning by communication is probably human specific. I have reviewed recent evidence showing that humans can transmit generic knowledge to young children and even to preverbal infants about artifact kinds, conventional behaviors, arbitrary referential symbols, cognitively opaque skills, and know-how embedded in means-end actions. These kinds of cultural contents can be transmitted by either linguistic communication or nonverbal demonstrations, and such types of knowledge transmission contribute to the stability of cultural forms across generations. The evidence summarized provides support for the proposal that by having evolved specific cognitive biases, human infants are prepared to be at the receptive side of such communicative knowledge transfer, which, together with adults' inclination to pass on their knowledge to the next generation, constitutes a system of "natural pedagogy" in humans.

REFERENCES

Brand, R. J., Baldwin, D. A., & Ashburn, L. A. (2002). Evidence for "motionese": modifications in mothers' infant-directed action. *Developmental Science, 5*, 72–83.

Brand, R. J., and Shallcross, W. K. (2008). Infants prefer motionese to adult-directed action. *Developmental Science, 11*, 853–861.

Brugger, A., Lariviere, L. A., Mumme, D. L., & Bushnell, E. W. (2007). Doing the right thing: Infants' selection of actions to imitate from observed event sequences. *Child Development, 78,* 806–824.

Casler, K., & D. Kelemen. (2005). Young children's rapid learning about artifacts. *Developmental Science 8,* 472–480.

Cimpian, A., & Markman, E. M. (2008). Preschool children's use of cues to generic meaning. *Cognition, 107,* 19–53.

Csibra, G. (2003). Teleological and referential understanding of action in infancy. *Philosophical Transactions of the Royal Society, London B, 358,* 447–458.

Csibra, G. (2010). Recognizing communicative intentions in infancy. *Mind & Language, 25,* 141–168.

Csibra, G., & Gergely, G. (2006). Social learning and social cognition: The case of pedagogy. In: M. H. Johnson, & Y. M. Munakata (Eds.), *Processes of Change in Brain and Cognitive Development. Attention and Performance, XXI* (pp. 249–274), Oxford: Oxford University Press.

Csibra, G., & Gergely, G. (2007). "Obsessed with goals": Functions and mechanisms of teleological interpretation of actions in humans. In B. Hommel, & S. Biro, (Eds.), *Becoming an Intentional Agent: The Development of Action Control.* A Special Issue of *Acta Psychologica, 124,* 60–78.

Csibra, G., & Gergely, G. (2009). Natural pedagogy. *Trends in Cognitive Sciences, 13,* 148–153.

Csibra, G., & Gergely, G. (2011). Natural pedagogy as evolutionary adaptation. *Philosophical Transactions of the Royal Society, London B, 366,* 1149–1157.

Deligianni, F., Senju, A., Gergely, G., and Csibra, G. (2010). Gaze-contingent objects elicit the illusion of communication in 8-month-old infants. *Developmental Psychology, 47,* 1499–1503.

Dunbar, R. (1997). *Grooming, Gossip and the Evolution of Language.* Cambridge, MA: Harvard University Press.

Egyed, K., Király, I., & Gergely, G. (in press). Communicating shared knowledge in infancy. *Psychological Science.*

Farroni, T., Csibra, G., Simion, F., & Johnson, M. H. (2002). Eye contact detection in humans from birth. *Proceedings of the National Academy of Sciences of the United States of America, 99,* 9602–9605.

Futó J., Téglás, E., Csibra, G., & Gergely, G. (2010). Communicative function demonstration induces kind-based artifact representation in preverbal infants. *Cognition, 117,* 1–8.

Gelman, S. A. (2003). *The Essential Child: Origins of Essentialism in Everyday Thought.* London: Oxford University Press.

Gergely, G. (2007). Learning "about" versus learning "from" other minds: Human pedagogy and its implications. In P. Carruthers, S. Laurence, & S. Stich (Eds.), *The Innate Mind: Foundations and the Future* (pp. 170–198). Oxford: Oxford University Press.

Gergely, G. (2010). Kinds of Agents: The origins of understanding instrumental and communicative agency. In U. Goshwami (Ed.). *Blackwell Handbook of Childhood Cognitive Development,* 2nd edition (pp. 76–105). Oxford: Blackwell Publishers.

Gergely, G., & Csibra, G. (2005). The social construction of the cultural mind: Imitative learning as a mechanism of human pedagogy. *Interaction Studies, 6,* 463–481.

Gergely, G., & Csibra, G. (2006). Sylvia's recipe: The role of imitation and pedagogy in the transmission of cultural knowledge. In S. Levenson, & N. Enfield (Eds.) *Roots of Human Sociality: Culture, Cognition, and Human Interaction* (pp. 229–255). Oxford: Berg Publishers.

Gergely, G. & Unoka, Zs. (2008). Attachment, affect-regulation and mentalization: The developmental origins of the representational affective self. In C., Sharpe, P. Fonagy, & I. Goodyer

(Eds.), *Social Cognition and Developmental Psychopathology* (pp. 303–340). Oxford: Oxford University Press.

Gergely, G., Bekkering, H., & Király, I. (2002). Rational imitation in preverbal infants. *Nature, 415*, 755.

Gergely, G., Király, I., & Egyed, K. (2007). On pedagody. *Developmental Science, 10*, 139–146

Grossmann, T., Johnson, M. H., Lloyd-Fox, S., Blasi, A., Deligianni, F., Elwell, C., et al. (2008). Early cortical specialization for face-to-face communication in human infants. *Proceedings of the Royal Society, London B, 275*, 2803–2811.

Heyes C., Huber, L., Gergely, G., and Brass, M. (2009). Evolution, development and intentional control of imitation, *Philosophical Transactions of The Royal Society B*, August 2009.

Johnson, S., Slaughter, V., & Carey, S (1998). Whose gaze would infants follow? The elicitation of gaze following in 12-month-olds. *Developmental Science, 1*, 233–238.

Király I. (2008): Memories for events in infants: goal relevant action coding. In T., Striano, & V. Reid (Eds.), *Social Cognition: Development, Neuroscience and Autism* (pp. 113–128). New York: Wiley-Blackwell.

Király, I., (2009). The effect of the model's presence and of negative evidence on infants' selective imitation. *Journal of Experimental Child Psychology, 102*, 14–25.

Király, I., & Gergely, G. (2011). Relevance or resonance: Selective imitation in communicative context by 14-month-olds. *Symposiumpaper presented at the SRCD Biennal Meeting*, Montreal, Canada, March 29–April 2.

Király, I., Csibra, G., & Gergely, G. (in press). Beyond rational imitation: Learning arbitrary means actions from communicative demonstrations. *Journal of Experimental Child Psychology, Special Issue on Early Rationality*.

Leslie, S-J. (2008). Generics: Cognition and Acquisition. *Philosophical Review, 117*, 1–47.

Mascaro, O., & Sperber, D. (2009). The moral, epistemic, and mindreading components of children's vigilence towards deception. *Cognition, 112*, 367–380.

Mithen, S. (2002). Mind, brain, and material culture: an archeological perspective. In: P. Carruthers, & A. Chamberlain (Eds). *Evolution and the Human Mind* (pp. 207–217). Cambridge: Cambridge University Press.

Moore, M. W. (2010). "Grammars of action" and stone flaking design space. In A. Nowell, & I. Davidson (Eds.), *Stone Tools and the Evolution of Human Cognition* (pp. 13–43). Boulder, CO: University Press of Colorado.

Movellan, J. R., & Watson, J. S. (2002). *The development of gaze following as a Bayesian systems identification problem.* UCSD Machine Perception Laboratory Technical Reports 2002.01

Nielsen, M. (2006). Copying actions and copying outcomes: Social learning through the second year. *Developmental Psychology, 42*, 555–565.

Perry, S. (2011). Social traditions and social learning in capuchin monkeys (*Cebus*). *Philosophical Transactions of the Royal Society: Biological Sciences, 366*, 988–996.

Piaget, J. (1954). *The Construction of Reality in the Child.* New York: Basic Books.

Rakoczy, H., Warneken, F., & Tomasello, M. (2008). The sources of normativity: Young children's awareness of the normative structure of games. *Developmental Psychology, 44*, 875–881.

Schick, K. D., & Toth, N. (1993). *Making Silent Stones Speak: Human Evolution and the Dawn of Technology.* New York: Simon & Schuster.

Sebanz, N., Bekkering, H, & Knoblich, G. (2006). Joint action: bodies and minds moving together. *Trends in Cognitive Sciences, 10*, 70–76.

Semaw, S. (2000). The world's oldest stone artefacts from Gona, Ethiopia: Their implications for understanding stone technology and patterns of human evolution between 2.6–1.5 million years ago. *Journal of Achaeological Science 27*, 1197–1214.

Senju, A. & Csibra, G. (2008) Gaze following in human infants depends on communicative signals. *Current Biology, 18*, 668–671.

Sperber, D. (1997). Intuitive and reflective beliefs. *Mind and Language, 12*, 67–83.

Sperber, D. (2000). Metarepresentations in an evolutionary perspective. In D. Sperber (Ed.), *Metarepresentations: A Multidisciplinary Perspective* (pp. 117–137). Oxford: Oxford University Press.

Sperber, D. (2006) An evolutionary perspective on testimony and argumentation. In R. Viale, D. Andler, and L. Hirschfeld (Eds.), *Biological and Cultural Bases of Human Inference* (pp. 177–189). Mahwah, NJ: Erlbaum.

Sperber, D., & Wilson, D. (1995). *Relevance: Communication and Cognition,* 2nd edition. Oxford: Blackwell.

Stout, D. (2005). The social and cultural context of stone-knapping skill acquisition. In V. Roux, & B. Bril (Eds.), *Stone Knapping: The Necessary Conditions for a Uniquely Hominin Behaviour* (pp. 331–340). Cambridge: McDonald Institute for Archaeological Research.

Stout, D. (2011). Stone toolmaking and the evolution of human culture and cognition. *Philosophical Transactions of the Royal Society: Biological Sciences 366*, 1050–1059.

Tehrani, J. J., & Riede, F. (2008). Towards an archaeology of pedagogy: learning teaching and the generation of material culture traditions. *World Archeology, 40*, 316–331.

Tomasello, M. (2008). *Origins of Human Communication*. Cambridge: MIT Press.

Tomasello, M., & Call, J. (1997). *Primate cognition*. Oxford: Oxford University Press.

Tomasello, M., Carpenter, M., Call, J., Behne, T., & Moll, H. (2005). Understanding and sharing intentions: The origins of cultural cognition. *Behavioral and Brain Sciences, 28*, 675–735.

Topál, J., Gergely, G., Miklósi, Á., Erdőhegyi, Á., & Csibra, G. (2008). Infants' perseverative search errors are induced by pragmatic misinterpretation. *Science, 321*, 1831–1834.

Topál, J., Gergely, G., Erdőhegyi, A., Csibra, G., & Miklósi, Á. (2009). Differential sensitivity to human communication in dogs, wolves and human infants. *Science, 325*, 1269–1272.

Warneken, F., & Tomasello, M. (2006). Altruistic helping in human infants and young chimpanzees. *Science, 311*, 1301–1303.

Whiten, A. (2000). Primate culture and social learning. *Cognitive Science, 24*, 477–508.

Whiten, A., and Custance, D. (1996). Studies of imitation in chimpanzees and children. In C. M. Heyes, & B. G. Galef (Eds), *Social learning in animals: The roots of culture* (pp. 347–370). NY: Academic Press.

Whiten, A., McGuigan, N., Marshall-Pescini, S., & Hopper, L. M. (2009). Emulation, imitation, over-imitation and the scope of culture for child and chimpanzee. *Philosophical Transactions of the Royal Society B, 364*, 2417–2428.

Whiten, A., & van Schaik, C. (2006). The evolution of animal "cultures" and social intelligence. *Philosophical Transactions of the Royal Society B, 362*, 603–620.

Xu, F., & Carey, S. (1996). Infants' metaphysics: The case of numerical identity. *Cognitive Psychology, 30*, 111–153.

Yoon, J. M. D., Johnson, M. H., & Csibra, G. (2008). Communication-induced memory biases in preverbal infants. *Proceedings of the National Academy of Sciences of the United States of America, 105*, 13690–13695.

8 Embodied Attention in Infant Pointing
Fabia Franco

IN THIS CHAPTER, I analyze the kind of knowledge that infants develop about sharing attention with other people, using evidence from experiments on declarative pointing by infants and toddlers. I also describe experiments that avoid problems that are inherent in studies of gesture production with preverbal participants, such as the distinction between spontaneous gestures and gestures associated with or elicited by some behavior of a social partner (Franco, Perucchini, & March, 2009).

If gaze following is defined as the displacement of one's attention to a target selected by another person, pointing is not simply its production twin (see also Carpenter & Call [chapter 2]). When a baby follows the gaze of an adult, typically cued by a head turn, we assume that this indicates the baby's acknowledgment that there must be something worthwhile to look at "over there." From a behavioral point of view, all that is required of the baby is to mirror the adult's visual action (but see Butterworth & Itakura, 2000; and Triesch, Teuscher, Deak, & Carlson, 2006, about the exact localization of a target). When a baby points, s/he takes the initiative to select a target and uses a symbolic gesture, pointing,[1] to elicit the displacement of another person's attention from her current focus to the infant's selected target. Not only is the action more complex than gaze following, but it may also fail to achieve its goal if care is not taken to coordinate the crucial gesture with the addressee's own attention and action.

Pointing emerges once infants have made the transition from mostly dyadic forms of communication (e.g., one-to-one social engagement implying mutual attention, vs. engagement with an object independent of social engagement) to triadic communication, involving a fluid coordination between a social partner and objects or events beyond the dyad, around which joint attention can develop (see, among others, Tomasello, 1995 for a discussion of this "9-month-revolution"). When pointing emerges, other gestures aiming to influence social partners are also produced (e.g., to make them give an out-of-reach toy and "pick-me-up" gestures) or to share meaning (e.g., clapping in enjoyment and "all-gone" gestures). This new set of communicative tools was first considered theoretically important by Bates, Camaioni, and Volterra (1975), as evidence of novel cognitive developments in means-to-end problem solving. Specifically, gestures were seen as new *means* to achieve preexisting goals (for instance, ritualized reaching replacing leaning toward and crying when wanting an object out of reach). However, more recent perspectives have emphasized that a particular subset of such communicative behaviors emerging at the end of the first year of life also announces the advent of novel interactional goals, namely *declarative goals* (Franco, 1997).

In contrast to instrumental behaviors (request), which require the addressee to act toward the referent and the baby (e.g., giving an out-of-reach toy to the baby), declarative gestures are aimed at manipulating the addressee's attention or knowledge, rather than her behavior (Franco & Butterworth, 1996; Tomasello & Camaioni, 1997; Tomasello, Carpenter, & Liszkowski, 2007). Pointing is the predominant gesture used by infants and toddlers when they intend to redirect their addressees' attention to specific targets (Cochet & Vauclair, 2010a, 2010b; Franco & Butterworth, 1996). Much of recent theoretical debates about pointing has revolved around the functional meaning of declarative pointing: when a 14-month old, sitting in her stroller at a pedestrian crossing, points to a dog while her mother is intently looking at the traffic lights, holding the point while switching gaze between mother and dog, can we assume that the baby has some understanding of attention as a mental state? Is this behavior different, and if so how, from a chimpanzee's pointing to an out-of-reach banana, alternating gaze between the banana and an experimenter (as observed in Leavens, Hopkins, & Thomas, 2004)?

Infant Pointing in Multimodal Communicative Events

Pointing is only occasionally produced in isolation, being most frequently associated with vocalizations, nonverbal expressive behaviors, and visual checking. Typical examples are illustrated in Figure 8.1A,B. Although these finely coordinated patterns of communicative actions get established within the first few weeks in which pointing starts to occur, observations conducted during the period of their emergence (9–12 months) reveal how the behaviors involved stem from different functions. When pointing is an emergent ability, babies sometimes engage in sequences such as: baby looks at the interesting event and vocalizes, then turns to look and point *toward the adult social partner* and vocalizes, then turns to look and point *toward the event* and vocalizes, then turns to look and point *toward the adult* again and vocalizes (Franco & Butterworth, 1996). In this kind of sequence, pointing switches back and forth between referent and addressee with a continuous movement, while infant gaze and pointing remain aligned. Subsequently, pointing will remain fixed on the referent and only the infant's gaze will travel between referent and addressee (as shown in Figs. 8.1 A, B examples).

What this suggests is that pointing emerges as a means to displace attention onto a specific target and to hold it there, whereas gaze takes the role of socializing attention and experience (i.e., checking on the addressee), and that vocalizations are likely to provide a rudimentary form of predication. Older toddlers appear to be aware of these interconnections; an 18-month-old watching an interesting event in front of her while sitting on her mother's lap may turn back to look at and point to her mother's eyes (her mother being her addressee), then draw a line between her mother's eyes and her target, finally turning back to check on her mother's direction of gaze (Franco, 2005). Pointing then embodies attention, and works as a communicative device to focus attention onto physical events,[2] thus allowing others to co-orient toward those events. Most recent debates have bypassed this question about the literal meaning of pointing, however, and have focused instead on the social cognition underlying pointing.

Even during the initial phase of pointing production, pointing gestures may be used in contexts suggesting different pragmatic meanings, such as instrumental, declarative, and interrogative. Examples would be, respectively:

- *Instrumental:* the adult has activated a toy and left it on a table, out-of-reach for the baby; the baby points to the toy, alternating gaze with the adult, and repeats until the adult gives the toy.
- *Declarative:* adult and baby are sitting near each other at a park; a hot air balloon flies by in the sky, the baby points to the balloon, smiles and turns to look at the adult; the adult looks at the balloon and shows surprise/smiles.
- *Interrogative:* adult and baby are walking by the pond, the baby points to the ducks excitedly while vocalizing "uh! uh!" and turns to look at the adult; the adult says "The ducks? Yeah, the ducks."

In terms of the agency attributed to the social partner, these three different forms of pointing can be differentiated by the kind of knowledge about the addressee implied by them, as follows:

- *Instrumental*—agent of action: the addressee is expected to do something.
- *Declarative*—agent of attention (and possibly other mental states or actions) and experiencer of feeling: the social partner is able to apprehend (eventually, know) the event of interest. No action is expected of the addressee, other than co-orientating herself to the target event, and possibly acknowledging the experience (for example, by showing an emotional reaction toward the referent). There are no necessary behavioral correlates of an experience corresponding to updating one's state of knowledge, other than possible emotional associations

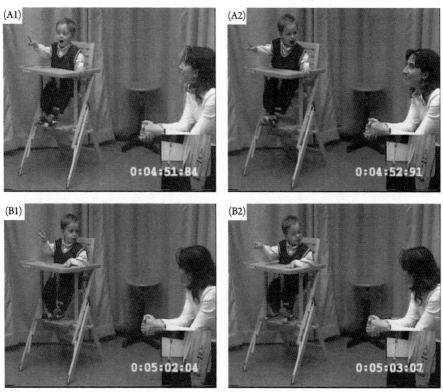

FIGURE 8.1 Typical Examples of Coordination between Pointing, Visual Checking, and Vocalizing in an 18-Month-Old Toddler. A1 → A2: Baby points and vocalizes, then turns to look at adult while vocalizing again, and adult turns back to look at target. B1 → B2: Baby points and turns to look at adult, adult turns to look at baby, and baby vocalizes while holding the point to the target (they "talk"). © D'Odorico, L., Assanelli, A., Franco, F., & Jacob, V.; see D'Odorico et al. (2007).

(see, however, Beebe et al. [chapter 5] for a description of an early perception of "shared states").

- *Interrogative*—cultural agent: no action is expected of the addressee, other than co-orientating herself to the target event, and then providing information (e.g., what is this called, what can we do with it?).

Given these three distinctive categories of pointing, there appears to be little disagreement that instrumental pointing does not necessarily imply the development of an infants' "mentalizing" (but see Leavens et al., 2004, for a different view). However, the two other categories of pointing are the subject of a controversy over their meaning. First, does declarative pointing really imply conceiving the addressee as an attentional/mental agent? It has been argued that babies may be pointing simply in order to get the adult to produce rewarding social behaviors (e.g., a display of positive affect; see Moore & D'Entremont, 2001; also Penn & Povinelli [chapter 3]; Perner, 1991). Second, how can we distinguish between the declarative and interrogative functions of pointing? If a baby is satisfied with any response associated with a co-orientation to the target by the adult, the function of pointing for babies may be that of seeking some information *from* the adult rather than of providing themselves information about the event *to* the adult (Gomez, Sarria & Tamarit, 1993; Southgate, van Maanen and Csibra, 2007).

Experiments performed by Franco, (2005) Franco & Gagliano (2001) and Liszkowski and colleagues (2004, 2006, 2007a, 2007b) sought to demonstrate that infants' declarative pointing was unambiguously referring to information not available to the addressee and thereby to clarify issues associated with the first question above. Tomasello et al. (2007) have also argued further that pointing, whose primary function is to convey information useful to the addressee, is rooted in a uniquely human altruistic motive to cooperate. In response to the second controversy point outlined above, Southgate et al. (2007) proposed that any claim that an infant's pointing seeks to obtain rather than provide information could be rejected only if we could demonstrate that infants point for each other, that is for a social partner who is unlikely to be a "good informant." Franco, Perucchini, & March (2009) did precisely that, and in the following section I will review evidence from our collected studies to support the view that although infant pointing may express all of the pragmatic functions that have thus far been attributed to it, it also specifically includes a declarative-informational one. As converging evidence is only partly available about the age of onset for informational pointing (12 months in Tomasello et al., 2007; 18 months in Franco, 2005), it will be suggested that some important changes occur during the second year, which underlie a transition in communication from *relevant to the self* (e.g., I want you to share with me excitement about this object—see this object over there? Isn't it exciting?) to *relevant to the addressee* (e.g., I want to let you know that there is an interesting event going on out there, which you are missing). The nature of such changes remains unspecified at present, as does the origin of the "altruistic" motive at 12 months as described in Tomasello et al. (2007). However, the central aspect of this transition is the link between attention and knowledge states in the self and in others.

Evidence: The Addressee as a Mental Agent

The research strategy used in the studies to be described in this section is based on four aspects derived from the paradigm introduced by Franco and Butterworth (1996):

1. Focusing on referential-declarative communication, in order to facilitate declarative pointing, two distal puppets were used at a distance of about 250 cm from the baby, at 30 degrees to the left and right of the baby's midline.

    The puppets were 50-cm tall and mounted on pedestals, making the target about 145-cm tall. The puppets were distally activated via a control box invisible to the baby, with a sequence of movement and pause in which one or the other puppet or both moved for 7 seconds and pauses were irregular (either 7 or 15 seconds).

When an adult partner was present, she was instructed to be moderately socially responsive to the infants' bids but not to start any communication bid herself.[3]

2. Pointing production was studied in association with gaze and vocalizing (quantified). Behaviors were coded as associated with a pointing gesture if they occurred within a time window −2/+2 s. with respect to gesture inception, and completion, respectively.

3. Other comparison gestures were included in the analyses whenever possible (e.g., reaching, waving "hello," "all-gone," iconic gestures referring to the puppets movements).

4. The experimental setting was kept constant across studies, whereas factors relevant to the occurrence of joint attention were manipulated.

DECLARATIVE POINTING IN PEER INTERACTION

If babies point for other babies, instrumental and interrogative motives are unlikely to play a major part in the pragmatics of infant pointing. In fact, it is thought rather unlikely that infants would be able to sustain focused, cooperative interactions around a common topic for any length of time before the end of the second year of life (Brownell, Ramani & Zerwas, 2006; Eckerman & Didow, 1989, among others). First of all, infant–peer interactions lack the type of scaffolding characteristically provided by the social partner in adult–infant interaction (Adamson & Bakeman, 1985; Bakeman & Adamson, 1986). For example, adults remain focused on the common activity/topic and follow the infant's attention, providing verbal comments, holding objects and so on—infant social partners do not. Furthermore, speech is missing in infant–peer interactions, particularly, attention-supporting speech, commonly referred to as infant directed speech—Fernald, 1989, 2000; Hurtado, Marchman, & Fernald, 2008; Liu, Kuhl, & Tsao, 2003). Thus, peer interaction in infancy represents a challenging context for joint attention.

As a result, the literature reports a characteristic *décalage* of approximately 3 months, with new communication abilities appearing first in adult–infant and then in infant–peer interaction (Adamson & Bakeman, 1985; Bakeman & Adamson, 1986; Hay, Caplan, Castle, & Stimson, 1991; Mayer & Musatti, 1992; Marcos & Verba, 1991; Vandell & Wilson, 1987). However, the experimental paradigm described above provides precisely what infants find difficult to sustain themselves: a common topic (the puppets event). Thus, Franco et al. (2009) found that, although pointing was more frequent in adult–infant than infant–peer interaction, declarative pointing was produced in peer interaction even by infants as young as 12 to 14 months.

Although these younger babies did not point for each other with great intensity, the frequency of pointing was nonetheless higher in peer interaction than when an infant watched the puppet event in a solitary condition. In other words, infants point (and in general, gesture and vocalize) less without the scaffolding interaction with a more competent adult, but they do point to share some interesting or puzzling experience with each other. Adult scaffolding, in terms of bringing a common focus back into the inter-action, responding systematically to the infant's bids, and supporting and extending the infant's communicative efforts, appears to be a facilitating factor but not an essential one for infant pointing to be produced. The presence of a social partner, however, is critical because pointing production virtually disappears in a solitary condition.

INFANTS INFORM THE ADULT ABOUT AN EVENT THAT HAPPENED IN HER ABSENCE OR OUT OF SIGHT

Although babies did not point to the puppets in the solitary condition, they "informed" the adults about the events on the adult's return by pointing to the puppets within 2 sec-onds of catching sight of the adult (Franco et al. 2009). Older babies did so more system-atically: respectively, 22% of 12- to 15-month-olds (1.4 points per baby) and 45% of 16- to 19-month-olds (1.9 points per baby) pointed to the puppets while alternating gaze with the returning adult. These observations were unplanned in the study and consequently the behavior of the returning adult had not been strictly controlled in its design. In order to gather more reliable data, spatial manipulations were therefore introduced in the next stage of the research, aiming to create challenging conditions for the achievement of joint attention.

Three conditions of visibility for the addressee were created using a large screen ori-ented in different ways, while infants had visual access to both puppets across the three adult viewing conditions: (1) full visibility—both puppets: whichever puppet a baby would point at, the target-puppet would be visible to the addressee; (2) zero visibility—neither puppet: whichever puppet a baby would point at, the puppet event would be hid-den from the addressee; (3) visibility of one puppet only—conflict: babies could choose to point toward the puppet visible to the addressee or toward the one remaining hidden from her. If infants were to point more often in conditions of limited (3) or no visibility (2) of the target for the adult, the intention to inform the addressee about the target would be the most likely motive for the gesture. However, if they were to point more often to the puppet event when both they and the adult could both see it (1), an expla-nation of pointing motives based on seeking a rewarding response from the addressee could not be ruled out. The conflict condition (3) was therefore a particularly useful test: Would toddlers point to either puppet (whichever grabbed their attention at a particular time)? or would they point more often to the puppet that they can see but the addressee cannot (hence informing the addressee about something that she doesn't know)? In the latter case, pointing would clearly have an underlying informative intention.

The pattern of results was clear: 18- to 36-month-old toddlers produced pointing ges-tures significantly more frequently when the visibility of the puppets was obstructed for the addressee than when the puppets were visually accessible. The results from the conflict condition further clarified that greater than 70% of pointing was directed to the puppet that was invisible to the addressee. Whether toddlers were pointing altruistically (to pass information about something fun) or in order to have a more interesting exchange with the adult, their pointing was certainly aimed at making the adult aware of something new, taking into account the adult's state of knowledge. In other words, the toddlers' behaviors in this task are based on a burgeoning understanding of the link between seeing and knowing (Franco & Gagliano, 2001).

SOCIALIZING ATTENTION THROUGH GAZE ALTERNATION

The last source of evidence that infant pointing encompasses knowledge of the addressee as a mental agent involves the consideration of the communicative behaviors associated with infant pointing, in particular visual checking with the addressee. Gaze alternation between referent and addressee is considered the hallmark of joint attention (Tomasello, 1995), and indicative of intentional interpersonal coordination of attention, but it is not unique to pointing; for example, in the second year requests supported by reaching or "give-me" gestures are also characterized by gaze alternation.

The proportion of pointing associated with visual checking to the addressee increases overall between 12 and 19 months. More importantly, the temporal pattern of pointing/ gaze coordination changes with age: initially, gaze alternation occurs *during* pointing execution, but by 18 months, pointing is characteristically associated with gaze *before* the gesture is initiated, often followed by gaze alternation during and after gesture completion. In the latter scenario, an infant watches something interesting, turns to look at the adult ("are you with me?"), and then points to the interesting event, often alternating gaze again between referent and addressee. This temporal pattern is unique to pointing, as infant requesting remains associated with gaze alternation only during the reaching gesture (Franco & Butterworth 1996). The development of such systematic *anticipatory* visual checks of the addressee, produced with pointing from 16 to 18 months, shows an emerging awareness of attentional states in others. It suggests that infants are aware that the addressee's attending is a precondition for (1) reorienting her attention to the baby's target, and (2) "referring" the baby's "comments" to their shared object of attention. Whereas the pointing gestures embody infants' attention to the designated target, making visual contact is how they recruit the addressee's attention to themselves before redirecting it to a distal event. Although the causal mechanism for this transition is still unclear, the addition of an anticipatory look to the social partner suggests a conceptual change underlying pointing in the middle of the second year—possibly a transition from implicit to explicit knowledge about social agents.

Analyses of the timing in gaze/pointing co-ordination are also providing convergent evidence in support of the "informative" function embedded in infant pointing (Franco, 2005; Franco & Butterworth, 1996; Franco & Gagliano, 2001). In our 18- to 36-month-olds: (1) the overall proportion of pointing associated with visual checking was more than twice as high in the zero- and one-puppet visibility conditions as in the full visibility condition; (2) anticipatory checking (gaze to addressee "before" pointing)

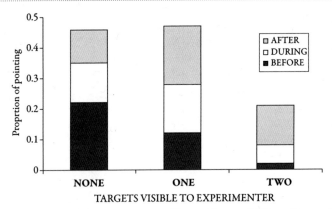

FIGURE 8.2 NONE, zero visibility, no puppets visible to addressee; ONE, conflict condition, only one target visible to addressee; TWO, full visibility, both puppets visible to addressee.

appeared to be directly proportional to the visibility conditions, occurring significantly more often with points produced in the zero–visibility condition overall, and still more often in the one-visibility than full visibility condition—see Figure 8.2.

In another experiment, data from younger children (12–26 months) were gathered in a context that manipulated the distance between adult, infant, and puppets (near, when within 100 cm vs. far, beyond 250 cm.). Overall, more visual checking with pointing was shown when the adult was far from the baby (about 10% more). Specifically, with the consistent results in younger infants complementing those of the previous study with older infants, a significantly higher proportion of points with anticipatory checking of the addressee was produced when the addressee was far than when she was near the infant, with a significant increase in this kind of checking in toddlers older than 18 months. Basic attentional signals (e.g., body orientation) are readily available and sameness of perspective may be assumed when sitting next to each other (near) but not when sitting apart (far). In the latter scenario, infants older than 18 months adjusted the temporal sequencing between pointing and visual checking, so as to maximize the opportunity to catch the addressee's attention and be able to exchange information about the event of interest.

Conclusion

The studies summarized above support the view that the pragmatic functions of infant pointing can not only be generically declarative, but also can be more specifically informational. However, the results appear to offer an explanation more conservative than that proposed in other current interpretations of infant pointing (e.g., Tomasello et al., 2007). It is suggested that in the second year, around 18 months of age, a transition can be described from declarative to informational communication, the latter being a sub-type of the former in which the infant shares with the addressee not just any piece of information, but specifically novel material (e.g., something that the addressee is not aware of—Halliday, 1975). Declarative pointing produced in conditions challenging joint attention reveals that infants of 18 months and older are sensitive to the addressee's states of (perceptual) knowledge and motivated to alter them in order to develop more interesting communicative exchanges. By bringing events that are peripheral to or unseen by the addressee into her attention, toddlers begin to free themselves from the restrictions of the here-&-now of proximal interaction.

In comparison with other mental states, attention presents at least some, however minimal, behavioral correlates.[4] For visual events such as those described in the studies mentioned, indicators of attention would certainly be body and head orientation, eyes open, temporal synchrony between these behaviors and the topical events, postural adjustments etc. Also, attention can be shared by acting it out. Infant pointing may be considered as embodied imagery allowing the alignment of cognitive states between social partners (experienced both as actor and recipient). In this respect, communicative experiences arising from pointing would provide the infant with an insight into the mental domain, supported by the comparison and integration of one's own and the addressee's perceptual experiences. The special relationship that has for long been suggested between pointing and language may stem from the extension of communication beyond the here-&-now, which is supported by informative pointing, for instance pointing to something that the addressee has not witnessed. This could instigate a new type of multimodal shared communication acts, thus facilitating the development of symbolic communication. For instance, McNeill (2006) and McNeill, Duncan, Franklin, Goss, et al. (2010) have recently introduced the concept of hyperphrases, described as acts of communication that are multimodal (including gestures, vocalizations, gesticulation, speech, etc.) and span across interlocutors. Such interpersonal structures may facilitate language development when one of the social partners—the adult owns a new system to encapsulate events beyond the here-&-now—language.

Acknowledgments

The studies reported here were supported by funding by ESRC (UK), MURST and CNR (Italy), and NFFR/Middlesex University (UK). Special thanks to Jennifer Wishart (University of Edinburgh) for comments on the manuscript.

NOTES

1. See Kita (2003) for a discussion of pointing as a universal gesture with cultural variants.

2. McNeill (1987) also describes instances of gesticulation during speech in adults, in which pointing may co-occur with a speaker's reference, for instance, to the past (a nonphysical entity), with the index finger pointing somewhere to the left or behind the speaker. For similar uses of pointing gestures in sign language, see Engberg-Pedersen (2003).

3. In some of the experiments, this was contrasted with a context aimed at facilitating infant's requests, in which the adult would activate an interesting toy in front of the baby, but then leave it out of reach of the infant. The adult's responses to the infant's communication bids were approximately equally distributed between just smiles and comments or reactivating the toy.

4. Hence higher imageability for infants when anticipating or predicting the effects of their pointing on their social partners (what to look for – did they get the message?).

REFERENCES

Adamson, L. B., & Bakeman, R. (1985). Affect and attention: Infants observed with mothers and peers. *Child Development, 56*, 582–593.

Bakeman, R., & Adamson, L. B. (1986). Infants' conventionalized acts: Gestures and words with mothers and peers. *Infant Behavior and Development, 9*, 215–230.

Bates, E., Camaioni, L., & Volterra, V. (1975). The acquisition of performatives prior to speech. *Merril-Palmer Quarterly, 21*, 205–226.

Beebe, B., Markese, S., Bahrick, L., Lachmann, F., Buck, K., Chen, H., et al. (2013). On knowing and being known in the 4-month origins of disorganized attachment: An emerging presymbolic theory of mind. In J. Metcalfe, & H. S. Terrace (Eds.), *Agency and Joint Attention* (pp. 100–124). New York: Oxford University Press.

Brownell, C. A., Ramani, G. B., & Zerwas, S. (2006). Becoming a social partner with peers: Cooperation and social understanding in one- and two-year-olds. *Child Development, 77*, 804–821.

Butterworth, G., & Itakura, S. (2000). How the eyes, head and hand serve definite reference. *British Journal of Developmental Psychology, 18*, 25–50.

Butterworth, G., & Jarrett, N. L. M. (1991). What minds have in common in space: Spatial mechanisms for perspective-taking in infancy. *British Journal of Developmental Psychology, 9*, 55–72.

Carpenter, M., & Call, J. (2013). How joint is the joint attention of apes and human infants? In J. Metcalfe, & H. S. Terrace (Eds.), *Agency and Joint Attention* (pp. 49–61). New York: Oxford University Press.

Cochet, H., & Vauclair, J. (2010a). Features of spontaneous pointing gestures in toddlers. *Gesture, 10*, 86–107.

Cochet, H., & Vauclair, J. (2010b). Pointing gestures produced by toddlers from 15 to 30 months: Different functions, hand shapes and laterality patterns. *Infant Behavior and Development, 33*, 432–442.

D'Odorico, L., Assanelli, A., Franco, F., & Jacob, V. (2007). A follow-up study on Italian Late Talkers: Development of language, short-term memory, phonological awareness, impulsiveness and attention. *Applied Psycholinguistics, 28*, 157–169.

Eckerman, C. O., & Didow, S. M. (1989). Nonverbal imitation and toddlers' mastery of verbal means of achieving coordinated action. *Developmental Psychology, 32*, 141–152.

Engberg-Pedersen, E. (2003). From pointing to reference and predication: Pointing signs, eyegaze, and head and body orientation in Danish Sign Language. In S. Kita, (Ed.), *Pointing: Where Language, Culture, and Cognition Meet* (pp. 269–292). Mahwah, NJ: Erlbaum.

Fernald, A. (1989). Intonation and communicative intent in mother's speech to infants: Is the melody the message? *Child Development, 60*, 1497–1510.

Fernald, A. (2000). Speech to infants as hyperspeech: Knowledge-driven processes in early word recognition. *Phonetica, 57*, 242–254.

Franco, F. (1997). The development of meaning in infancy: Early communication and social understanding. In S. Hala (Ed.) *The Development of Social Cognition* (pp. 95–160). Hove, UK: Psychology Press.

Franco, F. (2005). Infant pointing: Harlequin, servant of two masters. In N. Eilan, C. Hoerl, T. McCormack, & J. Roessler (Eds.) *Joint Attention: Communication and Other Minds. Problems in Philosophy and Psychology* (pp. 129–164). Oxford: Oxford University Press.

Franco, F., & Butterworth, G. (1996). Pointing and social awareness: Declaring and requesting in the second year. *Journal of Child Language, 23*, 307–336.

Franco, F., & Gagliano, A. (2001). Toddler's pointing when joint attention is obstructed. *First Language, 21*, 289–321.

Franco, F., Perucchini, P., & March, B. (2009). Is infant initiation of joint attention by pointing affected by type of interaction? *Social Development, 18*, 51–76.

Gomez, J. C., Sarria, E., & Tamarit, J. (1993). The comparative study of early communication and theories of mind: Ontogeny, phylogeny, and pathology. In S. Baron-Cohen, & H. Tager-Flusberg et al. (Eds.), *Understanding Other Minds: Perspectives from Autism* (pp. 397–426). New York: Oxford University Press.

Halliday, M. A. K. (1975). *Learning How to Mean: Exploration in the Development of Language.* London: Edward Arnolds.

Hay, D. F., Caplan, M., Castle, J., & Stimson, C. A. (1991). Does sharing become increasingly "rational" in the second year of life? *Developmental Psychology, 27*, 987–993.

Hurtado, N., Marchman, V. A., & Fernald, A. (2008). Does input influence uptake? Links between maternal talk, processing speed and vocabulary size in Spanish-learning children. *Developmental Science, 11*, F31–F39.

Kita, S. (Ed.) (2003). *Pointing: Where Language, Culture, and Cognition Meet.* Mahwah, NJ: Erlbaum.

Leavens, D. A., Hopkins, W. D., & Thomas, R. K. (2004). Referential communication by chimpanzees (Pan troglodytes). *Journal of Comparative Psychology, 118*, 48–57.

Liszkowski, U., Carpenter, M., Henning, A., Striano, T., & Tomasello, M. (2004). Twelve month-olds point to share attention and interest. *Developmental Science, 7*, 297–307.

Liszkowski, U., Carpenter, M., Striano, T., & Tomasello, M. (2006). Twelve- and 18-montholds point to provide information for others. *Journal of Cognition and Development, 7*, 173–187.

Liszkowski, U., Carpenter, M., & Tomasello, M. (2007a). Pointing out new news, old news, and absent referents at 12 months. *Developmental Science, 10*, F1–F7.

Liszkowski, U., Carpenter, M., & Tomasello, M. (2007b). Reference and attitude in infant pointing. *Journal of Child Language, 33*, 1–20.

Liu, H. M., Kuhl, P. K., & Tsao, F. M. (2003). An association between mothers' speech clarity and infants' speech discrimination skills. *Developmental Science, 6*, F1–F10.

Marcos, H., & Verba, M. (1991). Partager un thème dans la seconde année: aspects émotionnels et conventionnels. *Enfance, 1–2*, 25–38.

Mayer, S., & Musatti, T. (1992). Towards the use of symbol: Play with objects and communication with adult and peers in the second year. *Infant Behavior and Development, 15*, 1–13.

McNeill, D. (1987). *Psycholinguistics: A new approach.* Cambridge: Harper & Row.

McNeill, D. (2006). Gesture, Gaze, and Ground. In S. Renals and S. Bengio (Eds.), *Proceedings of Machine Learning for Multimodal Interaction 2005, LNCS 3869* (pp. 1–14). Berlin Heidelberg: Springer-Verlag.

McNeill, D., Duncan, S., Franklin, A., Goss, J., Kimbara, I., Parrill, F., et al. (2010). "Mind-merging." In E. Morsella (Ed.), *Expressing Oneself/Expressing One's Self: Communication, Language, Cognition, and Identity* (pp. 143–164). London: Taylor & Francis.

Moore, C., & D'Entremont, B. (2001). Developmental change in pointing as a function of attentional focus. *Journal of Cognition and Development, 2*, 109–129.

Penn, D. C, & Povinelli, D. J. (2013). The comparative delusion: the "behavioristic"/'mentalistic' dichotomy in comparative Theory of Mind research. In J. Metcalfe, & H. S. Terrace (Eds.), *Agency and Joint Attention* (pp. 62–81). New York: Oxford University Press.

Perner, J. (1991). *Understanding the representational mind.* Cambridge MA: MIT Press.

Southgate, V., van Maanen, C., & Csibra, G. (2007). Infant Pointing: Communication to Cooperate or Communication to Learn? *Child Development, 78*, 735–740.

Tomasello, M. (1995). Joint attention as social cognition. In C. Moore, & P.J. Dunham (Eds.), *Joint Attention: Its Origins and Role in Development* (pp. 103–130). Hillsdale: Erlbaum.

Tomasello, M., & Camaioni, L. (1997). A comparison of the gestural communication of apes and human infants. *Human Development, 40*, 7–24.

Tomasello, M., Carpenter, M., & Liszkowski, U. (2007). A New Look at Infant Pointing. *Child Development, 78*, 705–722.

Triesch, J., Teuscher, C., Deak, G., & Carlson, E. (2006). Gaze following: Why (not) learn it? *Developmental Science, 9*: 125–147.

Vandell, D.L., & Wilson, K.S. (1987). Infants' interactions with mothers, siblings, and peers: Contrasts and relations between interaction systems. *Child Development, 58*, 176–186.

9 Understanding the Structure of Communicative Interactions in Infancy

Athena Vouloumanos and Kristine H. Onishi

IN A TYPICAL day, humans engage in hundreds if not thousands of communicative interactions, some verbal ("a double non-fat latte please"), some written ("stuck @ café in massive Q, cu in 20"), some gestural (a shrug at the barista faced with a temperamental espresso machine). What are the basic components and structure of human communicative acts such that we can communicate in each of these interactions? And how do we build our understanding of human communication during development? Part of the difficulty in carving a communicative act at its joints stems from its intrinsic complexity (e.g., Bruner, 1981): It requires two (or more) agentive interlocutors who have a set of shared experiences, interacting with specific and intentional behaviors that transfer information both through the literal meaning of the communication and through the agents' intended meaning. Each of these aspects of communication must be resolved in order to participate in or evaluate a successful communicative interaction. We outline a framework for understanding some critical components of communicative acts, highlighting the critical roles of joint attention and agency, and propose that this framework can direct investigations into the developmental roots of understanding human communication.

Defining Communication

In the biological literature, communication is commonly defined as anything that influences the behavior of others, including for example, coloring and reflex displays (Maynard

Smith & Harper, 2003; Scott-Phillips, 2008). Here we restrict our discussion to communicative signals produced *intentionally* and *flexibly* to influence others (as in Tomasello, 2008; and similar to the non-natural, as opposed to natural, signs of Grice, 1957) with an assumption of *cooperation* between interlocutors (Clark, 1996 Grice, 1969; Levinson, 2000; Sperber & Wilson, 1995). Thus, communication is considered a cooperative act that occurs in the context of joint attention between at least two intentional agents. Further, we focus on the information-transferring properties of communication, rather than on the question of whether communication arises primarily from adaptations for cooperation or from formal properties of language (e.g., Tomasello, 2008).

Detecting Communicative Acts

How do we evaluate a particular behavior as communicative? Detecting a communicative act is not a trivial task (e.g., Scott-Phillips, Kirby, & Ritchie, 2009), as entities may engage in any number of behaviors, only some of which would count as communicative. How do observers of potentially communicative behaviors distinguish situations in which communication is being attempted from those in which it is not? Because we consider communication to be a cooperative act that occurs in the context of joint attention between at least two intentional agents, in order to evaluate an act as communicative, participants (and observers) must detect whether there is an interaction involving agents and whether the interaction is intentional.

From infancy, humans are sensitive to aspects of behavior that are relevant for communicative interactions such as intention, agency, and interaction. Much of the work in this area has focused on infants' sensitivity to the intentions of others (for reviews see Baldwin & Baird, 2001; Csibra, 2010; Meltzoff, 2007; Woodward, 2005; Woodward, Sommerville, & Gerson, 2009). As early as 5 to 6 months, infants interpret actions such as grasping as intentional (Woodward, 1998). By 9 months, infants behave differently toward a person who is unwilling and a person who is unable to perform an action (Behne et al., 2005), reflecting their understanding that a person's underlying intentions can change the interpretation of their actions. By 2 years, they understand the role of intentions in pretend scenarios (Rakoczy & Tomasello, 2006) and in interpreting others' drawings (Preissler & Bloom, 2008). Thus, understanding of others' intentions is discernable by 5 to 6 months of age, and develops over the next months and years.

Young infants distinguish between agents (entities with the capacity for intentional, goal-oriented behavior) and nonagents, and do so using a variety of cues such as self-propelled or variable motion (Csibra, 2008; Gergely, Nádasdy, Csibra, & Bíró, 1995; Luo & Baillargeon, 2005), eyes and eye gaze (Johnson, Slaughter, & Carey, 1998), having an effect on other objects (Bíró & Leslie, 2007; Király, Jovanovic, Prinz, Aschersleben, & Gergely, 2003), and contingent behavior (Johnson et al., 1998; Johnson, Shimizu, & Ok, 2007; Premack & Premack, 1997). Infants also differentiate between the interactions of agents and nonagents. By 6 months of age, infants expect people, but not objects, to respond contingently (Legerstee, 1997), and 15- to 18-month-olds have different expectations for human–human and human–chair interactions (Golinkoff, 1975; Golinkoff & Kerr, 1978). Unlike their expectations for the movements of inert objects, infants do not necessarily expect the actions of agents to be governed by spatial-temporal properties such as continuity (Kuhlmeier, Bloom, & Wynn, 2004), instead accepting that agents can act contingently and at a distance from other entities (Spelke, Phillips, & Woodward, 1995). For infants, the actions of agents are self-governed and can be contingent on the behaviors of other entities.

Although infants can evaluate an entity's intentions, differentiate between potential agents and nonagents, and hold different expectations about how people interact with people versus objects, their understanding of interlocutors' potential for interaction and agency as key structural components of communicative acts remains to be examined.

Functions of Communicative Acts

Even with the simplifying assumptions we have adopted in this chapter, communicative acts are diverse and challenging to characterize, due in part to the complexity introduced by the social context of language. Communication serves many functions, including behavior regulation (e.g., making requests, protesting), generating a state of joint attention (e.g., commenting on the world), and encouraging social interaction (e.g., attention seeking, social games; Bruner, 1981). (For more ways of classifying communicative functions, see Searle 1976; Tomasello, 2008.)

Children seem to understand that communicative acts can serve a range of functions. Infants produce different communicative acts that elicit specific reactions. An infant's cry quickly gets a parent's attention, whereas reaching up toward the ceiling often leads to getting picked up. Infants in ambiguous situations (e.g., when faced with a borderline slope that they have a 50% probability of successfully descending) actively seek emotional signals from trusted adults and use them to modulate their behavior (e.g., descending the borderline slope more often following their mother's positive than negative emotion; Tamis-LeMonda et al., 2008; see chapter 11). Older children appear to be sensitive to more sophisticated aspects of communicative acts; for example, differentiating the propositional content (an utterance's compositional meaning or meaning that can be derived from the individual words and their combination: "My homework is due tomorrow," meaning that a particular document must be delivered shortly) from the illocutionary force (the speaker's intent: "My homework is due tomorrow," meaning that the speaker can't go to the movies now; Searle, 1976). For example, 3-year-olds interpret assertive and imperative speech acts differently, correcting the speaker when she failed to describe actions correctly but correcting the receiver when she did not follow the speaker's instructions (Rakoczy & Tomasello, 2009). Children expect speech to be truthful, that is, to reflect the actual state of the world, and detect violations in truthfulness (consistent

with the Gricean maxim of Quality, be truthful, Grice, 1989; Koenig & Echols, 2003).
Children are also sensitive to the different communicative functions of gestures, correctly
inferring, for example, that an adult's gaze direction and pointing gesture indicate either
the location of a hidden toy (Behne, Carpenter, & Tomasello, 2005) or the referent of a
novel word (Gliga & Csibra, 2009). This sensitivity suggests that children are not just
following gaze, but also infer the intention underyling the gaze and have some understanding that both partners know that they are attending to the same location in a shared
psychological state (see chapter 2; Tomasello, 2008). In other words, children understand
shared communicative acts with others as states of joint attention and use their knowledge
of shared experience to determine the function of a given communicative act. Function,
however, is but one aspect of communicative acts. Understanding communicative acts
also requires understanding of their internal structure and constituent components.

Components of a Communicative Act

We identify several critical components of communicative acts based on the adult literature. These components underlie the success of communicative acts in transferring
information. First, *shared intentionality*: Communication is a joint activity requiring
coordinated action between interlocutors (the sender and the receiver; Clark, 2002),
which in turn requires shared psychological states between participants, or joint attention (Tomasello & Carpenter, 2007). Second, *directional signaling*: Communication
requires transfer of information from the sender (the source of the signal who has the
information) to the receiver. Third, *mutually readable formats*: The communicative signal
must be in a format that is understood by both sender and receiver, used by the sender to
encode information and the receiver to decode information. Fourth, *referential specificity*: The communicative signal must use specific forms titrated to the relevant level of
meaning (i.e., using the appropriate wording; Clark, 1979). Research on understanding
and development of communication has focused mainly on children's understanding of
shared intentionality and of referential specificity, but less is known about their understanding of the role of directional signaling and mutually readable formats for successful
communication.

SHARED INTENTIONALITY

Shared intentionality is a mental construct that can neither be observed nor can its
understanding be tested directly. However, observers have access to behavioral indices
of shared intentionality, including proximity of interlocutors, coordinated (contingent)
actions, and co-localized eye gaze. Shared intentionality provides a basis for making
inferences about the information states of interlocutors, and more specifically for establishing common ground between interlocutors, in which common ground includes the
history of the participants' interactions and the current information state of the sender

and receiver given the particular situation [this notion has also been discussed as "forms of life" (Wittgenstein, 1953), "joint attentional formats" (Bruner, 1981), and "common conceptual ground" (Clark, 1996; Tomasello, 2008)].

To understand the content of communicative acts, observers assume that others will communicate using principles of relevance (Sperber & Wilson, 1995) and informativeness (Grice, 1989), both of which rely on establishing common ground. In adult communication, information unknown to the receiver is identified as potentially relevant, and thus likely to be the content of the current communication (Sperber & Wilson, 1995), and the response of the recipient is expected to be appropriate to the communication (Albright, Cohen, Malloy, Christ, & Bromgard, 2004). Children appear to use relevance principles before informativeness principles to evaluate others' communication. By 3 to 5 years of age, children are sensitive to violations of Grice's maxim of Relation (be relevant), preferring the puppet who uses this relevance maxim over puppets who use only informativeness maxims: Quantity (say enough but not more than necessary) or Quality (be truthful; Eskritt, Whalen, & Lee, 2008). In some circumstances, 6-year-olds can appropriately use informativeness maxims. For example, consistent with the maxim of Quantity, when presented with several cards with clowns and asked to "give the clown," children selected a card with a clown alone over one with a clown with flowers or two clowns (because they presumably infer that if the speaker had wanted the cards with flowers or two clowns, they should have qualified their description; Surian & Job, 1987).

The ability to use joint attention contexts to infer shared intentionality has its roots in infancy. Even 18-month-olds behave in a manner consistent with the principle of relevance (see chapter 2; Moll, Koring, Carpenter, & Tomasello, 2006; Southgate, Chevallier, & Csibra, 2009). For example, 18-month-olds use others' discourse (e.g., "Oh, great, look!") to infer the focus of attention (i.e., the new object or object part) and therefore what is relevant (Moll et al., 2006). And when infants of this age were shown a toy moving into a house, if the goal location was mutually known to the infants and the experimenter, infants preferentially imitated the new information (about the manner of motion), suggesting that they considered this new information to be the relevant focus of the communication (Southgate et al., 2009). Thus, infants use behavioral indices of shared intentionality to interpret communicative acts.

More direct evidence for infants' understanding of shared intentionality comes from studies showing they respond differentially to information presented during interactions with and without ostensive communicative cues (direct eye gaze, child-directed speech; Gliga & Csibra, 2009; Senju & Csibra, 2008; Yoon, Johnson, & Csibra, 2008). These behavioral markers of joint attention signal to infants the presence of a knowledgeable speaker who is providing generalizable information.

Thus, although shared intentionality is not directly observable, children are sensitive to behavioral cues of shared intentionality that signal contexts of joint attention. Infants and young children thus seem to have a basic understanding of the role of shared intentionality in communicative acts.

DIRECTIONAL SIGNALING

Infants are sensitive to cause and effect, and causal direction within events (Bullock & Gelman, 1979; Golinkoff, 1975; Leslie & Keeble, 1987). Infants watching a third-party interaction understand that a communicative signal must travel in a particular direction, from an informed sender to an uninformed receiver, in order for information to be transferred (Martin, Onishi, & Vouloumanos, 2012). A related line of work suggests that older children understand something about the importance of the source of a communicative signal. For example, 3- and 4-year-olds preferentially learn a new word from a previously reliable rather than unreliable speaker (Birch, Vauthier, & Bloom, 2008; Pasquini, Corriveau, Koenig, & Harris, 2007; Vanderborght & Jaswal, 2009), demonstrating knowledge that the specific source of the signal matters. Children not only infer the causality of physical events and are selective in choosing the source of communicative signals, they also understand the abstract notion that transferring information requires directionality.

MUTUALLY READABLE FORMATS

Do children understand that certain formats (speech, pointing) allow for efficient communication of information, whereas others (coughing, nose-scratching) generally do not, and that these formats should be shared across interlocutors? Children seem to know that the communicative signal must use conventional means to accomplish a specific action or goal (Clark, 1979). For example, conventional requests ("What time do you close tonight?") are responded to with information ("at six"), whereas less conventionally worded requests ("Do you close before seven tonight?") receive a response to the question ("yes") as well as the information ("at six"). And even 13- and 19-month-old infants understand that speech is used conventionally across individuals, such that different people are expected to share labels for objects (Buresh & Woodward, 2007; Graham, Stock, & Henderson, 2006), although they are not expected to share, for example, preferences.

Although there is no evidence that younger infants understand the conventionality of communication formats, infants as young as 6 months show understanding that some formats are more efficient vehicles for information transfer. For example, based on hearing speech, infants can make some reasonable inferences: (1) that a human is present (Vouloumanos, Druhen, Hauser, & Huizink, 2009), (2) that a person shares the same language as other people (Kinzler, Dupoux, & Spelke, 2007), (3) that the entity spoken to is more likely to be another person than an inanimate object (Legerstee, Barna, & DiAdamo, 2000), and (4) that speech labels correspond to the number of objects (Xu, 2002) and to category membership (Fulkerson & Waxman, 2007). Although speech is a primary symbolic communicative signal for humans, humans may also communicate using other formats that infants also understand as transmitting information.

For example, infants can use a pointing gesture produced for a third party as a tool for finding a hidden toy (Gräfenhain, Behne, Carpenter, & Tomasello, 2009). Infants thus understand that some formats (speech, pointing) can transmit information, and that these are conventionally shared across individuals. Recent studies in our labs show that by the end of their first year, infants recognize that a sender's speech or point-ing gesture can communicate to a receiver which of two objects is the sender's target (Krehm, Onishi, & Vouloumanos, in press; Martin et al., 2012). Thus, although infants can evaluate some acts, but not others, as transferring information, there is as yet no direct evidence that children understand that the format of a communicative act must be mutually readable; that is, for a communicative act to be successful, that the sender must use a format that the receiver has the capability to perceive and knowledge to decode.

REFERENTIAL SPECIFICITY

The communicative signal must use specific forms with a level of specificity appropri-ate for the interlocutors' common ground and the situation (Clark, 1979). However, not all formats can titrate degrees of referential specificity equally. Speech is uniquely flexible in its capacity to express degrees of specificity. It allows a sender to merely draw attention to what is salient ("wow!") or to unambiguously pick out a specific entity in the world ("your grandmother's Eames chair"). Not every instance of speech is specific. If I say "chair" in a room full of chairs, I have not availed myself of speech's potential for specificity, but if I say the same utterance in a room full of tables and lamps, I likely have succeeded in being highly referentially specific. Throat-clearing, coughing, expressions of delight, disgust, or surprise do not unambiguously pick out a chair in a room of tables and lamps without some common ground–knowledge that the sender likes, dislikes, or is not expecting a chair, or some other concurrent cue like eye gaze. Nonspeech vocalizations are more dependent on deictic factors (temporal contiguity between the chair and the vocalization, simultaneous eye gaze or gestures toward the chair) whereas speech can be referentially specific, communicating meaning more independently of the context.

The appropriateness of a particular speech form for communicative success is modulated by the common ground between interlocutors. Common ground includes a range of levels of potential shared background knowledge including geo-graphical and cultural communities as well as specific individually shared knowledge (Brennan & Clark, 1996; Isaacs & Clark, 1987). For example, if you are a New Yorker (of a certain era) then you know about CBGBs; if you live in the United States, then you know about the Grand Canyon; and if you are human you know about fin-gers. Correct determination of group membership affects the appropriate referential form for an utterance ("fingers" vs. "the appendages at the tips of the upper limbs of the organism") and can even affect the message's content (for a child, a spleen is something found inside your body; for adults, an organ found in vertebrates for removing red blood cells).

The separation of common ground from privileged ground (information known only to oneself) may be challenging for children, and even adults (Keysar, Barr, & Horton, 1998). Children sometimes fail to use common ground in discourse, producing utterances that are ambiguous for others, and confusing ambiguous and informative utterances directed to them (Ackerman, 1981; Glucksberg, Krauss, & Weisberg, 1966; Rosenberg & Cohen, 1964). This failure in communication has been ascribed either to children being egocentric, in the Piagetian tradition, or to computational difficulties that arise when trying to map the communicative message to the set of possible referents (see Surian & Job, 1987).

Interestingly, it may be children's understanding of the agent's intention to communicate—that a speaker intends to communicate something to a receiver—that leads them to erroneously infer that communication has been successful even when the message lacks the appropriate level of referential specificity (by using illocutionary performative force instead of the locutionary content of the utterance, as in Austin, 1962). Children are thus fooled by ambiguous communicative attempts because they assume the receiver is cooperative and responding to the sender appropriately, even when the referent of the utterance is underspecified (Grice, 1989). Although children are biased toward interpreting utterances consistently with the speaker's intent (Shatz, 1978), they can be induced to evaluate the referential specificity of ambiguous communication appropriately when they cannot trust the intent of the speaker or the importance of the content is emphasized (Ackerman, 1981). Children's understanding of a critical component of communicative acts, intentionality, may thus interfere with their successful use of other components.

Children build their understanding of different communicative acts over time. By the age of 2 years, they can discuss specific topics and negotiate action; after 2, children can moderate politeness, deixis, and some forms of indirect speech. By 4, children can adjust utterances depending on the knowledge of the listener (Ninio & Snow, 1996). More direct evidence that common ground can modulate referential specificity comes from the finding that 5- and 6-year-old children adjust their speech to a partner's perspective and to information that is in common ground (Nadig & Sedivy, 2002). Recent work shows that rudimentary understanding of common ground may emerge earlier, as 4-year-olds can sometimes detect ambiguity in utterances (Nilsen, Graham, Smith, & Chambers, 2008), and even 2-year-olds take into account what others know when communicating; for example, gesturing more to the location of a hidden object when the receiver was absent than when she was present during a hiding event (Liszkowski, Carpenter, & Tomasello, 2007; O'Neill, 1996). Children can thus use and make judgments about the referential appropriateness of particular forms for transferring information between interlocutors, taking into account the interlocutors' common ground.

Conclusions

Human communication is complex. In order to understand communicative acts, observers must detect potentially communicative situations by (1) identifying agents, (2) detecting whether the agents are interacting, and (3) evaluating whether their interaction is intentional. Observers must further understand four critical components of communicative acts: (1) that the sender and receiver have shared intentionality established through joint attention, (2) the sender is directing a signal to a receiver, (3) that the signal format must be mutually readable, and (4) that the referential specificity of the signal is appropriate. Although infants can detect agents and intentions, whether they use this understanding in the service of understanding communicative acts is not fully known. More is known about children's understanding of shared intentionality, and how they produce and interpret utterances while taking into account common ground. However, much remains to be understood about children's understanding of the importance of the direction of the communicative signal and about the role of a mutually readable format for successful communicative interactions. Our proposed framework can guide investigations of how we build an understanding of human communication during development. A better understanding of the structure and components of communicative interactions elucidates the developmental roots of communicative competence, which provides a foundation for our social and cultural life as humans.

REFERENCES

Ackerman, B. P. (1981). Performative bias in children's interpretations of ambiguous referential communications. *Child Development, 52*, 1224–1230.

Albright, L., Cohen, A. I., Malloy, T. E., Christ, T., & Bromgard, G. (2004). Judgments of communicative intent in conversation. *Journal of Experimental Social Psychology, 40*, 290–302.

Austin, J. L. (1962). *How to Do Things with Words.* Oxford, UK: Clarendon Press.

Baldwin, D. A., & Baird, J. A. (2001). Discerning intentions in dynamic human action. *Trends in Cognitive Sciences, 5*, 171–178.

Behne, T., Carpenter, M., & Tomasello, M. (2005). One-year-olds comprehend the communicative intentions behind gestures in a hiding game. *Developmental Science, 8*, 492–499.

Birch, S. A. J., Vauthier, S. A., & Bloom, P. (2008). Three- and four-year-olds spontaneously use others' past performance to guide their learning. *Cognition, 107*, 1018–1034.

Bíró, S., & Leslie, A. M. (2007). Infants' perception of goal-directed actions: Development through cue-based bootstrapping. *Developmental Science, 10*, 379–398.

Brennan, S. E., & Clark, H. H. (1996). Conceptual pacts and lexical choice in conversation. *Journal of Experimental Psychology Learning Memory and Cognition, 22*, 1482–1493.

Bruner, J. (1981). The social context of language acquisition. *Language and Communication, 1*, 155–178.

Bullock, M., & Gelman, R. (1979). Preschool children's assumptions about cause and effect: Temporal ordering. *Child Development, 50*, 89–96.

Buresh, J. S., & Woodward, A. L. (2007). Infants track action goals within and across agents. *Cognition, 104,* 287–314.

Clark, H. H. (1979). Responding to indirect speech acts. *Cognitive Psychology, 11,* 430–477.

Clark, H. H. (1996). *Using Language.* New York: Cambridge University Press.

Clark, H. H. (2002). Conversation, structure of. *Encyclopedia of Cognitive Science.* New York: Macmillan.

Csibra, G. (2008). Goal attribution to inanimate agents by 6.5-month-old infants. *Cognition, 107,* 705–717.

Csibra, G. (2010). Recognizing communicative intentions in infancy. *Mind & Language, 25,* 141–168.

Eskritt, M., Whalen, J., & Lee, K. (2008). Preschoolers can recognize violations of the gricean maxims. *British Journal of Developmental Psychology, 26,* 435–443.

Fulkerson, A. L., & Waxman, S. R. (2007). Words (but not tones) facilitate object categorization: Evidence from 6- and 12-month-olds. *Cognition, 105,* 218–228.

Gergely, G., Nádasdy, Z., Csibra, G., & Bíró, S. (1995). Taking the intentional stance at 12 months of age. *Cognition, 56,* 165–193.

Gliga, T., & Csibra, G. (2009). One-year-old infants appreciate the referential nature of deictic gestures and words. *Psychological Science, 20,* 347–353.

Glucksberg, S., Krauss, R. M., & Weisberg, R. (1966). Referential communication in nursery school children: Method and some preliminary findings. *Journal of Experimental Child Psychology, 3,* 333–342.

Golinkoff, R. M. (1975). Semantic development in infants: The concepts of agent and recipient. *Merrill-Palmer Quarterly, 21,* 181–193.

Golinkoff, R. M., & Kerr, J. L. (1978). Infants' perception of semantically defined action role changes in filmed events. *Merrill-Palmer Quarterly, 24,* 53–61.

Graham, S. A., Stock, H., & Henderson, A. M. E. (2006). Nineteen-Month-Olds' understanding of the conventionality of object labels versus desires. *Infancy: The Official Journal of the International Society on Infant Studies, 9,* 341–350.

Gräfenhain, M., Behne, T., Carpenter, M., & Tomasello, M. (2009). One-year-olds' understanding of nonverbal gestures directed to a third person. *Cognitive Development, 24,* 23–33.

Grice, H. P. (1957). Meaning. *The Philosophical Review, 66,* 377–388.

Grice, H. P. (1969). Utterer's meaning and intention. *The Philosophical Review, 78,* 147–177.

Grice, H. P. (1989). *Studies in the Way of Words.* Cambridge, MA: Harvard University Press.

Isaacs, E. A., & Clark, H. H. (1987). References in conversation between experts and novices. *Journal of Experimental Psychology. General, 116,* 26–37.

Johnson, S., Slaughter, V., & Carey, S. (1998). Whose gaze will infants follow? The elicitation of gaze-following in 12-month-olds. *Developmental Science, 1,* 233–238.

Johnson, S. C., Alpha Shimizu, Y., & Ok, S. J. (2007). Actors and actions: The role of agent behavior in infants' attribution of goals. *Cognitive Development, 22,* 310–322.

Keysar, B., Barr, D. J., & Horton, W. S. (1998). The egocentric basis of language use: Insights from a processing approach. *Current Directions in Psychological Science, 7,* 46–50.

Kinzler, K. D., Dupoux, E., & Spelke, E. S. (2007). The native language of social cognition. *Proceedings of the National Academy of Sciences of the United States of America, 104,* 12577–12580.

Király, I., Jovanovic, B., Prinz, W., Aschersleben, G., & Gergely, G. (2003). The early origins of goal attribution in infancy. *Consciousness and Cognition: An International Journal, 12,* 752–769.

Koenig, M. A. & Echols, C. H. (2003). Infants' understanding of false labeling events: The referential roles of words and the speakers who use them. *Cognition, 87,* 179–208.

Krehm, M., Onishi, K. H., & Vouloumanos, A. (in press). Infants under 12 months understand that pointing is communicative. *Journal of Cognition and Development.*

Kuhlmeier, V. A., Bloom, P., & Wynn, K. (2004). Do 5-month-old infants see humans as material objects? *Cognition, 94,* 95–103.

Legerstee, M. (1997). Contingency effects of people and objects on subsequent cognitive functioning in three-month-old infants. *Social Development, 6,* 307–321.

Legerstee, M., Barna, J., & DiAdamo, C. (2000). Precursors to the development of intention at 6 months: Understanding people and their actions. *Developmental Psychology, 36,* 627–634.

Leslie, A. M., & Keeble, S. (1987). Do six-month-old infants perceive causality? *Cognition, 25,* 265–288.

Levinson, S. C. (2000). *Presumptive Meanings: The Theory of Generalized Conversational Implicature.* Cambridge, MA: MIT Press.

Liszkowski, U., Carpenter, M., & Tomasello, M. (2007). Pointing out new news, old news, and absent referents at 12 months of age. *Developmental Science, 10,* F1–F7.

Luo, Y., & Baillargeon, R. (2005). Can a self-propelled box have a goal? Psychological reasoning in 5-month-old infants. *Psychological Science: A Journal of the American Psychological Society/ APS, 16,* 601–608.

Martin, A., Onishi, K. H., & Vouloumanos, A. (2012). Understanding the abstract role of speech in communication at 12 months. *Cognition, 123,* 50–60. doi: 10.1016/j.cognition.2011.12.003

Maynard Smith, J. & Harper, D. D. (2003). *Animal Signals.* New York: Oxford University Press.

Meltzoff, A. N. (2007). The "like me" framework for recognizing and becoming an intentional agent. *Acta Psychologica, 124,* 26–43.

Moll, H., Koring, C., Carpenter, M., & Tomasello, M. (2006). Infants determine others' focus of attention by pragmatics and exclusion. *Journal of Cognition and Development, 7,* 411–430.

Nadig, A. S. & Sedivy, J. C. (2002). Evidence of perspective-taking constraints in children's online reference resolution. *Psychological Science, 13,* 329–336.

Nilsen, E. S., Graham, S. A., Smith, S., & Chambers, C. G. (2008). Preschoolers' sensitivity to referential ambiguity: Evidence for a dissociation between implicit understanding and explicit behavior. *Developmental Science, 11,* 556–562.

Ninio, A. & Snow, C. E. (1996). *Pragmatic Development.* Boulder, CO: Westview Press.

O'Neill, D. K. (1996). Two-year-old children's sensitivity to a parent's knowledge state when making requests. *Child Development, 67,* 659–677.

Pasquini, E. S., Corriveau, K. H., Koenig, M., & Harris, P. L. (2007). Preschoolers monitor the relative accuracy of informants. *Developmental Psychology, 43,* 1216–1226.

Preissler, M. A., & Bloom, P. (2008). Two-year-olds use artist intention to understand drawings. *Cognition, 106,* 512–518.

Premack, D., & Premack, A. J. (1997). Infants attribute value to the goal-directed actions of self-propelled objects. *Journal of Cognitive Neuroscience, 9*, 848–856.

Rakoczy, H., & Tomasello, M. (2006). Two-Year-Olds grasp the intentional structure of pretense acts. *Developmental Science, 9*, 557–564.

Rakoczy, H., & Tomasello, M. (2009). Done wrong or said wrong? Young children understand the normative directions of fit of different speech acts. *Cognition, 113*, 205–212.

Rosenberg, S., & Cohen, B. D. (1964). Speakers' and listeners' processes in a word-communication task. *Science, 145*, 1201.

Scott-Phillips, T. C. (2008). Defining biological communication. *Journal of Evolutionary Biology, 21*, 387–395.

Scott-Phillips, T. C., Kirby, S., & Ritchie, G. R. S. (2009). Signalling signalhood and the emergence of communication. *Cognition, 113*, 226–233.

Searle, J. R. (1976). A classification of illocutionary acts. *Language in Society, 5*, 1–23.

Senju, A., & Csibra, G. (2008). Gaze following in human infants depends on communicative signals. *Current Biology, 18*, 668–671.

Shatz, M. (1978). On the development of communicative understandings: An early strategy for interpreting and responding to messages. *Cognitive Psychology, 10*, 271–301.

Southgate, V., Chevallier, C., & Csibra, G. (2009). Sensitivity to communicative relevance tells young children what to imitate. *Developmental Science, 12*, 1013–1019.

Spelke, E. S., Phillips, A., & Woodward, A. L. (1995). Infants' knowledge of object motion and human action. In D. Sperber, D. Premack, & A. J. Premack (Eds.), *Causal Cognition: A Multidisciplinary Debate.* (pp. 44–78). New York: Clarendon Press.

Sperber, D., & Wilson, D. (1995). *Relevance: Communication and Cognition* (2nd ed.). Oxford, UK: Blackwell.

Surian, L., & Job, R. (1987). Children's use of conversational rules in a referential communication task. *Journal of Psycholinguistic Research, 16*, 369–382.

Tamis-LeMonda, C. S., Adolph, K. E., Lobo, S. A., Karasik, L. B., Ishak, S., & Dimitropoulou, K. A. (2008). When infants take mothers' advice: 18-month-olds integrate perceptual and social information to guide motor action. *Developmental Psychology, 44*, 734–746.

Tomasello, M. (2008). *Origins of Human Communication.* Cambridge, MA: MIT Press.

Tomasello, M. & Carpenter, M. (2007). Shared intentionality. *Developmental Science, 10*, 121–125.

Vanderborght, M. & Jaswal, V. K. (2009). Who knows best? Preschoolers sometimes prefer child informants over adult informants. *Infant and Child Development, 18*, 61–71.

Vouloumanos, A., Druhen, M. J., Hauser, M. D., & Huizink, A. T. (2009). Five-month-old infants' identification of the sources of vocalizations. *Proceedings of the National Academy of Sciences of the United States of America, 106*, 18867–18872.

Wittgenstein, L. (1953). *Philosophical Investigations.* Oxford, UK: Blackwell.

Woodward, A., Sommerville, J., & Gerson, S. (2009). The emergence of intention attribution in infancy. *The Psychology of Learning and Motivation, 51*, 187–222.

Woodward, A. L. (1998). Infants selectively encode the goal object of an actor's reach. *Cognition, 69*, 1–34.

Woodward, A. L. (2005). The infant origins of intentional understanding. *Advances in Child Development and Behavior, 33*, 229–262.

Xu, F. (2002). The role of language in acquiring object kind concepts in infancy. *Cognition, 85,* 223–250.

Yoon, J. M. D., Johnson, M. H., & Csibra, G. (2008). Communication-Induced memory biases in preverbal infants. *Proceedings of the National Academy of Sciences of the United States of America, 105,* 13690–13695.

10 Cognition in Action: A New Look at the Cortical Motor System

Vittorio Gallese and Corrado Sinigaglia

ANY ACTION, BEGINNING with the most basic, always allows for more than one description. Imagine stretching your arm to grab the glass in front of you. All this can be described in terms of mere physical aspects, such as arm and hand trajectories, joint displacements, muscular contractions and relaxations, force, and so on. Such description may be more or less fine-grained. For instance, it might take into account the trajectory and the velocity of the forearm–hand system; or it might take into account the joint displacements characterizing the various hand configurations during reaching, grasping, and lifting an object—not to mention the more properly dynamic aspects. However, no matter how detailed it may be, this kind of description is not intentional in any respect. Things are different if the movements you perform are described, let's say, in terms of grasping a glass, drinking, quenching one's thirst, taking a break, testing whether Pepsi is really different from Coke, and so on. Even in these cases it is possible to distinguish different kinds and/or levels of description. But in each of these descriptions, action is accounted for under a given intentional aspect.

For decades, neuroscientists, psychologists, and philosophers have been reluctant to think that neurophysiology could be involved with any research program aimed at investigating the intentional aspects of motor behavior. In particular, the target of neurophysiological research carried out in the cortical motor system of nonhuman primates and humans was, and according to some researchers still is, uniquely focused on the study of a multilayered system characterized exclusively in terms of physical features such as force, direction, and amplitude. However, a series of empirical results almost forces us to abandon our reluctance to deal with the intentional aspects of action, at least at the basic level.

Neurophysiological evidence shows that the cortical motor system in nonhuman primates and humans is organized in terms of motor goals and motor intentions rather than mere movements (Rizzolatti et al., 1988, 2000). This new account of the cortical motor system has important theoretical implications. Neuroscience shows that motor goals and motor intentions are the nuclear building blocks around which the interactions with the surrounding world are mapped and instantiated (Gallese et al., 2009). The motor cortex, long confined to the mere role of action programming and execution control, plays, in fact, a crucial role in cognitive abilities such as object and space representation and action understanding. A second consequence of the results reviewed here is that the functional architecture of the motor system, shaped by our situated pragmatic interaction with the world[1] gives intentional form to biological motions even when they can only be observed to be done by others, or imagined.

The present chapter shows how these cognitive functions of the cortical motor system have been assessed by discussing neuroscientific evidence collected during the last two decades both in nonhuman primates and humans. There are five sections. The first section addresses the topic of whether and to what extent intentional aspects of motor behavior are encoded in the cortical motor system. The second section investigates the role of motor goal encoding in perceiving and acting upon three-dimensional (3D) objects. The third section highlights the tight relationship between action and space representation. The fourth section deals with the primary ways of making sense of others' motor behavior. The chapter concludes that the intentional features of actions, at least at a basic level, can only be fully accounted for by the cognitive functions of the cortical motor system. From this definition of intentional action follows a unified neurophysiological explanatory frame for many aspects of our connected relations with the world.

Encoding Goals Within the Cortical Motor System

The cortical motor system is formed by the primary motor cortex (area F1), the mesial premotor cortices (areas F3 and F6), the dorsal premotor cortices (areas F2 and F7), and the ventral premotor cortices (areas F4 and F5) (Rizzolatti & Luppino, 2001). Furthermore, the motor role of areas located in the posterior parietal cortex has also being firmly established (Mountcastle, 1995; Rizzolatti & Luppino, 2001; Rozzi et al., 2008).

The most anterior region of the ventral premotor cortex of the macaque monkey controls hand and mouth movements (Hepp-Reymond, 1994; Kurata & Tanji, 1986; Rizzolatti et al., 1981, 1988). This sector, which has specific histochemical and cytoarchitectonic features, has been termed area F5 (Matelli et al., 1985). A fundamental functional property of area F5 is that most of its neurons do not discharge in association with simple movements (e.g., flexing the fingers), but are activated only and exclusively by the execution of movements accomplishing a given motor goal, such as grasping, tearing, holding, or manipulating objects (Rizzolatti et al., 1988). This seems to be true also for most of the motor neurons located in the mid-rostral part (areas PFG, AIP) of the inferior parietal lobule (IPL): The motor goal is what these neurons encode when they fire during the execution of a given motor act (Fogassi et al., 2005; Gallese, 2000; Jeannerod et al., 1995; Murata et al., 2000).

It is worth noting that F5 and IPL motor neurons encode the motor goal-relatedness of movements with different degrees of generality. Indeed, there are F5 neurons that are sensitive to a motor goal such as grasping a piece of food, irrespective of whether it is accomplished with left or right hand, or even with the mouth; other neurons are more selective, discharging only when the motor goal is achieved with a particular effector (grasping with right or left hand; grasping with the mouth) or with a specific grip (grasping with a whole hand prehension; grasping with a precision grip). However, even when selectivity is at its highest, the motor responses of F5 and IPL neurons cannot be interpreted in terms of single and merely physical movements. The neurons that discharge during certain movements (e.g., flexing a finger) performed with a specific motor goal (e.g., grasping), discharge weakly or not at all during the execution of those movements with a different motor goal (e.g., scratching) (Rizzolatti & Sinigaglia, 2008; Rizzolatti et al., 2004).

More recently, Umiltà et al. (2008) have shown that this motor goal-relatedness does not only pertain to hand-relatedness and mouth-relatedness, but also to tool-mediated motor acts, even when the distal goal of the tool requires opposite movements of the hand to be accomplished. In this study, hand-related neurons were recorded from premotor area F5 and the primary motor cortex (area F1) in monkeys trained to grasp objects using two different tools: "normal" and "reverse" pliers. These tools require opposite movements to grasp an object. With normal pliers the hand has to be first opened and then closed, as when grasping is executed with the bare hand. In contrast, with reverse pliers the hand has to be first closed and then opened. The use of the two tools enabled the researchers to dissociate the neural activity related to hand movement from that related to the goal of the motor act. All tested neurons in area F5 and half of the neurons recorded from area F1 discharged during the grasping phase in both conditions, regardless of the fact that diametrically opposite hand movements were required to achieve the goal.

A crucial step forward in the research on the functional properties of the cortical motor system has been provided by the discovery that IPL and F5 motor neurons, besides encoding a single motor goal, also encode the overall motor intention within which this goal is embedded. By recording single neurons from area PFG during eating and placing actions, Fogassi et al. (2005) found that most of the tested hand-grasping neurons are "action constrained," forming prewired motor chains and discharging differentially depending on whether the initial grasping occurred for eating or for placing. Bonini et al. (2010) also demonstrated the presence of "action-constrained" motor neurons in area F5. The comparison between PFG and F5 neuron properties seems to suggest that although the ventral premotor neurons are more sensitive to specific motor chains, the parietal motor neurons play a critical role in extending and generalizing their recruitment, thus allowing for more complex and flexible motor goal hierarchies.

Taken together, these findings clearly indicate that motor goal encoding is a distinctive functional feature upon which the cortical motor system is organized. F5 and IPL motor neurons encode the movements to be executed in terms of their intentional motor aspect. Thus, the motor behavior F5 and IPL neurons control can be described as something more than just "bare bones behavior," or mere physical movements. They code given motor acts directed to grasp a certain object, with a certain shape, a certain size, and so on. This is true not only for a single motor act per se, but also for a motor act carried out with a given motor intention; that is, for a chain of motor acts in which the single motor goals are organized according to a given motor goal hierarchy.

The existence in the cortical motor system of a specific neural format for motor goals and motor intentions allows for a more general and at the same time more economic characterization of the motor constrains relevant to action, as well as for a much simpler selection of particular goal-related motor acts within a given context, thus facilitating the fluidity of action that is a typical marker of intentional behavior.

Seeing with Hands

Beyond purely motor neurons, area F5 and IPL also contain two categories of sensory-motor neurons. Neurons of both categories have motor properties that are indistinguishable from those of the described purely motor neurons, whereas they have peculiar "visual" or, more generally, sensory properties. The neurons of the first category respond to the presentation of objects and are responsible for those sensory-motor transformations that are necessary for visually guided motor acts such as grasping, manipulating, and so on. These neurons have been called "canonical neurons" (Raos et al., 2006; Rizzolatti & Fadiga, 1998; Rizzolatti et al., 2000; Umiltà et al., 2007; for a review see Rizzolatti & Sinigaglia, 2008). The characterizing property of the neurons of the second category is that they discharge both when the monkey performs a given motor act and also when it observes someone else performing the same or a similar motor act. These latter sensory-motor neurons were called "mirror neurons" (Gallese et al., 1996; Rizzolatti et al., 1996; for a review, see Gallese et al., 2004; Rizzolatti & Craighero, 2004; Rizzolatti & Sinigaglia, 2010; Rizzolatti et al., 2001).

Let us have a closer look at the canonical neurons. Because most grasping actions are executed under visual guidance, a relationship has to be established between the most important relational features of 3D visual objects—their affordances—and the specific motor specifications they might engender whenever the individual is aiming at them. The sight of a graspable object in the visual space will immediately retrieve the appropriate motor schema of the intended type of hand–object relation. This process, in neurophysiological terms, implies that the same neuron must be able not only to code the motor acts it controls, but also to respond to the situated visual features triggering them.

Indeed, canonical neurons respond to the visual presentation of objects of different sizes and shapes, even when the monkey is just fixating them without being required to grasp them (Jeannerod et al., 1995; Murata et al., 1997; Raos et al., 2006; Rizzolatti, Fogassi, & Gallese, 2004; Rizzolatti et al., 1988; Umiltà et al., 2007). Very often, a strict congruence has been observed between the type of grip coded by a given neuron and the size or shape of the object effective in triggering its visual response (Murata et al., 1997; Raos et al., 2006). The most interesting aspect, however, is the fact that in a considerable percentage of neurons a congruence is observed between the response during the execution of a specific type of grip, and the visual response to objects that, although differing in shape, nevertheless all "afford" the same type of grip that excites the neuron when executed (see Murata et al., 1997; Raos et al., 2006).

Similar results have been found in humans. An early positron emission tomography (PET) study (Grafton et al., 1996) showed that the observation of manipulable objects activated the left premotor cortex even in the absence of any motor output. Further functional magnetic resonance imaging (fMRI) studies demonstrated that observing graspable objects activates the left premotor cortex and the superior parietal lobule (Chao & Martin, 2000) and that the degree of activation of this fronto-parietal circuit during the execution of a given hand grip co-varies with the hand grip afforded by the object (Grèzes et al., 2003). More recently, Buccino et al. (2009) adopted a transcranial magnetic stimulation (TMS) paradigm to investigate the excitability of the primary motor cortex while observing manipulable familiar objects, such as a mug. Interestingly, the handle of the objects could be broken or not, thus lessening the affordance of the object. Their results showed that motor evoked potentials (MEPs) were larger only when the handle was complete, suggesting that the cortical motor system is critically involved not only in the detailed programming and online control at the level of elementary movements, but also in the processing of the pragmatic features of the surrounding objects that enables us to perceive them in terms of actual possibilities for action; that is, in this case, as graspable or not.

Consistent with these neurophysiological and brain imaging data are a number of behavioral studies demonstrating that the mere sight of an object automatically triggers the corresponding action possibilities, even in absence of any effective interaction or intention to act (Craighero et al., 1999). In particular, it has been shown that task-irrelevant object information (e.g., the left-right orientation of the handle of a mug) may facilitate the execution of left–right hand motor acts when the orientation of the affording part of the object (e.g., handle) is spatially aligned with the responding hand (Tucker & Ellis, 1998; see also Ellis & Tucker, 2000; Tucker & Ellis 2001, 2004). An analogous compatibility effect between object orientation and motor act execution has been found by Phillips and Ward (2002). They presented participants with a visual manipulable object prime oriented toward or away from participants, or in a neutral position. The prime was followed by an imperative target requiring a response with the left or right hand, or a foot press. The results showed that the vision of motor affordances (e.g., the object handles) potentiates lateralized responses corresponding with a given orientation of the affordances.

In conclusion, the fact that the sight of an object evokes a motor activation in the observer's brain even in the absence of any overt motor behavior indicates that the object is encoded in the same way in both the execution and observation condition. The perception of an object, therefore, can be nothing but a preliminary form of action, a call to arms, so to speak, which regardless of whether we actually pick the object up, gives it to us as a virtual target of action; that is, as something present-at-hand (in Heidegger's terms; Heidegger, 1996), something that can be grasped with this or that body part (hand, mouth), this or that grip (whole hand prehension, precision grip), and so on. This suggests not only that object perception is strictly intertwined with action, but also that action constitutively shapes the content of perception, characterizing the perceived object in terms of motor acts it may afford—and this even in absence of any effective movement.

The claim that action plays a pivotal role in object perception is certainly not a novelty. Since Gibson (1979) inaugurated the ecological approach to perception, several authors have emphasized (Cutting & Kozlowky, 1997; Reed, 1996) the critical involvement of motor interaction in revealing perceptually relevant information, that is "perceptual" or "ecological invariants," without which no object perception can occur (Michaels & Carello, 1981). The constitutivity and pervasiveness of action in perceptual processes have been also stressed by the sensory-motor approach to perception (MacKay, 1987; Noë, 2004; Philipona et al., 2003), according to which the sensory-motor invariants have to be construed not just as mere sources of information but as constitutive parts of perceptual content (O'Reagan & Noë, 2001).

A detailed analysis of these approaches and a discussion of their similarities and differences are far beyond the scope of our chapter (see Hurley, 2001; Mossio & Taraborelli, 2008; Stoffregen, 2004). However, at least a point is worth noting here. Without questioning the relevance of either approach, the reviewed findings suggest a new way to conceive the function of action in perception, indicating that the motor potentialities for action are intrinsically involved in constituting the "pragmatic" object invariants that make our primary ways to perceive objects possible, even in the absence of any effective movement toward them.

A Space for Action

The relevance of action in shaping range and content of perception is also evident in the case of peripersonal space constitution. Peripersonal space is usually defined as the space that encompasses objects within reach. It differs from personal (or cutaneous) space as well as from extra-personal (or far) space. The latter is the space outside the body, including objects that are beyond our immediate reach.

There is considerable evidence that the neural circuit involved in encoding peripersonal space is formed by two main nodes: area F4, which lies in the caudal-dorsal portion of the ventral premotor cortex, and the ventral intraparietal area (VIP), which occupies the deepest part of both banks of the intraparietal sulcus. Single neuron studies showed that in area VIP there are two main classes of neurons responding to sensory stimuli: purely visual neurons and bimodal, visual, and tactile neurons (Colby et al., 1993). Bimodal VIP neurons respond independently to both visual and tactile stimuli. Tactile receptive fields are located predominantly on the face. Tactile and visual receptive fields are usually in register; that is, the visual receptive field encompasses a 3D spatial region around the tactile receptive field. Some bimodal neurons are activated preferentially or even exclusively when 3D objects are moved toward or away from the tactile receptive field. About 30% of VIP neurons encode the surrounding space in reference to the monkey's body.

Single neurons studies showed that most F4 neurons discharge in association with monkey's active movements (Gentilucci et al., 1988). The movements more represented are head and arm movements, such as head orientation toward or away from stimuli and arm reaching. Most F4 neurons also respond to sensory stimuli. As neurons in VIP, F4 sensory-driven neurons can be subdivided into two classes: unimodal, purely somatosensory neurons, and bimodal, somatosensory, and visual neurons (Fogassi et al., 1992, 1996a,b; Gentilucci et al., 1988). Tactile receptive fields, typically large, are located on the face, chest, arm, and hand. Visual receptive fields are also large. They are located in register with the tactile ones, and similarly to VIP, confined to the peripersonal space (Fogassi et al., 1992, 1996a,b; Gentilucci et al., 1983, 1988; Graziano et al., 1994). Subsequently, trimodal neurons responding also to auditory stimuli were described in F4 (Graziano et al., 1999).

In most F4 neurons visual receptive fields do not change position with respect to the observer's body when the eyes move (Fogassi et al., 1992, 1996a,b; Gentilucci et al., 1983; Graziano et al., 1994). The visual responses of F4 neurons do not signal positions on the retina, but positions in space relative to the observer's body. The spatial coordinates of the visual receptive fields are anchored to different body parts, and not to a single frame of reference, and they are coded in egocentric coordinates (Fogassi et al., 1996 a,b). Furthermore, visual receptive fields located around a certain body part (e.g., the arm) move when that body part is moved (Graziano et al., 1997).

To better appreciate what kind of space VIP-F4 neurons encode, let us briefly compare them with the frontal eye field (FEF) and the lateral intraparietal (LIP) neurons. As it is well known, the FEF-LIP neurons control rapid eye movements (saccadic), whose function is to bring the fovea onto targets located at the periphery of the visual field. Like the VIP-F4 neurons, they respond to visual stimuli and discharge in relation to particular types of movement. However, no further similarities exist. In fact, the LIP-FEF neurons (1) respond to a visual stimulus independently of the distance at which it is located; (2) their visual receptive fields are retino-centric; (3) their motor properties concern eye movements only (see Andersen et al., 1997; Colby & Goldberg, 1999). On the other hand, the VIP-F4 neurons (1) are mostly bimodal and respond more strongly to 3D objects than to simple luminous stimuli; (2) their receptive fields are coded in somatic coordinates and anchored to various parts of the body; (3) last but not least, the visual stimuli must appear close to the body parts to which their visual and somatosensory receptive fields are anchored.

VIP-F4 and LIP-FEF encode different kinds of spaces: peripersonal and extrapersonal space, respectively, typically also called near and far space. This distinction has been corroborated by a series of studies on deficits following lesions of FEF and F4 in the monkey. Unilateral lesion of the ventral premotor cortex impairs reaching movements and, even more interestingly, produces neglect for visual and tactile stimuli appearing in the contralateral near space (Fogassi et al., 2001; Rizzolatti et al., 1983; Schieber, 2000). Lesion of FEF prevents the monkey from moving its eyes toward the visual stimuli presented in the contralateral far space, whereas does not produce any deficit in the contralateral near space (Li et al., 1999; Rizzolatti et al., 1983; Wardak et al., 2004).

A similar distinction between near and far space has been observed in human patients affected by spatial neglect. In a reported case, the patients' neglect was more severe in their peripersonal space than in their extrapersonal space (Halligan & Marshall, 1991; see also Berti & Frassinetti, 2000; Rizzolatti, Berti, & Gallese 2000). The opposite form of neglect was also recorded, in which the impairment of the patients' extrapersonal space was much more severe than that of their peripersonal space (Cowey et al., 1994; see also Cowey et al., 1999; Frassinetti et al., 2001; Vuillemieur et al., 1998).

Overall, these data indicate that the defining properties of peripersonal space consist in its being multisensory (i.e., based on the integration of visual, tactile, auditory, and proprioceptive information), body-centered (encoded not in retinal, but in somatic coordinates), and motor in nature. Regarding the latter, however, the motor constitution of the peripersonal space cannot be accounted for in terms of mere bodily movements, because it is intrinsically action dependent. Indeed, both the multisensory character and the body centeredness of peripersonal space can be fully understood only in relation to the possibility to act. It is such possibility to act that enables us to grasp not only the nearness of the surrounding things, but also the dynamic plasticity that characterizes peripersonal space as action space and distinguishes it from any other form of space.

Empirical evidence in favor of the dynamic plasticity and action dependence of peripersonal space comes from a large number of studies in nonhuman primates and humans. Fogassi et al. (1996a) showed that the visual receptive field extension of F4 neurons increases in depth when the speed of an approaching stimulus also increases. The advantage of this dynamic mapping of space is quite obvious: The earlier the neuron discharges, the earlier the motor act it codes is evoked. This enables an efficient mapping of what is really near, thus permitting the animal to either take advantage of an opportunity or avoid a threat. Similar results are found in humans. Chieffi et al. (1992) asked subjects to reach for and grasp a sphere approaching them; across different trials the speed of the object was varied. When object speed was higher, participants moved their forelimb earlier in time and farther than at lower speed.

Further evidence comes from several studies on how tool use can extend the multi-sensory coding of peripersonal space into extrapersonal space. In a seminal experiment, Iriki et al. (1996; see also Ishibashi et al., 2000) showed that the visual receptive fields of monkey's parietal neurons can be modified by actions involving tool use. They trained monkeys to retrieve pieces of food with a small rake, and found that when the instrument was used repeatedly, the visual receptive fields anchored to the hand expanded to encompass the space around both the hand and the rake. If the animal stopped using the rake but continued to hold it, visual receptive fields shrank back to their normal extension.

Analogous results have been found in healthy (Maravita et al., 2002) and brain-damaged humans. Line-bisection studies on patients with selective neglect for the hemi-space close to (or far from) their body indicate that tool use might reduce or increase the neglect according to the status of the line to be bisected (reachable or out-of-reach) in relation to tool use. Such dynamical remapping is modulated both by the planned motor act and by tactile and visual feedback received during act execution (Ackroyd et al., 2002; Berti & Frassinetti, 2000; Neppi-Mòdona et al., 2007; Pegna et al., 2001). Finally, studies on patients with visuo-tactile extinction selectively confined to the space close to one hand showed that the severity of the extinction can be modified by tool use, which extends the reach of hand actions (Farnè & Làdavas, 2000; Maravita et al., 2001). This extension has been demonstrated to be tightly related to the functionally effective length of the tool (Farnè et al., 2005).

Both the electrophysiological and neuropsychological findings highlight that peripersonal space constitutively is an action space, with its boundaries defined by the effective reach of our motor acts (see Rizzolatti et al. 1997). To paraphrase Merleau-Ponty, the peripersonal space is "not a sort of ether in which all things float," and its varying range has to be construed in terms of "the varying range of our aims and our gestures" (1962, p. 243). As in the case of object perception, the action-dependence of peripersonal space does not involve the effective execution of movements, but it is revealed by the potentialities for action that shape the content of our perception of objects within reach even when we are not actually acting upon them.

Mirroring and Making Sense of Others

The tight relationship between action and perception is also evident at the level of the observed motor behavior of others. Single-cell recordings in the ventral premotor cortex (area F5) of macaque monkeys revealed the existence of a set of motor neurons (mirror neurons) discharging both during the execution and the observation of goal-directed movements (Gallese et al., 1996; Rizzolatti et al., 1996). Further experiments discovered neurons with similar properties in sectors (areas PF/PFG) of the inferior parietal lobule

(Fogassi et al., 2005; Gallese et al., 2002; Nelissen et al., 2005; Rozzi et al., 2008) reciprocally connected with area F5 (Rizzolatti & Luppino, 2001; Rozzi et al., 2008).

The relevance of these findings stems from the fact that, for the first time, a neural mechanism mapping the sensory description of an action onto its motor cortical representation has been identified. Solid evidence shows that the specific type of sensory-to-motor direct mapping enabled by mirror neurons goes far beyond the mere kinematic features of movement, because it occurs at the level of the motor goal–relatedness shared by the actively executed and the only imagined (Umiltà et al., 2001) or heard (Kohler et al., 2002) motor acts of someone else.

In a recent paper, Rochat et al. (2010) show that F5 mirror neurons respond to the execution and observation of motor acts—grasping objects—regardless of the effector (hand or pliers) and the movements required to accomplish the goal. In this experiment, mirror neurons activity was recorded during the observation and execution of grasping performed with the hand and with reverse pliers. The latter, tool-mediated grasp, requires opposite movements of the hand (fingers opening vs. fingers closing) with respect to natural grasping with the bare hand. In a third condition mirror neurons were recorded during the observation of an experimenter spearing objects with a stick. Virtually all neurons responding to the observation of hand grasping also respond to the observation of grasping with pliers and, many of them to the observation of spearing with a stick. Thus, what counts in triggering grasping mirror neurons is the identity of the goal (e.g., taking possession of an object) even when achieved with different effectors, controlled by means of different finger movements.

The study of Rochat et al. (2010) also demonstrates two important properties of F5 mirror neurons. The intensity of the discharge of the entire population of mirror neurons is significantly stronger during action execution than action observation. This means that the mirror mechanism is also sensitive to the issue of *who* is the agent. Also, the intensity and onset of mirror neurons response during hand and tools grasping observation correlates with the monkey's motor expertise. The strongest discharge and its earliest onset occurr during hand grasping observation, whereas the smallest and the latest during the observation of spearing.

Rochat et al. (2010) propose that grasping mirror neurons in area F5 map the goal of the observed motor act while simultaneously reflecting the reliability of this information with respect to the motor experience of the observing individual, by means of the intensity of their discharge.

Quite consistent are the results of a recent TMS study on humans in which motor evoked potentials (MEPs) were recorded from the observers' opponens pollicis during the observation of grasping performed with normal and reverse pliers (Cattaneo et al., 2009). The amplitude of the recorded MEPs is modulated by the goal of the observed motor act regardless of the movements required to accomplish it.

Functional magnetic resonance imaging evidence in humans shows that posterior parietal and ventral premotor areas, part of the network showing mirror mechanism-like functional properties, are activated by the observation of hand goal–related motor acts, when accomplished by a non-anthropomorphic robotic arm (Gazzola et al., 2007a), or when the observers are congenitally upper limb deficient, and thus could never practice hand grasping (Gazzola et al., 2007b). In the latter case, in the brain of the two patients the observed hand grasping maps onto the motor representations of mouth and foot grasping. All three motor representations, when activated, lead to the accomplishment of the same motor goal; hence their relative interchangeability when the motor goal of an observed motor act must be mapped and understood. In humans the parieto-premotor mirror mechanism can generalize motor goals also when relying—like in the monkey—on action sounds through the auditory channel (Gazzola et al., 2006). A similar functional property was also revealed in congenitally blind patients (Ricciardi et al., 2009).

Finally, a recent TMS adaptation study confirms the specific role of the motor system in generating a context-independent mapping of motor goal relatedness. Such a property appears to be absent in extrastriate visual areas sensitive to the observation of biological motion (Cattaneo et al., 2010). The intentional character of behavior as it is mapped by the cortical motor system enables a direct appreciation of purpose without relying on explicit inference. Indeed, an fMRI study by Brass et al. (2007) shows that when the observed goal-related motor act is unusual—like switching on the light with a knee—no matter if plausible (hands occupied) or not (hands free), it always leads to the activation of the mirroring mechanism.

Studies carried out in monkeys (Bonini et al., 2010; Fogassi et al., 2005) and humans (Cattaneo et al., 2009; Iacoboni et al., 2005) show that the mirror mechanism instantiated by parieto-premotor areas can also map basic motor intentions, such as eating, drinking, and putting objects away. This higher level of motor abstraction generates the possibility of executing, hence also of recognizing in the perceptual domain, an orderly sequence of motor acts appropriately chained to accomplish a distal goal. When such a level of motor mapping is present, motor behavior can be described at a higher level of abstraction, without implying an explicit language-mediated conceptualization. From the single-motor goal (e.g., grasping) we move up to the level of the goal hierarchy (e.g., grasping for eating) characterizing a whole motor action as such.

In the section on the pragmatic nature of peripersonal space, we stressed that its extension is produced by and therefore reflects our potentiality for action. Such potentiality for action has been recently shown to modulate the discharge of F5 mirror neurons during action observation (Caggiano et al., 2009). About half of recorded neurons respond to action observation only when the observed agent acts either inside or outside monkey's peripersonal space. Such modulation, however, doesn't simply measure the physical distance between agent and observer. A consistent percentage of mirror neurons not responding to the experimenter's grasping actions carried out near to the monkey resume firing when a transparent barrier is interposed between the object target of the action and the observing monkey. Blocking the monkey's potentiality for action on the target of the action of someone else remaps the spatial location of the observed agent according to a system of coordinates dictated by and expressing the monkey's relational potentiality for interaction.

The same potentiality for interaction most likely also explains the mirroring properties of bimodal neurons recorded in the VIP by Ishida et al. (2010). Body-centered visuotactile bimodal neurons exhibited visual responses to stimuli presented within the peripersonal space of equivalent body parts of the experimenter facing the monkey. Although motor responses have not been described by Ishida et al. (2009), area VIP is reciprocally connected with premotor area F4. As mentioned, F4 neurons' peripersonal visuo-tactile receptive fields are defined by the potentiality for action of the body parts to which they are dynamically anchored. It is likely that the mirroring visual responses of VIP neurons can be accounted for in motor terms.

Concluding Remarks

We presented neuroscientific evidence shedding new light on a variety of cognitive aspects of our daily life such as planning and controlling purposeful behavior, perceiving a world of objects that are primarily given to us as a virtual pole of potential interactive relations, the representation of the surrounding space, as the space of *our* own potentialities for action, and the possibility of seeing external moving physical bodies as acting bodies like us.

The main point of the present chapter is to show that all of these aspects of our cognitive nature find a minimal level of explanation only when considering how the cortical motor system is functionally organized and works. Our rich and complex social life is possible because most of the basic elements of the experience we make of what surrounds us (including other living bodies) are shared by all the members of our social consortium. Many of our direct social interactions are defined according to action-centered spatial coordinates. The same coordinates enable us to map the intentional relations of others as governed by the same spatial rules. All of these shared properties are shared at the level of the cortical motor system. Our behavior and the behavior of others can now be described and understood in a more refined way. By activating through mirroring a motor goal or a motor intention in the observers, others' behavior becomes intentionally graspable. This basic level of sense-making in social interactions is currently the most important cognitive expressions of the motor system as understood by neuroscience.

Of course this is only one part of the story. We described the cortical motor system without taking into account emotions and affects. Our actions are almost never divorced by the sense of emotionally charged personal involvement with the situation. It is indeed very important to investigate how these different dimensions interact at the level of the brain, in order to have research scenarios much closer to the *explanandum*, real life. Nevertheless, emotions and affects can be fully understood only when considering the role of the cortical motor functional organization in making sense of our and others' behavior.

NOTE

1. Both in terms of inherited behavioral schemata and of learned ones.

REFERENCES

Ackroyd K., Riddoch, M. J., Humphreys, G. W., Nightingale, S., & Townsend, S. (2002). Widening the sphere of influence: Using a tool to extend extrapersonal visual space in a patient with severe neglect. *Neurocase, 8,* 1–12.

Andersen, R. A., Snyder, L. H., Bradley, D. C., & Xing, J. (1997). Multimodal representation of space in the posterior parietal cortex and its use in planning movements. *Annual Review of Neuroscience, 20,* 303–330.

Berti, A., & Frassinetti, F. (2000). When far becomes near: Remapping of space by tool use. *Journal of Cognitive Neuroscience 12,* 415–420.

Bonini, L., Rozzi, S., Serventi, F. U., Simone, L., Ferrari, P. F., & Fogassi, L. (2010). Ventral premotor and inferior parietal cortices make distinct contribution to action organization and intention understanding. *Cerebral Cortex, 20,* 1372–1385.

Brass, M., Schmitt, R. M., Spengler, S., & Gergely. G. (2007). Investigating action understanding: inferential processes versus action simulation. *Current Biology, 17,* 2117–2121.

Buccino, G., Sato, M., Cattaneo, L., Rodà, F., & Riggio, L. (2009). Broken affordances, broken objects: A TMS study. *Neuropsychologia, 47,* 3074–3078.

Caggiano, V., Fogassi, L., Rizzolatti, G., Their, P., & Casile, A. (2009). Mirror neurons differentially encode the peripersonal and extrapersonal space of monkeys. *Science, 324,* 403–406.

Cattaneo, L., Sandrini, M., & Schwarzbach, J. (2010). State-dependent TMS reveals a hierarchical representation of observed acts in the temporal, parietal, and premotor cortices. *Cerebral Cortex, 20,* 2252–2258.

Cattaneo, L., Caruana, F., Jezzini, A., & Rizzolatti, G. (2009) Representation of goal and movements without overt motor behavior in the human motor cortex: A transcranial magnetic stimulation study. *Journal of Neuroscience, 29,* 11134–11138.

Chao, L. L., & Martin, A. (2000). Representation of manipulable man-made objects in the dorsal stream. *Neuroimage, 12,* 478–484.

Chieffi, S., Fogassi, L., Gallese, V., & Gentilucci, M. (1992). Prehension movements directed to approaching objects: Influence of stimulus velocity on the transport and the grasp components. *Neuropsychologia, 30,* 877–897.

Colby, C. L., & Goldberg, M. E. (1999). Space and attention in parietal cortex. *Annual Review of Neuroscience, 22,* 319–349.

Colby, C. L., Duhamel, J.-R., & Goldberg, M. E. (1993). Ventral intraparietal area of the macaque: Anatomic location and visual response properties. *Journal of Neurophysiology, 69,* 902–914.

Cowey, A., Small, M., & Ellis, S. (1994). Left visuo-spatial neglect can be worse in far than near space. *Neuropsychologia, 32,* 1059–1066.

Cowey, A., Small, M., & Ellis, S. (1999). No abrupt change in visual hemineglect from near to far space. *Neuropsychologia, 37,* 1–6.

Craighero, L., Fadiga, L., Rizzolatti, G., & Umiltà, C. (1999). Action for perception: A motor-visual attentional effect. *The Journal of Experimental Psychology: Human Perception and Performance, 25,* 1673–1692.

Cutting, J. E., & Koslowski, L. T. (1997). Recognizing friends by their walk: Gait perceptions without familiarity cues. *Bulletin of the Psychonomic Society, 9*, 353–356.

Ellis, R., & Tucker, M. (2000). Micro-affordance: The potentiation of components of action by seen objects. *British Journal of Psychology, 91*, 451–471.

Farnè, A., & Làdavas, E. (2000). Dynamic size-change of hand peripersonal space following tool use. *Neuroreport, 11*, 1645–1649.

Farné, A., Iriki, A., & Làdavas, E. (2005). Shaping multisensory action-space with tools: Evidence from patients with cross-modal extinction. *Neuropsychologia, 43*, 238–248.

Fogassi, L., Gallese, V., Di Pellegrino, G., Fadiga, L., Gentilucci, M., Luppino, G., et al. (1992). Space coding by premotor cortex. *Experimental Brain Research, 89*, 686–690.

Fogassi, L., Gallese, V., Fadiga, L., Luppino, G., Matelli, M., & Rizzolatti, G. (1996a). Coding of peripersonal space in inferior premotor cortex (area F4). *Journal of Neurophysiology, 76*, 141–157.

Fogassi, L., Gallese, V., Fadiga, L., & Rizzolatti, G. (1996b). Space coding in inferior premotor cortex (area F4): Facts and speculations. In F. Lacquaniti, & P. Viviani (Eds.), *NATO ASI Series: Multi-Sensory Control of Movement* (pp. 99–120). Dordrecht: Kluwer.

Fogassi, L., Gallese, V., Buccino, G., Craighero, L., Fadiga, L., & Rizzolatti, G. (2001). Cortical mechanism for the visual guidance of hand grasping movements in the monkey: A reversible inactivation study. *Brain, 124*, 571–586.

Fogassi, L., Ferrari, P. F., Gesierich, B., Rozzi, S., Chersi, F., & Rizzolatti, G. (2005). Parietal lobe: From action organization to intention understanding. *Science, 302*, 662–667.

Frassinetti, F., Rossi, M., & Làdavas, E. (2001). Passive limb movements improve visual neglect. *Neuropsychologia, 39*, 725–733.

Gallese, V. (2000). The inner sense of action: agency and motor representations. *Journal of Consciousness Studies, 7*, 23–40.

Gallese, V., Keysers, C., & Rizzolatti, G. (2004). A unifying view of the basis of social cognition. *Trends Cognitive Sciences, 8*, 396–403.

Gallese, V., Fadiga, L., Fogassi, L., & Rizzolatti, G. (1996). Action recognition in the premotor cortex. *Brain, 119*, 593–609.

Gallese, V., Fadiga, L., Fogassi, L., & Rizzolatti, G. (2002). Action representation and the inferior parietal lobule. In Prinz, W., & Hommel, B. (Eds.), *Common Mechanisms in Perception and Action: Attention and Performance* (Vol. XIX, pp. 247–266). Oxford, UK: Oxford University Press.

Gallese, V., Rochat, M., Cossu, G., & Sinigaglia, C. (2009). Motor cognition and its role in the phylogeny and ontogeny of intentional understanding. *Developmental Psychology, 45*, 103–113.

Gazzola, V., Aziz-Zadeh, L., & Keysers, C. (2006) Empathy and the somatotopic auditory mirror system in humans. *Current Biology, 16*, 1824–1829.

Gazzola, V., Rizzolatti, G., Wicker, B., & Keysers, C. (2007a). The anthropomorphic brain: The mirror neuron system responds to human and robotic actions. *Neuroimage, 35*, 1674–1684.

Gazzola, V., van der Worp, H., Mulder, T., Wicker, B., Rizzolatti, G., & Keysers, C. (2007b). Aplasics born without hands mirror the goal of hand actions with their feet. *Current Biology, 17*, 1235–1240.

Gentilucci, M., Scandolara, C., Pigarev, I. N., & Rizzolatti, G. (1983). Visual responses in the postarcuate cortex (area 6) of the monkey that are independent of eye position. *Experimental Brain Research, 50*, 464–468.

Gentilucci, M., Fogassi, L., Luppino, G., Matelli, M., Camarda, R., & Rizzolatti, G. (1988). Functional organization of inferior area 6 in the macaque monkey: I. Somatotopy and the control of proximal movements. *Experimental Brain Research, 71*, 475–490.

Gibson, J. J. (Ed.) (1979). *The Ecological Approach to Visual Perception*. Boston: Houghton-Mifflin.

Grafton S. T., M. A. Arbib, L. Fadiga, & Rizzolatti, G. (1996). Localization of grasp representations in humans by PET: 2. Observation compared with imagination. *Experimental Brain Research, 112*, 103–111.

Graziano, M. S. A., Yap, G. S., & Gross, C. G. (1994). Coding of visual space by premotor neurons. *Science, 266*, 1054–1057.

Graziano, M. S. A., Hu, X., & Gross, C. G. (1997). Visuo-spatial properties of ventral premotor cortex. *Journal of Neurophysiology, 77*, 2268–2292.

Graziano, M. S. A., Reiss, L. A. J., & Gross, C. G. (1999). A neuronal representation of the location of nearby sounds. *Nature, 397*, 428–430.

Grèzes, J., Tucker, M., Armony, J., Ellis, R., & Passingham, R. E. (2003). Objects automatically potentiate action: An fMRI study of implicit processing. *European Journal of Neuroscience, 17*, 2735–2740.

Halligan, P. W., & Marshall J. C. (1991). Left neglect for near but not far space in man. *Nature, 350*, 498–500.

Heidegger, M. (1996). *Being and Time*. Albany: State University of New York Press.

Hepp-Reymond, M.-C., Hüsler, E. J., Maier, M. A., & Qi, H.-X. (1994). Force-related neuronal activity in two regions of the primate ventral premotor cortex. *Canadian Journal of Biochemistry and Physiology, 72*, 571–579.

Hurley, S. (2001). Perception and action: Alternative views. *Synthese, 129*, 3–40.

Iacoboni, M., Molnar-Szakacs, I., Gallese, V., Buccino, G., Mazziotta, J., & Rizzolatti, G. (2005). Grasping the intentions of others with one's owns mirror neuron system. *PLOS Biology, 3*, 529–535.

Iriki, A., Tanaka, M., & Iwamura, Y. (1996). Coding of modified body schema during tool use by macaque postcentral neurones. *Neuroreport, 7*, 2325–2330.

Ishibashi, H., Hihara, S., & Iriki, A. (2000) Acquisition and development of monkey tool-use: Behavioral and kinematic analyses. *Canadian Journal of Biochemistry and Physiology, 78*, 958–966.

Ishida, H., Nakajima, K., Inase, M., & Murata, A. (2010). Shared mapping of own and others' bodies in visuotactile bimodal area of monkey parietal cortex. *Journal of Cognitive Neuroscience, 22*, 83–96.

Jeannerod, M., Arbib, M. A., Rizzolatti, G., & Sakata, H. (1995). Grasping objects: The cortical mechanisms of visuomotor transformation. *Trends in Neuroscience, 18*, 314–320.

Kohler, E., Keysers, C., Umiltà, M. A., Fogassi, L., Gallese, V., & Rizzolatti, G. (2002). Hearing sounds, understanding actions: Action representation in mirror neurons. *Science 297*, 846–848.

Kurata, K., & Tanji, J. (1986). Premotor cortex neurons in macaques: Activity before distal and proximal forelimb movements. *Journal of Neuroscience, 6*, 403–411.

Li, C.-S. R., Mazzoni, P., & Andersen, R. A. (1999). Effect of reversible inactivation of macaque lateral intraparietal area on visual and memory saccades. *Journal of Neurophysiology, 81*, 1827–1838.

MacKay, D. G. (1987). *The Organization of Perception and Action.* New York: Springer.

Maravita, A., Husain, M., Clarke, K., & Driver, J. (2001). Reaching with a tool extends visual-tactile interactions into far space: Evidence from cross-modal extinction. *Neuropsychologia, 39,* 580–585.

Maravita, A., Spence, C., Kennet, S., & Driver, J. (2002). Tool use changes multimodal spatial interactions between vision and touch in normal humans. *Cognition, 83,* 25–34.

Matelli, M., Luppino, G., & Rizzolatti, G. (1985). Patterns of cytochrome oxidase activity in the frontal agranular cortex of the macaque monkey. *Behavioral Brain Research, 18,* 125–137.

Merleau-Ponty, M. (1962). *The Phenomenology of Perception.* C. Smith (Trans.). London: Routledge and Kegan Paul.

Michaels, C. F., & Carello, C. (1981). *Direct Perception.* Englewood Cliffs, NJ: Prentice-Hall.

Mossio, M., & Taraborelli, D. (2008). Action-dependent perceptual invariants: From ecological to sensoimotor approaches. *Consciousness and Cognition, 17,* 1324–1340.

Murata, A., Fadiga, L., Fogassi, L., Gallese, V., Raos, V., & Rizzolatti, G. (1997). Object representation in the ventral premotor cortex (Area F5) of the monkey. *Journal of Neurophysiology, 78,* 2226–2230.

Murata, A., Gallese, V., Luppino, G., Kaseda, M., & Sakata, H. (2000) Selectivity for the shape, size and orientation of objects in the hand-manipulation-related neurons in the anterior intraparietal (AIP) area of the macaque. *Journal of Neurophysiology, 83,* 2580–2601.

Mountcastle, V. B. (1995). The parietal system and some higher brain functions. *Cerebral Cortex, 5,* 377–390.

Nelissen, K., Luppino, G., Vanduffel, W., Rizzolatti, G., & Orban, G. A. (2005). Observing others: Multiple action representation in the frontal lobe. *Science, 310,* 332–336.

Neppi-Mòdona, M., Rabuffetti, M., Folegatti, A., Ricci, R., Spinazzola, L., Schiavone, F., et al. (2007), Bisecting lines with different tools in right brain damaged patients: The role of action programming and sensory feedback in modulating spatial remapping. *Cortex, 43,* 397–410.

Noë, A. (2004). *Action in Perception.* Cambridge, MA: MIT Press.

O'Regan, J. K., & Noë, A. (2001). A sensorimotor account of vision and visual consciousness. *Behavioral and Brain Sciences, 24,* 939–1031.

Pegna, A. J., Petit, L., Caldara-Schnetzer, A. S., Khateb, A., Annoni, J. M., Sztajzel, R., et al. (2001). So near yet so far: Neglect in far or near space depends on tool use. *Annals of Neurology, 50,* 820–822.

Philipona, D., O'Regan, J. K., & Nadal, J.-P. (2003). Is there something out there? Inferring space from sensorimotor dependencies. *Neural Computation, 15,* 9.

Phillips, J. A., Humphreys, G. W., Noppeney, U., & Price, C. J. (2002) The neural substrates of action retrieval: An examination of semantic and visual routes to action. *Visual Cognition, 9,* 662–685.

Phillips, J. A., & Ward, R. (2002). SR correspondence effects of irrelevant visual affordance: Time course and specificity of response activation. *Visual Cognition, 9,* 540–558.

Raos, V., Umilta, M. A., Fogassi, L., & Gallese, V. (2006). Functional properties of grasping-related neurons in the ventral premotor area F5 of the macaque monkey. *Journal of Neurophysiology, 95,* 709–729.

Reed, E. S. (1996). *Encountering the World: Toward an Ecological Psychology.* New York: Oxford University Press.

Ricciardi, E., Bonino, D., Sani, L., Vecchi, T., Guazzelli, M., Haxby, J. V., et al. (2009). Do we really need vision? How blind people "see" the actions of others. *Journal of Neuroscience, 29,* 9719–9724.

Rizzolatti, G., Craighero, L. (2004). The mirror neuron system. *Annual Review of Neuroscience, 27,* 169–192.

Rizzolatti, G., & Fadiga, L. (1998). Grasping objects and grasping action meanings: The dual role of monkey rostroventral premotor cortex (area F5). *Novartis Found Symposium, 218,* 81–95.

Rizzolatti, G., & Luppino, G. (2001). The cortical motor system. *Neuron, 31,* 889–901.

Rizzolatti, G., & Sinigaglia, C. (2010). The functional role of the parieto-frontal mirror circuit: Interpretations and misinterpretations. *Nature Reviews Neuroscience, 11,* 264–274.

Rizzolatti, G., & Sinigaglia, C. (2008). *Mirrors in the Brain. How Our Minds Share Actions, Emotions, and Experience.* Oxford, UK: Oxford University Press.

Rizzolatti, G., Berti, A., & Gallese, V. (2000). Spatial neglect: Neurophysiological bases, cortical circuits and theories. In F. Boller, J. Grafman, & G. Rizzolatti (Eds.), *Handbook of Neuropsychology* (2nd ed., vol. I, pp. 503–537). Amsterdam: Elsevier Science B.V.

Rizzolatti, G., Fogassi, L., & Gallese, V. (2000). Cortical mechanisms subserving object grasping and action recognition: A new view on the cortical motor functions. In M. S.Gazzaniga, editor in chief), *The New Cognitive Neurosciences* (2nd ed., pp. 539–552). Cambridge, MA: MIT Press.

Rizzolatti G., Fogassi L., & Gallese V. (2001). Neurophysiological mechanisms underlying the understanding and imitation of action. *Nature Neuroscience Reviews, 2,* 661–670.

Rizzolatti, G., Fogassi, L., & Gallese, V. (2004). Cortical mechanisms subserving object grasping, action understanding and imitation. In M. S.Gazzaniga (editor in chief), *The New Cognitive Neurosciences* (3rd ed., pp. 427–440). Cambridge, MA: MIT Press.

Rizzolatti, G., Matelli, M., & Pavesi, G. (1983). Deficits in attention and movement following the removal of postarcuate (area 6) and prearcuate (area 8) cortex in macaque monkeys. *Brain, 106,* 655–673.

Rizzolatti, G., Fadiga, L., Gallese, V., & Fogassi, L. (1996). Premotor cortex and the recognition of motor actions. *Cognitive Brain Research, 3,* 131–141.

Rizzolatti, G., Fadiga, L., Fogassi, L., & Gallese, V. (1997). The space around us. *Science, 277,* 190–191.

Rizzolatti, G., Scandolara, C., Matelli, M., & Gentilucci, M. (1981). Afferent properties of periarcuate neurons in macaque monkey. II. Visual responses. *Behavioral Brain Research, 2,* 147–163.

Rizzolatti, G., Camarda, R., Fogassi, M., Gentilucci, M., Luppino, G., & Matelli M. (1988). Functional organization of inferior area 6 in the macaque monkey: II. Area F5 and the control of distal movements. *Experimental Brain Research, 71,* 491–507.

Rochat, M. J., Caruana, F., Jezzini, A., Escola, L., Intskirveli, I., Grammont, F., et al. (2010). Responses of mirror neurons in area F5 to hand and tool grasping observation. *Experimental Brain Research, 204,* 605–616.

Rozzi, S., Ferrari, P. F., Bonini, L., Rizzolatti, G., & Fogassi, L. (2008). Functional organization of inferior parietal lobule convexity in the macaque monkey: Electrophysiological characterization of motor, sensory and mirror responses and their correlation with cytoarchitectonic areas. *European Journal of Neuroscience, 28,* 1569–1588.

Schieber, M. H. (2000). Inactivation of the ventral premotor cortex biases the laterality of motoric choices. *Experimental Brain Research, 130*, 497–507.

Stoffregen, T. A. (2004). Breadth and limits of the affordance concept. *Ecological Psychology, 16*, 79–85.

Tucker, M., & Ellis, R. (1998). On the relations between seen objects and components of potential actions. *The Journal of Experimental Psychology: Human Perception and Performance, 24*, 830–846.

Tucker, M., & Ellis, R. (2001). The potentiation of grasp types during visual object categorization. *Visual Cognition, 8*, 769–800.

Tucker, M., & Ellis, R. (2004). Action priming by briefly presented objects. *Acta Psychologia (Amst), 116*(2), 185–203.

Umiltà, M. A., Kohler, E., Gallese, V., et al. (2001). "I know what you are doing": A neurophysiological study. *Neuron, 32*, 91–101.

Umiltà, M. A., Brochier, T., Spinks, R. L., & Lemon, R. N. (2007). Simultaneous recording of macaque premotor and primary motor cortex neuronal populations reveals different functional contributions to visuomotor grasp. *Journal of Neurophysiology, 98*, 488–501.

Umiltà, M. A., Escola, L., Intskirveli, I., Grammont, F., Rochat, M., Caruana, F., et al. (2008). How pliers become fingers in the monkey motor system. *Proceedings of the National Academy of Sciences, 105*, 2209–2213.

Vuillemieur, P., Valenza, N., Mayer, E., Reverdin, A., & Landis, T. (1998). Near and far space in unilateral neglect. *Annals of Neurology, 43*, 406–410.

Wardak, C., Olivier, E., & Duhamel, J. R. (2004). A deficit in covert attention after parietal cortex inactivation in the monkey. *Neuron, 42*, 501–508.

11 Early Sensitivity to Emotion Cues: Precursors of Social Referencing?
Stefanie Hoehl

IN OUR EVALUATION of the environment we are strongly affected by emotional cues we receive from others. This is particularly the case when we encounter a novel or ambiguous situation. Others' expressions help us to discern whether a situation entails danger and how to behave in an unfamiliar context. Infants are constantly faced with situations and objects, which, for them, are novel. In numerous studies it has been shown that infants show "social referencing" behavior by the end of the first year. That is, when faced with a novel object, infants by 9 to 12 months of age search for emotional signals from adults and adjust their behavior toward the object in accordance with the adults' emotional, facial, and vocal expressions (Hertenstein & Campos, 2004; Hornik, et al., 1987; Moses, et al., 2001; Mumme & Fernald, 2003). Infants' responses depend on referential information and cannot be solely explained by emotional contagion. For instance, infants do not alter their behavior toward an object if the adult expressing an emotion is out of sight, and they actively search for referential information if it is not clearly given (Moses, et al., 2001). Furthermore, infants adjust their behavior only toward target objects and not toward simultaneously presented distracters (Hertenstein & Campos, 2004; Hornik, et al., 1987; Mumme & Fernald, 2003).

These findings have been replicated using various settings and stimuli. However, the developmental onset and social-cognitive prerequisites of social referencing remain largely unknown. The earliest accounts of social referencing behavior in a classic paradigm using vocal emotion cues have been reported at 8.5 months (Campos, et al., 2003). Younger infants can hardly be tested using classic paradigms because of their limited motor abilities and memory capacities. However, even younger infants may be capable of social-cognitive functions contributing to social referencing. Because social referencing is a very complex behavior, it likely follows a gradual developmental trajectory rather than a sudden onset by the end of the first year.

Full-fledged social referencing entails (1) seeking information from adults in novel or ambiguous situations, (2) associating the referent with the social message, and (3) regulating behavior in response to the provided information (Feinman, et al., 1992). In order to show this complex behavior, infants must be able to discern different emotional expressions and understand their respective meanings or at least their valence. Infants must also be able to follow referential signals such as eye gaze and understand that an adult's emotional expression refers to the cued object, person, or situation. In this chapter I outline that both sensitivity to emotional expressions and gaze following can be observed very early in development. New evidence suggests that even 3-month-old infants' attention toward an unfamiliar object is enhanced by an adult's frightened expression that is directed toward the object (Hoehl, et al., 2008b). However, these early abilities may initially be based on automatic neural mechanisms and subcortical processing pathways. More sophisticated and controlled processes presumably underlie social referencing behavior by the end of the first year. I summarize recent research on early basic abilities and later more elaborate skills and discuss which neural networks may underlie the observed developmental changes.

Infants' Attention toward Referential Emotional Expressions

Infants are able to discriminate emotional facial expressions already in the first months after birth (Leppänen & Nelson, 2006). However, discrimination may be based on a merely perceptual comparison of low-level differences between stimuli and does not necessarily imply an understanding of the underlying emotion. Recent findings suggest that infants' attention is affected by emotional expressions depending on the referent of the expression.

In an event-related potential study, 7-month-old infants responded with an increased negative central (Nc) component to angry faces who directed eye gaze straight at them compared with angry faces with eye gaze averted to the side (Hoehl & Striano, 2008). The Nc is a midlatency component on frontocentral channels that has been associated with attention allocation (Reynolds & Richards, 2005). Enhanced Nc amplitude is usually taken to signal enhanced attention allocation toward a salient stimulus. Thus, infants showed increased attention for angry faces directing gaze toward them.

In the same study, infants did not show different brain responses for fearful faces with direct and averted gaze. It is possible that fearful faces with direct eye gaze and gaze averted to the side are too ambiguous with respect to the referent of the expression. Whereas an angry face with direct gaze is an immediate indicator of threat for the self, a fearful face may become more salient if it is directed toward a concrete source of threat in the environment. We tested this hypothesis in another study with 7-month-old infants (Hoehl, et al., 2008a). Infants showed an increased Nc for fearful faces looking toward an object next to the face compared with neutral faces looking toward an object and fearful faces looking straight ahead. This finding suggests that fearful faces are particularly salient for infants when they indicate a concrete source of potential threat in the environment. This shows that fearful faces are processed depending on the social context by 7 months of age. The same effect was found in 6-month-olds, but not in 3-month-old infants (Hoehl & Striano, 2010). Nine-month-olds are more attentive to fearful faces than to neutral faces regardless of gaze direction and context (Hoehl & Striano, 2010). This fits nicely with results showing that enhanced attention to fearful faces emerges between 5 and 7 months of age (Peltola, et al., 2009). Interestingly, this effect can be found even in younger infants when happy faces are presented. Using a very similar paradigm with 3-month-olds, an increased Nc was found for happy versus neutral faces looking toward an object, but not if eye gaze was directed toward empty space (Hoehl & Striano, 2009). Presumably the effect can be found earlier with happy faces because these are more familiar for very young infants. In the first months infants most frequently perceive positive expressions, and only by 7 to 8 months are they confronted more and more frequently with negative expressions as they start to locomote and put themselves into dangerous situations more often (Campos, et al., 2000). Correspondingly, happy expressions are most consistently discriminated from other expressions in the first months (Leppänen & Nelson, 2006) and even shortly after birth (Farroni et al., 2007).

To conclude, even very young infants do not only discriminate emotional expressions based on low-level perceptual differences. There is converging evidence that infants are sensitive to referential gaze cues when processing an emotional facial expression (see summary in Table 11.1). In particular, infants' attention to happy and fearful faces is enhanced when the face is looking toward an immediate referent in the environment. An angry face, in contrast, seems to be most salient when directing gaze toward the infant.

TABLE 11.1

Summary of results by Hoehl & Striano (2008, 2009, 2010) and Hoehl et al. (2008a)

Age Group	Sensitivity to Referential Emotional Expressions
3 months	Increased attention for happy vs. neutral faces looking toward an object, no effect for fearful vs. neutral faces
6–7 months	Increased attention for fearful vs. neutral faces looking toward an object and for angry faces looking straight ahead vs. to the side
9 months	Increased attention for fearful vs. neutral faces regardless of gaze direction and referent

Effects of Emotional Expressions and Eye Gaze on Young Infants' Object Processing

The studies reviewed here thus far have shown that even young infants process emotional facial expressions and gaze direction in conjunction. Infants' attention toward faces is affected by gaze direction and the presence or absence of objects as referents of the expression. However, is young infants' processing of novel objects also affected by emotional expressions?

We presented 3-month-old infants with neutral and fearful faces gazing toward small colorful objects next to the face (Hoehl, et al., 2008b). Then face and object disappeared for a short amount of time and the object reappeared in the middle of the screen alone. Infants showed an increased Nc amplitude for objects that were previously gaze-cued by a fearful face. This effect was not found if a different object followed the face plus object stimulus or if the face did not look toward the object. Furthermore, infants showed the effect only for fearful faces, but not for happy faces (Hoehl & Striano, 2009). In sum, infants responded with increased attention specifically to those objects that were gaze-cued by a fearful face. Thus, infants by 3 months show referential specificity when processing novel objects in the context of a fearful face.

We also tested 6-month-olds and 9-moth-olds using the same paradigm and stimuli (Hoehl & Striano, 2010). Six-month-olds showed the same effect as the younger infants and responded with an increased Nc for objects that were gaze-cued by a fearful face. No effect was found in the control condition in which faces directed eye gaze away from the objects. Nine-month-olds, in contrast, showed an increased Nc for objects that were gaze-cued by a neutral face compared to a fearful face. Again, no effect was found when faces averted eye gaze away from the objects, suggesting that infants in this age group also acquired information from the adult's gaze direction. Around 9 months of age social referencing can first be observed on a behavioral level (Campos, et al., 2003). Between 9 and 12 months a number of social cognitive skills and joint attention indices can be observed more and more robustly and more frequently (Carpenter, et al., 1998). Whereas 3- and 6-month-olds' responses may reflect relatively automatic processes of attention allocation in response to emotionally salient stimuli, 9-month-olds' responses may be indicative of more elaborate processing (see summary in Table 11.2). What neural systems may underlie the observed results?

Neural Processes Involved in Infants' Attention to Emotional Stimuli

The amygdala is a crucial structure for emotion processing in adults (Adolphs, 2002). Importantly, the amygdala is also involved in social learning processes (Hooker, et al., 2006) and in particular in social learning of fear (Olsson & Phelps, 2007). It is conceivable that the amygdala is involved in the processing of fearful faces and social learning

TABLE 11.2

Summary of results by Carver & Vaccaro (2007), Hoehl et al. (2008b), and Hoehl & Striano (2010)

Age Group	Effects of Emotional Expression on Infants' Aattention Toward Objects
3 months	Increased attention for toy objects cued by a fearful vs. neutral face; no effect for noncued objects
6 months	Increased attention for toy objects cued by a fearful vs. neutral face; no effect for noncued objects
9 months	Increased attention for toy objects cued by a neutral vs. fearful face; no effect for noncued objects
12 months	Increased attention for ambiguous objects cued by a disgusted vs. neutral or happy face

already in infancy. In functional neuroimaging studies with adults, the amygdala is consistently activated by fearful faces (Morris, et al., 1996). Amygdala activation is even enhanced in a social learning context when the expression is directed toward an object relative to the expression alone (Hooker, et al., 2006). Adults possess a rapid subcortical face-detection system including the superior colliculus located in the mesencephalon, the pulvinar nucleus of the thalamus, and the amygdala. These structures rapidly process and enhance attention toward fearful faces (Vuilleumier, 2005). Johnson (2005) has argued that this subcortical pathway may be functional from birth. Presumably, the amygdala enhances cortical processing of socially relevant stimuli like faces and thus helps to establish and fine-tune the cortical social brain network (Johnson, 2005). In fact, infants show certain perceptual biases toward faces, direct eye contact, and biological motion from birth (Farroni, et al., 2002; Johnson, et al., 1991; Simion, et al., 2008). The amygdala may mediate these inherent perceptual biases to biologically salient stimuli and boost experience-dependent fine-tuning of cortical areas specialized for the processing of social information (Leppänen & Nelson, 2009).

Amygdala activation cannot be directly measured using electrophysiological measures. However, amplitude of the Nc component is a useful index of attentional processes in infancy. Cortical sources of the Nc include the inferior and medial frontal gyri and anterior cingulate cortex (Reynolds & Richards, 2005). The anterior cingulate cortex (ACC) is involved in the conscious perception of threat stimuli (Öhmann, 2005) and is highly interconnected with the amygdala in processing fearful affect (Das, et al., 2005; Bissiere, et al., 2008). It is supposable that fearful faces looking toward objects activate the amygdala in 3- and 6-month-old infants, which in turn enhances ACC activation in the subsequent processing of the cued object. The fact that we did not find an Nc modulation for the fearful faces in 3-month-olds, but only for the subsequently presented objects, suggests that this pathway may not be mature in terms of processing speed at 3 months and may function rather slowly in this age group. At 6 months, responses for fearful faces gazing toward objects are enhanced as well as subsequent responses to the cued objects alone. At 9 months, fearful faces elicit enhanced processing regardless of the gaze direction, suggesting that fearful faces are recognized as informative and salient regardless of the presence of immediate referents of the expression by that age. However, why did 9-month-olds not show the expected enhanced Nc in response to fearfully cued objects?

Presumably, the early attention biases toward fearful faces and fearfully cued objects in 3- and 6-month-olds are mediated by an automatic and rapid subcortical pathway including the amygdala. The amygdala may be sensitive to certain biologically relevant stimuli from birth and enhances infants' attention to those stimuli. In the second half of the first year, infants become more and more able to deliberately regulate attention allocation. Early attention biases may now become less effective and may be overridden by more conscious cognitive control mechanisms. Previous research has demonstrated infants' ability to down-regulate negative affect and distress to novelty and this has been attributed to increasing attentional control accomplished through the ACC during the first year (Posner & Rothbart, 1998). Increased attentional control may be reflected in the response pattern of the Nc component in 9-month-olds in our study. We presented colorful harmless toy objects, which do not themselves implicate any threat. When we tested a small sample of adults with the same stimuli, they reported that they found the stimuli—especially the fearful faces looking at the toys—rather funny. Possibly, even 9-month-old infants perceived fearful faces in the context of toy objects as implausible. Nc amplitude for objects in the fear condition may have been attenuated in 9-month-olds rather than enhanced as in the younger subjects. Infants' reactions to ambiguous or threatening objects, on the other hand, are much more susceptible to an adult's emotional displays as shown in a study with 12-month-olds using life displays of negative emotion toward threatening toy robots (Carver & Vaccaro, 2007). Indeed, there is evidence that social referencing is more likely to occur in 12-month-olds in ambiguous than in unambiguous situations and infants may even laugh when their mothers pose a frightened expression in a nonambiguous context (Campos et al., 2003).

From Early Attention Biases to Social Referencing

Recent electrophysiological research has revealed infants' early sensitivities for referential emotional expressions. Questions regarding the function of these sensitivities remain open. Is there a developmental trajectory from early sensitivities and attention biases to later social referencing? Social referencing entails active searching for emotional information. Although newborn infants already preferentially orient toward faces and facelike stimuli (Johnson, et al., 1991), active searching for an emotional expression in an ambiguous situation (e.g., when faced with a barking dog toy) has been documented at the earliest by seven months of age (Striano & Rochat, 2000; Striano & Vaish, 2006). It is not clear whether younger infants actively search for emotional expressions in ambiguous or potentially dangerous situations. In the electrophysiological studies reviewed above, infants were passively presented with emotional expressions and objects. Infants' attention biases in these studies are most probably automatic responses that are relatively independent from previous learning and experience, especially regarding fearful expressions that are rare in young infants' typical environment. These early observable processes may still continue to exist later in development. In fact, automatic attention biases toward angry and fearful facial expressions are well documented in human adults and have been linked to the amygdala (Öhmann, 2005; Vuilleumier, 2005). Angry and fearful expressions capture our attention automatically (Öhmann, 2005). In adults, the amygdala is particularly responsive to the same kind of emotional stimuli that infants respond to the most in event-related potential studies. Amygdala activation is greater for happy and fearful faces that are associated with objects in a social learning context compared with the emotional faces alone (Hooker, et al., 2006). The amygdala is also more activated by angry faces looking toward the observer compared to angry faces looking away (Sato, et al., 2004). However, given enough processing time and cognitive effort, activation of the amygdala can be down-regulated in adults even in response to highly aversive stimuli (Ochsner, et al., 2004). Thus, young infants' attention biases toward fearful expressions and objects associated with fearful expressions may persist throughout development, but may be overridden by more controlled processes later in development when attention can be deliberately regulated, at least if cognitive resources are available.

By the end of the first year, infants' social referencing is remarkably selective. Following an ambiguous event 10-month-olds look more toward an experimenter who is attentive to them compared to an experimenter who ignores them (Striano & Rochat, 2000), and 12-month-olds look more toward an experimenter who vocally responds to them immediately compared to a temporally noncontingent experimenter (Striano et al., 2006). At 12 months of age, infants also seem to take into account the expertise of the adult in the given context (Stenberg & Hagekull, 2007). Contrary to attachment accounts of social referencing, infants look more toward an experimenter compared to their own caregiver in an ambiguous experimental context. This has been attributed to the fact that infants may judge the experimenter to be the expert in the unfamiliar experimental context rather than their own caregiver (Stenberg & Hagekull, 2007). By 14 months of age, infants also seem to distinguish between information an experimenter provides on his or her individual attitudes toward an object versus generalizable information that is universally valid (Gergely et al., 2007). In order to be able to take into account another person's attention focus, temporal contingency, presumed expertise, and communicative intent, much more complex social-cognitive skills are required than the ability to detect and identify an emotional expression and its referent, which can be found even in very young infants. The crucial prerequisite for social referencing by the end of the first year seems to be the ability to identify others as intentional and communicative agents. In an ambiguous situation it makes sense to actively turn toward another person who is attentive to me, who knows the situation better than I do (and better than other people who may also be present), and who is willing to communicate his or her evaluation of the situation to me. By the end of the first year, infants already take into account all of these factors when turning toward other people in novel and ambiguous situations. Longitudinal studies on the development of social referencing and related social-cognitive skills are still warranted, to better understand this fascinating phenomenon and its developmental trajectory as well as the relationship of early attention biases toward emotional stimuli and later social referencing.

Conclusion

Even in the first months, infants show attention biases to referential emotional expressions and toward objects, which are associated with a fearful face. These early biases may function automatically and rely on subcortical brain structures such as the amygdala. In the second half of the first year, infants gain more and more control over attention allocation mechanisms and increasingly show selective social referencing behavior, which may primarily rely on the ability to identify others as intentional and communicative agents. Longitudinal studies should further explore the function of early attention biases and the development of more sophisticated social referencing skills.

Acknowledgments

The writing of this chapter was supported by the German Research Foundation (Deutsche Forschungsgemeinschaft, DFG) grant # HO 4342/2-1.

REFERENCES

Adolphs, R. (2002). Recognizing emotion from facial expressions: Psychological and neurological mechanisms. *Behavioral and Cognitive Neuroscience Reviews, 1*, 21–62.

Bissiere, S., Plachta, N., Hoyer, D., McAllister, K. H., Olpe, H. R., Grace, A. A., et al. (2008). The rostral anterior cingulate cortex modulates the efficiency of amygdala-dependent fear learning. *Biological Psychiatry, 63*, 821–831.

Campos, J. J., Anderson, D. I., Barbu-Roth, M. A., Hubbard, E. M., Hertenstein, M. J., & Witherington, D. (2000). Travel Broadens the Mind. *Infancy, 1*, 149–219.

Campos, J. J., Thein, S., & Owen, D. (2003). A Darwinian legacy to understanding human infancy—Emotional expressions as behavior regulators. *Annals of the New York Academy of Sciences, 1000*, 110–134.

Carpenter, M., Nagell, K., & Tomasello, M. (1998). Social cognition, joint attention, and communicative competence from 9 to 15 months of age. *Monographs of the Society for Research in Child Development, 63*, i–vi, 1–143.

Carver, L. J., & Vaccaro, B. G. (2007). 12-month-old infants allocate increased neural resources to stimuli associated with negative adult emotion. *Developmental Psychology, 43*, 54–69.

Crockenberg, S. C., & Leerkes, E. M. (2004). Infant and maternal behaviors regulate infant reactivity to novelty at 6 months. *Developmental Psychology, 40,* 1123–1132.

Das, P., Kemp, A. H., Liddell, B. J., Brown, K. J., Olivieri, G., Peduto, A., et al. (2005). Pathways for fear perception: modulation of amygdala activity by thalamo-cortical systems. *Neuroimage, 26,* 141–148.

Farroni, T., Csibra, G., Simion, F., & Johnson, M. H. (2002). Eye contact detection in humans from birth. *Proceedings of the National Academy of Sciences USA, 99,* 9602–9605.

Farroni, T., Menon, E., Rigato, S., & Johnson, M. H. (2007). The perception of facial expressions in newborns. *European Journal of Developmental Psychology, 4,* 2–13.

Feinman, S., Roberts, D., Hsieh, K.-F., Sawyer, D., & Swanson, D. (1992). A critical review of social referencing in infancy. In S. Feinman (Ed.), *Social Referencing and the Social Construction of Reality in Infancy* (pp. 15–54). New York: Plenum Press.

Gergely, G., Egyed, K., & Kiraly, I. (2007). On pedagogy. *Developmental Science, 10*(1), 139–146.

Hertenstein, M. J., & Campos, J. J. (2004). The retention effects of an adult's emotional displays on infant behavior. *Child Development, 75,* 595–613.

Hoehl, S., Palumbo, L., Heinisch, C., & Striano, T. (2008a). Infants' attention is biased by emotional expressions and eye gaze direction. *Neuroreport, 19,* 579–582.

Hoehl, S., & Striano, T. (2008). Neural processing of eye gaze and threat-related emotional facial expressions in infancy. *Child Development, 79,* 1752–1760.

Hoehl, S., & Striano, T. (2010). Infants' neural processing of positive emotion and eye gaze. *Social Neuroscience, 5,* 30–39.

Hoehl, S., & Striano, T. (2010). The development of emotional face and eye gaze processing. *Developmental Science, 13,* 813–825.

Hoehl, S., Wiese, L., & Striano, T. (2008b). Young infants' neural processing of objects is affected by eye gaze direction and emotional expression. *PLoS ONE, 3,* e2389. doi:10.1371/journal. pone.0002389.

Hooker, C. I., Germine, L. T., Knight, R. T., & D'Esposito, M. (2006). Amygdala response to facial expressions reflects emotional learning. *Journal of Neuroscience, 26,* 8915–8922.

Hornik, R., Risenhoover, N., & Gunnar, M. R. (1987). The effects of maternal positive, neutral, and negative affective communications on infant responses to new toys. *Child Development, 58,* 937–944.

Johnson, M. H. (2005). Subcortical face processing. *Nature Reviews Neuroscience, 6,* 766–774.

Johnson, M. H., Dziurawiec, S., Ellis, H., & Morton, J. (1991). Newborns' preferential tracking of face-like stimuli and its subsequent decline. *Cognition, 40,* 1–19.

Leppänen, J. M., & Nelson, C. A. (2006). The development and neural bases of facial emotion recognition. *Advances in Child Development and Behavior, 34,* 207–246.

Leppänen, J. M., & Nelson, C. A. (2009). Tuning the developing brain to social signals of emotions. *Nature Reviews Neuroscience, 10,* 37–47.

Morris, J. S., Frith, C. D., Perrett, D. I., Rowland, D., Young, A. W., Calder, A. J., et al. (1996). A differential neural response in the human amygdala to fearful and happy facial expressions. *Nature, 383,* 812–815.

Moses, L. J., Baldwin, D. A., Rosicky, J. G., & Tidball, G. (2001). Evidence for referential understanding in the emotions domain at twelve and eighteen months. *Child Development, 72,* 718–735.

Mumme, D. L., & Fernald, A. (2003). The infant as onlooker: learning from emotional reactions observed in a television scenario. *Child Development, 74*, 221–237.

Ochsner, K. N., Ray, R. D., Cooper, J. C., Robertson, E. R., Chopra, S., Gabrieli, J. D., et al. (2004). For better or for worse: neural systems supporting the cognitive down- and up-regulation of negative emotion. *Neuroimage, 23*, 483–499.

Öhmann, A. (2005). The role of the amygdala in human fear: Automatic detection of threat. *Psychoneuroendocrinology, 30*, 953–958.

Olsson, A., & Phelps, E. A. (2007). Social learning of fear. *Nature Neuroscience, 10*, 1095–1102.

Peltola, M. J., Leppänen, J. M., Maki, S., & Hietanen, J. K. (2009). Emergence of enhanced attention to fearful faces between 5 and 7 months of age. *Social Cognitive and Affective Neuroscience, 4*, 134–142.

Posner, M. I., & Rothbart, M. K. (1998). Attention, self-regulation and concsiousness. *Philosophical Transactions of the Royal Society of London B, 353*, 1915–1927.

Reynolds, G. D., & Richards, J. E. (2005). Familiarization, attention, and recognition memory in infancy: an event-related potential and cortical source localization study. *Developmental Psychology, 41*, 598–615.

Sato, W., Yoshikawa, S., Kochiyama, T., & Matsumura, M. (2004). The amygdala processes the emotional significance of facial expressions: an fMRI investigation using the interaction between expression and face direction. *Neuroimage, 22*, 1006–1013.

Simion, F., Regolin, L., & Bulf, H. (2008). A predisposition for biological motion in the newborn baby. *Proceedings of the National Academy of Science U S A, 105*, 809–813.

Stenberg, G., & Hagekull, B. (2007). Infant looking behavior in ambiguous situations: Social Referencing or Attachment Behavior? *Infancy, 11*, 111–129.

Striano, T., & Rochat, P. (2000). Emergence of selective social referencing in infancy. *Infancy, 1*, 253–264.

Striano, T., & Vaish, A. (2006). Seven- to 9-month-old infants use facial expressions to interpret others' actions. *British Journal of Developmental Psychology, 24*, 753–760.

Striano, T., Vaish, A., & Henning, A. (2006). Selective looking by 12-month-olds to a temporally contingent partner. *Interaction Studies, 7*, 233–250.

Vuilleumier, P. (2005). How brains beware: neural mechanisms of emotional attention. *Trends in Cognitive Sciences, 9*, 585–594.

12 Linking Joint Attention and Joint Action
Anne Böckler and Natalie Sebanz

IN MOST OF our everyday social interactions, attending jointly and acting jointly are intrinsically and naturally linked. Both watching and working together are required when it comes to holding the door for someone, passing the salt, or jointly carrying furniture. Research addressing the mechanisms underlying joint attention and joint action, however, has largely been carried out in separation. Whereas joint attention has mainly been studied from a developmental point of view with a strong focus on the emergence of higher-level cognition, research on joint action has primarily investigated motor coordination in time and space.

The aim of this chapter is to discuss the role of joint attention for successful joint action and to highlight the overlap in research questions that have challenged scientists in both fields. First, we will briefly outline the main topics that have been addressed separately in each field. Subsequently, the role of joint action and joint attention for three core abilities underlying social interaction will be discussed. How are shared representations formed? How is interpersonal coordination achieved? How do people manage to keep self and other apart? By addressing these abilities, we show that focusing on the interplay between joint attention and joint action can provide new perspectives on questions treated separately in the two fields.

Joint Attention: A Brief Review

Two aspects of joint attention have dominated psychological research: the perceptual component of processing and following someone else's gaze on the one hand, and the conceptual component of knowing about others' attention and experiencing shared attention on the other hand. Concerning perception, a large amount of evidence suggests that others' gaze automatically shifts our attention and provides a perceptual benefit for the attended location (Ristic, Friesen, Kingstone, 2002). For instance, when people try to detect objects while simultaneously seeing someone's face, they cannot help but follow the other's gaze, even when they know that the objects are less likely to appear at the gazed at location (Driver, Davis, Ricciardelly, Kidd, Maxwell, & Baron-Cohen, 1999). The ability to track conspecifics' gaze has been revealed in animals (e.g., ravens, Bugnyar, Stöwe, & Heinrich, 2004; goats, Kaminski, Riedel, Call, & Tomasello, 2005; great apes, Bräuer, Call, & Tomasello, 2005) and in infants from the ages of 3 to 6 months (D'Entremont, Hains, & Muir, 1997; see also Meltzoff & Brooks, 2007).

As to sharing attention, research has mainly focused on epistemic and motivational aspects. Although some nonhuman animals seem to be aware of what conspecifics can and cannot see (Hare, Call, Agnetta, & Tomasello, 2002; Itakura, 2004), it has been claimed that the motivation to share attention with conspecifics just for the sake of sharing is specific to humans (Tomasello & Carpenter, 2007). Indeed, already very young infants engage in triadic joint attention with adults, helping the infants to focus on relevant aspects of the environment (Striano, Reid, & Hoehl, 2006). For instance, when jointly attending to novel objects with adults, children are much better at generalizing information that is provided by the adults than when attending alone, indicating that joint attention fosters learning (Csibra & Gergely, 2009). In sum, besides the urge to rapidly follow others' gaze, humans are inclined to share attention and exploit it as a vehicle for learning.

Joint Action: A Brief Review

Joint attention naturally takes place in social context, and both gaze following and shared attention is involved when people perform actions together. But how do we manage to act jointly? This question has been addressed on different levels of analysis, ranging from motor control (Meulenbroek, Bosga, Hulstijn, & Miedl, 2007; Richardson, Marsh, & Schmidt, 2005; Vesper, Soutschek, & Schubö, 2009) to action planning (Sebanz, Knoblich, & Prinz, 2003) and questions about collective intentionality (Bratman, 1993; Gilbert, 1989). As to the latter, researchers have asked what individuals need to share conceptually in order to act jointly. It has been argued that a main requirement for joint action is the uniquely human ability to engage in "shared intentionality," referring to the deliberate and mutual sharing of psychological states (Tomasello & Carpenter, 2007).

On the level of action planning, evidence suggests that people represent coactors' actions in a functionally equivalent way as their own. In particular, when taking turns with someone else in responding to visual stimuli, participants display a response pattern that is similar to when they perform both parts of the task alone, but different from when they only complete their part without a co-acting person (Hommel, Colzato, & van den

Wildenberg, 2009; Sebanz, Knoblich, & Prinz, 2003; Tsai, Kuo, Jing, Hung, & Tzeng, 2006; Welsh, Elliott, Anson, Dhillon, Weeks, Lyons, & Chua, 2005). Thus, people are sensitive to what the other is doing because common representations underlie their own and the other's actions.

These results have been related to ideomotor theories, according to which perception and action involve the same mental representations (James, 1890; Prinz, 1997). The discovery of "mirror neurons" in the macaque brain and the finding that motor areas in the human brain are active not only when planning and executing an action oneself, but also when observing others' actions (Rizzolatti & Craighero, 2004), provide a neural basis for such direct interpersonal links. Common mechanisms resulting from shared representations of own and others' actions may also support temporal coordination across people. In particular, people seem to employ the same simulation processes for making temporal predictions about their own actions as well as others' actions (Wilson & Knoblich, 2005).

Links between Joint Attention and Joint Action

The studies of joint attention and joint action have both elicited fruitful, but largely separate fields of research. Joint attention and joint action are, however, tightly linked in social interaction. In fact, successful joint action crucially depends on joint attention, and both areas might benefit from taking into account the approaches and discoveries of the other field. In the following, we will address the interplay between joint attention and joint action by discussing three abilities that are crucial for social interaction, namely how shared representations are formed, how rapid and concise temporal coordination is accomplished, and finally, how coacting and coattending individuals manage to keep self and other apart.

SHARING REPRESENTATIONS IN ATTENTION AND ACTION

Successful joint action requires coactors to predict and keep track of each other's actions and goals. This is based on shared perceptual and action representations. For example, when jointly transporting a piano down the stairs it is crucial to know for each actor how the other is going to perform her part of the joint task. Will she carry the piano on her shoulders or in her hands? Will she walk behind or next to the piano when going round the corner? As sketched above, research on coaction has shown that people form representations of each other's actions when performing tasks together (Sebanz et al., 2003). This may help them predict what the other is going to do next.

However, coordinating actions in a changing and complex environment requires coactors to take into account physical constraints and flexibly adjust their actions online. In the piano example, the steepness and narrowness of the staircase will influence how each actor is performing her part of the task. Joint attention provides a crucial mechanism for implementing action plans in a particular environment. By attending jointly, coactors can establish perceptual common ground and become aware of each other's action opportunities or limitations (Sebanz, Bekkering, & Knoblich, 2006).

Experimental evidence for the extensive use of others' gaze and attention behavior in a joint action task was reported by Clark and Krych (2004). Pairs of participants assembled Lego models in such a way that a "director" told a "builder" which pieces to select and how to attach them. When directors had visual access to the builders' workspace, the builders made information about their gaze direction more salient as compared to when directors were "blind." The directors, in turn, followed the builders' gaze and immediately incorporated this information in their next instruction, leading pairs in the joint attention setting to be much faster and more accurate. Joint attention thus allows us to make use of information that others' eye gaze offers about their action goals.

More specifically, following others' gaze allows people to match their perception with that of others, which enhances the chance of detecting the same affordances and enables the prediction and understanding of others' actions. For instance, when pairs of participants communicated about visual scenes that were displayed before them (taken from the sitcom "Friends"), the listener's understanding of the speaker's information improved the closer their eye movements matched (Richardson & Dale, 2005). This held when the speaker had previously been videotaped as well as in online face-to-face conversations (Richardson, Dale, & Kirkham, 2007).

When acting together, however, coactors often operate from different positions, implying that they also have different perspectives on the jointly attended objects. Joint attention allows people to infer what the other's gaze is directed at, but are they also able to align their perception with the other's, given different perspectives? That is, do they know what the other perceives even when attending to an object or scene from a different perspective? Samson and colleagues (2010) recently addressed this question. Participants had to judge the amount of dots on virtual walls from either their own perspective or from the perspective of a virtual avatar that was present in the scene. When participants reported how many dots they saw themselves, the avatar's perspective interfered with their own, reflected in slower responses when the avatar saw a different amount of dots. This indicates that we rapidly and effortlessly compute what others perceive when attending to objects from different perspectives. It has been suggested that this ability is essential for predicting others' actions and, consequently, for smooth interaction (Apperley & Butterfill, 2009).

Together with findings that demonstrated co-representation of other people's actions (Sebanz et al., 2003), the computation of others' perception points toward humans' ability to represent what conspecifics see and do. Sharing perceptual and action representations seems to come naturally when we act together. In this context, both the role of joint attention in action co-representation and the role of joint action for the computation of others' perceptions are interesting topics for future research.

COORDINATING ATTENTION AND ACTION IN TIME

Many joint actions require rapid and precise temporal coordination. Thus, besides knowing what action the coactor is planning, partners need to predict the time course of each others' actions. This holds for the onset of joint action as well as for its progression (Clark, 1996). For example, the two carriers of the piano have to precisely time the initiation of the lifting and they need to temporally adjust their steps as they continue down the stairs.

It has been suggested that this ability is achieved by means of simulating the other's actions on the basis of one's own motor system (Wilson & Knoblich, 2005). The idea is that internal simulations generate not only precise temporal predictions about the sensory consequences of our own actions, but can also be applied to predict the timing and outcome of others' actions (Sato, 2008; Wolpert, Doya, & Kawato, 2003). For example, when watching hand-, arm-, or body movements or when listening to music pieces, people are most accurate at predicting the timing and the outcome of their own as compared to others' actions, indicating that they are employing simulation processes, which are most accurate for their own performance (Knoblich & Flach, 2001; Knoblich, Seigerschmidt, Flach, & Prinz, 2002; Repp & Knoblich, 2004). Similarly, synchronization in a piano duet was best when pianists played along with an earlier recording of themselves as compared to earlier recordings of other pianists (Keller, Knoblich, & Repp, 2007).

Moreover, it has been shown that when rehearsing duets together, pianists increase the amount of eye gaze to enhance temporal accuracy (Williamson & Davidson, 2002) and they synchronize and exaggerate jointly attended visual cues such as finger and head movements when auditory feedback is absent (Goebl & Palmer, 2009). This finding points toward an important role of ostensive cues not only for learning (Csibra & Gergely, 2009), but also for timing—an issue that could be of interest for future research.

What underlies the use of eye gaze in temporal coordination? A potential answer is suggested by studies in which participants performed and observed visually guided actions (Flanagan and Johansson, 2003). It was found that not only the performer but also the observer carried out predictive (rather than reactive) eye movements relative to the performer's hand movements. That is, eye gaze in the actor closely preceded and predicted the respective actions. At the same time, eye gaze during observation reflected action expectations in the observer. The authors argued that simulating perceived actions in one's own motor system relies on the same eye–hand coordination programs that are involved in performing the respective actions oneself. In support of this claim, it was shown that predictions of the outcome of both perceived grasping actions and perceived eye movements rely on the same motor structures in the brain (Pierno, Becchio, Wall, Smith, Turella, & Castiello, 2006).

Thus, humans seem to be very well equipped for rapidly and efficiently simulating and predicting others' (looking) behavior. Direct experimental manipulation of the information available about the other's gaze might shed additional light on the strength and the time course of the connection between attention and temporal action coordination.

SELF AND OTHER IN ATTENTION AND ACTION

Acting together involves not only shared representations and temporal coordination, but also requires conceiving of the other as an intentional agent with mental states as well as keeping both the intentions and actions of self and other apart (Knoblich & Sebanz, 2008). Both of our two piano carriers ascribe to the respective other the goal to get the piano down the stairs—preferably without damaging either the piano or themselves. At the same time, they need to distinguish their own motor contribution from the other's to decide how much force to apply or how to correct errors (see van der Wel & Knoblich, [chapter 15]).

Two accounts have highlighted the importance of joint attention and action for developing an understanding of others as mental agents. First, according to Barresi and Moore (1996), humans become capable of representing their own and others' mental states and actions equally well, despite the fact that the information available about self and other is quite different (e.g., proprioception for our own and vision for access to others' mental states and actions). The understanding of our own and others' minds heavily depends on directing attention to both sources of information, the opportunity for which is provided in joint action contexts. Only when we manage to attend to and integrate first and third person information at the same time, so the argument goes, do we achieve the concept of us and others as being mental agents who can, for example, perceive one and the same situation differently.

Second, social-affective accounts have stressed the role of sharing attention for the development of understanding others as having mental states (Hobson, 1989; Hobson & Hobson, 2007). According to these accounts, joint attention, by fostering the sharing of emotional states, also underlies the development of joint action capabilities (Hobson, 1989). Indeed, children with autism, who displayed less attempts to share attention than controls when interacting with caretakers (García-Pérez, Lee, & Hobson, 2006; Hobson & Hobson, 2007) were impaired at correctly imitating the caretaker's behaviour (Hobson & Hobson, 2007; but see Southgate & Hamilton, 2008 for a different view).

But how do we keep others apart from ourselves? It has been argued that experiencing oneself as the object of others' attention triggers emotional self-consciousness in the first months of infancy (Beebe, Jaffe, Feldstein, Mays, & Alson, 1985) and underlies the development of a conceptual understanding of self and other (Reddy, 2003). Later in infancy, the differentiation of self and other was suggested to depend on the experience of jointly relating to objects (Hobson & Hobson, 2007). By attending to or acting with an object and at the same time observing someone else relating to it, we have access to a first and to a third person relation to one and the same object. Having different perspectives while attending and acting jointly may further support the ability to keep mental states of self and other apart. When seeing something from different visual angles, the difference between self and other might become more salient.

Whereas developmental approaches have regarded the experience of joint attention as a prerequisite for understanding self and other as distinct mental agents, a joint action view suggests that keeping actions of self and other apart at a nonconceptual, motor level could form the basis for more conceptual self–other distinctions. In particular, it is well established that both perceptual and sensorimotor cues contribute to our experience of agency (the experience of being the cause of action effects; Metcalfe [chapter 14]; van der Wel & Knoblich [chapter 15]). Acting together provides opportunities for learning to keep action effects resulting from one's own movements and action effects resulting from others' movements apart (Sebanz, 2007). A first step toward integrating conceptual developmental views and perception-action oriented joint action accounts could be to experimentally address the role of joint attention for agency.

Conclusions

Social interaction requires the ability to share representations, to coordinate actions in time, and to keep self and other apart. These requirements depend both on mechanisms of joint attention and mechanisms of joint action. Although joint attention and joint action have been studied in separation, there is evidence for overlapping mechanisms (e.g., Flanagan & Johansson, 2003), mutual influences of these abilities on each other in development (e.g., Barresi & Moore, 1996; Hobson & Hobson, 2007; Sebanz, 2007), as well as emergent properties when joint attention and joint action mechanisms are combined (e.g., Goebl & Palmer, 2009). Insight into the role of joint attention for different levels of joint action (from joint motor control and action planning to the development of joint intentionality) may be gained by experimentally manipulating the availability of information about coactors' gaze and the extent of shared attention. Similarly, varying joint action requirements and joint action opportunities can serve to study how acting together shapes effects of joint attention. Bringing together joint attention and joint action promises to enhance our understanding of social cognition.

REFERENCES

Apperley, I. A., & Butterfill, S. A. (2009). Do humans have two systems to track beliefs and belief-like states? *Psychological Review, 116*, 953–970.

Barresi, J., & Moore, C. (1996). Intentional relations and social understanding. *Behavioral and Brain Sciences, 19*, 107–154.

Beebe, B., Jaffe, J., Feldstein, S., Mays, K., & Alson, D. (1985). Interpersonal timing: The application of an adult dialogue model to mother-infant vocal and kinesic interactions. In T. M. Field, & N. A. Fox (Eds.), *Social Perception in Infants* (pp. 217–248). Notwood, NJ: Ablex.

Bratman, M. E. (1993). Shared intention. *Ethics, 104*, 97–113.

Bräuer, J., Call, J., & Tomasselo, M. (2005). All great ape species follow gaze to distant locations and around barriers. *Journal of Comparative Psychology, 119*, 145–154.

Bugnyar, T., Stöwe, M., & Heinrich, B. (2004). Ravens, Corvus corax, follow gaze direction of humans around obstacles. *Proceedings of the Royal Society B, 271*, 1331–1336.

Clark, H. H. (1996). *Using language*. Cambridge, UK: Cambridge University Press.

Clark, H. H., & Krych, M. A. (2004). Speaking while monitoring addressees for understanding. *Journal of Memory and Language, 50*, 62–81.

Csibra, G., & Gergely, G. (2009). Natural pedagogy. *Trends in Cognitive Sciences, 13*, 148–153.

D'Entremont, B., Hains, S. M. J., Muir, D. W. (1997). A demonstration of gaze following in 3- to 6-month-olds. *Infant Behavior and Development, 20*, 569–572.

Driver, J., Davis, G., Ricciardelli, P., Kidd, P., Maxwell, E., Baron-Cohen, S. (1999). Gaze perception triggers reflexive visuospatial orienting. *Visual Cognition, 6*, 509–540.

Flanagan, J. R., & Johansson, R. S. (2003). Action plans used in action observation. *Nature, 424*, 769–771.

García-Pérez, R. M., Lee, A., & Hobson, R. P. (2006). On intersubjective engagement in autism: A controlled study of nonverbal aspects of conversation. *Journal of Autism and Developmental Disorders, 37*, 1310–1322.

Gilbert, M. (1989). *On Social Facts*. London: Routledge.

Goebl, W., & Palmer, C. (2009). Synchronization of timing and motion among performing musicians. *Music Perception, 26*, 427–438.

Hare, B., Call, J., Agnetta, B., & Tomasello, M. (2000). Chimpanzees know what conspecifics do and do not see. *Animal Behaviour, 59*, 771–785.

Hobson, R. P. (1989). On sharing experiences. *Development & Psychopathology, 1*, 197–203.

Hobson, J. A., & Hobson, R. P. (2007). Identification: the missing link between joint attention and imitation? *Development & Psychopathology, 19*, 411–431.

Hommel, B., Colzato, L. S., & van den Wildenberg, W. P. M. (2009). How social are task representations? *Psychological Science, 20*, 794–798.

Itakura, S. (2004). Gaze-following and joint visual attention in nonhuman animals. *Japanese Psychological Research, 46*, 216–226.

James, W. (1890). *The Principles of Psychology*. New York: NY Holt.

Kaminski, J., Riedel, J., Call, J., & Tomasello, M. (2005). Domestic goats follow gaze direction and use social cues in an object choice task. *Animal Behaviour, 69*, 11–18.

Keller, Knoblich, & Repp (2007). Pianists duet better when they play with themselves. *Consciousness and Cognition, 16*, 102–111.

Knoblich, G. & Flach, R. (2001). Predicting the effects of actions: interactions of perception and action. *Psychological Science, 12*, 467–472.

Knoblich, G., Seigerschmidt, E., Flach, R., & Prinz, W. (2002). Authorship effects in the prediction of handwriting strokes: evidence for action simulation during action perception. *Quarterly Journal of Experimental Psychology, A55*, 1027–1046.

Knoblich, G., & Sebanz, N. (2008). Evolving intentions for social interaction: from entrainment to joint action. *Philosophical Transactions of the Royal Society B: Biological Sciences, 363*, 2021–2031.

Meltzoff, A. N. & Brooks, R. (2007). Eyes wide shut: The importance of eyes in infant gaze following and understanding other minds. In R. Flom, K. Lee, & D. Muir (Eds.), *Gaze Following: Its Development and Significance* (pp. 217–241). Mahwah, NJ: Erlbaum.

Metcalfe, J. (2013). "Knowing" that the self is the agent. In J. Metcalfe, & H. S. Terrace (Eds.), *Agency and Joint Attention* (pp. 238–255). New York: Oxford University Press.

Meulenbroek, R. G. J., Bosga, J., Hulstijn, M., & Miedl, S. (2007). Joint action coordination in transferring objects. *Experimental Brain Research, 180*, 333–343.

Pierno, A.C., Becchio, C., Wall, M.B., Smith, A.T., Turella, L., & Castiello, U. (2006). When gaze turns into grasp. *Journal of Cognitive Neuroscience, 18,* 2130–2137.

Prinz, W. (1997). Perception and action planning. *European Journal of Cognitive Psychology, 9,* 129–154.

Reddy, V. (2003). On being the object of attention: Implications for self–other consciousness. *Trends in Cognitive Sciences, 7,* 397–402.

Repp, B. H., & Knoblich, G. (2004). Perceiving Action Identity. *Psychological Science, 15,* 604–609.

Richardson, D. C., & Dale, R. (2005). Looking to understand: The coupling between speakers' and listeners' eye movements and its relationship to discourse comprehension. *Cognitive Science, 29,* 1045–1060.

Richardson, D. C., Dale, R., & Kirkham, N. Z. (2007). The art of conversation is coordination: Common ground and the coupling of eye movements during dialogue. *Psychological Science, 18,* 407–413.

Richardson, M. J., Marsh, K. L., & Schmidt, R.C. (2005). Effects of visual and verbal interaction on unintentional interpersonal coordination. *Journal of Experimental Psychology: Human Perception and Performance, 31,* 62–79.

Ristic, J., Friesen, C. K., & Kingstone, A. (2002). Are eyes special? It depends on how you look at it. *Psychonomic Bulletin & Review, 9,* 507–513.

Rizzolatti, G., & Craighero, L. (2004). The mirror-neuron system. *Annual Review of Neuroscience, 27,* 169–192.

Samson, D., Apperly, I. A., Braithwaite, J. J., Andrews, B. J., & Scott, S. E. B. (2010). Seeing it their way: Evidence for rapid and involuntary computation of what other people see. *Journal of Experimental Psychology: Human Perception and Performance, 36,* 1255–1266.

Sato, A. (2008). Action observation modulates auditory perception of the consequence of others' actions. *Consciousness and Cognition, 17,* 1219–1227.

Sebanz, N., Knoblich, G., & Prinz, W. (2003). Representing others' actions: just like one's own? *Cognition, 88,* 11–21.

Sebanz, N., Bekkering, H., & Knoblich, G. (2006). Joint action: Bodies and minds moving together. *Trends in Cognitive Sciences, 10,* 70–76.

Sebanz, N. (2007). The emergence of self: Sensing agency through joint action. *Journal of Consciousness Studies, 14,* 234–251.

Southgate, V., & Hamilton, A. F. de C. (2008). Unbroken mirrors: challenging a theory of autism. *Trends in Cognitive Sciences, 12,* 225–229.

Striano, T., Reid, V. M. & Hoehl, S. (2006). Neural mechanisms of joint attention in infancy. *European Journal of Neuroscience, 23,* 2819–2823.

Tomasello, M., & Carpenter, M. (2007). Shared intentionality. *Developmental Science, 10,* 121–125.

Tsai, C.-C., Kuo, W.-J., Jing, J.-T., Hung, D. L., & Tzeng, O. J.-L. (2006). A common coding framework in self-other interaction: Evidence from joint action task. *Experimental Brain Research, 175,* 353–362.

van der Wel, R., & Knoblich, G. (2013). Cues to agency: Time can tell. In J. Metcalfe, & H. S. Terrace (Eds.), *Agency and Joint Attention* (pp. 256–267). New York: Oxford University Press.

Vesper, C., Soutschek, A., & Schubö, A. (2009). Motion coordination affects movement parameters in a joint pick-and-place task. *Quarterly Journal of Experimental Psychology, 62,* 2418–2432.

Welsh, T. N., Elliott, D., Anson, J. G., Dhillon, V., Weeks, D. J., Lyons, J. L., et al. (2005). Does Joe influence Fred's action? Inhibition of return across different nervous systems. *Neuroscience Letters, 385,* 99–104.

Williamson, A., & Davidson, J. W. (2002). Exploring coperformer communication. *Musicae Scientiae, 6,* 53–72.

Wilson, M., & Knoblich, G. (2005). The case for motor involvement in perceiving conspecifics. *Psychological Bulletin, 131,* 460–473.

Wolpert, D. M., Doya, K., Kawato, M. (2003). A unifying computational framework for motor control and social interaction. *Philosophical Transactions of the Royal Society B: Biological Sciences, 358,* 593–602.

13 Do You See What I See? The Neural Bases of Joint Attention

Elizabeth Redcay and Rebecca Saxe

IN THE SIMPLEST social interactions, two people look at each other. For example, gazing face-to-face is infants' first social experience with their parents. Most social interactions between humans, however, don't stop with mutual gaze. Instead, people quickly switch to sharing attention on an object or topic of communication. I point out the flowers; you mention your sister's graduation; and we both smile at the thought. In each of these cases, our social interaction has at least three elements: two people, coordinating attention (and perception, and emotional reactions) on a third element. These core elements of social interaction are called "joint attention" (or sometimes "triadic attention," to make the distinction from simple mutual gaze).

These triadic interactions provide an infant with a platform by which she can learn about her world. Similarly, they provide the caretaker with a platform by which she can guide the infant's learning. Joint attention continues to be an important tool throughout life; however, it is particularly critical in infancy and early childhood when social interaction is the primary means of learning. Before an infant has acquired abstract symbols (words) for objects, her medium of communication (and learning) about her world with others is constrained to points, gaze shifts, and head turns. The simple ability and motivation to share attention with another person on an object is highly correlated with a host of cognitive and social advances later in life. For example, joint attention ability is correlated with later language ability (Baldwin, 1991; Morales, Mundy, & Rojas, 1998; Mundy & Newell, 2007) emotion regulation (Morales, Mundy, Crowson, Neal, & Delgado, 2005), social competence (Vaughan Van Hecke et al., 2007), and theory of mind (or reasoning about others' mental states) (Nelson, Adamson, & Bakeman, 2008).

Neuroscientists have only recently begun to investigate the neural mechanisms of joint attention. New noninvasive neuroimaging techniques now let scientists peer directly into the brains of healthy human adults, children, and even infants while they engage in simple social interactions. Neuroscience studies can inform what brain systems mediate a behavior. This neural information can often provide greater sensitivity than the study of behavior alone for several reasons. First, a behavior may be the same but the mechanism that produces it differs. For example, if I view a person look to my left or see an arrow point to my left, I will likely shift my own gaze to the left; however, orienting to a person's gaze relies on overlapping but distinct brain regions (and thus mechanisms) than does orienting to a nonsocial directional cue (Engell et al., 2010). Second, neural sensitivity can serve as evidence for stimulus discrimination if an overt behavioral response is not reliably measurable. This is particularly true when studying infants and young children who may have more sophisticated abilities that are belied by their poor motor and attentional control. Finally, the identification of brain regions that underlie a given behavior in typical, healthy individuals provides a baseline by which atypical populations can be compared.

Almost all neuroscience studies focus on a simple example of joint attention (although as we shall see, this example is complicated enough): Person A sees person B looking at object C, and so person A shifts their visual attention to object C. Furthermore, neuroscience studies are largely restricted to the perspective of person A—the "responder." In the following we describe the few studies that have looked at the neural correlates for the "initiator" of joint attention. However, the bulk of this chapter follows the literature, and tries to characterize the cognitive and neural mechanisms that allow people to detect a bid for joint attention and respond appropriately.

From the responder's perspective, engaging in joint attention requires at least four steps. First, the responder must attend to, or at least be aware of, the initiator as a potential social partner. Second, the responder must detect a shift in the attention of the initiator towards an object, for example, by perceiving the initiator's gaze shift, head turn and/or point. Third, the responder must shift attention to the object. And fourth, the responder must monitor the ongoing relationship among the initiator's attention, his or her own attention, and the object to ensure that joint attention is successfully achieved and maintained. Although the first, second, and third components are relatively easy to isolate and examine in typical neuroimaging experiments, the fourth provides technical and methodological challenges. However, in many ways the fourth is the essence of joint attention. Joint attention can only fully occur if two people actively coordinate attention and are aware of each other's attention on the same thing. In a typical functional magnetic resonance imaging (fMRI) experiment, participants lie flat on their back in a magnetic tube (the MRI bore). Activation is detected by looking for changes in MRI signal in small regions of the brain (about 45 mm^3); a resolution that requires participants to remain motionless. Acquisition of these data produces a very loud repetitive and high-frequency sound. Let's remember now the goal of our study: to understand the neural bases underlying active coordination of attention with another person in the context of a social interaction. The challenges of creating a natural social interaction while in the scanner are daunting. As described in the following, this challenge is only beginning to be overcome.

The first section of this chapter describes what is known about the neural mechanisms of each of these four steps of joint attention. The second section discusses how and whether neural evidence can help to address questions about the development of joint attention in human infancy.

Neural Mechanisms of Joint Attention in Adulthood

ATTENDING TO A POTENTIAL SOCIAL PARTNER

In adults, attending to the presence of a social partner appears to depend on the dorsal medial prefrontal cortex (dMPFC). The dMPFC is located on the medial wall of the frontal lobe, anterior and superior to the cingulate gyrus; or about half an inch behind the middle of the forehead. Activity has been observed in the dMPFC during a whole range of different tasks that require participants to think about, or interact with, another person.

Activity in the dMPFC is critical to a social interaction in two ways. First, it appears to reflect the sense that another person is *present* as a social partner and second, it supports reasoning about the person's psychological or emotional traits (Harris, Todorov, & Fiske, 2005; Mitchell, Heatherton, & Macrae, 2002; Mitchell, Neil Macrae, & Banaji, 2005), which typically occurs in a social interaction. Dorsal medial prefrontal cortex activity is specifically enhanced when the potential social partner deliberately draws the subject's attention to himself. A bid for attention can occur via direct mutual gaze (to catch your attention, I look you in the eye), or via calling the target's name. Both of these social cues elicit enhanced activity in the dMPFC (Kampe, Frith, & Frith, 2003). A particularly strong social cue occurs if the person walks toward the subject, looks toward him or her, and then makes a social gesture (e.g., a smile, raised eyebrows). These cues elicit dMPFC activity (Schilbach et al., 2006; but see Pelphrey, Viola, & McCarthy, 2004). The duration of mutual gaze is also correlated with higher dMPFC activity (Kuzmanovic et al., 2009).

In sum, in a joint attention episode, dMPFC activity may initially support attending to a potential social partner, especially if the social partner is deliberately eliciting that attention, signaling the beginning of an interaction.

DETECTING A SHIFT IN ATTENTION

Once the responder is attending to the initiator, the second step of a joint attention interaction occurs when the initiator shifts attention to another object. The responder must detect and accurately represent that shift. To accurately do this, the observer must understand that the attentional shift was intentional. Considerable neuroscientific evidence, from both animal and human models, implicates the right posterior superior temporal sulcus (pSTS) in these calculations. The superior temporal sulcus runs the length of the temporal lobe; the region implicated in perceived shifts of attention, at least in humans, is near the posterior end, above the right ear.

In macaque monkeys, neurons in the pSTS respond to specific orientations of the head and eyes (Perrett, Hietanen, Oram, & Benson, 1992). Some of these neurons appear to literally code the observed direction of an actor's attention. For example, an individual neuron might prefer (i.e., discharge more action potentials when viewing an image of) a face in which the head is pointed toward location A but not B. If the head is inverted the same cell will fire only if the head is facing toward A (even though the direction of head orientation will be different) (Hasselmo, Rolls, Baylis, & Nalwa, 1989). Similarly, another neuron might prefer leftward gaze (as compared with rightward), regardless of the orientation of the head; however, if the eyes are occluded, the same neuron prefers a left-facing head to a straight or right-facing head, regardless of overall body orientation; and if the head is occluded, then the same neuron prefers a leftward pointing body (Jellema, Baker, Wicker, & Perrett, 2000). These neurons thus appear to implement a very abstract code, representing the direction of another person's attention based on the best available evidence (eyes > head > body orientation). In humans, fMRI studies have similarly reported right pSTS activation when people observe (and attend to) another person's gaze shifts (Kingstone, Tipper, Ristic, & Ngan, 2004; Hooker et al., 2003; Pelphrey, Singerman, Allison, & McCarthy, 2003; Materna, Dicke, & Thier, 2008). Distinct regions of the pSTS appear to respond to motion in the eyes, mouth, and hands (Puce, Allison, Bentin, Gore, & McCarthy, 1998).

Importantly, the STS does not just respond to moving eyes or bodies, but appears to integrate the eye movement with the surrounding context in order to interpret the person's action. People don't just move their eyes; they look at specific objects. For example, in one experiment, participants saw an animated face that occasionally gazed toward one of the four corners of the screen. Immediately before the gaze shift, a flashing checkerboard would appear either in the target-of-gaze position (congruent) or somewhere else (incongruent). Both conditions elicited activation in the pSTS; however, the incongruent condition engaged the pSTS to a greater extent (Pelphrey et al., 2003). That is, when gaze shifts are incongruous with the visible context, pSTS activity is enhanced (as if the pSTS is "working harder" to interpret the unexpected action). This incongruency effect has been shown with other types of actions, such as reaching and walking (Brass, Schmitt, Spengler, & Gergely, 2007; Pelphrey, Morris, & McCarthy, 2004; Saxe, Xiao, Kovacs, Perrett, & Kanwisher, 2004).

There is also some evidence that activity in the pSTS is enhanced when an action (e.g., gaze shift or point) reflects a communicative intention. In one study, activity in the pSTS was higher when an animated character with averted gaze shifted his gaze toward the participant to make eye contact, compared with when he shifted his gaze further away from the participant (Pelphrey, Viola, et al., 2004). Thus, the pSTS may play a role in interpreting actions within a communicative context.

In sum, pSTS appears to be involved in perceiving and interpreting other people's biological actions, including particularly gaze and head orientation shifts. The pSTS allows the responder to detect and interpret the initiator's movements as evidence of a shift of her attention, providing the invitation for the responder to follow. The pSTS is recruited more if this biological action requires that the observer think about the intention behind the action.

SHIFTING ONE'S OWN ATTENTION

Another person's gaze shift is a powerful cue that elicits a shift in the observer's attention. This responsive shift of attention can occur both automatically, and under deliberate control. To illustrate the difference: If you are focused on reading a chapter at your desk but colleagues are talking loudly outside your door, attention will be automatically oriented to your colleagues (i.e., exogenously). This is distinct from voluntary (endogenous) control of attention orienting such as subsequently choosing to focus back on your chapter. Exogenous and endogenous attention processes rely on distinct, but overlapping, neural mechanisms (Corbetta & Shulman, 2002; Rosen et al., 1999). Responding to joint attention involves both.

Orienting to another person's gaze or point has been shown to be a reflexive, automatic process, engaging the exogenous attention network. This has been tested a number of times through variations of a simple cueing paradigm (Posner, 1980). In this paradigm, participants are told to push a button as soon as they see a target on the left or right side of the screen. Before the target appears, a face in the center of the screen will shift gaze to the right or left of the screen but the shift does not predict the location of the target. Even though the subjects are aware that the gaze cue is not informative, the subject will take longer to detect a cue if it appears on the side that was not cued by the gaze shift (Kingstone et al., 2004; Stevens, West, Al-Aidroos, Weger, & Pratt, 2008). Exogenous control relies on a ventral frontoparietal network of brain regions, including the right inferior and middle frontal gyrus (R IFG and R MFG) and a region within the temporoparietal junction (TPJ) (Corbetta & Shulman, 2002). Thus, these regions play a role in automatic shifting of attention during perception of a gaze or point cue.

Although viewing another person's gaze automatically orients attention to where that person is looking, joint attention also requires controlled and voluntary shifts of attention (endogenous attention). This endogenous attention recruits a network of regions within the dorsolateral frontal parietal system, including the frontal eye fields (FEF) and intraparietal sulcus (IPS) (Corbetta & Shulman, 2002). This system is recruited during eye movements, as well as covert shifts of attention (Corbetta et al., 1998; Nobre, Gitelman, Dias, & Mesulam, 2000). The FEF region plays a role in motor control and planning of eye movements, whereas the IPS with the superior parietal lobule (SPL) may play a role in deployment and maintenance of spatial attention (Hopfinger, Buonocore, & Mangun, 2000; Molenberghs et al., 2007; Yantis & Serences, 2003). The IPS may play a key role in the fourth stage of joint attention (described in the following) as it is more active when attention must shift between different features (e.g., object and person), whereas the SPL is active during any shift of spatial attention (i.e., even if an object remains the same but moves to a new location) (Molenberghs et al., 2007).

Thus, both the exogenous (or reflexive) and endogenous (or controlled) attention systems rely on regions within frontal and parietal cortex that are distinct from those involved in other components of joint attention. Depending on the context, either system may be recruited to make a shift of attention (reflexive or controlled) during a joint attention interaction.

MONITORING THE RELATIONSHIP BETWEEN ONE'S OWN ATTENTION, ANOTHER'S ATTENTION, AND AN OBJECT (TRIADIC ATTENTION)

After the responder shifts attention to an object, she must be able to detect and monitor that the initiator is also sharing attention with her. Joint, or triadic, attention only lasts as long as both people know that they are each attending to the object and each other. This knowledge or sense that you are sharing attention with another person *intentionally* is the essential component in joint attention. This shared experience is what allows joint attention to be truly communicative and such a successful platform for learning.

Joint attention can be either concrete, such as physically looking at the same object in their shared environment, or abstract, such as a common topic of conversation. These joint interactions within the scanner have been difficult to study given that they require that a person in the scanner interact with another person in a manner that communicates something about an object or goal. As described, the challenge behind creating a naturalistic social interaction while lying motionless and alone in a noisy tube is not trivial. Through several lines of research, this challenge is beginning to be overcome.

Triadic Attention with an Alleged Partner

One solution to the problem of collecting neuroimaging data during a triadic interaction is to have the participants think they are interacting with another person in a common task. For example, participants are engaged in a trust or decision-making game with an alleged human partner (who they can not see). These studies compare patterns of activation during engagement in a game in which participants are told they are playing a person (who is not visible) or a computer. When participants think they are engaged in a collaborative game with a person, greater activation is most consistently found in medial prefrontal cortex (Fukui et al., 2006; Gallagher, Jack, Roepstorff, & Frith, 2002; Kircher et al., 2009; Rilling et al., 2002; Rilling, Sanfey, Aronson, Nystrom, & Cohen, 2004). One interpretation is that, similar to a social interaction, participants need to monitor the other player's thoughts and beliefs in relation to their own to achieve a shared goal. This representation of another is only required when playing a human.

Triadic Attention with a Visible Person

Recent studies have come up with novel methods to allow participants to interact face-to-face with another person (real, virtual, or a video of a real person). Participants are engaged in a joint attention game in which a visible experimenter and subject share attention on an object, simulating (or actually creating in some cases) a joint attention experience. These studies (Bristow, Rees, & Frith, 2007; Materna et al., 2008; Redcay et al., 2010a ; Schilbach et al., 2009; Williams, Waiter, Perra, Perrett, & Whiten, 2005) have identified recruitment of regions within the medial prefrontal cortex (Bristow et al., 2007; Redcay et al., 2010a ; Schilbach et al., 2009; Williams et al., 2005) and posterior superior temporal sulcus (Materna et al., 2008; Redcay et al., 2010a) while participants share attention on an object with another person. In each study, the design used to elicit joint attention varied widely; however, the regions engaged during these joint attention tasks are consistent.

One dimension by which the studies differ is how the participant and "experimenter" achieve shared attention. In one study (Williams et al., 2005) joint attention was achieved coincidentally, rather than intentionally. Study participants were instructed to follow a ball that was moving in the lower half of the screen. In the upper half of the screen, a video of a man's face was presented. The man also followed the ball—leading to an experience of joint attention among the man, subject, and ball—or did not follow the ball (non–joint attention). In this study joint as compared with non–joint attention differentially recruited activity in both the MPFC as well as posterior cingulate cortex. Thus these regions appear to be engaged during the experience of shared attention even if neither party initiated or responded to a bid for joint attention.

In the remainder of the studies joint attention is achieved by following the experimenter's gaze cue in order to share attention with the experimenter and achieve a goal (Materna et al., 2008; Redcay et al., 2010a; Schilbach et al., 2009). These studies varied by whether a real or virtual character was used and by the condition used to control for properties of the interaction not relevant to joint attention. In one of these studies (Schilbach et al., 2009), participants were cued by a virtual character towards one of 3 squares. When the participant and the virtual character both looked at the square, the square lit up. In the comparison condition the subjects were told to look at a square that was not cued by the virtual character. In this case, the square that the subjects looked at, not the virtual character, lit up. This study identified medial prefrontal cortex as differentially recruited during the joint attention condition as compared to the control (Schilbach et al., 2009).

A second study presented subjects with a virtual character that would both shift her gaze towards one of five targets on the screen and her iris would change color to match one of the five targets on each trial (Materna et al., 2008). On joint attention trials, participants were told to look at the same target at which the face was looking. On non–joint attention trials, participants were told to look at the target that matched the color of the woman's iris. Thus, in both conditions the participant observed a gaze shift; however, only in joint attention trials did the participant use that gaze shift to direct their own attention and share attention with the face image. Activation was seen in right posterior superior temporal cortex in joint as compared to non-joint attention conditions.

Finally, in the third study (Redcay et al., 2010a) participants were engaged in an interactive game with an experimenter in a face-to-face interaction (via a live video feed). The participant was told their goal was to "catch the mouse." In the joint attention condition, the experimenter would receive a cue as to which of the four corners of the screen the mouse was "hiding." The experimenter would then look at that corner. The subject would detect the experimenter's gaze shift and follow her gaze to the appropriate corner. When the subject also looked to the corner the mouse was "caught" and appeared on the screen. In the control (non-joint attention) condition, the subject received the cue as to where the mouse was "hiding" and simply looked to that corner of the screen in order to "catch" the mouse. The experimenter opened and closed her eyes at the start of each trial in order to control for the presence of biological motion and make explicit to the subject that the experimenter was not involved in the game. Joint as compared with non–joint attention recruited regions within bilateral posterior superior temporal cortex with the strongest focus of activation in the right posterior superior temporal sulcus as well as a region within dorsal medial prefrontal cortex.

Thus, the posterior STS appears to be recruited not only to use a gaze cue to shift one's attention but also to share attention with another on an object (Materna et al., 2008; Redcay et al., 2010a). The medial prefrontal cortex also appears to be recruited when attention is shared intentionally between two people and an object (Redcay et al., 2010a; Schilbach et al., 2009).

Initiating Joint Attention

Until now, we've focused on just one side of a joint attention interaction: that of the responder. However, unlike detecting a gaze shift, monitoring the relationship between one's own attention, another's, and an object is required by both the responder and initiator in a joint attention episode. Thus, a powerful test of the regions important to this fourth component is to examine whether the same regions are engaged during joint attention in both the initiator and responder.

The ability to study the initiation of a joint attention episode poses a significant challenge during fMRI data acquisition for two reasons: (1) as with responding to joint attention, initiating joint attention requires that the subject believe she is in a joint attention episode with another person and (2) the response of the experimenter must be contingent on the subjects, which is unique to joint attention. The preceding section addressed how studies have overcome challenge 1. In the following we describe how the second challenge is just beginning to be addressed.

One way to accomplish the second challenge is to use eye-tracking technology to detect exactly where a participant is looking at all times. In this way, the stimuli can be programmed in such a way that the subject's gaze behavior determines which stimuli are presented to the subject. This method was recently developed (Wilms et al., 2010) and used in a study of joint attention (Schilbach et al., 2009). Participants viewed a virtual character but they were told that this character mimicked the behavior of an actual person. The authors used a design in which gaze was either followed (joint attention) or not followed (non–joint attention) and in which either the subject (self) or experimenter (other) initiated the gaze shift. In the self (initiating) joint attention condition, when the eye-tracking software detected the subject's gaze over one of the three squares, the virtual character's gaze would shift to that block, allowing for a contingent joint attention interaction. Both types of joint attention combined (initiating and responding), as compared to non–joint attention, conditions recruited multiple brain areas including the medial prefrontal cortex.

A second way to overcome the challenge is to develop a set-up in which a real person can interact with a subject face-to-face (via video feed) and in real time. Recently, we developed such a set-up (Redcay et al., 2010a). During the experiment participants engaged in simple and highly scripted interactive games with an experimenter. This experiment did not explicitly test joint attention; however, numerous episodes of joint attention occurred within the interaction. In the "live" condition, the experimenter and subject engaged in a real-time, live interaction, whereas in the "recorded" conditions, subjects responded to a recording of the experimenter. Thus, the essential difference between these conditions is that only in the live condition are the experimenter's actions directly contingent on the subject's gaze behavior. Comparison of live versus recorded conditions revealed greater activation in a number of brain regions, including the right posterior STS, which is consistent with its role in monitoring another person's attention and actions in relation to your own, as is required in a joint attention interaction (Redcay et al., 2010a).

Using the same face-to-face set-up, we examined the neural bases underlying initiating joint attention specifically (Redcay et al., 2010b; Redcay et al., 2012). This study used a similar design to that described in the Redcay et al. (2010a) joint attention study in which participants were instructed to play an interactive game called "catch the mouse" with a live experimenter. In addition to responding to joint attention and control conditions described in the preceding, a third condition, initiating joint attention, was included. In this condition, the subject received a clue as to where the mouse was hiding on his screen. Based on the subject's gaze, the experimenter shifted her gaze to that location and the mouse was then caught. Comparison of both responding to and initiating joint attention conditions with the control condition revealed activation in dMPFC and bilateral pSTS.

The Medial Prefrontal Cortex and Posterior Superior Temporal Sulcus
Are Essential Players in Joint Attention

In sum, the MPFC and pSTS clearly play an essential role in joint attention; however, the specific role remains undetermined. Each plays a distinct role in components of joint attention. The MPFC is recruited when someone is perceived as a social partner. The pSTS is recruited to detect a shift in another person's attention. However, both are recruited when participants are required to share attention with another person on an object. These regions are recruited whether or not the participant responds to a gaze cue or initiates a gaze cue. Designs have varied widely and reveal differential involvement of these two regions (described in the preceding), but the reason for these differences is not yet clear.

A major question for future research is whether the MPFC and pSTS play distinct roles in the essential component of joint attention; namely, the intentional, active coordination of attention between two people and an object. One possibility is that both together serve a function during joint attention that cannot be isolated to one or another region. Another possibility is that each is engaged during a joint attention context, but represent slightly different aspects of that interaction. For example, the MPFC may represent the "what" of another person's attention and the pSTS may represent the "where." In other words, the MPFC is recruited to monitor what the other person is attending to in relation to your own attention (e.g., an abstract game or the properties of an object), whereas the pSTS is recruited to represent where the other person's attention is in relation to your own.

Although the specific roles of each region remain unclear, the involvement of the MPFC and pSTS in joint attention in adults is clear. Comparatively less is known about the neural bases of joint attention in infancy.

Neural Mechanisms of Joint Attention in Development

As defined, joint attention depends on (1) detection of a potential social partner, (2) detection of a shift in another's attention, (3) shifting attention to the appropriate location, and (4) monitoring the relation between another person's attention in relation to one's own and a third entity. Similar to the adult literature, research has focused mostly on the first, second, and third components because these are easier to isolate and study in infants. The challenge in infancy is how to measure whether infants are simply orienting to others' shifts in attention or they understand the intention behind these shifts in attention. As Call and Tomasello note, joint attention is not simply looking at the same thing as another person, but rather it is *knowing* both of you are looking at the same thing at the same time (Call & Tomasello, 2005). This active, intentional coordination is a critical component of joint attention behavior. When this *knowing* emerges in development is a matter of debate. Some suggest joint attention does not emerge until infants have the capacity to understand others' intentions, which develops at the end of the first year of life (Tomasello, Carpenter, Call, Behne, & Moll, 2005). Others suggest that joint attention emerges as early as 4 months of age (Grossmann & Johnson, 2010). The following section reviews both behavioral and neuroscience evidence examining when joint attention emerges and what neural and cognitive systems underlie its emergence.

WHAT CAN NEUROIMAGING MEASURES PROVIDE?

Neuroimaging measures can provide insight into two questions for which behavioral evidence alone may not be sufficient. First, neuroimaging can provide greater sensitivity to ask questions of very young infants who cannot or will not give reliable overt behavioral responses. These measures can reveal discrimination among different stimuli without requiring any measure of overt behavior. Second, neuroimaging measures can provide information about what regions or processes are differentially engaged. Our review pays particular attention to whether neuroimaging has yet lived up to its potential. Has neuroimaging provided us with anything additional beyond what we know from behavior?

WHAT DO WE KNOW FROM BEHAVIORAL STUDIES?

Full joint attention is thought to emerge between 9 and 12 months of age (Tomasello et al., 2005). However, components, or precursors, of this process are present early and develop throughout the first few years of life. For example, infants appear biased to social stimuli from the first minutes of life (Johnson, Dziurawiec, Ellis, & Morton, 1991) and can discriminate faces with direct gaze as compared with averted gaze (Farroni, Csibra, Simion, & Johnson, 2002). As early as 2 to 3 months of age infants can detect the contingency between their own and another's actions within a social interaction (Murray & Trevarthen, 1985). Thus, there is evidence that the first component of joint attention, detecting another as a social partner, is present as early as the first few months of life.

By 3 to 4 months of age, infants are able to use directional cues to shift their attention. Also around this age, infants begin to be able to volitionally disengage attention from their current focus (Colombo, 2001; Hood, Willen, & Driver, 1998; Hunnius, 2007; Richards, 2003). Initially, infants can only shift attention if the object is already within their field of view. The ability to detect less salient directional cues (e.g., gaze shift vs. head turn) improves well into the second year of life (Butterworth & Jarrett, 1991; but see Moll & Tomasello, 2004). Nonetheless, the first signs of the ability to shift attention based on another's shift of attention is present by 3 to 4 months of age. Thus, behaviorally, there is compelling evidence that portions of joint attention are present from very early on, as young as 4 months of age.

Evidence for the fourth component is trickier. When do infants actively monitor their own attention and another's in relation to an object? When do they *know* they are attending to the same thing as another person? Although one may be able to use another's gaze as a directional cue, the understanding of the intention behind that shift is necessary to achieve joint attention. Similarly, to monitor the relation between one's own and another's attention on an object requires an understanding that both parties are intending to attend to that object together. Much behavioral evidence suggests this "knowing" is not present until close to the end of the first year of life (see chapter 2 for further discussion).

For example, infants at 9 months of age will look just as long at a toy that a woman turned toward with her eyes open or with her eyes closed. By 10 to 11 months of age, however, infants look longer at the toy only if the woman turned toward it with her eyes open (Brooks & Meltzoff, 2005). In a separate series of studies, infants were first habituated to a woman who gazed at either a bear or a ball (Woodward, 2003). On new object trials the woman looked to the same side of the screen but the object changed. On new side trials the woman looked to the other side of the screen but the object remained the same. Only infants 12 months of age looked longer on new object trials but not new side trials, suggesting that 12-month-olds, but not 7- to 9-month-olds, are able to represent the goal or intention behind another's gaze shift (i.e., to look at the object). These findings suggest that by 10 to 11 months, but not earlier, infants understand the referential intent of others' gaze shifts.

WHAT DO WE KNOW FROM NEUROIMAGING MEASURES?

Here we draw on neuroimaging as a possible tool to ask whether there is evidence for an early representation of the referential intention behind a gaze shift. The majority of neuroimaging in infancy has been conducted through the use of event-related potentials (ERPs) (Nelson & McCleery, 2008). Event-related potentials are recorded from a cap placed over the scalp that contains electrodes (sensors) that detect electrical activity coming from the brain. Brain cells firing generate this electrical activity. In the ERP method, the activity is time-locked to the presentation of a stimulus, allowing for a measure of how a stimulus affects the amplitude of the signal over time. Amplitude can be positive or negative, and both reflect increased firing. These signals are described as components, which are simply terms that reflect the time at which a relative peak in amplitude is detected and whether the activity is positive or negative. For example, the N170 component describes electrical activity that occurs at 170 milliseconds after a stimulus and is negative in amplitude. Many of these components are associated with different processes, such as attention or memory. In this way, ERPs can index whether an infant is paying more or less attention to a stimulus without having to rely on behavior. On the other hand, ERPs provide fairly limited information about where the activity is coming from, so it makes comparison to the adult fMRI results difficult. The next section examines studies that have used the ERP method to examine when infants show evidence for triadic attention. In these studies, similar to the adult fMRI literature, the participant (i.e., the infant) is typically responding to joint attention while the experimenter (i.e., the adult) is initiating joint attention. Little data exist on the neural bases of initiating joint attention in infancy.

When Are Infants Sensitive to Joint Attention?

Using ERPs, two studies have examined 9-month-old infants' neural sensitivity to joint attention contexts (Senju, Johnson, & Csibra, 2006; Striano, Reid, & Hoehl, 2006). In a novel, live interactive set-up, Striano et al. (2006) showed that 9-month-olds process objects differently if they are observed in a joint compared with non-joint attention context. In the joint attention condition, the adult (the initiator) first made eye contact with the infant (the responder) and then looked at the object on the screen. In the non-joint attention condition the adult just looked at the object on the screen. Event-related potentials were analyzed during presentation of the objects in either joint or non-joint attention contexts. A fronto-central negativity (known as the Nc component), which is thought to reflect attentional processing (Courchesne, Ganz, & Norcia, 1981) showed larger amplitudes to the objects that were viewed during joint attention situations than non-joint attention situations (Striano et al., 2006), suggesting greater attentional resources are devoted to processing objects when they are in a joint attention context.

In a second study (Senju et al., 2006), 9-month-old infants (and adults) were presented with a screen containing an image of a woman's face. During each trial, an object would appear on the left or right of the screen and then the woman would shift gaze either toward (object-congruent) or away (object-incongruent) from the object. Both infants and adults showed greater negativity in components over occipito-temporal sites to object-*incongruent* gaze shifts. These findings suggest some continuity in the response to object-incongruent gaze shifts between 9 months and adulthood. However, unlike adults, infants showed greater negativity (N200 and N400) in anterior electrode sites during object-congruent gaze shifts. One possible interpretation of the anterior negativity in the infants, but not adults, is that the neural response in infants is less specialized than that of adults; thus, greater cortical resources are engaged during joint attention behaviors (Johnson, Grossmann, & Cohen Kadosh, 2009).

INFANTS SHOW DISCRIMINATION OF JOINT ATTENTION CONTEXTS AS YOUNG AS 4 MONTHS

As noted, a major potential contribution of neuroimaging in infancy is to ask when behaviors emerge. Studies have examined even younger ages in an attempt to answer just that. Infant ERP measures reveal that by 4 months of age infants can detect that a person is looking at an object; process an object more if gazed at by another; and use another's emotional information to modulate object-processing (review, Striano & Reid, 2006). Four-month old infants show a greater positive slow wave (PSW), which is thought to be a measure of encoding (Nelson, 1996), if an adult's gaze is directed at an object versus not at an object (Hoehl, Reid, Mooney, & Striano, 2008). They show a smaller PSW if they view an object that they had previously seen an adult gaze at, than if they view an object that an adult had not gazed at, suggesting the object had already been encoded during the joint attention episode (Reid, Striano, Kaufman, & Johnson, 2004).

Infants as young as 4 months old also show some evidence that they expect an adult to look toward an object. Specifically, if an object appears and an adult looks to the other side of the screen, infants show a larger Nc component (an index of attentional processing) than if the adult looks toward the object (Hoehl, Reid, et al., 2008). They also show a larger Nc if they view an object that was previously viewed by an adult with a fearful as compared with neutral gaze, suggesting the infant is able to detect an adult's negative emotion and map it onto the object the adult is viewing (Hoehl, Wiese, & Striano, 2008).

In sum, ERP studies suggest sensitivity to joint attention contexts as early as 4 months of age. This early neural sensitivity is intriguing given behavioral results, suggesting that infants do not map the intention behind a gaze shift until closer to the end of the first year of life. One possibility is many of the neural results are interpretable in the context of low-level properties. For example, direction of attention may serve as a directional cue to infants, similar to a non-social stimulus such as an arrow. With a directional cue toward an object the infant may process that object more, simply because the infant's own attention is now on the object. Similarly, another person's fearful expression may make the directional cue more salient or induce an arousal response in the infant allowing for more attentional resources devoted to the object.

On the other hand, ERP studies provide some evidence for continuity in the neural response to joint attention between infants and adults. For example, greater occipito-temporal negativity to an object-incongruent gaze shift is observed in infant ERPs, adult ERPs, and adult fMRI (in the pSTS) (Senju et al., 2006). In adults this activity likely reflects the fact that an object-incongruent gaze shift violates the observer's expectation of the experimenter's action, thus requiring greater processing of the true intention behind that action. Could infants have such a representation of other's intentions at only 4 months of age? Compelling evidence would be if ERPs were recorded during a similar paradigm to that of Woodward (2003). If infants show neural discrimination between new object (goal) and new side trials this would suggest infants have a neural representation of the goal of the reach. To our knowledge no such study has been conducted.

What Brain Regions Are Engaged During Joint Attention?

One way to examine whether the infant brain is sensitive to the intention behind another's gaze shift is to see if the same regions that are recruited in adults (who we know are sensitive to intention) are also recruited in infants during a joint attention episode. Review of the adult literature suggests that the MPFC and pSTS are essential players in active and intentional sharing of attention with another person on an object in adults. Are the same regions engaged in infants?

The adult studies relied on fMRI because it is a noninvasive method that has good spatial resolution (i.e., can identify which brain regions are involved at the resolution of about 45 mm³). However, fMRI is very challenging to use with infants because it requires that infants remain almost motionless in a big, noisy tube while focusing attention on a mirror above their head. A relatively new technique, near-infrared spectroscopy (NIRS) eliminates a number of these challenges (Lloyd-Fox, Blasi, & Elwell, 2010). Near-infrared spectroscopy, like fMRI, uses changes in blood volume (or flow) as an index of neuronal activity, which allows for some comparison across methodologies. Near-infrared spectroscopy works by shining a light across the scalp and measuring the amount of light absorbed. The absorption level will vary based on the volume of hemoglobin in that area, an indirect index of neural activity. The resolution is not as good as fMRI but can still give some degree of localization. Instead of lying in a tube, infants wear a lightweight hat and as a result the images are less affected by infant head motion. Thus, in principle NIRS offers an exciting avenue for direct comparison of adult neuroimaging results to findings from infants and children using NIRS.

DORSAL MEDIAL PREFRONTAL CORTEX RECRUITED DURING TRIADIC INTERACTION AT 5 MONTHS

The one study to examine triadic attention in infancy with NIRS (Grossmann & Johnson, 2010) did so in 5-month-old infants (before the age at which infants are thought to understand intentions behind others' actions). They find that a region within the left dorsal medial prefrontal cortex (dMPFC) is selectively recruited during a joint attention episode in which an adult engages an infant in a communicative interaction (by making eye contact) and then shifts attention to an object. This same selectivity is not seen if the adult either does not look at the infant first or looks away from the object. The study only examined regions within the frontal cortex, so it is not clear if posterior areas were engaged during this joint attention episode. Nonetheless, engagement of dMPFC suggests that even at 5 months, infants recruit a similar neural region as older infants and adults.

THE DORSAL MEDIAL PREFRONTAL CORTEX AND POSTERIOR SUPERIOR TEMPORAL SULCUS ARE RECRUITED DURING DYADIC INTERACTION AT 4 MONTHS

A second NIRS study examined regions within both frontal and posterior areas in 4-month-olds (Grossmann et al., 2008). This study only examined the first component of joint attention, namely, engaging in a social interaction in 4-month-old infants. Using NIRS, they found that like in adults (Kampe et al., 2003; Pelphrey, Viola, et al., 2004; Redcay et al., 2010a; Schilbach et al., 2006), the dMPFC and right pSTS were recruited during engagement in a social interaction. Specifically, sensors over the medial prefrontal cortex and posterior superior temporal cortex show greater activation if a virtual character looked toward the infant and made a communicative expression (raised eyebrows and a smile) than if the character looked away from the infant and also made the same communicative expression.

CONTINUITY IN BRAIN REGIONS UNDERLYING JOINT ATTENTION
BETWEEN INFANTS AND ADULTS

In sum, recent evidence suggests that infants as young as 4 to 5 months of age and adults recruit similar neural regions to both detect another as a potential social partner and to engage in a joint attention episode. Like adults, infants rely on the dorsal medial prefrontal cortex and the posterior superior temporal cortex.

One possible conclusion is that the continuity in neural regions supporting joint attention between infancy and adulthood provides evidence that intention understanding is a robust and very early-emerging phenomenon. If true, this would be a case in which neuroimaging measures can provide a more sensitive measure of infant cognition. However, this claim should be taken with caution given that we know the MPFC and pSTS are also recruited during the early components of joint attention: The detection of another as a social partner and perception of gaze direction. Thus, recruitment of these regions in infants does not necessarily imply intention understanding.

An alternative possibility is that these regions may serve as an early-emerging social-communicative system that is initially only partially functional and serves to bias infants toward communicative cues (similar to Grossmann & Johnson, 2007). Detection of these communicative cues is critical for the infant to take maximal advantage of learning opportunities within his or her social world (Csibra & Gergely, 2009). Later development of these systems may allow for the more complex representation of the intention behind one's attention.

Current evidence cannot rule out the possibility that other systems may be critical to joint attention and its development. Evidence from the adult suggests that attention systems are involved in some components of joint attention. Similarly (as discussed in chapter 10), systems implicated in representing one's own and another's actions (known as the mirror neuron system) may also play a role. The mirror neuron system is comprised of regions of neurons within ventral premotor cortex and inferior parietal lobe that fire both during observation and execution of the same action, or in some cases, goal. Thus, one could imagine that the mirror neuron system may provide an early link between the third and fourth components of joint attention, as defined in this chapter; that is, the detection of a shift in attention in another person and a shift in your own attention to match the other person's attention. In fact, compelling behavioral evidence suggest that an infant's experience in the first year of life provides a necessary foundation for understanding another's actions (Meltzoff & Brooks, 2008; Sommerville, Woodward, & Needham, 2005). The infant NIRS studies do not give a measure of whole-brain activity and the ERP studies do not provide sensitive information on localization of function. Thus, it is possible that other regions and systems (e.g., mirror neuron and attention systems) are differentially recruited during the emergence and development of joint attention (for review, Mundy & Newell, 2007 and Mundy, Sullivan, & Mastergeorge, 2009). Replicating the same studies over other regions of cortex would give insight into whether the pattern of neural response across the whole brain is the same in infants as in adults.

CONCLUSION

Exciting advances in neuroimaging technologies have allowed us to identify the regions that are critical to our ability to engage in a social interaction, follow another's attention, and shift our own attention. Identifying regions that are critical to active, intentional coordination of attention has proved to be a more challenging endeavor. Nevertheless, recent creative experimental designs and technological advances (e.g., Redcay et al., 2010a; Redcay et al., 2012; Schilbach et al., 2009) have opened a new avenue of research. The first experiments reveal that the MPFC and pSTS are recruited during this process. Recent strides have been made in investigating this question in infants through the use of noninvasive imaging methods, including ERP and NIRS. By 4 months, infants are sensitive to a joint attention context and the same regions are recruited as in adults.

CLINICAL IMPLICATIONS

The beginning of this chapter posited that the third significant contribution of neuroimaging measures is to provide a baseline by which atypical populations can be compared. Advances in understanding the neuroscience of joint attention may be particularly pertinent to individuals with autism spectrum disorder (ASD), a developmental disorder characterized by impairments in social interaction and communication. Individuals with ASD show robust and early impairments in joint attention, both in initiating and in responding to others' attention shifts (Charman et al., 1997; Mundy, Sigman, Ungerer, & Sherman, 1986). Given the critical role of joint attention in later language acquisition, emotion regulation, and Theory of Mind, these early impairments may have a cascading effect on linguistic, emotional, and social development in these children (Charman, 2003; Mundy et al., 2007, 2009). Some preliminary neuroscience work in autism has already revealed that the posterior STS is recruited to the same extent when an ASD subject perceives someone shift gaze either toward or away from an object, suggesting a lack of intention–attribution to the gaze shift (Pelphrey, Morris, & McCarthy, 2005). Other work has shown that, unlike controls, individuals with autism do not show greater ERP responses to faces with direct than averted gaze (Senju, Tojo, Yaguchi, & Hasegawa, 2005), suggesting a lack of attention to another as a potential social partner. We recently used the live face-to-face paradigm described in a preceding section to examine brain differences between ASD and neurotypical participants during both initiating and responding to joint attention (Redcay et al., in press). This study revealed reduced differentiation between joint attention (IJA and RJA) and solo attention conditions in the ASD group within the pSTS and dMPFC, suggesting a possible lack of functional specialization. Future work using interactive designs to examine the developmental trajectory of functional specialization to joint attention contexts holds promise to uncover the mechanism underlying this early and fundamental impairment in ASD.

REFERENCES

Baldwin, D. A. (1991). Infants' contribution to the achievement of joint reference. *Child Development, 62*, 875–890.

Brass, M., Schmitt, R. M., Spengler, S., & Gergely, G. (2007). Investigating action understanding: Inferential processes versus action simulation. *Current Biology, 17*, 2117–2121.

Bristow, D., Rees, G., & Frith, C. D. (2007). Social interaction modifies neural response to gaze shifts. *Social Cognitive and Affective Neuroscience, 2*, 52–61.

Brooks, R., & Meltzoff, A. N. (2005). The development of gaze following and its relation to language. *Developmental Science, 8*, 535–543.

Butterworth, G., & Jarrett, N. (1991). What minds have in common is space: Spatial mechanisms serving joint visual attention in infancy. *British Journal of Developmental Psychology, 9*, 55–72.

Call, J., & Tomasello, M. (2005). What chimpanzees know about seeing, revisited: An explanation of the third kind. In N. Eilan, C. Hoerl, T. McCormack & J. Roessler (Eds.), *Joint Attention: Communication and Other Minds* (pp. 45–64). Oxford, UK: Clarendon Press.

Charman, T. (2003). Why is joint attention a pivotal skill in autism? *Philosophical Transactions of the Royal Society of London B, 358*, 315–324.

Charman, T., & et al. (1997). Infants with autism: An investigation of empathy, pretend play, joint attention, and imitation. *Developmental Psychology, 33*, 781–789.

Colombo, J. (2001). The development of visual attention in infancy. *Annual Review of Psychology, 52*, 337–367.

Corbetta, M., Akbudak, E., Conturo, T. E., Snyder, A. Z., Ollinger, J. M., Drury, H. A., et al. (1998). A common network of functional areas for attention and eye movements. *Neuron, 21*, 761–773.

Corbetta, M., & Shulman, G. L. (2002). Control of goal-directed and stimulus-driven attention in the brain. *Nature Reviews of Neuroscience, 3*, 201–215.

Courchesne, E., Ganz, L., & Norcia, A. M. (1981). Event-related brain potentials to human faces in infants. *Child Development, 52*, 804–811.

Csibra, G., & Gergely, G. (2009). Natural pedagogy. *Trends in Cognitive Science, 13*(4), 148–153.

Engell, A. D., Nummenmaa, L., Oosterhof, N. N., Henson, R. N., Haxby, J. V., & Calder, A. J. (2010). Differential activation of frontoparietal attention networks by social and symbolic spatial cues. *Social Cognitive and Affective Neuroscience, 5*, 432–440.

Farroni, T., Csibra, G., Simion, F., & Johnson, M. H. (2002). Eye contact detection in humans from birth. *Proceedings of the National Academy of Science U S A, 99*, 9602–9605.

Fukui, H., Murai, T., Shinozaki, J., Aso, T., Fukuyama, H., Hayashi, T., et al. (2006). The neural basis of social tactics: An fMRI study. *Neuroimage, 32*, 913–920.

Gallagher, H. L., Jack, A. I., Roepstorff, A., & Frith, C. D. (2002). Imaging the intentional stance in a competitive game. *Neuroimage, 16*(3 Pt 1), 814–821.

Grossmann, T., & Johnson, M. H. (2007). The development of the social brain in human infancy. *European Journal of Neuroscience, 25*, 909–919.

Grossmann, T., & Johnson, M. H. (2010). Selective prefrontal cortex responses to joint attention in early infancy. *Biology Letters, 6*, 540–543.

Grossmann, T., Johnson, M. H., Lloyd-Fox, S., Blasi, A., Deligianni, F., Elwell, C., et al. (2008). Early cortical specialization for face-to-face communication in human infants. *Proceedings of the Royal Society of Biological Sciences, 275*, 2803–2811.

Harris, L. T., Todorov, A., & Fiske, S. T. (2005). Attributions on the brain: Neuro-imaging dispositional inferences, beyond theory of mind. *Neuroimage, 28*, 763–769.

Hasselmo, M. E., Rolls, E. T., Baylis, G. C., & Nalwa, V. (1989). Object-centered encoding by face-selective neurons in the cortex in the superior temporal sulcus of the monkey. *Experimental Brain Research, 75*, 417–429.

Hoehl, S., Reid, V., Mooney, J., & Striano, T. (2008). What are you looking at? Infants' neural processing of an adult's object-directed eye gaze. *Developmental Science, 11*, 10–16.

Hoehl, S., Wiese, L., & Striano, T. (2008). Young infants' neural processing of objects is affected by eye gaze direction and emotional expression. *PLoS One, 3*, e2389.

Hood, B. M., Willen, D., & Driver, J. (1998). Adult's eyes trigger shifts of visual attention in human infants. *Psychological Science, 9*, 131–134.

Hooker, C. I., Paller, K. A., Gitelman, D. R., Parrish, T. B., Mesulam, M. M., & Reber, P. J. (2003). Brain networks for analyzing eye gaze. *Brain Research: Cognitive Brain Research, 17*, 406–418.

Hopfinger, J. B., Buonocore, M. H., & Mangun, G. R. (2000). The neural mechanisms of top-down attentional control. *Nature Neuroscience, 3*, 284–291.

Hunnius, S. (2007). The early development of visual attention and its implications for social and cognitive development. *Progress in Brain Research, 164*, 187–209.

Jellema, T., Baker, C. I., Wicker, B., & Perrett, D. I. (2000). Neural representation for the perception of the intentionality of actions. *Brain Cognition, 44*, 280–302.

Johnson, M. H., Dziurawiec, S., Ellis, H., & Morton, J. (1991). Newborns' preferential tracking of face-like stimuli and its subsequent decline. *Cognition, 40*, 1–19.

Johnson, M. H., Grossmann, T., & Cohen Kadosh, K. (2009). Mapping functional brain development: Building a social brain through interactive specialization. *Developmental Psychology, 45*, 151–159.

Kampe, K. K., Frith, C. D., & Frith, U. (2003). "Hey John": signals conveying communicative intention toward the self activate brain regions associated with "mentalizing," regardless of modality. *Journal of Neuroscience, 23*, 5258–5263.

Kingstone, A., Tipper, C., Ristic, J., & Ngan, E. (2004). The eyes have it! An fMRI investigation. *Brain Cognition, 55*, 269–271.

Kircher, T., Blumel, I., Marjoram, D., Lataster, T., Krabbendam, L., Weber, J., et al. (2009). Online mentalising investigated with functional MRI. *Neuroscience Letters, 454*, 176–181.

Kuzmanovic, B., Georgescu, A. L., Eickhoff, S. B., Shah, N. J., Bente, G., Fink, G. R., et al. (2009). Duration matters: Dissociating neural correlates of detection and evaluation of social gaze. *Neuroimage, 46*, 1154–1163.

Lloyd-Fox, S., Blasi, A., & Elwell, C. E. (2010). Illuminating the developing brain: The past, present and future of functional near infrared spectroscopy. *Neuroscience Biobrhavioral Reviews, 34*, 269–284.

Materna, S., Dicke, P. W., & Thier, P. (2008). Dissociable roles of the superior temporal sulcus and the intraparietal sulcus in joint attention: A functional magnetic resonance imaging study. *Journal of Cognitive Neuroscience, 20*, 108–119.

Meltzoff, A. N., & Brooks, R. (2008). Self-experience as a mechanism for learning about others: A training study in social cognition. *Developmental Psychology, 44*, 1257–1265.

Mitchell, J. P., Heatherton, T. F., & Macrae, C. N. (2002). Distinct neural systems subserve person and object knowledge. *Proceedings of the National Academy of Science U S A, 99,* 15238–15243.

Mitchell, J. P., Neil Macrae, C., & Banaji, M. R. (2005). Forming impressions of people versus inanimate objects: Social-cognitive processing in the medial prefrontal cortex. *Neuroimage, 26,* 251–257.

Molenberghs, P., Mesulam, M. M., Peeters, R., Vandenberghe, R. R. C. (2007). Remapping attentional priorities: Differential contribution of superior parietal lobule and intraparietal sulcus. *Cerebral Cortex, 17,* 2703–2712.

Moll, H., & Tomasello, M. (2004). 12- and 18-month-old infants follow gaze to spaces behind barriers. *Developmental Science, 7,* F1–F9.

Morales, M., Mundy, P., Crowson, M., Neal, A. R., & Delgado, C. (2005). Individual differences in infant joint attention skills, joint attention, and emotion regulation. *International Journal of Behavioral Development, 29,* 259–263.

Morales, M., Mundy, P., & Rojas, J. (1998). Following the direction of gaze and language development in 6-month-olds. *Infant Behavior & Development, 21,* 373–377.

Mundy, P., Block, J., Delgado, C., Pomares, Y., Van Hecke, A. V., & Parlade, M. V. (2007). Individual differences and the development of joint attention in infancy. *Child Development, 78,* 938–954.

Mundy, P., & Newell, L. (2007). Attention, joint attention, and social cognition. *Curr Dir Psychol Sci, 16,* 269–274.

Mundy, P., Sigman, M., Ungerer, J., & Sherman, T. (1986). Defining the social deficits of autism: The contribution of non-verbal communication measures. *Journal of Child Psychology and Psychiatry and Allied Disciplines, 27,* 657–669.

Mundy, P., Sullivan, L., & Mastergeorge, A. M. (2009). A parallel and distributed-processing model of joint attention, social cognition and autism. *Autism Research, 2,* 2–21.

Murray, L., & Trevarthen, C. (1985). Emotional regulation of interactions between two-month-olds and their mothers. In T. M. Field, & N. A. Fox (Eds.), *Social Perception in Infancy* (pp. 177–198). Norwood, NJ: Ablex.

Nelson, C. A. (1996). Electrophysiological correlates of memory development in the first year of life. In H. Reese, & M. Franzen (Eds.), *Biological and Neuropsychological Mechanisms: Life Span Developmental Psychology* (pp. 95–131). Hillsdale, NJ: Erlbaum.

Nelson, C. A., 3rd, & McCleery, J. P. (2008). Use of event-related potentials in the study of typical and atypical development. *Journal of the American Academy of Child & Adolescent Psychiatry, 47,* 1252–1261.

Nelson, P. B., Adamson, L. B., & Bakeman, R. (2008). Toddlers' joint engagement experience facilitates preschoolers' acquisition of theory of mind. *Developmental Science, 11,* 847–852.

Nobre, A. C., Gitelman, D. R., Dias, E. C., & Mesulam, M. M. (2000). Covert visual spatial orienting and saccades: Overlapping neural systems. *Neuroimage, 11,* 210–216.

Pelphrey, K. A., Morris, J. P., & McCarthy, G. (2004). Grasping the intentions of others: the perceived intentionality of an action influences activity in the superior temporal sulcus during social perception. *Journal of Cognitive Neuroscience, 16,* 1706–1716.

Pelphrey, K. A., Morris, J. P., & McCarthy, G. (2005). Neural basis of eye gaze processing deficits in autism. *Brain, 128*(Pt 5), 1038–1048.

Pelphrey, K. A., Singerman, J. D., Allison, T., & McCarthy, G. (2003). Brain activation evoked by perception of gaze shifts: The influence of context. *Neuropsychologia, 41*, 156–170.

Pelphrey, K. A., Viola, R. J., & McCarthy, G. (2004). When strangers pass: Processing of mutual and averted social gaze in the superior temporal sulcus. *Psychological Science, 15*, 598–603.

Perrett, D. I., Hietanen, J. K., Oram, M. W., & Benson, P. J. (1992). Organization and functions of cells responsive to faces in the temporal cortex. *Philosophical Transactions of the Royal Society of London B, 335*, 23–30.

Posner, M. I. (1980). Orienting of attention. *Quarterly Journal of Experimental Psychology, 32*, 3–25.

Puce, A., Allison, T., Bentin, S., Gore, J. C., & McCarthy, G. (1998). Temporal cortex activation in humans viewing eye and mouth movements. *Journal of Neuroscience, 18*, 2188–2199.

Redcay, E., Dodell-Feder, D., Pearrow, M. J., Mavros, P. L., Kleiner, M., Gabrieli, J. D., et al. (2010a). Live face-to-face interaction during fMRI: A new tool for social cognitive neuroscience. *Neuroimage, 50*, 1639–1647.

Redcay, E., Dodell-Feder, D., Pearrow, M. J., Kleiner, M., Mavros, P.L., Gabrieli, J.D.E., Saxe, R. (2010b). *Do you see what I see? The neural correlates of joint attention*. Poster presented at the Cognitive Neuroscience Society Meeting, April 2010.

Redcay, E., Kleiner, M., Saxe, R. (2012). Look at this: the neural correlates of initiating and responding to bids for joint attention. *Frontiers in Human Neuroscience, 6*(169). 1–14.

Redcay, E., Dodell-Feder, D., Mavros, P. L., Kleiner, M., Pearrow, M. J., Triantafyllou, C., Gabrieli, J. D., Saxe, R. (in press). Atypical brain activation patterns during a face-to-face joint attention game in adults with autism spectrum disorder. *Human Brain Mapping*.

Reid, V. M., Striano, T., Kaufman, J., & Johnson, M. H. (2004). Eye gaze cueing facilitates neural processing of objects in 4-month-old infants. *Neuroreport, 15*, 2553–2555.

Richards, J. E. (2003). The development of visual attention and the brain. In M. de Haan, & M. H. Johnson (Eds.), *The Cognitive Neuroscience of Development* (pp. 73–93). New York: Psychology Press.

Rilling, J., Gutman, D., Zeh, T., Pagnoni, G., Berns, G., & Kilts, C. (2002). A neural basis for social cooperation. *Neuron, 35*, 395–405.

Rilling, J. K., Sanfey, A. G., Aronson, J. A., Nystrom, L. E., & Cohen, J. D. (2004). The neural correlates of theory of mind within interpersonal interactions. *Neuroimage, 22*, 1694–1703.

Rosen, A. C., Rao, S. M., Caffarra, P., Scaglioni, A., Bobholz, J. A., Woodley, S. J., et al. (1999). Neural basis of endogenous and exogenous spatial orienting. A functional MRI study. *Journal of Cognitive Neuroscience, 11*, 135–152.

Saxe, R., Xiao, D. K., Kovacs, G., Perrett, D. I., & Kanwisher, N. (2004). A region of right posterior superior temporal sulcus responds to observed intentional actions. *Neuropsychologia, 42*, 1435–1446.

Schilbach, L., Wilms, M., Eickhoff, S. B., Romanzetti, S., Tepest, R., Bente, G., et al. (2009). Minds made for sharing: Initiating joint attention recruits reward-related neurocircuitry. *Journal of Cognitive Neuroscience, 22*, 2702–2715.

Schilbach, L., Wohlschlaeger, A. M., Kraemer, N. C., Newen, A., Shah, N. J., Fink, G. R., et al. (2006). Being with virtual others: Neural correlates of social interaction. *Neuropsychologia, 44*, 718–730.

Senju, A., Johnson, M. H., & Csibra, G. (2006). The development and neural basis of referential gaze perception. *Social Neuroscience, 1*, 220–234.

Senju, A., Tojo, Y., Yaguchi, K., & Hasegawa, T. (2005). Deviant gaze processing in children with autism: An ERP study. *Neuropsychologia, 43*, 1297–1306.

Sommerville, J. A., Woodward, A. L., & Needham, A. (2005). Action experience alters 3-month-old infants' perception of others' actions. *Cognition, 96*, B1–B11.

Stevens, S. A., West, G. L., Al-Aidroos, N., Weger, U. W., & Pratt, J. (2008). Testing whether gaze cues and arrow cues produce reflexive or volitional shifts of attention. *Psychonomic Bulletin and Review, 15*, 1148–1153.

Striano, T., & Reid, V. M. (2006). Social cognition in the first year. *Trends in Cognitive Science, 10*, 471–476.

Striano, T., Reid, V. M., & Hoehl, S. (2006). Neural mechanisms of joint attention in infancy. *European Journal of Neuroscience, 23*, 2819–2823.

Tomasello, M., Carpenter, M., Call, J., Behne, T., & Moll, H. (2005). Understanding and sharing intentions: The origins of cultural cognition. *Behavioral Brain Science, 28*, 675–691; discussion 691–735.

Vaughan Van Hecke, A., Mundy, P. C., Acra, C. F., Block, J. J., Delgado, C. E., Parlade, M. V., et al. (2007). Infant joint attention, temperament, and social competence in preschool children. *Child Development, 78*, 53–69.

Williams, J. H., Waiter, G. D., Perra, O., Perrett, D. I., & Whiten, A. (2005). An fMRI study of joint attention experience. *Neuroimage, 25*, 133–140.

Wilms, M., Schilbach, L., Pfeiffer, U., Bente, G., Fink, G. R., & Vogeley, K. (2010). It's in your eyes—using gaze-contingent stimuli to create truly interactive paradigms for social cognitive and affective neuroscience. *Social Cognitive and Affective Neuroscience, 5*, 98–107.

Woodward, A. (2003). Infants' developing understanding of the link between looker and object. *Developmental Science, 6*, 297–311.

Yantis, S., & Serences, J.T. (2003). Cortical mechanisms of space-based and object-based attentional control. *Current Opinion in Neurobiology, 13*, 187–193.

14 "Knowing" that the Self is the Agent
Janet Metcalfe

THE IDEA THAT our minds are transparent with respect to themselves; that is, that we know infallibly, immediately, and with certainty, what we, ourselves, are doing or thinking as well as that we are the agent, enjoys great popularity. For example, Epley, Caruso, and Bazerman (2006) stated:

> People perceive the world directly through their own sensory organs and interpret those perceptions by using schemas and expectations that are firmly planted in their own brains. This means that one's own unique perspective on the world is immediately and easily available, whereas others' perspectives must be deliberately inferred.

This commonsense view—that knowledge of oneself is essentially automatic, whereas knowing about another is a complicated inferential affair—has been criticized on a number of grounds (see Carruthers, 2011 for a review and interesting alternative perspective; and also see Prinz, 2012). And, consistent with critiques of this view, there is now considerable evidence that it is not only patients with psychoses such as schizophrenia but also ordinary people who can make faulty self-attributions of agency (e.g., Wegner & Wheatley, 1999). Instead of being transparent and obvious, judgments of agency, appear, like other metacognitive judgments, to depend on specific cues.

At first blush it might be supposed from, for example, the authority accorded confession in attributions concerning people's responsibility, that the agency cues used by healthy people are usually veridical. As noted by van der Wel and Knoblich (chapter 15), it appears that most of the time, most people are right. Nevertheless, it has been demonstrated many times that it is possible to trick the system in ways that can sometimes be flamboyant, ranging from Ouija boards to false confessions (see Wegner, 2002). These demonstrations indicate that the agency detection system is fallible, and that even normally valid cues may be interpreted incorrectly or given insufficient weight in the causal chain that indicates the person's perceived responsibility for an act. This chapter discusses and evaluates several sources of information that people use in making agency judgments. One of these sources—the intention/outcome discrepancy information, which is discussed first (also see chapter 15), provides agency information that is potentially accurate. However, other cues provide either no veridical information, or even the wrong information. For instance, actions by others, the goodness of the outcome, and personal force or effort are cues that people appear to use in making attributions concerning the extent to which an individual, including the self, is to be credited or blamed for an act. However, each of these cues can be irrelevant or, worse, misleading. Despite the compelling feeling that we know infallibly when we are the agent, it will be argued that systematically biased judgments of agency are often produced based on misleading cues.

The Relation Between Intention and Outcome

One cue that appears to be focal in allowing the correct determination of whether the self was causal in an action is the timely match or mismatch between the individual's intentions and the perceived outcome. This cue, which is often investigated at the motor level, fits well with our folk psychological notion of will (see, e.g., Pacherie, 2008): We intend to do something, see that it has been done just as we had intended, and, therefore, infer that we did it. When this intention–outcome match or mismatch is assessed at the motor level, it can be a powerful and accurate diagnostic cue to agency. If the outcome matches the person's intentions and plan on a moment-to-moment basis and with no observable discrepancies, then the person thinks that he or she did it. If it does not, then that mismatch provides evidence for external intervention or control.

Much research has been devoted to this idea, and a highly successful model investigating this discrepancy cue, called the "comparator" model, has been proposed (e.g., Wolpert & Ghahramani, 2000). This model was originally proposed to solve the problem of how people are able to make fine motor corrections (e.g., Frith, Blakemore, & Wolpert, 2000; Wolpert & Kawato, 1998), but also specifies in some detail how a process of action monitoring at the motor level could work. The core idea is that there are separate cortical streams for the person's plan of an action and the feedback resulting from the actual action, which run off simultaneously and meet at some comparison point. If the plan and the outcome are the same—no discrepancy results—then no motor alteration is needed. If, however, the two streams mismatch, then it is likely that something external to the person produced the lack of smooth control coming between the intention and the outcome. As a result, a correction in the motion is needed. If the discrepancy information that is the signal for motion correction were also to feed into a second order metacognitive monitor, that monitor could use this information to consciously make self or other attributions (e.g., Blakemore, Wolpert, & Frith, 2002). Furthermore, such a monitor would operate with some considerable degree of objective accuracy.

IS THE METACOGNITIVE MONITORING PROCESS SEPARATE FROM ACTION MONITORING?

There is a considerable amount evidence pointing to an action monitoring circuit (see chapter 15) and its use in controlling movement at an implicit level of processing that is dissociable from an explicitly conscious judgment process. For example, in an experiment by Fourneret and Jeannerod (1998), participants sometimes moved their hand directly to a target and saw it move to the target as expected (in a situation in which they saw visual feedback about their motion via a computer). Sometimes though, to reach the target the participants had to compensate by moving their hand more to the left or the right as a result of a distortion that was introduced by the computer in the location of the target. Although the participants were able to make the compensatory movements, they were unable to consciously report how they had moved their hand to do so, suggesting that normal participants can be unaware of the signals generated by their own movements even when they can appropriately use those signals to correct their movements. Action monitoring functioned independently of the metacognition.

Knoblich, Stottmeister, and Kircher (2004) have also shown that motor correction can occur without the person being aware of the circumstances leading to the correction. In their experiment, people with schizophrenia as well as control participants were able to correct their motor movements to keep a stylus on a trajectory, in spite of a perturbation introduced by the experimenter. However, although the motor performance of both the patients and the controls was good, the patients were less aware than the control participants of having to make a correction. This result suggests that action monitoring may occur without conscious awareness, but that it feeds into a conscious agency monitoring mechanisms to which the control participants had better access than the patients with schizophrenia.

Metcalfe and Greene (2007; Metcalfe, Eich, & Castel, 2010) have interposed noise between the position of a mouse that the participants control and the position of the cursor that they are trying to control to play a game of touching downward streaming Xs on the screen. Under conditions of externally interposed turbulence, all participants—including elders and children as well as college students and community adults—whom we have tested (except people with schizophrenia, see Metcalfe et al., 2012), have rated themselves as lacking in control (i.e., their judgment of control was less than their judgment of performance). When there was a mismatch between what they did with the mouse and what happened with the cursor, they felt out of control. These are, of course, the very circumstances in which the comparator model would detect a discrepancy between the person's plan and the outcome.

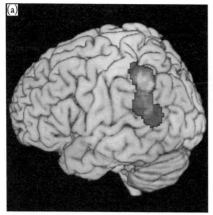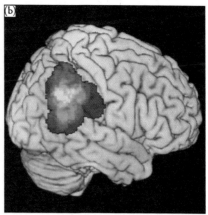

FIGURE 14.1 The resultant activation map from Miele et al.'s (2011) meta-analysis of recent agency monitoring studies. The map, which was thresholded first at the voxel-level ($p < .05$) and then at the cluster-level ($p < .05$), yielded large clusters in the left (-50, -50, 34; $K_E = 1,469$) and right TPJ (54, -50, 32; $K_E = 1,021$) that included portions of the angular gyrus, supramarginal gyrus, and superior temporal gyrus, as well as smaller clusters that included portions of the supramariginal gyrus (56, -30, 30; $K_E = 841$), the middle temporal gyrus (52, -58, 12; $K_E = 721$), the angular gyrus (42, -60, 48; $K_E = 463$), and inferior parietal lobule (-46, -50, 44; $K_E = 331$). (Based on the data reported in Miele, D. M., Wager, T. D., Mitchell, J. P., & Metcalfe, J. (2011). Dissociating neural correlates of action monitoring and metacognition of agency. *Journal of Cognitive Neuroscience, 23,* 3620–3636.)

When fMRI imaging was conducted on people while doing this task, the contrast between the turbulence condition and the condition in which the participants were in full control of the cursor, showed up as activation primarily in the temporal parietal junction (Miele et al., 2011), in keeping with much other research (Decety & Lamm, 2007; Farrer, Franck, Georgieff, Frith, Decety, & Jeannerod, 2003; and see chapter 13, for this and other functions of this area) pointing to this locale as being critical for action monitoring. Figure 14.1 presents a meta-analysis conducted by Miele et al. (2011) of activation associated with such discrepancy detection in agency tasks.

However, it was not this "action monitoring" region that was activated when participants were making judgments of agency (compared with judgments of performance). Instead, the medial frontal areas (and especially BA10—a metacognitive area; see Fleming et al., 2010) were activated during people's judgments of whether they were or were not in control. It would seem, then, that the action monitoring, evidenced by TPJ activation, feeds into a higher "meta"-level conscious evaluation process that determines agency over and above motor control.

IMPAIRMENT OF THE DISCREPANCY MONITORING SYSTEM
IN SCHIZOPHRENIA AND AUTISM

People with schizophrenia appeared to be impervious to both externally interposed turbulence, which in our agency experiments and those of Knoblich et al. (2004) produced a real distortion in people's control, and also to temporal delay in the effect of the mouse movements on the cursor, again, a discrepancy in objective control. Similar intention/outcome discrepancy cues were not used by people with schizophrenia in the experiments of Synofzik, Thier, Leube, Schlotterbeck, and Lindner (2010) or Voss, Moore, Hauser, Gallinat, Heinz, and Haggard (2010). Indeed, the only cue that people with schizophrenia used in our experiments was their judgment of performance—a cue that will be discussed shortly and is not inherently diagnostic of agency.

An interesting variant on the intention/outcome discrepancy phenomenon on people's perceptions of self-causality—which provides converging evidence that there is an impairment in the intention/action discrepancy monitoring ability of schizophrenics—was demonstrated by Blakemore, Frith, and Wolpert (1998, 2000). They first noted that when there is a match between the plan and the outcome in the comparator model (and note, this is the condition in which the person feels him- or herself to be in control or to be the causal agent), the person's sensation concerning the outcome of the action is also dampened. Thus, if one intentionally touches one's own chin, there is less sensation of the touch than if another person touches one's chin. They have suggested that this dampening of the sensation of self-generated actions is why an individual cannot tickle him- or herself. Interestingly, this inability to tickle oneself obtains even when one's actions are transferred through a robotic stimulator, so long as the participant intends the action and the effect is immediate: The robot that the participant controls still fails to produce the ticklish sensation. However, when the authors interposed a delay between the person's actions and the outcome produced by the robotic stimulator, the tickle sensation returned. It appears that when there is a discrepancy between intention and outcome, the tickle sensation is perceived, and when there is not—a situation that usually corresponds to being the agent—tickle sensation is not perceived. Healthy people cannot tickle themselves. Patients with schizophrenia, however, were able to tickle themselves (Blakemore, Frith, & Wolpert, 2000) a capability that points to a breakdown in the intention/action discrepancy (or in this case *lack* of discrepancy) detection mechanism.

Although the intention/outcome discrepancy cue can be subverted, and may also be impaired in pathological cases, under normal circumstances it provides information that is valid concerning whether the self was in control or not. The same is not true for all cues, however. The next three sections outline cues in which the metacognitive system appears to be affected by information that is inherently nondiagnostic.

Action and Words by Others

When an individual observes an action or hears an utterance done by someone else it would seem self-evident that the individual should attribute that action or that verbalization to the other and not to the self. Oddly then, people apparently partially ascribe other people's actions to themselves, and they may mistake others' words as signaling their own intent. I first describe some data suggesting that people internalize others' actions, and then briefly turn to a similar internalization of others' words. The underlying neurological basis of self-attribution of others' actions at least presumably, is the mirror neuron system.

The discovery of mirror neurons (see chapter 10; Iacoboni, 2009; Rizzolatti, Foggassi, & Gallese, 2001) provides support for the notion that people comprehend the utterances, thoughts, and actions of others by internally "doing" the actions that they see others do. Indeed, the characteristic that has so captured the attention of researchers and theorists about the biological basis of mind is that these neurons fire indiscriminately regardless of whether the action was one's own or the act of another. But although the system related to mirror neurons is crucial for internalizing and understanding another person's perspective, such indiscriminant firing poses a problem for keeping one's own boundaries straight and knowing whether it is the self who is doing the acting or the other, as noted by Daprati et al. (1997), Georgieff and Jeannerod (1998), and others. Allocation of one's own resources and effort to joint action in response to others' contributions to an action (see chapter 12) may also be complicated by the fact that the others' actions are apparently represented in our minds as if they were our own. It would appear, then, that understanding other minds comes at a cost of partial loss of our own autonomy.

Is there any evidence, other than the finding that mirror neurons exist and we can understand one another, that other people's actions contribute to one's own feelings of agency? People who were taking credit for others' actions as their own would exhibit an egocentrism bias—thinking that in a joint action situation they were doing more than their fair share. This bias should come about if they were internalizing the action of the partner, and claiming it as if it were their own. Interestingly, van der Wel, Sebanz, and Knoblich (2012) found that people working in dyads to control a pendulum together, each ascribed to themselves more that 50% of the credit for the action. And, indeed, there is a considerable literature on egocentrism bias supporting the contention that people may, in good faith, feel responsible for other people's actions.

The classic example of egocentrism bias involves marital couples' self-evaluation of their relative contribution to domestic tasks. Ross and Sicoly (1979) gave individual members of couples a questionnaire in which they were asked to assess their own degree of responsibility for doing 20 activities, such making breakfast, doing dishes, cleaning house, shopping for groceries, caring for the children, and so on. The total responsibility claimed over both members of the couples on most items appraised was significantly more than 100%. On average, people thought they were doing more than they were. The study found similar results in naturally occurring discussion groups, on basketball teams, and in groups assembled in the laboratory. And, similarly, people interacting with one another on a daily basis all thought they were doing more than they could possibly have been doing, as would be expected if one were taking credit not only for what one did oneself, but also to some extent for what the other did—as the mirror neuron hypothesis would suggest.

Interestingly, Kruger and Gilovitch (1999) showed that married individuals self-ascribed more than their fair share of responsibility both for desirable *and* undesirable activities—suggesting that the effect was not merely self-congratulatory or aggrandizing. Participants had a 5.2% and 3.8% self-related overestimation (i.e., increase beyond 100%) for desirable and undesirable activities, respectively. The participants expected, however, that their partners would claim much more of the fair share of responsibility for desirable activities (9.7%), but less than their fair share (−16.1%) for undesirable activities. Thus, in this case at least, the egocentric bias seen in the attribution of responsibility was not self-serving (although the participants were cynical concerning their partners' attributions). If this egocentrism were only based on a self-serving bias, rather than being a genuine over-internalization of the other's actions, it seems that people should have shown the pattern they expected of the partner. Instead, the pattern they exhibited in their own self-evaluation, which did not eschew responsibility in the undesirable cases, is consistent with the hypothesis of the self-internalization of all of the other's actions, good and bad.

Caruso, Epley, and Bazerman (2006) noted that people working together on joint projects and even on research tend to think they have contributed more than their place in the authorship list indicates. Furthermore, egocentric biases have been cited as one of the essential reasons for people's dissatisfaction with the fairness of collaborative groups and their role in them (e.g., Babcock & Loewenstein, 1997). Accordingly, Caruso et al. (2006) set out to overcome these biases. To do so, they had people focus on the contributions of the other people involved, rather than their own. Although this strategy was somewhat, although not entirely, successful in counteracting people's egocentric biases, focusing on others' contributions also produced an unexpected negative consequence: The more active contributors to the task became less happy about the collaboration. Presumably, they had not previously paid much attention to the fact that the others in the group were loafing, while at the same time taking more than their share of the credit. Social loafing may result because people overestimate their own contribution having incorporated the contributions of others into their own agency assessments. They may then try to equalize the contributions across people by decreasing their own.

But although the kind of results outlined in the preceding suggest the possibility that people internalize the actions of others and take credit for them as if they were their own actions, it must be acknowledged that such egocentric biases might also have occurred for other reasons. For most people, there is selective attention to self-performed actions. Self-relevant information is more salient, engaging, and interesting than information about someone else, and these attentional differences ensure a hyperencoding that results in better memory for actions done by the self than for actions done by the other—the "enactment effect" (e.g., Nyberg, Petersson, Nilsson, Sandblom, Åberg, & Ingvar, 2001; Zimmer & Engelkamp, 2003). The pattern of egocentrism seen in the cited studies, then, could have resulted because of a misattribution of others' acts to the self, but it could also have resulted from preferential memory encoding for events enacted by or related to the self.

Furthermore, observation of another's actions in tasks similar to one's own does not always result in increased feelings of agency. The impact of the presence of another person can sometimes be complex (see e.g., Prinz, Försterling, & Hauf, 2005). In a leader–follower paradigm in which participants pointed to the letters from A–Z on a glass sheet (Sparrow, 2007), a confederate also sometimes pointed to the letters either one step ahead or one step behind the participant. Although this action of the confederate had no direct physical effect on the participant; nevertheless, the presence of the confederate doing this related task affected people's judgments of agency. Although it seems intuitive that people would feel most in control when they were the leader in this pointing task, in fact people's judgments of agency were highest when they acted alone (see Experiment 2, Sparrow, 2007).

It is notable that in this situation, the confederate's actions were *in conflict with* rather than being concordant with the participant's own actions, both when the confederate was one step ahead, but also when she was one step behind. If this discrepancy between intention and action were internalized, one would expect a decrease in the felt agency by the comparator-model rationale outlined in the preceding. However, the notable point in this case is that it was not a discrepancy in one's own actions but rather those of the other. The presence of another agent doing something discrepant with what one was oneself intending and doing, siphoned off one's own feelings of being in control.

The work of Sebanz, Bekkering, and Knoblich (2006; and see chapter 12) underlines this same point. They have shown that the presence, or indeed even the assumed but not physically observable presence, of another person responding in a different way to the stimulus to which the participant is responding, is enough to interfere with the participant's own responses. We appear to be unable to ignore other people: Their presence, or even their *assumed* presence, may systematically disrupt our own judgments of agency.

Furthermore, a most dramatic example of people's misperception of their own agency, due to the language of another, was demonstrated by Wegner and Wheatley (1999). In their experiment, people experienced misperceptions of their own agency when they were primed by the words of another, apparently mistaking the other's word for their own intention. In their "I spy" study, two people (a participant and a confederate) were jointly moving a mouse that ostensibly shifted control between participants. On a signal, they would stop on particular images, and they would have to make attributions of agency, that is, of whether they felt they had been the one moving the mouse. Both were wearing headphones. The confederate heard instructions to move the mouse to a particular image on the critical trials during which she controlled the mouse. The participant heard music most of the time, but was sometimes primed by hearing a word on the headphones that was the name of the object on which the mouse, controlled by the confederate, landed. When this priming happened, the participant had an inflated sense of agency; that is, the participant disproportionately thought she or he was responsible for intentionally moving to that image. It seems, then, that the words we hear may not be completely distinguishable from our own thoughts, and this conflation may result in illusions of agency. Similarly, Wenke, Fleming, and Haggard (2010; and see Chambon, Wenke, Fleming, Prinz, & Haggard, 2012) have shown that subliminal priming can influence a person's metacognition of agency. These experiments provide examples whereby people internalize external words or signals as if they were one's own internally generated intentions. Additionally, there are many real-world cases of unconscious plagiary, of course, that no doubt further support the difficulty of distinguishing others words and ideas from our own thoughts and intentions. Our language itself, then, not only interconnects us but also appears to make it easy to confuse our own agency with that of another.

EXCEPTIONS

Although the mirroring cues from others' acts appear to be used by typically developing participants, we might expect to see abnormalities in agency monitoring in clinical populations who have a deficit in the mirror neuron system. It would be interesting if impairment of this nonvalid cue sometimes resulted in more veridical judgments and memory performance. There has been some research indicating that people with autism spectrum disorder have a deficit in the mirror neuron system (Dapretto, Davis, Pfeifer, Scott, Sigman, Bookheimer, & Iacaboni, 2006; Oberman, Hubbard, McCleery, Altschuler, Ramachanran, & Pineda, 2005; Théoret, Halligan, Kobayashi, Fregni, Tager-Flusberg, & Pascual-Leone, 2005). This deficit corresponds well with the function of the mirror system and the characteristic symptoms of the syndrome.

Interestingly, several reports have indicated that people with autism sometimes fail to show the enactment effect (Millward, Powell, Messer, & Jordan, 2000; Russell & Jarrold, 1999; c.f., Hill & Russell, 2002). Unlike typical participants, people with autism sometimes do not show a memorial advantage for acts they did themselves as contrasted to the actions of others. In Millward, Powell, Messer, and Jordan's (2000) experiment, children with autism, as contrasted with children with mild learning disabilities, participated in two walks through, for example, a horse sanctuary, a park, a shopping precinct, where they experienced events that were designed to be of interest to the children. The events were underlined by the experimenter's narrative (e.g., "Do you want to go on the slide?") and nonverbal techniques (e.g., pointing to the horses) and target items that would become the to-be-remembered items, were preidentified by the experimenter. Sometimes the participant child him- or herself engaged in an event, whereas sometimes the partner child did. The finding of interest is that the children with autism (unlike the children with learning disabilities) did not show better recall for the events that they themselves experienced and they sometimes showed worse recall. In short, they failed to show the typical egocentric enactment effect.

Furthermore, college students who have high autism quotients, as measured by a questionnaire, showed less of an effect of the presence of others in the leader follower task described in the preceding study (Sparrow, 2007). And recently, Zalla, Herbrecht, Leboyer, and Metcalfe (2011) reported atypical patterns of judgments of agency in highly functioning patients with Aspergers' syndrome. Further investigations with this population may allow more detailed specification of what is undoubtedly a complex relation between people's understanding of the acts of others and their understanding of those of the self.

Perceived Performance

Although the mirroring cue outlined in the foregoing section may contribute (speciously) to people's judgments of agency, it is not the only cue to do so: There is also a performance-related cue that is separable from those of another actor. The person's assessment of performance-success per se appears to be used in assessing agency. This cue has an impact despite the fact that success or failure does not necessarily stem from the individual's own actions and could be, and often is, increased or decreased for other reasons, such as chance, systematic external intervention, reward availability, and so on. Nevertheless, perception of performance in several experiments (Metcalfe & Greene, 2007; Metcalfe, Eich, & Castel, 2010; Metcalfe, Van Snellenberg, DeRossa, Balsam, & Malhotra, 2012; Miele, Wager, Mitchell, & Metcalfe, 2011) has been found to be a primary contributor to people's judgments of agency.

In these agency/performance experiments, sometimes the participant is objectively in perfect control of the cursor, but sometimes the experimental program on a particular trial will intervene with noise, or a temporal lag, both of which hurt performance. The participant's judgment about performance on the just-completed trial is the single strongest contributor to the judgment of agency: If people perceive good performance, they give a high judgment of agency; if they perceive poor performance, they give a low judgment of agency, regardless of whether said participant is a typical college student, a community member recruited from Craig's list, an older adult, an elementary school child, a person with Asperger's syndrome, or schizophrenia. The dominant cue that contributes to their agency judgment is their perception of performance.

Similarly, Dewey, Seiffert, and Carr (2010), in a task in which participants had to steer a simulated boat that could get closer to a goal or further away due to non-subject controlled noise, found that people felt less in control when performance was altered to be worse by the manipulations in the simulation, and more in control when it was altered to be better. But in fact the participants were not causal in whether performance got better or worse. This study highlights the fact that the performance variable, although perhaps providing a rough guide under normal circumstances as to whether or not the outcome was favorable, is not in general diagnostic of agency.

In some of our agency experiments, in which people used the cursor to touch down-wardly streaming Xs and avoid Os, we included one condition in which participants were credited with a hit even when they got moderately close to the target X, whereas in the other conditions they had to actually touch the target. When they only had to get close, of course, their performance was inflated. But it was not inflated because they themselves were doing anything better or more efficiently or had better control. Instead they were "given" the answer by what we called "magic." Logically they should not have given a higher rating of control in this condition than they did when they were com-pletely in control of the cursor but did not get the "free" hits. However, participants' judgments of agency increased in the magic condition. To the credit of our college students, who were perhaps hyperaware of the possibility of artificially inflated perfor-mance (cheating, plagiarism, etc.), their judgments of agency did not increase as much as did their judgments of performance—indicating that they were somewhat aware that they were not completely responsible for the increase in performance. The same was not true for elementary school children (Metcalfe et al., 2010). They took full credit in the magic condition.

Interestingly, very small children may not yet understand the distinction between desire and intention. They may tend to say that they were responsible for an action if its outcome satisfies a desire they have; that is, if performance is good. Astington (2001), for example, showed that young children tended to say accidental action was intended if its outcome was favorable. Similarly, Shultz and Wells (1985) showed that 3- and 7-year-old children relied nearly exclusively on a matching rule in which they claimed an action was intentional if it matched the desired outcome, whereas 11-year-old children, although still relying heavily on this rule, also began to take other factors into account.

These findings are consistent with the literature on self-efficacy. "Positive" psycholo-gists (e.g., Bandura, 2001; Deci & Ryan, 2000) generally have equated self-efficacy with feelings of control, and apply both of these terms only to situations in which being "in control" results in favorable rather than unfavorable outcomes. Indeed, in the learned helpless literature, people feel powerless and out of control when they continually are unable to eventuate the hoped-for outcome (Alloy & Abramson, 1979). The reward, the contingency, and the action, appear to matter (Tricomi, Delgado, & Fiez, 2004) both for the feeling of being in control or empowered, and also for people's subsequent actions and their feelings of depression.

EXCEPTIONS?

Interestingly, perceived performance was the *only* factor that contributed to judgments of agency in people with schizophrenia (Metcalfe et al., 2012). Other experimental factors such as interposed turbulence or lag that should have influenced judgments of control were not considered. Thus, even among people exhibiting profound deficits in their metacognition of agency, perceived performance is used as a proxy for control.

Access to performance cues alone, failing access to other more diagnostic and directly relevant cues, appears insufficient to allow the individual to adequately monitor whether she or he really was in control and responsible.

Personal Force and Effort

When people assess credit for activities, the amount of effort invested in the endeavor seems to play a part. Credit (or blame) due seems synonymous with the extent of causal impact due to self, and such causal impact requires effort. For this reason it seems intuitive that personal force or effort is a cue that people probably use in assessing agency. As Wegner and Bargh (1998) have put it:

> Control must be understood not only as a psychological process but as a feeling, an experience one has of controlling or being in control. Control requires effort, and this effort as it is expended, yields a continuous sense that one is doing something, not just allowing something to happen. Both the actual expenditure of cognitive effort, and the phenomenal experience of effortfulness, appear to be at a maximum during conscious control. (p 458)

But although effort seems like a likely candidate for an agency cue, the experimental literature directly investigating the relation between feelings of agency and effort is small. Indeed, although a number of theorists discuss the purported role of effort, we have been able to find only one study that experimentally investigated its direct role in altering people's attributions of their own agency. Preston and Wegner (2007) had participants jointly engaged in an anagram-solving task while simultaneously doing a motor task that required varying degrees of effort. The concurrent task was unrelated to the anagram solving. Nevertheless, people were more likely to wrongly think that they, rather than their partner, had solved the anagrams when they had allocated more rather than less effort to the concurrent task.

Although the evidence is less direct, differential attributions of moral responsibility due to another person for an act, as a function of effort or personal force, also bear on people's use of this cue. Presumably moral culpability accrues to the extent the individual actor is accorded agency. The responsibility that people, at least in theory, allocate to themselves and others has been investigated by means of the trolley problem. People are presented with a "switch" scenario in which they are asked to imagine that they are standing on a train platform and can see that if the incoming train continues on its course five people will be hit and killed by the train. The conductor will not have enough time to put on the brakes. However, if the subject pulls a switch, she or he can divert the train to a different track where one person is standing. That person, however, will be killed. Most people agree that the subject should pull the switch.

Interestingly, though, the degree of personal effort and force used is important in the evaluation of the moral credit or culpability for the action. In a variant called the footbridge dilemma the subject is faced with the prospect of saving the five people by pushing someone else off a footbridge and into the trolley's path, still killing one person. Although most people approve of the act in the case of the switch, few approve in the case of the footbridge (Greene et al., 2001; Petrinovich, O'Neill, & Jorgensen, 1993). The felt responsibility concerning the action changed when the low effort act of pulling the switch was altered to be a high effort action of pushing the person.

Greene et al. (2009) investigated whether this difference was because the person who pushed the other had direct physical contact with the victim, or whether it was because of the use of force (or effort). In all four conditions in the experiment the participants were told that a train was headed down a track, and that if it stayed on its current course it would kill five people. In the standard condition the agent pushed the victim off the footbridge using physical force and his hands. In the remote condition, the subject dropped the victim onto the tracks using a trap door and a remote switch. The footbridge "pole" condition was identical to the standard condition except that the agent used a pole rather than his hands to push the victim, but personal force was involved. Finally, the switch condition was identical to the remote condition except that the agent and the switch were adjacent to the victim, and so physically proximal. The results indicated that it was the physical force or effort that figured most strongly into the attribution of moral responsibility.

These results all suggest that the more effortful the act, the more agentic the person should feel. Even so, other considerations indicate that the relation between effort and agency may not be entirely straightforward. Within the comparator model discussed in the preceding, increased effort to reach a goal may indicate less rather than more control. Obstructions and deviations from the plan caused by external forces require the individual to exert more effort to achieve the goal, but such effort exerted to overcome external obstructions means, within that framework, that the individual was less rather than more in control.

There are also circumstances—related to the construct of "flow," "being in the zone," or the Buddhist notions of the "action of inaction" or of "doing without doing"—in which a feeling of effortlessness while acting is both related to control, in some sense, but also to a lack of the kind of self-consciousness that seems to be associated with agency. So, on the one hand, greater effort would seem to indicate greater agency by some views, whereas just the opposite could also be argued by others. At the present time, there is no synthesis of these apparently contradictory interpretations of effort cues with respect to agency.

Conclusion

How does one know that the self was the agent? The answer to this question is anything but transparent. The factors that affect these central judgments concerning one's own responsibility are not necessarily valid. The straightforward answer—that one knows that one was the agent because there are veridical internal cues that designate whether one's plans and intentions were carried out at the time and in the sequence that one planned them, can only partially account for the data. Under some circumstances, people do use such concordance (or discrepancy) cues as part of the information utilized in evaluating their own agency. Even using these often-valid cues, people can be wrong in these assessments, and some patient populations are systematically incorrect. Nevertheless, this intention/outcome discrepancy cue, on balance, provides some accurate information that relates to whether it was in fact the self who was responsible for an action.

But it appears that people also incorporate into their metacognitions about their own agency a number of other cues, and these additional cues can be systematically misleading. In this chapter, three of these potentially highly fallible cues have been discussed, and further investigation is likely to uncover more. Although cues such as perceived goodness of performance, the presence of another person, and the amount of effort exerted provide little information specifying whether an individual was the agent or not, they nevertheless factor into people's metacognitive assessments about culpability or credit.

In summary, then, metacognition of agency is, both behaviorally and neurally, separate from action monitoring. The latter provides information to the former that, at least in principle, allows some veridicality of assessment. But the metacognitive judgments rely not only on this usually valid source of information, but also on a number of sources of information that are much more fallible. These other factors may have adaptive origins. It is undoubtedly useful, in a general way, to internalize the actions of others. Such an ability provides a basis for the understanding and appreciation of others and has broad implications for self-consciousness (Carruthers, 2011; Prinz, 2012). The cost of an individual wrongly taking some credit or blame for another's actions seems a small price to pay for such understanding. Similarly, taking credit for favorable outcomes is undoubtedly ego protective, elating, and invigorating. Disavowing such credit (even if correctly) is undoubtedly maladaptive to the health and happiness of the individual. So the price paid in accuracy of agency judgments may be well spent. And taking credit when much effort has been exerted seems to underlie basic principles of fairness, and is no doubt grounded in our evolutionary past. But in our world, in which the amount of effort exerted is not so tightly related to responsibility for an outcome—a tap may be more effective than a bludgeon—this cue no longer works. Although these non-valid cues may have been incorporated into people's metacognitive judgments of agency for adaptive reasons, nevertheless, their use clouds the transparency of the relation between our own causal connection to the world and our assessment of that connection.

REFERENCES

Alloy, L. B., & Abramson, L. A. (1979). Judgment of contingency in depressed and nondepressed students: Sadder but wiser? *Journal of Experimental Psychology: General, 108,* 441–485.

Astington, J. W. (2001). The paradox of intention: Assessing children's metarepresentational understanding. In B. F. Malle, L.J. Moses, & D. A. Baldwin (Eds.), *Intentions and Intentionality, Foundation of Social Cognition.* (pp 85–103). Cambridge MA: MIT Press.

Babcock, L., & Loewenstein, G. (1997). Explaining bargaining impasse: The role of self-serving biases. *Journal of Economic Perspectives, 11,* 109–126.

Bandura, A. (2001). Social cognitive theory: An agentic perspective. *Annual Review of Psychology, 52,* 1–26.

Blakemore, S.-J., Wolpert, D. M., & Frith, C. D. (1998). Central cancellation of self- produced tickle sensation. *Nature Neuroscience, 1,* 635–640.

Blakemore, S.-J., Frith, C. D., & Wolpert, D. M. (2000). Why can't you tickle yourself? *Neuroreport, 11,* R11–R16.

Blakemore, S.-J., Wolpert, D. M., & Frith, C. D. (2002). Abnormalities in the awareness of action. *TRENDS in Cognitive Sciences, 6,* 237–242.

Böckler, A., & Sebanz, N. (2013). Linking joint attention and joint action. J. Metcalfe, & H. S. Terrace (Eds.), *Agency and Joint Attention.* New York: Oxford University Press.

Carruthers, P. (2011). *The Opacity of Mind.* New York: Oxford University Press.

Caruso, E. M., Epley, N., & Bazerman, M. H. (2006). The costs and benefits of undoing egocentric responsibility assessments in groups. *Journal of Personality and Social Psychology, 91,* 857–871.

Chambon, V., Wenke, D., Fleming, S.M., Prinz, W., & Hggard, P. (2012). On online neural substrate for sense of agency, *Cerebral Cortex,* published online April 17, 2012.

Daprati, E., Franck, N., Georgieff, N., Proust, J., Pacherie, E., Dalery, J., et al. (1997). Looking for the agent: an investigation into consciousness of action and self-consciousness in schizophrenic patients. *Cognition, 65,* 71–86.

Dapretto, M., Davies, M. S., Pfeifer, J. H., Scott, A. A., Sigman, M., Bookheimer, S., Y., & Iacoboni, M. (2006). Understanding emotions in others: Mirror neuron dysfunction in children with autism spectrum disorders. *Nature Neuroscience, 9,* 28–30.

Decety, J., & Lamm, C. (2007). The role of the right temporo-parietal junction in social interaction: How low-level computational processes contribute to meta- cognition. *Neuroscientist, 13,* 580–593.

Deci, E. L., & Ryan, R. M. (2000). The "What" and "Why" of goal pursuits: Human needs and the self-determination of behavior. *Psychological Inquiry, 11,* 227–268

Dewey, J. A., Seiffert, A. E., & Carr, T. H. (2010). Taking credit for success: The phenomenology of control in a goal-directed task. *Consciousness and Cognition, 19,* 48–62.

Epley, N., Caruso, E. M., & Bazerman, M. H. (2006). When perspective taking increases taking: Reactive egoism. *Social Interaction Journal of Personality and Social Psychology, 91,* 872–889.

Farrer, C., Franck, N., Georgieff, N., Frith, C.D., Decety, J., Jeannerod, M. (2003). Modulating the experience of agency: a positron emission tomography study. *Neuroimage. 18,* 324–333.

Fleming, S. M., Weil, R. S., Nagy, Z., Dolan, R. J., & Rees, G. (2010). Relating introspective accuracy to individual differences in brain structure. *Science, 329,* 1541–1543.

Fourneret, P., & Jeannerod, M. (1998). Limited conscious monitoring of motor performance in normal subjects. *Neuropsychologia, 36,* 1133–1140.

Frith, C. D., Blakemore, S., & Wolpert, D. M. (2000). Interactive report explaining the symptoms of schizophrenia: Abnormalities in the awareness of action. *Brain Research Reviews, 31,* 357–363.

Gallese, V., & Sinigaglia, C. (2013). Cognition in action: A new look at the cortical motor system. In J. Metcalfe, & H. S. Terrace (Eds.), *Agency and Joint Attention*. New York: Oxford University Press.

Georgieff, N., & Jeannerod, M. (1998) Beyond consciousness of external reality. A "Who?" system for consciousness of action and self-consciousness. *Consciousness and Cognition, 7*, 465–477.

Greene, J. D., Sommerville, R. B., Nystrom, L. E., Darley, J. M., & Cohen, J. D. (2001). An fMRI investigation of emotional engagement in moral judgment. *Science, 293*(5537), 2105–2108.

Greene, J. D., Cushman, F. A., Stewart, L. A., Lowenberg, K., Nystrom, L. E., & Cohen, J. D. (2009). Pushing moral buttons: The interaction between personal force and intention in moral judgment. *Cognition, 111*, 364–371.

Hill, E. L., & Russell, J. (2002). Action memory and self-monitoring in children with autism: Self versus other. *Infant and Child Development, 11*, 159–170.

Iacoboni, M. (2009). Imitation, empathy, and mirror neurons. *Annual Review of Psychology, 60*, 653–670

Knoblich, J., Stottmeister F., & Kircher, T. (2004). Self-monitoring in patients with schizophrenia. *Psychological Medicine, 34*, 1561–1569.

Kruger, J., & Gilovitch, T. (1999). "Naive cynicism" in everyday theories of responsibility assessment: On biased assumptions of bias. *Journal of Personality and Social Psychology, 76*, 743–753.

Metcalfe, J., Eich, T. S., & Castel, A. (2010). Metacognition of agency across the lifespan. *Cognition, 116*, 267–282.

Metcalfe, J., & Greene, M. J. (2007). Metacognition of agency. *Journal of Experimental Psychology: General, 136*, 184–199.

Metcalfe, J., Van Snellenberg, J. X., DeRossa, P., Balsam, P., & Malhotra, A. K. (2012). Judgments of agency in schizophrenia: An impairment in autonoetic metacognition. *Proceedings of the Royal Society B, Special Issue on Metacognition.367*, 1391–1400.

Miele, D. M., Wager, T. D., Mitchell, J. P., & Metcalfe, J. (2011). Dissociating neural correlates of action monitoring and metacognition of agency. *Journal of Cognitive Neuroscience, 23*, 3620–3636.

Millward, C., Powell, S., Messer, D., & Jordan, R. (2000). Recall for self and other in autism: Children's memory for events experienced by themselves and their peers. *Journal of Autism and Developmental Disorders, 30*, 15–28.

Nyberg, L., Petersson, K. M., Nilsson, L.-G., Sandblom, J., Åberg, C., & Ingvar, M. (2001). Reactivation of motor brain areas during explicit memory for actions. *Neuroimage, 14*, 521–528.

Oberman, L. M., Hubbard, E. M., McCleery, J. P., Altschuler, E. L., Ramachanran, V. S., & Pineda, J. A. (2005). EEG evidence for in autism spectrum disorders. *Cognitive Brain Research, 24*, 190–198.

Pacherie, E. (2008). The phenomenology of action: A conceptual framework. *Cognition, 107*, 179–217.

Petrinovich, L., O'Neill, P., & Jorgensen, M. (1993). An empirical study of moral intuitions: Toward an evolutionary ethics. *Journal of Personality and Social Psychology, 64*, 467–478.

Preston, J., & Wegner, D. W. (2007). The eureka error: Inadvertent plagiarism by misattributions of effort. *Journal of Personality and Social Psychology, 92*, 575–584.

Prinz, W. (2012). *Open minds: The Social Making of Agency and Intentionality*. Cambridge, MA: MIT Press.

Prinz, W., Försterling, F., & Hauf, P. (2005). Of minds and mirrors: An introduction to the social making of minds. *Interaction Studies*, *6*, 1–19.

Redcay, E., & Saxe, R. (2013). Do you see what I see? The neural bases of joint attention. In J. Metcalfe, & H. S. Terrace (Eds.), *Agency and Joint Attention*. New York: Oxford University Press.

Rizzolatti, G., Fogassi, L., & Gallese, V. (2001). Neurophysiological mechanisms underlying the understanding and imitation of action. *Nature Neuroscience*, *2*, 661–670.

Ross, M., & Sicoly, F. (1979). Egocentric biases in availability and attribution. *Journal of Personality and Social Psychology*, *37*, 322–336.

Russell, J., & Jarrold, C. (1999). Memory for actions in children with autism: Self versus other. *Cognitive Neuropsychiatry*, *4*, 303–331

Sebanz, N., Bekkering, H., & Knoblich, G. (2006). Joint action: Bodies and minds moving together. *Trends in Cognitive Sciences*, *10*, 70–76.

Shultz, T. R., & Wells, D. (1985). Judging the intentionality of action–outcomes. *Developmental Psychology*, *21*, 83–89.

Sparrow, B. (2007). *Where is your intention? Authorship processing in co-action.* Ph.D. dissertation. Cambridge, MA: Harvard University.

Synofzik, M., Vosgerau, G., & Newen, A. (2008). Beyond the comparator model: A multifactorial two-step account of agency. *Conscious and Cognition*, *17*, 219–239.

Synofzik, M., Thier, P., Leube, D.T. Peter Schlotterbeck, P., & Lindner, A. (2010). Misattributions of agency in schizophrenia are based on imprecise predictions about the sensory consequences of one's actions. *Brain*, *133*, 262–271.

Theoret, H., Halligan, E., Kobayashi, M., Fregni, F., Tager-Flusberg, H., & Pascual- Leone, A. (2005). Impaired motor facilitation during action observation in individuals with autism spectrum disorder. *Current Biology*, *15*, R84–R85.

Tricomi, E. M., Delgado, M. R., & Fiez, J. A. (2004). Modulation of caudate activity by action contingency. *Neuron*, *41*, 281–292.

van der Wel, R., & Knoblich, G. (2013). Cues to agency: Time can tell. In J. Metcalfe, & H. S. Terrace (Eds.), *Agency and Joint Attention*. New York: Oxford University Press.

van der Wel, R. Sebanz, N., & Knoblich, G. (2012). The sense of agency during skill learning in individuals and dyads. *Consciousness and Cognition*, *15*, 423–432.

Voss, M., Moore, J., Hauser, M., Gallinat, J., Heinz, A., & Haggard, P. (2010). Altered awareness of action in schizophrenia: A specific deficit in predicting action consequences. *Brain*, *133*, 3104–3112.

Wegner, D. M. (2002). *The Illusion of Conscious Will.* Cambridge, MA: MIT Press.

Wegner, D. M., & Bargh, J. A. (1998). Control and automaticity in social life. In D. Gilbert, S. T. Fiske, & G. Lindzey (Eds.), *Handbook of Social Psychology* (4th ed., vol. 1, pp. 446–496). New York: McGraw-Hill.

Wegner, D. M., & Wheatley, T. (1999). Apparent mental causation: Sources of the experience of will. *American Psychologist*, *54*, 480–492.

Wenke, D., Fleming, S. M., & Haggard, P. (2010). Subliminal priming of actions influences sense of control over the effects of action. *Cognition*, *115*, 25–38.

Wolpert, D. M., & Ghahramani, Z. (2000). Computational principles of movement neuroscience. *Nature Neuroscience*, *3*(Suppl.), 1212–1217.

Wolpert, D. M., & Kawato, M. (1998). Multiple paired forward and inverse models for motor control. *Neural Networks*, *11*, 1317–1329.

Zalla, T., Herbrecht, E., Leboyer, M., & Metcalfe, J. (May 27, 2011). *Metacognition of agency in adults with high functioning autism.* Paper presented at the 23rd Annual Convention of the Association for Psychological Science, Washington, DC.

Zimmer, H. D., & Engelkamp, J. (2003). Signing enhances memory like performing actions. *Psychonomic Bulletin & Review, 10*, 450–454.

15 Cues to Agency: Time Can Tell
Robrecht van der Wel and Günther Knoblich

IN SOME SITUATIONS, people incorrectly attribute events they did not cause to themselves, or ascribe events they did cause to another source (e.g., Sato & Yasuda, 2005; Wegner & Wheatley, 1999; Wegner, Fuller, & Sparrow, 2003). This happens particularly in situations in which the actions of different people may cause the same environmental effect, such as when two people simultaneously press what appears to be a light switch and as a consequence the light goes on. Such situations raise questions about how people establish a sense of agency, a term referring to the feeling of being the causal source of a behavior (Sato & Yasuda, 2005). How do people know whether they themselves caused a change in the environment, or if somebody else did? Which factors determine whether and how strongly people experience a sense of agency?

Different perspectives for how the sense of agency arises have emerged. One prominent view is expressed in the theory of apparent mental causation (Wegner, 2002). This theory was developed to provide a general account of the mechanisms that trick humans into experiencing "the illusion of conscious will." For the present purposes, we will focus on those aspects of the theory that are relevant for experiencing control over one's actions and their outcomes. This experience is often referred to as the sense of agency. The experience of conscious will is a broader concept because it can, in principle, arise independently of the experience of agency (e.g., it is perfectly possible to have the conscious will to lift off and fly).

The theory of apparent mental causation states that actors may experience agency over an action when three criteria are met. These criteria are priority, consistency, and exclusivity. Priority dictates that a thought needs to precede an action. Consistency dictates that the thought needs to be consistent with the action. Finally, exclusivity dictates that no

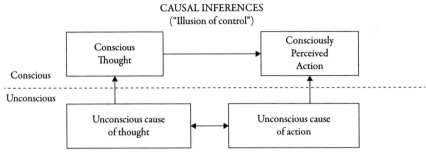

FIGURE 15.1 The Theory of Apparent Mental Causation Adopted from Wegner, D. M., & Wheatley, T. (1999). Apparent mental causation: Sources of the experience of will. *American Psychologist, 54*, 480–492.

alternative causes for the action are perceived or known. To the extent that these criteria are violated the sense of agency is reduced. A second central assumption of the theory is that an unconscious cause of a thought and an unconscious cause of an action may arise at approximately the same time (see Fig. 15.1). These two sources may be linked through an unconscious path.

Importantly, with a certain time delay the unconscious cause of a thought gives rise to an actual thought and the unconscious cause of an action gives rise to an actual action. These two causal paths are independent. If the transformation from the unconscious action to the actual action takes longer than the transformation from the unconscious thought into an actual thought, then the actual thought will precede the actual action in time. In such cases, people may incorrectly attribute mental causation and think that their conscious thought caused the consciously perceived action even though in reality the causal mechanisms are entirely unconscious. Thus, illusions in the experience of agency can emerge under such conditions.

Note that the distinction between conscious thoughts and unconscious thoughts in Wegner's model refers to a person's experience and does not necessarily imply any commitment at a neural level of explanation. Therefore, it is not as straightforward as it may seem at first glance to link Wegner's model to findings demonstrating that certain neural activities precede the conscious intention to act (Libet, Gleason, Wright & Pearl, 1983). In Wegner's model, any neural measure could reflect either conscious or unconscious processing and it is thus not quite clear how to interpret the Libet results. The most provocative aspect of Wegner's (2002) model is his doubt about whether our experience of being a causal agent is at all veridical. Although this possibility appears rather pessimistic, it is of theoretical and societal importance to consider whether and when our sense of agency is illusory.

Perhaps because it was developed to provide a provocative account of conscious will, the theory of apparent mental causation downplays the validity of perceived information about the timing and perceptual outcomes of intended actions that could actually support a truthful sense of agency (Metcalfe & Greene, 2007; Pacherie, 2008). In particular, the theory neglects that when people act they have partial conscious access to sensorimotor and perceptual cues that can help them link actions to their consequences. Sensorimotor cues arise from the generated movements themselves and are private in nature. In contrast, perceptual cues relate to the perceivable (i.e., visual and auditory) effects of actions that people share through the external environment. Lack or distortions of this access result in grave psychiatric disorders such as delusion and hallucinations in schizophrenia (Fletcher & Frith, 2009; Frith, Blakemore, & Wolpert, 2000).

Therefore, a comprehensive theory for the experience of agency needs not only to explicate when people fail to be accurate in their sense of agency but also whether and how people use sensorimotor and perceptual information to determine whether they have control over their own actions and the external events that are caused by these actions or not. Two alternative accounts focus on the use of two types of cues for sensing agency: sensorimotor cues and perceptual cues. Sensorimotor accounts do not predict difficulties in determining agency, but accounts in which perceptual cues are of central importance do predict such difficulties. We discuss these accounts in turn.

Sensorimotor Cues and the Sense of Agency

The sensorimotor account for the sense of agency emerged from studies in the domain of motor control (Wolpert & Kawato, 1998; Wolpert, Doya, & Kawato, 2003). This account states that when people perform an action they form a prediction or forward model about the sensory consequences of the action (e.g. Wolpert & Kawato, 1998). People experience themselves to have caused an action when the sensory consequences match the contents of the forward model (e.g. Blakemore, Wolpert, & Frith, 2002; Haggard, 2005; Tsakiris, Prabhu, & Haggard, 2006). For example, when writing a note to a friend, the experience of agency over producing pen strokes arises because the motor commands sent to the hand match the sensory feedback from moving the hand. Thus, our central nervous system has information about the exact motor commands that were issued to generate the action and the sensory consequences they should cause. This information provides a central, unambiguous cue for agency in the sensorimotor account.

Perceptual Cues and the Sense of Agency

In other theories of action planning, perceptual cues are crucial for determining agency. Within this account, actions are planned in terms of the perceptual events they cause in the environment rather than in terms of motor commands. For example, the common coding theory for action (Hommel, Müsseler, Aschersleben, & Prinz, 2001; Prinz, 1997) asserts that observing and executing an action relies on a similar action code. Common coding provides a parsimonious mechanism for action observation and action execution, but creates a problem for the attribution of agency (Jeannerod, 1999). If the two rely on common codes, then it is impossible for people to know from the availability of that code whether they performed an action or observed one. Before discussing this further, we'll sketch empirical evidence supporting the assumption of common coding.

Behaviorally, it has been shown that motor expertise influences action observation (e.g., Abernethy, Zawi, & Jackson, 2008; Aglioti et al., 2008; Calvo-Merino et al., 2005, 2006; Casile & Giese, 2006; Cross et al., 2006, 2009; Hecht, Vogt, & Prinz, 2001; Knoblich & Flach, 2001; Knoblich et al., 2002; Sebanz & Shiffrar, 2009), and that motor laws hold for action perception (Grosjean, Shiffrar, & Knoblich, 2007; Eskenazi et al., 2009; Viviani, Baud-Bovy, & Redolfi, 1997). For instance, Aglioti et al. (2008) showed that basketball experts were much better in predicting the outcome of incipient basketball throws than reporters with comparable visual experience of observing basketball throws. Grosjean et al. (2007) demonstrated that people's judgments of whether an observed actor could perform a movement at a particular speed or not corresponded to Fitts's law (this law defines a very general relationship between the speed and accuracy of biological movements). Such results support the assumption of common coding theory that perception of others' actions is fundamentally affected by a perceiver's motor skills (Schütz-Bosbach & Prinz, 2007; see Repp & Knoblich, 2007 for an example in the auditory domain).

Mirror neurons in macaque monkeys' premotor and parietal cortices (e.g., Gallese & Sinigaglia [chapter 10]; Rizzolatti & Craighero, 2004) are active both for action production and action observation and may provide a possible neural substrate for common coding of perception and action. These neurons discharge both when a macaque monkey performs an object-directed action, such as grasping a peanut, and when the monkey observes another individual performing the same action, such as when the monkey sees the experimenter grasp a peanut (Gallese, Fadiga, Fogassi, & Rizzolatti, 1996). Thus, these neurons "mirror" others' actions as if one would perform them oneself, providing a previously unexpected, direct link between individuals.

Numerous brain imaging studies demonstrate that premotor and parietal areas of the human brain are active when people observe others acting (Rizolatti & Sinigaglia, 2010). How much these brain areas are activated through observation depends on the observer's expertise in performing the observed action. One study investigated whether dancers trained in a particular style would show more activation in brain areas linked to performance when observing someone dancing in their own style (Calvo-Merino et al., 2005). Indeed, ballet dancers showed more activation in premotor cortex when observing ballet dancing than when observing capoeira, a martial art style dance that was unfamiliar to them. Skilled capoeira dancers showed the reverse pattern, more activation when observing capoeira dancing than when observing ballet dancing.

Jeannerod et al. (e.g., Daprati et al., 1997; Georgieff & Jeannerod, 1998; Jeannerod, 2009) were the first to point out that the overlap of representations for action production and action observation may generate ambiguity for the sense of agency. This is so because in many instances it is virtually impossible to disentangle an action producing a perceptual event from the perceptual event produced by the action itself, especially if the perceptual event is auditory or visual. At the same time, it is well known that people tend to be unaware of their movements. To illustrate, people may rely more on ambiguous perceptual information about a tone than on less ambiguous sensorimotor information about their movement in relation to the tone to determine whether they have produced a tone with a key press (see Knoblich & Repp, 2009). In other words, public perceptual cues may dominate agency, although more accurate private sensorimotor cues to agency are available.

Fourneret and Jeannerod (1998) tested this assumption in an experiment in which they asked people to trace straight lines by moving their hand on an occluded writing pad. Participants could only see a visual trace of their movement and they could only feel the movement of their hand because it was occluded from view. In some trials, angular perturbations ($-10°$ to $10°$) were introduced between the actual movement and its visual consequences on the screen. Participants judged their movements to be straight ahead, even when they were actually bent. This experiment suggests that people may rely more on visual information rather than proprioceptive information when judging agency.

In a similar paradigm study in which participants were drawing circles instead of tracing straight lines, Knoblich and Kircher (2004) asked for an explicit judgment of when people started to feel that a distortion was affecting the relation between proprioception and vision. This manipulation was very similar to changing the ratio between the movement of a computer mouse and the visual cursor observed on a computer screen. Surprisingly, participants' sensitivity to such changes was very low. Rather than using the sensorimotor cues arising from the distortion to detect loss of agency, these sensorimotor cues were used to automatically compensate for the distortions. This made it actually harder for the participants to detect loss of agency through the distortions in the visual trajectories they were producing. Thus more ambiguous perceptual information dominated over less ambiguous sensorimotor information when people judged their agency.

In a recent study, we (van der Wel, Sebanz, & Knoblich, 2012) examined the sense of agency over actions people learned to perform together with an action partner. Such joint actions provide an interesting case with regards to sensing agency, because the perceptual effects of actions are intended together with somebody else. Do people predominantly derive a sense of agency for joint actions based on this perceptual information, or do they place emphasis on their sensorimotor contributions to distinguish their own contributions as well? To address this question, pairs of participants moved a pendulum back and forth between two targets by pulling on cords attached to each side of the apparatus (for a description, see van der Wel, Knoblich, & Sebanz, 2011). While they did so, we measured the quality of their performance (available to participants from the perceptual information), as well as the forces each participant contributed to the movements (related to sensorimotor information). After each trial, we then asked participants to rate how strongly they felt in control during the preceding performance. Correlational analyses revealed that participants relied heavily on perceptual information, but not on sensorimotor information for their sense of agency during joint action.

People have also been shown to be able to identify their own previous actions based on perceptual cues alone (Knoblich & Flach, 2003, Repp & Knoblich, 2004). For instance, Knoblich and Prinz (2001) demonstrated that people are able to recognize recordings of dynamic traces of their writing from a single moving dot. Similarly, Flach et al. (2004) demonstrated that people are able to recognize recordings of their clapping from basic temporal parameters such as tempo and rhythmic idiosyncrasies. Such findings suggest that a sequence of perceptual events is often sufficient to determine agency and they are in line with the common coding assumptions that actions are planned based on their perceptual effects. As a result, agency misattributions may occur due to ambiguities in the perceptual domain.

What are the necessary conditions for experiencing agency? Of course, one needs to have a code or representation that in some way corresponds to the particular action. However, having such an action code is not sufficient condition to support a "veridical" sense of agency as the code may originate from action production or action observation. In other words, it is inherently ambiguous with regard to whether oneself or somebody else has caused the action. In the next section, we propose one way in which this ambiguity may be resolved.

Towards a Comprehensive Model for the Sense of Agency

Although people correctly attribute agency most of the time, their reliance on perceptual cues raises the question of whether there are particular self-monitoring systems that deal with the inherent ambiguity of these cues with regard to agency. This led Georgieff and Jeannerod, (1998) to postulate that there is a "who-system" in the brain, a dedicated self-monitoring system that serves to consciously monitor perceptual events with regard to agency, thus explicitly assigning perceptual events that potentially result from action to self and others. So far, research on the who-system has focused on identifying the underlying neural networks (Jeannerod, 2009).

But how exactly does the who-system work functionally? One possibility to further specify the workings of the who-system is to assume that perceptual events are tagged differently by the who-system depending on whether or not they follow an action or an action sequence that the actor has previously initiated. In other words the who-system could provide a time-tag that signifies when an intentional action was generated. If an action code becomes available that temporally matches the issuing of a time-tag provided by the who-system, then an agent may experience having caused the action. Thus a private, possibly sensorimotor, mechanism is thought to provide a time tag, and this tag is then linked to the action codes. This account provides a way of integrating sensorimotor and perceptual accounts of agency, in that private (sensorimotor) cues are matched up with shared perceptual cues, thus exploiting all available cues for agency.

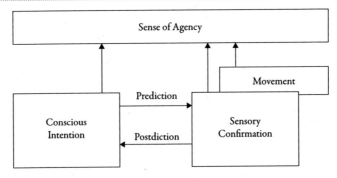

FIGURE 15.2 Multiple Sources of Agency Scheme. In this scheme, the conscious intention to act, sensorimotor commands from the movement itself (somatosensory reafference), and sensory confirmation based on external action effects are integrated to give rise to the sense of agency. The conscious intention to act is caused by preparation for action (not shown). Preparation for action, movement, and action effects are objective physical events, whereas conscious intentions, sensory confirmation, and the resulting sense of agency concern the subjective domain. Modified from Haggard, P., & Tsakiris, M. (2009). The experience of agency. *Current Directions in Psychological Science, 18*(4), 242–246.

Recently, Haggard and Tsakiris (2009) put forth a scheme that suggests a similar integration of sensorimotor and perceptual accounts for the sense of agency (see Fig. 15.2). In this scheme, the conscious intention to act, the forward model related to the executed movement, and the sensory effects of the action all influence the extent to which people experience agency over an action. Although both sensorimotor and perceptual cues can influence the experience of agency, no indication is given about how these cues are weighed against each other, and how they interact. In addition, the importance of the timing of different cues is not specified. Thus the scheme effectively integrates major assumptions made in different existing theoretical frameworks, but it lacks specificity concerning the precise role of the timing of different cues and their integration for the sense of agency. In the remainder of this chapter, we argue that the timing of perceptual and sensorimotor cues plays a central role for establishing a sense of agency.

Time Can Tell

The timing of actions and their perceptual consequences is of fundamental importance for the sense of agency. All theories of agency acknowledge this fact. In Wegner's (2002) framework, priority is one of the key factors that determine whether people feel control over actions and events but the theory does not specify specific processes for timing events that result from one's own and others' actions. Sensorimotor theories have stressed the additional information that is available for self-performed action, including sensorimotor information about when they initiated an action (see also Steele & Lau [chapter 18]). In addition, perceptual events arising from actions and the relative timing of such events in an event sequence (rhythm) could provide information about who is producing these events. How do people use perceptual timing cues to establish a sense of agency?

As briefly mentioned previously, one way to assess people's sensitivity to perceptual cues for identifying their own actions is to expose people to recordings of their own and others' previous actions, and ask them to indicate if the replayed perceptual effects stem from their own previous actions or not. Repp and Knoblich (2004) employed this approach to measure sensitivity to perceptual cues in the auditory domain by asking professional piano players to recognize their own previous performances. Several piano pieces were first played by and recorded for each participant, either while they could hear what they played or while they played on a silent keyboard. Several months later, the pianists returned and listened to recordings of their own and other participants' previous performances. The performances were edited to remove any obvious errors. The participants then were asked to indicate on a five-point scale to what extent they thought they were listening to their own performance. The results of this first recognition test revealed that on average participants gave higher ratings for their own performances (indicating self-recognition) than for those of others. This result did not depend on whether the performances were recorded on a normal or a silent keyboard. In a second and third recognition test conducted a few months later, the performances were further stripped so that they preserved only the articulation, dynamics, and timing (ATD test), or only the articulation and timing (AT test) information. The results indicated that removing this information did not influence the recognition pattern. Thus, recognition was equally good based in the initial test compared to the ATD test and the AT test. These results thus suggest that the timing of perceptual cues may constitute a major information source that people use to distinguish their own perceptual effects from those of others.

The results of Repp and Knoblich (2004) suggest that people are quite sensitive to the timing of perceptual cues. This raises the question of whether such sensitivity transfers to how people establish a sense of agency. To investigate this issue, Repp and Knoblich (2007; Knoblich & Repp, 2009) used a paradigm in which participants were to detect switches in agency (gaining or losing control over perceptual events). Participants were either musical experts (Repp & Knoblich, 2007) or nonmusicians (Knoblich & Repp, 2009; Experiment 1). In half of the conditions, participants actively performed a finger-tapping task. In the other half of the conditions, participants passively listened. In both cases, they heard a tone sequence that corresponded either to their own tapping (self-control), or was computer-generated with a fixed interval between taps (external control). The tones switched from one form of control to the other at some unpredictable point in the sequence. Participants indicated when they perceived such switches from one mode of control to the other. By eliminating action production in the passive listening conditions, the contribution of sensorimotor and perceptual cues for sensing agency could be distinguished. In the active conditions participants could use both sensorimotor cues and perceptual cues, whereas in the passive conditions participants could only use perceptual cues. Signal-detection theory was used to determine the sensitivity to different cues.

First, participants were generally better at detecting switches in agency in the active compared to the passive conditions, although this finding appears to depend on musical expertise. This result indicates that especially musical experts successfully used sensorimotor cues to detect agency. Second, the results indicate that participants were sensitive to switches in agency based on perceptual cues alone (i.e., the passive conditions), especially when control switched from external to self. These results suggest that both sensorimotor and perceptual cues are integrated over time to establish a sense of agency. The generality of these findings was confirmed in two additional experiments that used a modified procedure (Knoblich & Repp, 2009). Other studies further substantiate the observation that people are sensitive to the timing of different cues for detection of agency (e.g. Daprati et al., 2007; Flach, Knoblich, & Prinz, 2003, 2004).

Conclusions

The findings discussed above suggest that conscious and unconscious processing are likely not as clearly distinct as Wegner et al. suggest. Although errors in the sense of agency may arise from a mismatch between conscious and unconscious causality, sensorimotor as well as perceptual information can become conscious and, therefore, be used to establish an at least partially veridical sense of agency. Thus, usually, the conscious perception of these cues corresponds to the underlying unconscious machinery generating these cues. Our studies of timing cues provide strong evidence that people clearly establish this sensitivity to the timing of perceptual cues. These findings illustrate that theories of agency need not only address biased or illusionary experiences of agency, but that they also need to further explicate the mechanisms that allow sensorimotor and perceptual cues to inform the experience of agency. An interesting implication of this "psychophysical" approach to agency is that the sense of agency may increase as people master perceptual and motor skills. It remains to be seen whether timing cues to agency are indeed more telling for concert pianists and Formula 1 racecar drivers than for musical novices and pilots of road cruisers.

REFERENCES

Abernethy, B., Zawi, K., & Jackson, R.C. (2008). Expertise and attunement to kinematic constraints. *Perception, 37,* 931–948.

Aglioti, S. M., Cesari, P., Romani, M., & Urgesi, C. (2008). Action anticipation and motor resonance in elite basketball players. *Nature Neuroscience, 11,* 1109–1116.

Blakemore, S. J., Wolpert, D. M., & Frith, C. D. (2002). Abnormalities in the awareness of action. *Trends in Cognitive Sciences, 6,* 237–242.

Calvo-Merino, B., Glaser, D. E., Grezes, J., Passingham, R. E., & Haggard, P. (2005). Action observation and acquired motor skills: An fMRI study with expert dancers. *Cerebral Cortex, 15,* 1243–1249.

Calvo-Merino, B., Grèzes, J., Glaser, D. E., Passingham, R. E., & Haggard, P. (2006). Seeing or doing? Influence of visual and motor familiarity in action observation. *Current Biology, 16,* 1905–1910.

Casile, A., & Giese, M.A. (2006). Non-visual motor learning influences the recognition of biological motion. *Current Biology, 16*, 69–74.

Cross, E. S., Hamilton, A. F., & Grafton, S. T. (2006). Building a motor simulation de novo: Observation of dance by dancers. *NeuroImage, 31*, 1257–1267.

Cross, E. S., Kraemer, D. J. M., Hamilton, A. F. D. C., Kelley, W. M., & Grafton, S. T. (2009). Sensitivity of the action observation network to physical and observational learning. *Cerebral Cortex, 19*, 315–326.

Daprati, E., Franck, N., Georgieff, N., Proust, J., Pacherie, E., Dalery, J., & Jeannerod, M. (1997). Looking for the agent: an investigation into consciousness of action and self-consciousness in schizophrenic patients. *Cognition, 65*, 71–86.

Daprati, E., Wriessnegger, S., & Lacquaniti, F. (2007). Kinematic cues and recognition of self-generated actions. *Experimental Brain Research, 177*, 31–44.

Eskenazi, T., Grosjean, M., Humphreys, G., & Knoblich, G. (2009). The role of motor simulation in action perception: A neuropsychological case study. *Psychological Research, 73*, 477–485.

Flach, R., Knoblich, G., & Prinz, W. (2003). Off-line authorship effects in action perception. *Brain and Cognition, 53*, 503–513.

Flach, R., Knoblich, G., & Prinz, W. (2004). Recognizing one's own clapping: The role of temporal cues in self-recognition. *Psychological Research, 69*, 147–156.

Fletcher, P. C., & Frith, C. D. (2009). Perceiving is believing: a Bayesian approach to explaining the positive symptoms of schizophrenia. *Nature Reviews Neuroscience, 10*, 48–58.

Fourneret, P., & Jeannerod, M. (1998). Limited conscious monitoring of motor performance in normal subjects. *Neuropsychologia, 36*, 1133–1140.

Frith, C. D., Blakemore, S.-J., Wolpert, D. M. (2000). Abnormalities in the awareness and control of actions. *Philosophical Transactions of the Royal Society London: Series B, 355*, 1771–1788.

Gallese, V., Fadiga, L., Fogassi, L., & Rizzolatti, G. (1996). Action recognition in the premotor cortex. *Brain, 119*, 593–609.

Gallese, V., & Sinigaglia, C. (2013). Cognition in action: A new look at the cortical motor system. In J. Metcalfe, & H. S. Terrace (Eds.), *Agency and Joint Attention* (pp. 178–195). New York: Oxford University Press.

Georgieff, N., & Jeannerod, M. (1998). Beyond consciousness of external reality: a "who" system for consciousness of action and self-consciousness. *Consciousness and Cognition, 7*, 465–477.

Grosjean, M., Shiffrar, M., & Knoblich, G. (2007). Fitts' law holds in action perception. *Psychological Science, 18*, 95–99.

Haggard, P. (2005). Conscious intention and motor cognition. *Trends in Cognitive Sciences, 9*, 290–295.

Haggard, P., & Tsakiris, M. (2009). The experience of agency. *Current Directions in Psychological Science, 18*, 242–246.

Hecht, H., Vogt, S., & Prinz, W. (2001). Motor learning enhances perceptual judgment: A case for action-perception transfer. *Psychological Research, 65*, 3–14.

Hommel, B., Müsseler, J., Aschersleben, G., & Prinz, W. (2001). The Theory of Event Coding (TEC): A framework for perception and action planning. *Behavioral and Brain Sciences, 24*, 849–937.

Jeannerod, M. (1999). The 25th Bartlett Lecture. To act or not to act: Perspectives on the representation of action. *Quarterly Journal of Experimental Psychology: Human Experimental Psychology, 52A*, 1–29.

Jeannerod, M. (2009). The sense of agency and its disturbances in schizophrenia: a reappraisal. *Experimental Brain Research, 192*, 527–532.

Knoblich, G., & Flach, R. (2001). Predicting the effects of actions: Interactions of perception and action. *Psychological Science, 12*, 467–472.

Knoblich, G., & Flach, R. (2003). Action identity: evidence from self-recognition, prediction, and coordination. *Consciousness and Cognition, 12*, 620–632.

Knoblich, G., & Kircher T. (2004). Deceiving oneself about being in control: Conscious detection of changes in visuo-motor coupling. *Journal of Experimental Psychology: Human Perception and Performance, 30*, 657–666.

Knoblich, G., & Repp, B. (2009). Inferring agency from sound. *Cognition, 111*, 248–262.

Knoblich, G., Seigerschmidt, E., Flach, R., & Prinz, W. (2002). Authorship effects in the prediction of handwriting strokes. *Quarterly Journal of Experimental Psychology, 55A*, 1027–1046.

Knoblich, G., & Prinz, W. (2001). Recognition of self-generated actions from kinematic displays of drawing. *Journal of Experimental Psychology: Human Perception and Performance, 27*, 456–465.

Libet, B., Gleason, C. A., Wright, E. W., & Pearl, D. K. (1983). Time of conscious intention to act in relation to onset of cerebral activity (readiness-potential). The unconscious initiation of a freely voluntary act. *Brain, 106*, 623–642.

Metcalfe, J., & Greene, M. J. (2007). Metacognition of agency. *Journal of Experimental Psychology: General, 136*, 184–199.

Pacherie, E. (2008). The phenomenology of action: A conceptual framework. *Cognition, 107*, 179–217.

Prinz, W. (1997). Perception and action planning. *European Journal of Cognitive Psychology, 9*, 129–154.

Repp, B. H., & Knoblich, G. (2004). Perceiving action identity: How pianists recognize their own performances. *Psychological Science, 15*, 604–609.

Repp, B. H., & Knoblich, G. (2007). Action can affect auditory perception. *Psychological Science, 18*, 6–7.

Rizzolatti, G., & Craighero, L. (2004). The mirror-neuron system. *Annual Review of Neuroscience, 27*, 169–192.

Rizzolatti, G., & Sinigaglia, C. (2010). The functional role of the parieto-frontal mirror circuit: interpretations and misinterpretations. *Nature Reviews Neuroscience, 11*, 264–274.

Sato, A., & Yasuda, A. (2005). Illusion of self-agency: Discrepancy between the predicted and actual sensory consequences of actions modulates the sense of self-agency, but not the sense of self-ownership. *Cognition, 94*, 241–255.

Schütz-Bosbach, S., & Prinz, W. (2007). Perceptual resonance: Action-induced modulation of perception. *Trends in Cognitive Sciences, 11*, 349–355.

Sebanz, N., & Shiffrar, M. (2009). Detecting deception in a bluffing body: The role of expertise. *Psychonomic Bulletin and Review, 16*, 170–175.

Steele, S., & Lau, H. The function of consciousness in controlling behavior. In J. Metcalfe, & H. S. Terrace (Eds.), *Agency and Joint Attention* (pp. 304–320). New York: Oxford University Press.

Tsakiris, M., Prabhu, G., & Haggard, P. (2006). Having a body versus moving your body: How agency structures body-ownership. *Consciousness and Cognition, 15*, 423–432.

van der Wel, R. P. R. D., Knoblich, G., & Sebanz, N. (2011). Let the force be with us: Dyads exploit haptic coupling for coordination. *Journal of Experimental Psychology: Human Perception and Performance, 37*, 1420–1431.

van der Wel, R. P. R. D., Sebanz, N., & Knoblich, G.K. (2012). The sense of agency during skill learning in individuals and dyads. *Consciousness and Cognition, 21,* 1267–1279.

Viviani, P., Baud-Bovy, G., & Redolfi, M. (1997). Perceiving and tracking kinesthetic stimuli: Further evidence of motor-perceptual interactions. *Journal of Experimental Psychology: Human Perception and Performance, 23,* 1232–1252.

Wegner, D.M. (2002). *The Illusion of Conscious Will.* Cambridge, MA: MIT Press.

Wegner, D. M., Fuller, V. A., & Sparrow, B. (2003). Clever hands: Uncontrolled intelligence in facilitated communication. *Journal of Personality and Social Psychology, 85,* 5–19.

Wegner, D. M., & Wheatley, T. (1999). Apparent mental causation: Sources of the experience of will. *American Psychologist, 54,* 480–492.

Wolpert, D. M., Doya, K., & Kawato, M. (2003). A unifying computational framework for motor control and social interaction. *Philosophical Transactions of the Royal Society, 358,* 593–602.

Wolpert, D. M., & Kawato, M. (1998). Multiple paired forward and inverse models for motor control. *Neural Networks, 11,* 1317–1329.

16 The Meaning of Actions: Cross-Talk between Procedural and Declarative Action Knowledge
Wolfgang Prinz, Christiane Diefenbach, and Anne Springer

AGENCY IS AN ambiguous concept because it can be used at both the cognitive and the metacognitive level. At the cognitive level it stands for the human capacity to select and initiate goal-directed actions, including elements like goal-setting, intention formation, action authorship, top-down control, etc. In other words, the term "agency" stands at this level for functional characteristics of the machinery for volition. In this regard, we may speak of a *craft of agency*.

At the metacognitive level, the concept of agency refers to the way in which individuals perceive and understand intentional action—either performed by themselves or perceived being performed by others. Here the notion of agency stands for awareness of volition (i.e., for characteristics of the mental experience of producing and perceiving intentional action). In that regard we may speak of a *sense of agency*.

Research on the foundations of agency follows several strands. One classical strand is concerned with sources of a sense of agency and ways it is rooted in volitional mechanisms (see chapters by Pacherie [chapter 19] and van der Wel & Knoblich [chapter 15]). Relatedly, a further strand of research traces the ontogenetic trajectories of agency at the cognitive and the metacognitive level as well as their mutual relationships (Russell, 1996; Zelazo, Astington, & Olson, 1999).

In this chapter we focus on a third strand, which concerns representational underpinnings of agency. Our main issue will be to examine the representational resources on which action perception and production draw. More specifically, we will address the alleged divide between contributions of *procedural knowledge for action* and *declarative knowledge about action* to the representational grounds of agency. A side issue will be to examine how representational resources for own action and foreign action may be related to each other. This issue is necessarily entailed in the logic of our experimental paradigms, which combine action production with action perception. Here we encounter a further alleged divide, this time between production and perception.

In a nutshell we will show that both divides are less deep than is often thought: procedural and declarative knowledge are closely interlinked, and perception and production draw on common representational resources.

The Great Divide

Social interaction can be described and explained in various ways and at various levels. Psychological inquiry tends to focus on the level of individuals as they act and interact with others. Research of social interaction is at that level concerned with what people do in response to, or anticipation of what others do. In a way, then, the study of interaction comes down to the study of the interplay between action perception (watching what others are doing) and action production (acting in response to/anticipation of their doings).

That interplay may be examined at two levels, symbolic and embodied. At the symbolic level, language provides ample resources for capturing both the surface and the deep structure of human action. In everyday conversation we use language to give an account of what people do, how they do it, and why they do it. Actually we spend a considerable portion of our lifetime with communicative exchange about own and foreign action, aiming at understanding the meaning of people's doings. At the embodied level we may also study those actions themselves, rather than studying talk about them. Here we consider the way people perceive/anticipate the actions of others and produce their own complementary actions. Research at that level tries to understand how body movements instantiating meaningful actions are perceived and generated, focusing on the kinematics of their movements rather than the semantics of their actions.

In this chapter we discuss two experimental paradigms that address the issue of cross-talk between action semantics and movement kinematics or, for that matter, between symbolic, declarative knowledge *about* action and embodied procedural knowledge *for* action perception and production. As we show, both paradigms demonstrate interactions and mutual dependencies between the two kinds of knowledge. They add to the increasing body of evidence that is now challenging the great divide that is often seen to exist between symbolic versus embodied, declarative versus procedural, and conceptual versus sensorimotor modes of representation and processing.

That divide is perhaps more implicitly inherent in the way psychological textbooks are organized rather than being explicitly expressed in overarching theoretical statements. Textbooks have, on the one hand, chapters on knowledge representation and language processing, and, on the other hand, on object and event perception and action production. These chapters have their respective topics and theories, but when one tries to relate them to each other one begins to see that styles of theorizing are quite distinctive. Theories on the declarative side explain *what* people believe and think, while theories on the procedural side explain *how* people perceive and act.

Not surprisingly, the great divide is not only a divide between styles of theorizing but at the same time a divide between research communities and literatures cultivating those styles. Traditionally the community of those who study the semantics of action knowledge and its role in social interaction and communication has been quite distinct from the community of those who study the syntax underlying the perception and production of movements that instantiate human action. The first community covers fields like cognition, language, volition, and social cognition, whereas the second field covers more low-level fields like perception, attention, and motor control.

Although the great divide is thus deeply inherent in the systematics of psychology and cognitive science, it hasn't gone unchallenged. One major challenge is as old as experimental psychology itself. In psychological experiments we use verbal instructions (in the declarative mode) in order to set the stage for participants' subsequent acting (in the procedural mode). In doing so we are assuming that participants have a way of translating, as it were, declarative instructions into procedural operations. In fact, such instructions are efficient: We can successfully instruct others what to do, under what conditions to do it, and how to do it. Trivial as it may be, this simple observation already illustrates that the divide cannot be as great and deep as the organization of our textbooks suggests.

What the efficacy of commands and instructions demonstrates is that declarative knowledge can set the stage for subsequent procedural processing. What they demonstrate are, in other words, offline interactions between declarative and procedural knowledge, without implying any kind of online cross-talk. Yet, in a number of recent studies such online cross-talk has been shown to exist as well. Although some of them have approached the declarative/procedural interface from the symbolic/semantic side, others have approached it from the embodied/motor side.

Starting from the symbolic/semantic side, numerous studies have demonstrated that processing verbal and conceptual information is closely linked to information processing in sensory and motor domains in the sense that each and every token of activation of semantic knowledge goes along with, and perhaps even relies on, tokens of concomitant activation of sensory and/or motor knowledge (e.g., Barsalou, 2003, 2005, 2008; Glenberg, 2008; Glenberg, 2008 Kiefer, 2007, 2008; Mahon & Caramazza, 2008, 2009; Martin, Ungerleider, & Haxby, 2000; Pulvermüller, 1999, 2005, 2008). Likewise, starting from the embodied/motor side, many studies have shown that motor control may be closely linked to semantic and conceptual processing in the sense that the kinematics of ongoing movements may be affected by the semantics of concurrently processed words and concepts (e.g., Boulenger, Roy et al., 2006; Boulenger, Silber et al., 2008; Gentilucci, Benuzzi, Bertolani, Daprati, & Gangitano, 2000; Glover, Rosenbaum, Graham, & Dixon, 2004; Jeannerod, 1994).

While these studies converge on questioning the great divide, they come with diverse (and actually divergent) proposals on how to bridge the gap. Whereas some of them believe that the bridge results from declarative knowledge being grounded in procedural knowledge, others believe that it results from procedural knowledge being associated with mandatory entries at the declarative level. Which one is true? Does declarative knowledge depend on procedural knowledge or vice versa—or can the two views even be combined? For the rest of this chapter we discuss findings from two paradigms that may shed some light on this issue. One starts on the declarative side and studies interactions with concurrent action (action language). The other starts on the procedural side and addresses interactions with concurrent language processing (action simulation).

Action Language

Over the past 10 years a number of studies have addressed the so called action-sentence compatibility effect (ACE) (e.g., Borreggine & Kaschak, 2006; Glenberg & Kaschak, 2002; Zwaan & Taylor, 2006). This effect is meant to demonstrate online interactions between language comprehension and action selection. More specifically it is meant to show content-specific cross-talk between sentence comprehension (SC) and response selection (RS) and, hence, to support the notion of grounding of the processing of declarative knowledge (SC) in procedural processing (RS). The paradigm combines a sentence comprehension task with an action selection task.

The sentence comprehension task requires participants to determine whether or not a given sentence is meaningful (yes vs. no response). All sentences that are presented refer to human actions, either *meaningful* ("You give Peter the book") or *meaningless* ("You sing Peter the book"). The crucial manipulation is that meaningful sentences are of two kinds: *away* ("You give Peter the book") and *toward* ("Peter gives you the book"). Responses are recorded on a vertically oriented response panel, with a home button in the center and buttons for the *YES* and the *NO* response in the far or near position to the body (cf. Fig. 16.1). Importantly, there are two response conditions, differing in the mapping of the two responses to the two buttons: *YES-IS-FAR (and no-is-near)* and *YES-IS-NEAR (and no-is-far)*. Thus, depending on the response condition, the yes response to a meaningful sentence has to be delivered by moving the finger either to the *far* button (*away* from the body) or to the *near* button (*toward* the body).

The ACE obtained in this task is a content-based compatibility effect between two kinds of action information: semantic information (entailed in the sentence) and motor information (entailed in the to-be-selected response). Responses to away-sentences are

Conditions

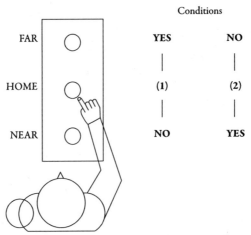

FIGURE 16.1 Response Panel and Mapping Conditions in the ACE Paradigm. (1): YES-IS-FAR (and no-is-near); (2): YES-IS-NEAR (and no-is-far).

initiated faster in the YES-IS-FAR condition than in the YES-IS-NEAR condition, whereas the reverse is true for toward sentences. In other words, the content of the sentence (away/toward) seems to prime the selection of the response to that sentence. This has been taken to support the notion that language comprehension may be grounded in motor processes: one primes the other when both address a common spatial feature (away/toward).

In a recent collaboration with Art Glenberg we started working on the ACE (Diefenbach, 2010; Diefenbach, Rieger, Massen, & Prinz, in prep.). Our initial research question was meant to address the relative contributions of two factors: movements and movement effects. In order to pursue this question we dissociated movements from their effects (e.g., combining a movement directed away from the body with a movement effect located near the body). Yet our results showed that the ACE was unreliable (even in control conditions in which movement direction and effect location were not dissociated). Importantly, however, the effect was unreliable in the interesting sense of occasionally turning into the opposite, emerging as a substantial and reliable negative compatibility effect.

An example of both the standard (positive) ACE and the inverted (negative) ACE is shown in Table 16.1. The results are taken from an experiment in which we manipulated the time at which the instruction was delivered (as explained in more detail below). The instruction (i.e., YES-IS-FAR vs. YES-IS-NEAR) was either given at the onset of sentence presentation or after a delay. We obtained a positive ACE when instructions were delivered at the onset of presentation (stimulus onset asynchrony (SOA) = 0 ms). In this condition, responses to away sentences were faster when directed away from the body than when directed toward the body (compatible vs. incompatible trials) and vice versa. However, when we delayed the instruction (SOA = 500 ms), a negative ACE was

TABLE 16.1

Mean Response Times (ms) for Compatible and Incompatible Trials under Two
Instruction Conditions (SOA between Sentence Onset and Mapping Instructions)

	Compatible Trials	Incompatible Trials
SOA = 0 ms	2120	2171
SOA = 500 ms	2145	2085

SOA = stimulus onset asynchrony.

obtained. In this case, responses to away sentences were faster when directed toward the body than when directed away from the body (incompatible vs. compatible trials).

On the one hand, the occasional occurrence of an inverted effect made it impossible to further pursue our initial research question. On the other hand, we thought that a negative compatibility effect is by itself at least as interesting as a positive effect is. Accordingly, we became interested in a novel research question pertaining to conditions under which the effect becomes negative. How does a negative ACE emerge and what does it mean?

Figure 16.2 sketches two frameworks for the ACE, minimal and extended. The upper panel provides an outline for a minimal framework that is needed to account for the basic effect (i.e., the positive ACE). The example refers to the case of processing an awaysentence ("You give Peter the book") under YES-IS-FAR instructions. To understand the effect, we need to consider two subsequent phases, sentence comprehension (SC) and response selection (RS). If it is true that SC and RS draw on common representational resources, the early operation (SC) may prime the late ones (RS) if they share common features. For instance, in the example in Figure 16.2, SC refers to a meaningful away sentence that requires a yes response which, under given instructions, has to be translated into a movement away from the body (far). Accordingly, semantic content (away) may prime the subsequent motor response (far), and as a result we may see faster responses on compatible than on incompatible trials. Notably, no such priming can be expected to occur when an away sentence is processed under YES-IS-NEAR instructions, or when a toward sentence like "Peter gives you the book" is processed under YES-IS-FAR instructions.

Although this scheme helps us to understand the positive compatibility effect (ACE+) it does not explain the reverse effect (ACE−). Consider the lower panel of Figure 16.2 in which a slightly extended framework is applied to the same example. The extension refers to the early phase which now has two operations running in parallel: sentence comprehension (as before) and motor preparation (SC and MP, respectively). Suppose that motor preparation reflects a bias in favor of the yes direction as specified in the instruction (i.e., here in favor of the far response). Accordingly, this scenario implies two concurrent operations (SC and MP) of which we assume that they both draw on common representational resources. This time, however, the two operations may impair each other

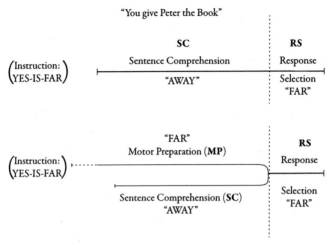

FIGURE 16.2 Two Frameworks of the ACE. Upper panel: Basic framework of ACE+. Lower panel: Extended framework of combining ACE+ and ACE−.

because they address the same representational resources at the same time. Such interference between perception and production of overlapping action events has been observed in a number of different paradigms (see Schütz-Bosbach & Prinz, 2007, for an overview). It seems to reflect a structural limitation of the number of operations in which a given representation can be engaged at a time (Hommel, Müsseler, Aschersleben, & Prinz, 2001; Müsseler & Hommel, 1997). Accordingly, we may expect that MP (pertaining to the far response) interferes with concurrent SC (pertaining to the away sentence)—to the effect that SC may be slower on compatible as compared with incompatible cases. Accordingly, the extended framework can not only account for ACE+ (resulting from SC priming RS), but also for ACE− (resulting from interference between MP and SC).

The logic of this reasoning is based on the assumption that compatibility may help or hurt, depending on conditions. Compatibility helps when the same representational resources are addressed in two subsequent operations such that the activation of these resources in the first operation may prime their use in the second (as is the case in the relationship between SC and RS in the upper panel). This is the standard interpretation of compatibility effects. On the other hand, as has been shown in a number of studies (Hommel, Müsseler, Aschersleben, & Prinz, 2001; Müsseler & Hommel, 1997), compatibility may hurt when a given representational resource is simultaneously addressed by two concurrent operations (as is the case in the competition between MP and SC in the lower panel).

Although the extended framework may help us to understand how the ACE may turn from positive into negative, it leaves us with a serious problem. We now have two compatibility effects counteracting each other: an early ACE− presumably caused by interference between motor preparation and sentence comprehension, and a late ACE+ presumably caused by priming of response selection through sentence comprehension.

Importantly, both effects build on compatibility due to shared resources for semantic and motor processing. Thus, if the extended framework holds true, the ACE must be inherently ambiguous because its net effect reflects an additive combination of early interference and late priming.

How can a framework like this be tested? An indirect way of testing is to study the impact of factors that are likely to affect one of the two effects more than the other. Consider, for example, the impact of comprehension skills. As reflected in different levels of response times, participants are not equally fast at constructing the meaning of a sentence. Accordingly, slow comprehenders who take relatively long to understand a sentence should be exposed to the early interference effect (ACE−) for a longer period than fast comprehenders. As a result, we may expect that the net ACE becomes more negative for slow than for fast comprehenders. Indeed, we found the net ACE to be modulated by participants' comprehension speed in the predicted way (Diefenbach, 2010).

As a further example, consider the role of response biases and the timing of instructions. The extended framework predicts that the early interference effect depends on SC and MP concurrently drawing on the same representational resource. Importantly, there may be two directions of such interference arising from different temporal constellations of SC and MP according to the timing of response instructions. Instructions can occur before or after the sentence is processed. Either SC or MP may become impaired, depending on which of them addresses the shared resource in the first place. In one case, the negative ACE may result from SC being impaired. When MP starts before the sentence is being processed (SC), the common resource may already be occupied by MP and thus be less accessible when needed for SC. In the reverse case, the negative ACE may result from MP being impaired. When MP starts after the crucial components of the sentence have been processed, the common resource may be temporarily occupied by SC which should hamper MP. Because MP prepares for RS, its impairment may delay RS and thus lead to slower responses on compatible trials. In fact, we found indications for both directions of interference by manipulating the point in time (relative to sentence onset) at which participants were instructed how to give the yes response in a given trial (i.e., yes-is-far vs. yes-is-near). Providing the instruction one second before sentence presentation should result in an early MP and thus act to impair SC. Consistent with this expectation, the error rates in this condition were higher on compatible than on incompatible trials, yielding a negative net ACE. On the other hand, when instructed about the yes direction during sentence presentation, SC should already have addressed and occupied the common resource before MP starts, thus acting to impair MP. As expected, response times were slower on compatible than on incompatible trials, thus showing a negative net ACE under this condition, too (see Table 16.1, SOA = 500 ms).

As described earlier, the extended framework predicts that a positive net ACE will arise when the contribution of the early interference effect is reduced as compared with the late priming effect. In fact, the early interference effect should disappear when SC and MP address the common resource at the same point in time (i.e., before it is occupied by either one or the other operation). To test this assumption, we instructed participants about the yes direction at sentence onset, implying that MP and SC are initiated at the same point in time. Because the verb denoting the movement was consistently provided soon after sentence onset, and because it takes a few hundred milliseconds from address-ing the resource to its occupation (Stoet & Hommel, 2002), both SC and MP may address the common resource while it is still accessible. Consequently, the late priming of RS through SC should be predominant and result in a positive net ACE. This is exactly what we observed (see Table 16.1, SOA = 0 ms) (Diefenbach, 2010).

We take these observations as preliminary evidence in support of the logic inherent in the extended framework of the ACE. That framework invokes shared representational resources for semantic and motor processing. Drawing on these resources may help or hurt, depending on whether two concurrent operations compete for them or whether the first operation preactivates, or primes resources addressed by a second, subsequent operation. In any case, the framework invokes that cross-talk may go either way, from movements to meanings and from meanings to movements.

Action Simulation

Whereas the ACE is meant to tap the procedural grounding of declarative processing, action simulation opens a window to the role of declarative knowledge for procedural processing. The specific project we are addressing here is concerned with the way in which task-irrelevant semantic primes modulate the internal simulation of others' actions under conditions of temporary occlusion.

Imagine watching a child playing on a playground. When others cross your line of vision the child disappears from sight for a moment. Textbook wisdom has it that per-ception fills in what is invisible and, hence, unseen. Stationary objects, for example do not vanish when they get temporarily occluded; it is for the perceiver as if they are still there. Likewise, events or actions do not just terminate when they get occluded; it is for the perceiver as if they are still going on. These observations are usually taken to indicate that perceivers are, at least to some extent, capable of substituting, or simulating what they cannot see under given circumstances: When an object or event gets occluded they somehow fill in, based on what they have seen before.

We developed a paradigm that allows addressing issues concerning the representa-tional bases and the time course of action simulation (Graf, Reitzner, Corves, Casile, Giese, & Prinz, 2007). In this paradigm participants are, on each given trial, exposed to the following sequence of events: first, over a period of 2 to 4 seconds, they see a point-light character performing an action. Then that action gets occluded for a time period in the range of 100 to 700 ms. Finally, when the occlusion is over, a point-light pose is shown and the task is to determine whether or not the test pose is derived from the character's current action (yes/no response). The test poses shown in the experiment are either taken from that action (in which they require a yes response) or they are slightly tilted around their vertical axes (in which case they require a no response). From participants' responses we recorded both error rates and response times. As it turned out in pilot studies, the error rates for yes responses tend to range between 10% and 30%, indicating that the task can be performed above chance level but is still difficult enough to deliver substantial error rates.

We manipulated two factors: *occluder time* (the duration of occlusion, i.e., the time after occlusion onset at which the test pose is presented) and *pose time* (the time at which the snapshot shown after occlusion was actually taken from the occluded movement). These two factors were manipulated independently, and each of them could take three values (100, 400, 700 ms). As a result, there are nine conditions, differing in the relationship between occluder times and pose time (absolute time distances; see Fig. 16.3). The three cells on the diagonal stand for conditions in which the two times match perfectly. In these conditions the snapshot is presented just in time. Four other conditions in the table exhibit a time distance of 300 ms. In these conditions the presentation of the test pose either precedes or follows the time at which the snapshot would be taken from the movement by 300 ms. Finally, two other conditions exhibit a time distance of 600 ms.

Recording performance in this task should allow one to assess internal real-time simulations of occluded action. Running a simulation of unseen action means to run and update an internal reference against which the external test pose is eventually matched. Thus if the simulation runs in real-time, that internal reference would, in the 0 ms distance conditions, always precisely match the test pose being presented, whereas that match must be much weaker in the 300 ms condition—and even weaker at a temporal distance of 600 ms. In other words, real-time simulation of unseen action should disclose itself in what we may call a monotonic distance function, that is, a monotonic decrease of response performance as temporal distance increases (see Fig. 16.3). This is in fact what we observed in our previous study (Graf et al., 2007) and what several further experiments from our lab have since replicated (e.g., Springer, & Prinz, 2010).

In recent experiments we studied how the representational resources involved in real-time simulation might be related to the resources involved in semantic processing of verbal content (Springer & Prinz, 2010; Springer, Huttenlocher, & Prinz, 2012.). In one of our experiments, the action simulation task was always preceded by a lexical decision task. The lexical task was to determine whether the word shown is a legitimate German verb (which was the case in 75% of trials, whereas pseudo-verbs were shown in the residual 25%). Although all verbs were action verbs, one half implied high motor activity (like *springen—to jump*) whereas the other half implied low motor activity (like *stehen—to stand*). Assignment to the high versus low motor activity category was based on an independent word rating.

On each given trial, the lexical decision was immediately followed by the action simulation task. Importantly, the two tasks were instructed to be entirely unrelated to

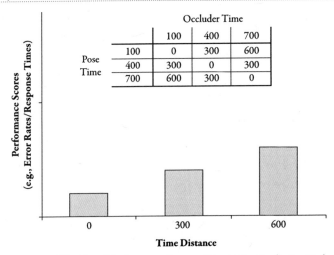

FIGURE 16.3 Design and Predicted Performance Scores of the Action Prediction Task. Cell entries in the table give the absolute time distances between occluder times and pose times (0, 300, 600; all values in ms). Predicted performance scores are plotted as a function of absolute time distances between the occluder time and the pose time. Action simulation predicts that task performance decreases with increasing time distance (monotonic distance function).

each other. Still, as our results indicated there was a strong impact of verbal content on simulation performance: When the simulation followed lexical decisions involving high-activity verbs, the monotonic distance function turned out to be more pronounced and steeper as compared with trials in which action simulation was preceded by lexical decisions involving low-activity verbs. A similar result was even obtained under conditions wherein the verbs were masked by visual symbols and did not require any response, thus avoiding the potential involvement of deliberate response strategies due to conscious awareness of the verbal prime (e.g., Forster, 1998; van den Bussche, van den Noortgate, & Reynvoet, 2009).

Further experiments addressed semantic interference rather than priming effects. Whereas the priming paradigm allowed participants to finish verb processing before turning to the simulation, the interference paradigm was designed to require concurrent processing of semantic input and visual motion information. In each given trial the presentation of a high- or low-activity verb was immediately followed by the action simulation task (as described above). Participants were asked to keep the verb in memory while observing the point-light character up to the point of occlusion. During occlusion another verb appeared that was either identical to the first one or new. Participants were required to respond to the test pose shown after occlusion on identical trials (80%) and to refrain from responding on new trials (20%). Thus, because the verb presented during occlusion indicated whether or not the action continuation had to be assessed, the task required maintaining verbal information in working memory while observing the point-light action.

In this experiment, too, we found the slope of the temporal distance function was modulated by the activity entailed in the memorized verbs. Although there was a pronounced monotonic temporal distance function for high-activity verbs, the slope of that function was close to zero for low-activity verbs. We may therefore conclude that observations from both priming and interference experiments suggest an impact of declarative content presented in a verbal processing task on procedural operations involved in a subsequent action simulation task.

In order to better understand the nature of that impact, we need to take a closer look at the details of the putative simulation process and its underlying machinery. More specifically, we need to understand how the functional details of that machinery are reflected in the behavioral performance recorded from the simulation task—and vice versa. For instance, the observation that the slope of the distance function is steeper for high-activity as compared with low-activity trials could invite (at least) two different functional interpretations. One option is to invoke a direct impact of verbal semantics on simulation dynamics—for instance in the sense that the degree of activity entailed in the action verbs affects the speed of simulation (faster after processing high-activity verbs as compared with low-activity verbs). The other option is that the distance function actually reflects a blend of performance resulting from two modes of solving the task: dynamic updating and static matching. Whereas dynamic updating relies on real-time updating of the internal reference against which the test pose is matched, static matching relies on an internal reference that is static and may, for example, be derived from the last posture seen before occlusion.

As we have shown elsewhere (Springer & Prinz, 2010; Springer, Huttenlocher, & Prinz, 2012), our results lend in fact support to the idea that simulation performance is best regarded as a blend of outcomes of static and dynamic processes. That view opens a new perspective on the nature of the cross-talk between declarative content and procedural simulation. Declarative content may now be seen to modulate the relative contributions of two processes, static matching and dynamic updating: High-activity content invites stronger contributions from dynamic processing than does low-activity content, whereas low-activity content invites stronger contributions of static processing.

Conclusions

Our observations on the reversal of the ACE and on semantic modulation of action simulation add to the growing body of evidence challenging the great divide from which we started in this chapter. The cross-talk that we observed between meanings and movements suggests that verbal semantics and motor kinematics may draw on shared representational resources. As discussed in the introductory section, related studies have shown that action language may affect overt action execution (e.g., Boulenger, Roy et al., 2006; Boulenger, Silber et al., 2008; Gentilucci et al., 2000; Glover et al., 2004) or, conversely, that motor expertise may affect action language processing (Beilock, Lyons, Mattarelia-Micke, Nusbaum, & Small, 2008).

We believe that these observations have important implications for both the foundations of agency and the workings of joint action. On the one hand, they suggest that the craft of agency equally draws on both procedural and declarative action knowledge, thus challenging the great divide between embodied and symbolic foundations of mental life. In this regard our findings suggest that embodied and symbolic resources jointly contribute to both action perception and action production.

On the other hand, our observations demonstrate that the craft of agency also draws on common representational resources for perception and production of action, thus also challenging the divide between the afferent and the efferent side of mental life. Since such common coding for perception and production offers a shared representational basis for production of own action and perception of foreign action, it may be seen to lay the ground for joint action and social interaction (Hommel, Müsseler, Aschersleben, & Prinz, 2001; Prinz, 1990, 1997, 2008).

To conclude, we come back to the great divide between (declarative) semantic processing and (procedural) motor processing. Basically, there are two major ways of challenging that divide—and perhaps a third one emerging from combining the two. They share the belief that the dividing line that we are used to draw between the declarative and the procedural side of mental life is not justified by a corresponding functional divide between declarative and procedural operations.

One such challenge comes from what we may call the *Meaning-is-Embodied* claim. That claim is mainly derived from studies trying to understand how declarative knowledge may emerge and on what kinds of representational resources it may be grounded (e.g., Barsalou, 2003, 2005, 2008; Hauk, Shtyrov, & Pulvermüller, 2008; Kiefer, 2007, 2008; Mahon & Caramazza, 2008, 2009; Pulvermüller, 1999, 2005, 2008). For this approach the *explanandum* resides at the level of declarative processing, whereas procedural processing takes the role of the *explanans*. The basic assumption is that the gap between the two is bridged by semantic information being grounded in motor information (see left hand panel in Fig. 16.4). As the motor grounding loop indicates, meaning is grounded in movement—to the effect that there can be no meaning without movement. The other option for challenge comes from what we may call the *Movement-is-Symbolic* claim. Here the focus is on explaining the cognitive underpinnings of movement. For this approach, the *explanandum* resides at the level of procedural processing whereas resources and operations at the declarative level take the role of the *explanans*. The basic assumption is that motor information is grounded in semantic information (see right hand panel in Fig. 16.4). Accordingly, as the semantic grounding loop indicates, movements are always grounded in meaning—to the effect that there can be no movements without meaning.

These two options challenge the great divide by positing permanent cross-talk between the movements and meanings, and the grounding loops imply that each and every entry in one domain is associated with mandatory entries in the other domain. The *Meaning-is-Embodied* claim holds that declarative meaning is grounded in procedural operations

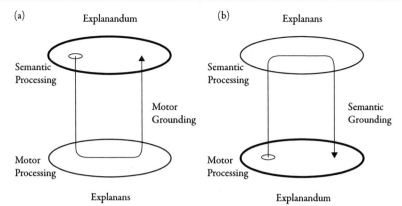

FIGURE 16.4 Two Options for Bridging the Gap between (Declarative) Semantic Processing and (Procedural) Motor Processing through Grounding. (a) The *Meaning-is-Embodied* claim, positing motor grounding. (b) The *Movement-is-Symbolic* claim, positing semantic grounding.

and—one step further—that declarative knowledge even arises from procedural knowledge. Conversely, in the *Movement-is-Symbolic* claim the semantic grounding loop posits that procedural acts like movements and actions get mandatorily represented at the declarative level—in precisely the same way as other perceived events are registered at that level. Either of these two claims can account for the experimental findings reported above. Both hold that the great divide, though it may still exist in terms of a structural divide between domains for semantic or motor processing, is permanently bridged by automatic and mandatory cross-talk between the two.

Contrasting the two options may even invite a third, more radical option—more radical in the sense that it even relinquishes the structural divide between the two domains. That option comes to mind when one takes the claim serious that movements and actions are meaningful events and therefore always subject to automatic and mandatory semantic interpretation. If so, one may regard motor processing *as* semantic processing (a particular kind thereof) rather than being grounded in it. Accordingly, the machinery for motor processing must be considered part and parcel of the machinery for semantic processing. With that view there is no structural divide anymore, and no grounding loop is needed to bridge it. As a consequence the ellipses at the bottom of Figure 16.4 would have to move into the areas covered by the ellipses at the top and become included in them. Future textbooks may wish to consider a radical view like this as well.

REFERENCES

Barsalou, L. W. (2003). Abstraction in perceptual symbol systems. *Philosophical Transactions of the Royal Society of London: Biological Sciences, 358,* 1177–1187.

Barsalou, L. W. (2005). Situated conceptualization. In H. Cohen, & C. Lefebvre (Eds.), *Handbook of Categorization in Cognitive Science* (pp. 619–650). St. Louis: Elsevier.

Barsalou, L. W. (2008). Grounded Cognition. *Annual Review of Psychology, 59,* 617–645.

Beilock, S. L., Lyons, I. M., Mattarelia-Micke, A., Nusbaum, H. C., & Small, S. L. (2008). Sports experience changes the neural processing of action language. *Proceedings of the National Academy of Science of the United States of America, 105,* 13269–13273.

Borreggine, K. L., & Kaschak, M. P. (2006). The action-sentence compatibility effect: It's all in the timing. *Cognitive Science, 30,* 1097–1112.

Boulenger, V., Roy, A. C., Paulignan, Y., Deprez, V., Jeannerod, M., & Nazir, T. A. (2006). Cross-talk between language processes and overt motor behavior in the first 200 msec of processing. *Journal of Cognitive Neuroscience, 18,* 1606–1615.

Boulenger, V., Silber, B. Y., Roy, A. C., Paulignan, Y., Jeannerod, M., & Nazir, T. A. (2008). Subliminal display of action words interferes with motor planning: A combined EEG and kinematic study. *Journal of Physiology—Paris, 102,* 130–136.

Diefenbach, C. (2010). *Interactions between sentence comprehension and concurrent action: The role of movement effects and timing.* (Doctoral thesis, Max Planck Institute for Human Cognitive and Brain Sciences, Leipzig, Germany).

Diefenbach, C., Rieger, M., Massen, C., & Prinz, W. (in preparation). Action-sentence compatibility: The role of action effects and timing.

Forster, K. I. (1998). The pros and cons of masked priming. *Journal of Psycholinguistic Research, 27,* 203–233.

Gentilucci, M., Benuzzi, F., Bertolani, L., Daprati, E., & Gangitano, M. (2000). Language and motor control. *Experimental Brain Research, 133,* 468–490.

Glenberg, A. M. (2008). Toward the integration of bodily states, language, and action. In G. R. Semin, & E. R. Smith (Eds.), *Embodied Grounding: Social, Cognitive, Affective and Neuroscientific Approaches* (pp. 43–70). New York: Cambridge University Press.

Glenberg, A. M., & Kaschak, M. P. (2002). Grounding language in action. *Psychonomic Bulletin & Review, 9,* 558–565.

Glover, S., Rosenbaum, D. A., Graham, J., & Dixon, P. (2004). Grasping the meaning of words. *Experimental Brain Research, 154,* 103–108.

Graf, M., Reitzner, B., Corves, C., Casile, A., Giese, M., & Prinz, W. (2007). Predicting point-light actions in real-time. *NeuroImage, 36,* T22–T32.

Hauk, O., Shtyrov, Y., & Pulvermüller, F. (2008). The time course of action and action-word comprehension in the human brain as revealed by neurophysiology. *Journal of Physiology—Paris, 102,* 50–58.

Hommel, B., Müsseler, J., Aschersleben, G., & Prinz, W. (2001). The theory of event coding (TEC): A framework for perception and action planning. *Behavioral and Brain Sciences, 24,* 849–878.

Jeannerod, M. (1994). The representing brain: Neural correlates of motor intention and imagery. *Behavioral and Brain Sciences, 17,* 187–246.

Kiefer, M., Sim, E.-J., Liebich, S., Hauk, O., & Tanaka, J. (2007). Experience-dependent plasticity of conceptual representations in human sensory-motor areas. *Journal of Cognitive Neuroscience, 19,* 525–542.

Kiefer, M., Sim, E.-J., Herrnberger, B., Grothe, J., & Hoenig, K. (2008). The sound of concepts: Four markers for a link between auditory and conceptual brain systems. *The Journal of Neuroscience, 28,* 12224–12230.

Mahon, B. Z., & Caramazza, A. (2008). A critical look at the embodied cognition hypothesis and a new proposal for grounding conceptual content. *Journal of Physiology—Paris, 102,* 59–70.

Mahon, B. Z., & Caramazza, A. (2009). Concepts and categories: A cognitive neuropsychological perspective. *Annual Review of Psychology, 60,* 27–51.

Martin, A., Ungerleider, L. G., & Haxby, J. V. (2000). Category specificity and the brain: The sensory-motor model of semantic representations of objects. In M. Gazzaniga (Ed.), *The New Cognitive Neuroscience,* 2nd ed. (pp. 1023–1036). Cambridge, MA: MIT Press.

Müsseler, J., & Hommel, B. (1997). Blindness to response-compatible stimuli. *Journal of Experimental Psychology: Human Perception and Performance, 23,* 861–872.

Prinz, W. (1990). A common coding approach to perception and action. In O. Neumann, & W. Prinz (Eds.), *Relationships Between Perception and Action: Current Approaches* (pp. 167–201 p.). Berlin: Springer.

Prinz, W. (1997). Perception and action planning. *European Journal of Cognitive Psychology, 9,* 129–154.

Prinz, W. (2008). Mirrors for embodied communication. In I. Wachsmuth, M. Lenzen, & G. Knoblich (Eds.), *Embodied Communication in Humans And Machines* (pp. 111–128). Oxford: Oxford University Press.

Pulvermüller, F. (1999). Words in the brain's language. *Behavioral and Brain Sciences, 22,* 253–279.

Pulvermüller, F. (2005). Brain mechanisms linking language and action. *Nature Reviews Neuroscience, 6,* 576–582.

Pulvermüller, F. (2008). Grounding language in the brain. In M. d. Vega, A. M. Glenberg, & A. C. Graesser (Eds.), *Symbols and Embodiment. Debates on Meaning and Cognition* (pp. 85–116). New York: Oxford University Press.

Russell, J. (1996). *Agency: Its role in Mental Development.* Hove, UK: Erlbaum.

Schütz-Bosbach, S., & Prinz, W. (2007). Perceptual resonance: action-induced modulation of perception. *Trends in Cognitive Sciences, 11,* 349–355.

Springer, A. & Prinz, W. (2010). Action semantics modulate action prediction. *The Quarterly Journal of Experimental Psychology, 63,* 2141–2158.

Springer, A., Huttenlocher, A., & Prinz, W. (2012). Language-induced modulation during the prediction of others' actions. *Psychological Research, 76,* 456–466.

Stoet, G., & Hommel, B. (2002). Interaction between feature binding in perception and action. In W. Prinz, & B. Hommel (Eds.), *Common Mechanisms in Perception And Action: Attention & Performance XIX* (pp. 538–552). Oxford, UK: Oxford University Press.

van den Bussche, E., van den Noortgate, W., & Reynvoet, B. (2009). Mechanisms of masked priming: A meta-analysis. *Psychological Bulletin, 135,* 452–477.

Zelazo, P. D., Astington, J. W., & Olson, D. R. (Eds.). (1999). *Developing Theories of Intention: Social Understanding and Self-Control.* Mahwah, NJ: Erlbaum.

Zwaan, R. A., & Taylor, L. J. (2006). Seeing, acting, understanding: motor resonance in language comprehension. *Journal of Experimental Psychology: General, 135,* 1–11.

17 The Three Pillars of Volition: Phenomenal States, Ideomotor Processing, and the Skeletal Muscle System

Ezequiel Morsella, Tanaz Molapour, and Margaret T. Lynn

WHAT IS THE difference between a blink and a wink? Most people would argue that, unlike blinking, which is usually carried out without any conscious intention on the part of the "doer," winking is *voluntary*. To the doer, the difference between a voluntary and involuntary actions is felt to be as sharp as that between night and day: The actions of glancing at a wall clock, coughing to grab someone's attention, and winking to a friend simply feel "voluntary," whereas the physically similar acts of reflexively glancing at a bright flash, coughing in a knee-jerk manner, and blinking every so often (or in response to an object approaching the eye) tend to feel "involuntary." However, to an observer who is not privy to the mental state of the doer (e.g., what the doer *wills*), drawing a principled distinction between voluntary and involuntary actions is less than straightforward, for *willing*, *desiring*, and *intending* cannot be observed externally. To the casual observer and even the scientist, a blink and a wink are both seen only as motor acts in which the eyelids approach each other, closing momentarily.

For this and many other reasons, detecting and understanding *willing*, *desiring*, and *intending* is a major challenge for science. More profoundly, the very notion of volition is at odds with everything else that is understood about the physical world. As far as we know, computers, tables, and door knobs do not desire or will anything. Chomsky (1988) proposed that, though it makes intuitive sense that a machine or creature could be designed in such a way that it responds in a prescribed manner when confronted with certain situations (as in the case of a reflexive automaton), it makes absolutely no sense whatsoever that a creature or machine should ever, not only be compelled to act in a certain way, but also be *inclined* to act in that way. In the rest of the physical world it appears that things either *do* or *do not do*—there is no in-between, as in the case of desiring to do something but then not doing it. Thus, the conceptual scientific framework with which we understand the nuts and bolts of behavior has not yet found an explanatory home for inclinations, desires, and volitions, although they are a very dear part of our lives and are what separate a blink from a wink.

Despite the challenges, some progress regarding the difference between blinks and winks, and, more generally, between voluntary and involuntary actions, has been made. This research has examined the phenomena of volition *inductively* and *descriptively*. Before reviewing the research, it is important to appreciate the nature of an inductive and descriptive approach.

An Inductive and Descriptive Approach

When adopting an inductive approach, one reasons from detailed facts to general conclusions. (In a *deductive* approach, one does the opposite and explains data by appealing to overarching general principles.) In such a "bottom-up" approach, there are no strong a priori (previously held) general conclusions that guide how one should construe the phenomenon under investigation. In the case of volition, because so little is understood about its nature and how it arises from the brain, from an inductive standpoint it is premature to hold strong views about what it is and what it does. One such commonly held and historically recurring strong view is that, as a conscious state (defined below), volition is "epiphenomenal," serving no function whatsoever in a nervous system that achieves what it achieves only through the workings of non-willing, unconscious neurons. This view is nonscientific from an inductive standpoint: Until one understands the place of a given phenomenon in nature, and how it emerges from nature, one cannot make the strong claim that the phenomenon is epiphenomenal. (Consider that more was known about the thymus gland than was ever known about volitional states when the thymus gland was prematurely believed to be functionless. Today it is known that the thymus gland serves an important role in the immune system.)

Our approach is also descriptive: processes in humans are described *as they are* and not *as they should be* or *could be* (which would be a *normative* approach). From this point of view, although one can envision a zombie-like creature that performs all our human actions but is devoid of any volitional states, this reflects more our powers of imagination than what has resulted from the happenstance and tinkering process of evolution, where bizarre, counterintuitive, and even suboptimal strategies may be selected to solve challenges (Lorenz, 1965; Gould, 1977; Mayr, 2001). Consider that the way that we envision how a heart should be (the artificial heart) is nothing like the actual heart, much like artificial locomotion (wheels) is nothing like biological locomotion (legs). To understand something like volition, one must describe it from the point of view of a naive naturalist, respectful of the fact that nature does not always resolve its challenges the way we would. It may well be that Mother Nature and the artificial intelligence theorist have reached different solutions regarding how adaptive behavior should be implemented (Marr, 1982).

This inductive, descriptive, and bottom-up approach has revealed that, when attempting to unravel a phenomenon as perplexing and multifaceted as voluntary action, it is useful to distinguish the *high-level properties* of the phenomenon from its constitutive *basic components*, that is, from the primary building blocks that seem necessary for the phenomenon to exist. Fire, for example, has countless properties, including the capacity to illuminate a room, warm up one's hands, destroy things, or be incessantly waving and flickering around, but it has fewer constitutive components: oxygen, combustible, and a spark. In this spirit, in this chapter we first review the high-level properties of voluntary action, including cognitions such as the *sense of agency* (the sense that the self is responsible for the occurrence of a physical or mental act; Engbert, Wohlschläger, & Haggard, 2007; Synofzik, Vosgerau, & Newen, 2008; Sato, 2009) and less intuitive properties, such as the distortions in time perception caused by volitional processes and the ability of volitional processes to influence that which enters conscious awareness, as described below. Most of these properties would have been overlooked from a normative, deductive approach. Second, we examine how the instantiation of voluntary action seems to rest upon three basic, primary components: the phenomenal state (the most basic form of consciousness), ideomotor processing (a form of action control), and the skeletal muscle output system (the only effector in the body that can be controlled voluntarily). Last, we discuss how the interdependences among these three components provide a unique portal through which to understand the mechanisms of voluntary action and nature of human agency.

The High-Level Properties of Voluntary Action

In this section we review phenomena that, at first glance, appear to be high-level properties of voluntary action. Many of these properties would have never been predicted based on a priori notions about this peculiar form of processing in the brain. The section thus reveals some of the earliest fruits of our inductive, experimental approach.

Research reveals that there are properties of voluntary action that are not shared by other (e.g., involuntary) forms of action. For reasons unknown, in *intentional binding*, for example, the perceived elapsed time between a voluntary action and its consequence is shorter than the actual time span (Haggard, Clark, Kalogeras, 2002), as if the two events were temporally attracted to each other. Thus, when striking a bell voluntarily, the experiences of striking the bell and of hearing the gong of the bell are perceived to occur more closely together in time than they actually did. Although there may have been a half-second delay between observing the strike and hearing the gong, one would perceive the delay as shorter than a half-a-second. In this way, one also binds the actions and outcomes performed by others (Engbert, Wohlschläger, Thomas, & Haggard, 2007). For example, when observing someone else strike the bell, one also would reduce the delay time between watching the bell being struck and hearing the gong. Why this phenomenon of intentional binding occurs—a phenomenon that would have never been predicted from a deductive approach—remains a matter of substantial investigation and theorizing.

Time perception is also affected in other ways by voluntary action. In one case, exerting a voluntary action that conflicts with an automatic (involuntary) action can produce distortions in the perception of time. This, for example, can occur through a laboratory paradigm such as the classic Stroop task (Stroop, 1935). In this task, participants are instructed to name the color in which a word is written. When the word and color are incongruous (e.g., RED presented in blue), response conflict leads to increased error rates, response times, and reported urges to make a mistake (Morsella, Gray, Krieger, & Bargh, 2009a). When the color matches the word (e.g., RED presented in red), or is presented on a neutral stimulus (e.g., a series of x's as in "XXXX"), there is little or no interference (see review in MacLeod & MacDonald, 2000). It has been proposed that, in the incongruent condition, there is conflict between word-reading and color-naming plans (Cohen, Dunbar, & McClelland, 1990). Current research has revealed that, during the kind of conflict instantiated in the incongruent condition, time perception is distorted systematically (cf., Corallo, Sackur, Dehaene, & Sigman, 2008). These unexpected temporal effects are now an object of current theorizing and investigation (Wenke & Haggard, 2009).

Recent research has revealed other, unexpected properties of voluntary processing, properties that would not have been foreseen from a deductive approach. For instance, under some circumstances, voluntary processes can influence that which enters conscious awareness, revealing the intimate liaison between voluntary action and consciousness. This is obvious in the case of "subvocalization," that is, when one talks silently "within one's head." Through the act of subvocalization one can quickly change the contents of one's consciousness with minimal effort (Baddeley, 2007). At the drop of a hat, one can occupy one's consciousness with, say, the sound of one's name or of any other phonological form. It is interesting to ponder which other acts of "executive function" (Baddeley, 2007) can so quickly change the contents of consciousness.

A more surprising finding revealing how voluntary processing can influence entry into consciousness is found in the binocular rivalry paradigm. In this paradigm, subjects are trained to respond in certain ways when presented with certain visual stimuli (e.g., to button-press when presented with the image of a house). After training, a different stimulus is presented to each eye (e.g., an image of a house to one eye and of a face to the other eye). Surprisingly, the subject does not consciously perceive both objects (e.g., a face overlapping a house), but responds as if perceiving only one object at a time (e.g., a house followed by a face), though both images are continuously present and each exerts a nontrivial influence over nervous processing. There is evidence that brain regions are processing both the conscious percept and the one that is unconscious or "suppressed" (Alais & Blake, 2005). For example, if the suppressed image is of something scary (e.g., a spider), there is evidence that emotional areas of the brain (e.g., the amygdala) are activated, even though the experimental subject does not perceive the stimulus consciously (Williams et al., 2004).

Using the binocular rivalry paradigm, Maruya, Yang, and Blake (2007) demonstrated that voluntary action during binocular rivalry can influence which of the two percepts involved in the rivalry enters conscious awareness. Specifically, the object that happens to move in synchrony with participants' voluntary movements remain conscious for longer periods of time (and unconscious for shorter periods of time), elucidating that, "conflict between two incompatible visual stimuli tends to be resolved in favor of a stimulus that is under motor control of the observer viewing that stimulus" (Maruya et al., 2007; p. 1096; see related finding in Wohlschläger, 2000). Complementary psychophysiological research reveals that, during binocular rivalry, it is only the neural processing of the conscious percept that is associated to both activations in perceptual areas of the brain and to motor-related processes in frontal cortex (Doesburg, Green, McDonald, & Ward, 2009). This reveals the intimate link between conscious states and motor action. Why this occurs remains unknown. Again, it is an observation furnished by nature that would have never been anticipated in a deductive approach.

Less startling properties of voluntary action include the *sense of agency* and *authorship processing* (i.e., attributing actions to oneself; Wegner, 2003), which are based on several high-level processes, including the perception of a lawful correspondence between *action intentions* and *action outcomes* (Wegner, 2003). If one intends to flex one's finger and then the finger happens to flex, one is likely to believe that the movement was "willed" by "the self" (Prinz, 2003; Berti & Pia, 2006; Pacherie, 2008). Similarly, if one intends to imagine the shape of a triangle and then happens to experience the relevant imagery, one is likely to believe that the imagery arose voluntarily, even when the percept may have been caused by an experimental trick, as in the Perky effect (Perky, 1910). In this effect, experimental subjects are fooled into believing that they are imagining an image that is actually presented physically on a screen.

In this way, experimentally manipulating the nature of the *intention-outcome* correspondence leads to systematic distortions in the sense of agency/authorship, such that subjects can be fooled into believing that they caused actions that were in fact caused by someone else (Wegner, 2002). By manipulating contextual factors, a plethora of experiments have demonstrated such authorship illusions (Wegner, 2002). For example, when a participant's hand controls a computer-drawing device behind a screen such that the participant cannot see his or her hand in motion, the participant can be fooled into thinking (through false feedback on the computer display) that the hand intentionally moved in one direction when it actually moved in a different direction

(Fourneret & Jeannerod, 1998). One limitation of this kind of paradigm is that veridical proprioceptive and perceptual feedback from participants' own (true) actions limit the extent to which participants can be fooled. It is important to note that, had participants been allowed to see their hand movements, or had the proprioceptive feedback from the action yielded a stronger sensory signal, it is unlikely that any illusion would have arisen. In a paradigm designed to circumvent these limitations to some extent, participants in another study were tricked into believing that they could control the movements of stimuli on a computer screen through a phony brain-computer interface. In this study (Lynn, Berger, Riddle, & Morsella, 2010), participants were instructed to move a line on the computer screen by use of the phony brain-computer interface. Line movements were actually controlled by computer program. Demonstrating the *illusion to intend*, participants reported more intentions to move the line when it moved frequently than when it moved infrequently. Unlike in previous studies (e.g., Fourneret & Jeannerod, 1998), in this study, proprioceptive feedback from actual action production was not available to diminish the illusion.

When intentions and outcomes mismatch, as in action slips and spoonerisms, people are less likely to perceive actions as originating from the self (Wegner, 2002). Similar self-versus-other attributions are found in intrapsychic conflicts (Livnat & Pippenger, 2006), as captured by the "monkey on one's back" metaphor that is often used to describe the tendencies associated with aspects of addiction. Accordingly, in the Stroop task described before, participants perceive the activation of the undesired word-reading plans as less associated with the self when the plans conflict with intended action (e.g., in the incongruent condition) than when the same plans lead to no such interference (e.g., in the congruent condition; Riddle & Morsella, 2009).

What happens when processes are not conflicting, but harmonious, as in the congruent condition? The hypothesis of *synchrony blindness* proposes that, during harmonious processing, not only may one not experience any conflict, but one may also be unaware that more than one process yielded the same intention/action plan (Molapour, Berger, & Morsella, 2011). Accordingly, in the Stroop task, participants reported less of an urge to err (by reading) when words were presented in the congruent condition (e.g., RED presented in red) than when the very same words were presented in standard font color, suggesting that awareness of word-reading was diminished experimentally (Molapour, Berger, & Morsella, 2011).

Regarding the sense of agency, it is worth mentioning that neuroscientific research has revealed some startling findings (see chapter 18). For example, direct electrical stimulation of parietal areas of the brain gives rise to the subjectively experienced will to perform an action, and that increased activation makes subjects believe that they actually executed the corresponding action, even though no action was performed (Desmurget et al., 2009; Desmurget & Sirigu, 2010). Activating motor areas (e.g., premotor areas) can lead to the actual action, but subjects believe that they did not perform any action (see also Fried et al., 1991).

The Basic Components of Voluntary Action

In this section, we will analyze the basic, primary components of voluntary action/processes from a descriptive (rather than a normative) standpoint. When describing the component processes of volition, one must first deal with *the component that should not be*, namely, the homunculus.

No Homunculus Necessary

To explicate how an organism carries out a function in terms of its component parts and processes (e.g., brain areas and cognitive mechanisms), one must explain organismic action at a *suborganismic* level. Although it is tempting to propose that an action is "voluntary" only when "one" intends to do it, there are strong a priori considerations and empirically-based considerations (e.g., Libet, 2004) that render such a position unscientific. The proposal is fallacious because it compels one to then ask how the intraorganismic agent itself functions. Does it too have yet another agent within itself calling the shots? If so, does that internal agent too carry out its function in virtue of another agent within itself? This obviously leads to the fallacy of *ad infinitum*. Sooner or later, one must explain voluntary action at sub-agent level of description. For this reason, "homuncular" accounts of volition should be avoided.

With this in mind, descriptive accounts of action production have illuminated the basic components of volition, all while avoiding "homuncular" descriptions in which volition is explained by invoking the actions of a "supervisory system" (Angell, 1907; Norman & Shallice, 1980), "central executive" (Baddeley, 1986), or another, homuncular-like agent in the brain. (For supporting evidence, see Kimberg, D'Esposito, & Farah, 1997; Roepstorff & Frith, 2004; Curtis & D'Esposito, 2009.) The spirit of this nonhomuncular approach is evident in article titles with phrases such as, *What's at the Top in the Top-Down Control of Action?* (Roepstorff & Frith, 2004), *In Search of the Wild Homunculus* (Logan, 2003), and *Banishing the Homunculus* (Hazy, Frank, & O'Reilly, 2006). Regarding the empirical evidence, research reveals that, during the kind of conflict instantiated in the Stroop task, there is no homunculus in charge of suppressing one action in order to express another action, consistent with the idea that "no single area of the brain is specialized for inhibiting all unwanted actions" (p. 72, Curtis & D'Esposito, 2009). For example, in the morning, action plan *A* may oppose plan *B*; and in the evening plan *C* may conflict with plan *D*, with there never being the same third party (a homunculus) observing each conflict. Approaches in action production have arrived at a similar conclusion: Lotze and James's "acts of express fiat" (see below) referred not to a homunculus reining action in, but rather to the actions of an incompatible idea (i.e., a competing action plan). Instead of a homunculus, there exists a forum in which representations vie for action control. It has been proposed that the phenomenal state, one of the primary components of volition, provides such a forum.

Phenomenal States

Atypical and associated with only a subset of all brain regions and processes (cf., Morsella, Krieger, & Bargh, 2010), phenomenal states appear to furnish the nervous system with a form of internal communication ("crosstalk") that integrates neural activities and information-processing structures that would otherwise be independent, allowing diverse kinds of information to be gathered in some sort of global workspace (the *integration consensus*; see reviews in Dehaene & Naccache, 2001; Baars, 2002; Morsella, 2005; Merker, 2007). This integration leads to adaptive actions. In contrast, actions that are decoupled from conscious states lack this form of integration and often appear impulsive or irrational (Morsella & Bargh, 2011), as if the processes giving rise to these actions fail to take certain kinds of information into account when producing overt behavior.

One limitation of the integration consensus is that it appears that not all kinds of information/processes require conscious integration (e.g., neural activity related to reflexes, vegetative functions, unconscious motor programs, and low-level perceptual analyses). This leads to the question of which kinds of integration require consciousness?

By contrasting interactions that are *consciously impenetrable* (e.g., pupillary reflex, peristalsis, and intersensory conflicts) with *conscious conflicts*, a dramatic class of conscious interactions between different information-processing systems (e.g., holding one's breath underwater, withstanding pain; Morsella et al., 2009a), Supramodular Interaction Theory (SIT; Morsella, 2005) builds on the integration consensus by proposing that phenomenal states are required to integrate information, *but* only certain kinds of information. Specifically, phenomenal states are required to integrate information from specialized, high-level (and often multi-modal) systems that are unique in that their goals may conflict with skeletal muscle plans, as described by the principle of parallel responses into skeletal muscle (PRISM; Morsella, 2005). These *supramodular* systems are usually defined in terms of their "concerns" (e.g., bodily needs) rather than in terms of their sensory afference (e.g., visual, auditory), the latter being the more historical approach to system categorization in the brain. Each system can influence action directly and unconsciously, as in the case of *unintegrated* action (e.g., reflexively inhaling or dropping a hot dish; Morsella & Bargh, 2011). It is only through consciousness that these systems can influence action collectively, leading to *integrated actions* (Morsella & Bargh, 2011) such as holding one's breath or performing an incongruent trial in the Stroop task.

From this standpoint, in the nervous system there are three distinct kinds of integration or "binding" in the brain (see review in Morsella & Bargh, 2011). *Afference binding* is the binding of perceptual processes and representations, as in intersensory binding (e.g., the McGurk effect; McGurk & MacDonald, 1976) and in intrasensory, feature binding (e.g., the binding of shape to color; Zeki & Bartels, 1999). For example, the McGurk effect (McGurk & MacDonald, 1976) involves interactions between visual and auditory processes: An observer views a speaker mouthing "ga" while presented with the sound "ba." Surprisingly, the observer is unaware of any intersensory interaction, perceiving only "da." (As outlined below, unconscious interactions and bindings also occur in motor control [Grossberg, 1999; Rosenbaum, 2002] and in the control of smooth muscle [Morsella et al., 2009a]). Afference binding reveals that phenomenal states are unnecessary to integrate information from sources as diverse as different sensory modalities.

Another form of binding, linking perceptual processing to action/motor processing, is known as *efference binding* (Haggard, Aschersleben, Gehrke, & Prinz, 2002), a kind of stimulus-response binding that allows one to learn to press a button when presented with a cue in a laboratory paradigm. Research has shown that responding on the basis of efference binding can occur unconsciously. For example, Taylor and McCloskey (1990) demonstrated that, in a choice response time task, response times for responses to subliminal (masked) stimuli were the same as those for responses to supraliminal stimuli, suggesting that "appropriate programs for two separate movements can be simultaneously held ready for use, and that either one can be executed when triggered by specific stimuli without subjective awareness" (p. 62). (For reviews of other kinds of masking-based, efference binding, see Hallett, 2007, and Neisser, 1967.) See Figure 17.1 for a schematic depiction of all the forms of binding that can occur unconsciously.

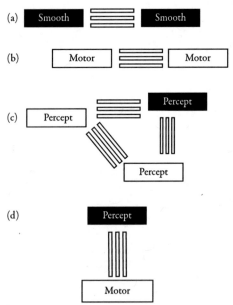

FIGURE 17.1 The Many Forms of Interaction (Or "Crosstalk") That Can Occur Unconsciously in the Nervous System (a) Unconscious interactions in the control of smooth muscle effectors, as in the case of the consensual processes in the pupillary reflex. (b) Unconscious interactions in motor control. (c) Unconscious crosstalk between perceptual systems within a sensory modality (signified by the boxes sharing the same hue) and between different sensory modalities (signified by the boxes bearing distinct hues). (d) Unconscious interactions between perceptual and motor processes, as in the case of unconscious efference binding.

Responsible for integrated actions, the third kind of binding, *efference-efference binding*, occurs when two streams of efference binding are trying to influence skeletomotor action simultaneously, as in the incongruent conditions of interference paradigms, in which stimulus dimensions activate competing action plans. It also occurs when one holds one's breath, suppresses a prepotent response, or experiences another form of conscious conflict. In the SIT framework, it is the instantiation of conflicting efference-efference binding that requires conscious processing and is most associated with the sense of agency (see quantitative review of evidence for SIT in Morsella, Berger, & Krieger, 2011). Phenomenal states are the crosstalk medium that allows such actional processes to influence action collectively (Fig. 17.2). Absent these states, behavior can be influenced by only one of the efference streams, leading to unintegrated actions such as unconsciously inhaling while underwater, button-pressing to a subliminal stimulus, or reflexively removing one's hand from a hot object. One can certainly imagine integration among systems occurring without anything like phenomenal states, but, in our descriptive approach, and for reasons that only the tinkering and happenstance process of evolution could explain, it was these states that were selected to solve this particular integration problem in the brain (Morsella, 2005).

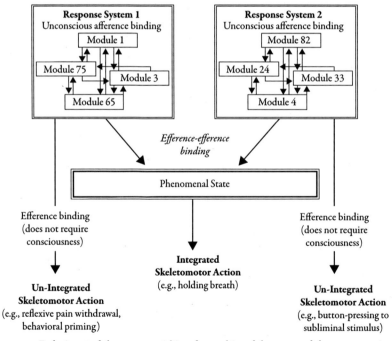

FIGURE 17.2 Fodorian modules operate within a few multimodal, supramodular response systems, each defined by its concern. Afference binding within systems can be unconscious. Although response systems can influence action directly (illustrated by the lateral arrows), only by virtue of conscious states they interact and influence action collectively, as when one holds one's breath. The sense of agency is most intimately associated to this efference-efference binding, a process that has been associated with the ventral processing stream.

Thus, phenomenal states permit a form of crosstalk in the brain that is essential for *integrated action-goal selection*, a process that has historically been linked to the "ventral processing stream" of the brain (Goodale & Milner, 2004). Substantial evidence from diverse sources (Grossberg, 1999; Rosenbaum, 2002), including research on the properties of the dorsal visual processing stream (Goodale & Milner, 2004), reveals that online motor control and other forms of action can occur unconsciously (cf., Morsella & Bargh, 2011). But this should not be taken to mean that the properties of conscious perceptual representations (e.g., the kind associated with the ventral processing stream; Goodale & Milner, 2004) are in a realm far removed from overt action. As Goodale and Milner (2004) conclude, "the primary role of perceptual representations is not in the *execution* of actions, but rather in helping the person or animal arrive at a decision to act in a particular way" (Goodale & Milner, 2004, p. 48). In the ventral stream, information about the world is represented in a unique manner (e.g., representing the *invariant* aspects of the world, involving *allocentric* coordinates), one unlike that of the dorsal stream (e.g., representing the *variant* aspects of the world, using *egocentric* coordinates). Regarding the latter, during everyday actions such as reaching for a cup, highly-flexible "online" adjustments are made unconsciously (Rosenbaum, 2002; Goodale & Milner, 2004). Because the physical spatial relationship between the objects of the world and one's body is seldom unchanging (e.g., a pen is sometimes at left or right), each time an action is performed, new motor programs are generated online in order to deal with peculiarities of each setting, and then these "use only once" unconscious representations are scrapped and no conscious memory is made from them (Grossberg, 1999; Rosenbaum, 2002). In contrast, representations of the ventral stream reflect unchanging aspects of the world that can be used, not just to travel down memory lane, but as knowledge to constrain future action (Schacter & Addis, 2007).

Not requiring such crosstalk, unconscious perceptual processes (e.g., as in the attentional blink; Raymond, Shapiro, & Arnell, 1992) involve smaller networks of brain areas than phenomenal processes (Sergent & Dehaene, 2004), and automatic behaviors (e.g., reflexive pharyngeal swallowing) are believed to involve substantially fewer brain regions than their intentional counterparts (e.g., volitional swallowing; Kern et al., 2001; Ortinski & Meador, 2004). Research reveals that the phenomenal state is intimately related to our second proposed component of volition, the skeletal muscle output system.

The Skeletal Muscle Output System

More than any other effector system, skeletal muscle is influenced by distinct (and often opposing) systems/regions of the brain. It is well known that simple motor acts (e.g., grabbing a cup) suffer from the "degrees of freedom" problem, because there are countless ways to instantiate a motor act such as grasping a handle (Rosenbaum, 2002), but *action selection*, too, suffers from this problem. There are simply too many things that one could decide to do next, and there are many disparate sources of information (including cultural knowledge and inborn approach/avoidance inclinations) that are action-relevant and should be constraining action. For action selection, this "multidetermination" problem is met, not by unconscious motor algorithms controlling motor efference such as those of the dorsal pathway, but by the ability of phenomenal states to constrain what *we do* by having the inclinations (or "votes") of multiple systems constrain skeletomotor output. Thus, multiple systems in the brain are simultaneously controlling the same "steering wheel" (i.e., the skeletal muscle system) of the nervous system. This is captured conceptually by the PRISM principle: Just as a prism combines different colors to yield a single hue, phenomenal states integrate simultaneously activated tendencies to yield adaptive skeletomotor action. Consistent with the principle, consider that expressing (or suppressing) inhaling, blinking, pain withdrawal, and micturating all involve, specifically, skeletal muscle actions/plans. Accordingly, regarding processes such as digestion, one is conscious of only those phases requiring coordination with skeletomotor plans (e.g., chewing, micturating) and none of those that do not (e.g., peristalsis). Conversely, no skeletal muscle plans are directly involved in unconscious processes such as the pupillary reflex, peristalsis, bronchial dilation, and vasoconstriction (all involving smooth muscle). Though often functioning unconsciously (as in blinking and breathing), skeletal muscle is the only effector that can be consciously controlled, but why this is so has never been explained. PRISM introduces a reinterpretation of this age-old fact: *Skeletomotor actions are at times "consciously mediated" because they are directed by multiple, encapsulated systems that, when in conflict, require consciousness to yield adaptive action* (Morsella, 2005).

The Contents of Phenomenal States

In SIT, consciousness crosstalks information and behavioral inclinations that were already generated and analyzed unconsciously (Shepard, 1984; Jackendoff, 1990; Wegner & Wheatley, 1999). Thus, consciousness is not so much a doer, but more of a talker, and it cross-talks relatively few kinds of information. The little of that which we are conscious of tends to reflect what in everyday life is called "perception," or, more scientifically, "perceptual products" and "evaluative products," such as objects in the world (Fodor, 1983) or, importantly, inclinations that are experienced subjectively (Gray, 1995, 2004). This is consistent with the view that one is conscious only of the "outputs" of processes, including urges and inclinations toward certain acts, and not of the processes themselves (Lashley, 1951). (See Morsella & Bargh [2010] for a treatment of the notion of "output" in the nervous system.) Again, it seems that we do not have direct, conscious access to low-level perceptual processes, nor to programs for behavioral control (Grossberg, 1999; Rosenbaum, 2002), including those for language (Levelt, 1989), emotional systems (e.g., the amygdala; Anderson, & Phelps, 2002;

Öhman, Carlsson, Lundqvist, & Ingvar, 2007), or executive control (Crick & Koch, 2000; Suhler & Churchland, 2009).

If the function of phenomenal states is to achieve integration among systems by broadcasting information, then we should expect that the nature of phenomenally accessible representations is to have a high *broadcast ability* (i.e., should be "understood" by the greatest number of action systems). This is indeed the case. Independent of phenomenological observations, and based instead on the requirements of isotropic information processing, it has been proposed a priori that it is the perceptual-like (object) representation that has the best broadcast ability (Fodor, 1983; Morsella, Lanska, Berger, & Gazzaley, 2009b). It seems that some kinds of representations (e.g., linguistic/propositional representations) cannot be "understood" by some systems, especially by those that are phylogenetically old (Morsella et al. 2009b). Thus, it may be no accident that it is the perceptual-like kind of representation (e.g., visual objects or linguistic objects such as phonemes; Fodor, 1983) that happens to be phenomenally accessible (Gray, 1995). (Convergent evidence for this stems from research elucidating why motor programs are unconscious, e.g., Gray, 1995; Grossberg, 1999; Prinz, 2003.) Interestingly, the same, perceptual-like representation constitutes that which is phenomenally accessible in several different contexts—normal action, dreams, and when observing the actions of others (Rizzolatti, Sinigaglia, & Anderson, 2008). For example, it is the phonological representation (and not, say, the motor-related, articulatory code) that one is conscious of during both spoken and subvocalized speech, or when perceiving the speech of others (Fodor, 1983; Rizzolatti et al., 2008). Although these disparate approaches can begin to illuminate the nature of the content of conscious representations (i.e., why they happen to represent, of all that could be represented, that which they happen to represent), the approaches of course do not attempt to explain why these representations must be processed in this phenomenal mode in order to be broadcasted among systems.

At this stage of understanding, perhaps a more tractable question is the following. How do these phenomenally accessible representations that are so important for action selection, but so divorced from motor efference, influence skeletomotor action at all?

Ideomotor Processing

The nature of ideomotor processing is evident in the following anecdote. The television program *60 Minutes* recently presented a news story about how patients can control robotic arm/limb prostheses. In the episode, the *60 Minutes* interviewer was surprised to learn that a soldier who had lost his lower arm in combat could, in just a few practice trials, control the grasping motions of a robotic hand, a prosthesis that was connected to electrodes attached to the muscles of the remaining part of the soldier's upper arm. The soldier had never interacted with such a device before. The interviewer asked the soldier how he knew which muscles to activate in order to enact the action. The soldier replied that he had no idea regarding which muscles to activate, nor what the muscles were actually doing. Instead, the soldier claimed that, to enact the action on the part of the robotic arm, all he had to do was imagine the grasping action (Berger & Morsella, 2012). This image (or *Effektbild*; Harleß 1861) was somehow translated (unconsciously) into the kind of muscular activation that would normally result in the grasping action. Is this how people generally guide and perceive their own actions?

According to James's (1890) popularization of *ideomotor processing*, the answer is yes. Originating in the times of Lotze (1852), Harleß (1861), and Carpenter (1874), the hypothesis states that action guidance and action knowledge are limited to perceptual-like representations (or, *event codes*; cf., Hommel, Müsseler, Aschersleben, & Prinz 2001) of action outcomes (e.g., the "image" of one's finger flexing), with the motor programs/events actually responsible for enacting the actions being unconscious (Gray 1995; Rossetti 2001; Rosenbaum 2002; Gray 2004; Jeannerod 2006). (See neuroimaging evidence for the ideomotor principle in Melcher, Weidema, Eenshuistra, Hommel, & Gruber 2008.) From this standpoint, conscious contents regarding ongoing action are primarily of the perceptual consequences of action (Jeannerod 2006). (For a computational explanation of why motor programs should be unconscious and explicit memories should be not formed for them, see Grossberg 1999.) Consistent with contemporary ideomotor-like approaches (e.g., Greenwald 1970; Hommel, Müsseler, Aschersleben, & Prinz 2001; Hommel 2009; Hommel & Elsner 2009), James (1890) proposed that the conscious mind later uses these conscious perceptual-like representations to voluntarily guide the generation of motor efference, which itself is an unconscious process.

Ideomotor approaches (Greenwald, 1970; Hommel, Müsseler, Aschersleben, & Prinz, 2001; Hommel, 2009) propose that it is through perceptual-like representations that action is controlled voluntarily. According to James, for example, the mere thoughts of actions produce impulses that, if not curbed or controlled by "acts of express fiat," result in the performance of those actions (James, 1950, pp. 520–524; based on Lotze, 1852). He added that this was how voluntary actions are learned and generated: The image of the sensorial effects of an action leads to the corresponding action—effortlessly and without any explicit knowledge of the motor programs involved. Once an action outcome (e.g., flexing the finger) is selected, unconscious motor efference enacts the action by activating the right muscles at the right time, unless one entertains an incompatible idea (e.g., to not move the finger; Jeannerod 2006). (It is important to note that not all ideomotor acts are conscious acts; consider the kind of unconscious efference binding involved in responses to subliminal stimuli.) Akin to Skinner's (1953) *operants*, action goals (i.e., effects upon the body or world) can be instituted by various motor programs and effectors, resulting in phenomena such as "motor equivalence" (Lashley, 1942).

Unlike affective states, which cannot be modulated directly (Öhman & Mineka, 2001), instrumental goals (e.g., moving a finger) can be implemented instantaneously by ideomotor processing, a kind of *direct cognitive control* (Morsella et al., 2009b). Few cognitive processes can be influenced by direct cognitive control (Öhman & Mineka, 2001; Morsella, 2005; Bargh & Morsella, 2008), which is perhaps best exemplified by one's ability to immediately control thinking (or imagining) and the movements of a finger, arm, or other skeletal muscle effector. Each of these kinds of processes requires the activation of, again, perceptual-like representations: one for constituting mental imagery (Farah, 2000) and the other for action selection (Hommel et al., 2001). From this standpoint, one can snap one's finger at will but one cannot make oneself feel scared or joyous with the same immediacy. For the latter, one may employ *indirect cognitive control*. For example, to make oneself scared or joyous, one may activate the perceptual symbols that can then trigger the neural processes responsible for these states (Morsella et al., 2009b).

To summarize, ideomotor approaches (see chapter 16) have provided the best framework for understanding how phenomenal states (e.g., conscious perceptual-like representations) can lead to voluntary actions through the skeletal muscle output system.

Conclusion

In synthesis, regarding the basic components of voluntary action, phenomenal states are required to establish crosstalk among the involved actional systems. More specifically, phenomenal states are required to establish the crosstalk necessary for *integrated action selection*, a process that has been associated with the ventral thalamocortical processing stream in the brain. Without these states, actions can arise but they will be unintegrated (e.g., reflexively inhaling); integrated actions such as holding one's breath require the instantiation of these elusive states. It is important to note that the current approach may identify what phenomenal states are for, but it sheds no light on why "subjectivity" is associated with the tightly circumscribed, integrative function that these states appear to subserve.

For action to be influenced by top-down "direct cognitive control," the component mechanisms of ideomotor processing and skeletal muscle action must be at play. Within this framework, the activation of action plans countering one's goals are perceived to be less associated to the self (Riddle & Morsella, 2009), as captured by the "monkey on one's back" metaphor. Similarly, metacognitions such as urges, the sense of agency, and intentional binding (and less understood phenomena such as distortions in time perception and modulation of that which enters attentional awareness) are properties of voluntary action, a peculiar form of action production. These high-level properties appear to not be shared by other forms of action. In this way, phenomenal states, ideomotor processing, and the skeletal muscle system are the pillars of voluntary action.

We adopted an inductive and descriptive approach, one in which nervous function is described as is, and not as it (perhaps) should be. In our approach, intuitions regarding how the nervous system should work took a back seat to data revealing how it actually works, whether the system works optimally or suboptimally. Appreciating the many components and properties of volitional processing reveals that identifying what is special about voluntary action—that which distinguishes a blink from a wink—is a much more complicated affair than what everyday experience suggests.

NOTE

1. Often referred to as "subjective experience," "qualia," "sentience," "consciousness," and "awareness," the phenomenal state (or basic consciousness) has proven to be difficult to describe and analyze but easy to identify, for it constitutes the totality of our experience. Perhaps this basic form of consciousness has been best defined by Nagel (1974), who claimed that an organism has phenomenal states if there is *something it is like* to be that organism—something it is like, for example, to be human and experience pain, love, breathlessness, or yellow afterimages. Similarly, Block (1995) claimed, "the phenomenally conscious aspect of a state is what it is like to be in that state" (p. 227).

REFERENCES

Alais, D., & Blake, R. (2005). *Binocular Rivalry*. Cambridge, MA: The MIT Press.
Anderson, A. K., & Phelps, E.A. (2002). Is the human amygdala critical for the subjective experience of emotion? Evidence of intact dispositional affect in patients with amygdala lesions. *Journal of Cognitive Neuroscience, 14*, 709–720.
Angell, J. R. (1907). The province of functional psychology. *Psychological Review, 14*, 61–91.
Baars, B. J. (2002). The conscious access hypothesis: Origins and recent evidence. *Trends in Cognitive Sciences, 6*, 47–52.
Baddeley, A. D. (1986). *Working Memory*. Oxford: Oxford University Press.
Baddeley, A. D. (2007). *Working Memory, Thought and Action*. Oxford: Oxford University Press.
Bargh, J. A., & Morsella, E. (2008). The unconscious mind. *Perspectives on Psychological Science, 3*, 73–79.
Berger, C. C., & Morsella, E. (2012). The 'what' of doing: Introspection-based evidence for James's ideomotor principle. *Psychology of Self-Control* (pp. 145–160). New York: Nova.
Berti, A., & Pia, L. (2006). Understanding motor awareness through normal and pathological behavior. *Current Directions in Psychological Science, 15*, 245–250.
Block, N. (1995). On a confusion about a function of consciousness. *Behavioral and Brain Sciences, 18*, 227–287.
Carpenter, W. B. (1874). *Principles of Mental Physiology*. New York: Appleton.
Chomsky, N. (1988). *Language and Problems of Knowledge: The Managua Lectures*. Cambridge, MA: MIT Press.
Cohen, J. D., Dunbar, K., & McClelland, J. L. (1990). On the control of automatic processes: A parallel distributed processing account of the Stroop effect. *Psychological Review, 97*, 332–361.
Corallo, G., Sackur, J., Dehaene, S., & Sigman, M. (2008). Limits on introspection: Distorted subjective time during the dual-task bottleneck. *Psychological Science, 19*, 1110–1117.
Crick, F., & Koch, C. (2000). The unconscious homunculus. In T. Metzinger (Ed.), *Neural Correlates of Consciousness* (pp. 103–110). Cambridge, MA: The MIT Press.

Curtis, C. E., & D'Esposito, M. (2009). The inhibition of unwanted actions. In E. Morsella, J. A. Bargh, & P. M. Gollwitzer (Eds.), *Oxford Handbook of Human Action* (pp. 72–97). New York: Oxford University Press.

Dehaene, S., & Naccache, L. (2001). Towards a cognitive neuroscience of consciousness: Basic evidence and a workspace framework. *Cognition, 79*, 1–37.

Desmurget, M., Reilly, K. T., Richard, N., Szathmari, A., Mottolese, C., & Sirigu, A. (2009). Movement intention after parietal cortex stimulation in humans. *Science, 324*(5928), 811–813.

Desmurget, M., & Sirigu, A. (2010). A parietal-premotor network for movement intention and motor awareness. Trends in Cognitive sciences, 13, 411–419.

Doesburg, S. M., Green, J. L., McDonald, J. J., & Ward, L. M. (2009). Rhythms of consciousness: Binocular rivalry reveals large-scale oscillatory network dynamics mediating visual perception. *PLOS, 4*, 1–14.

Engbert, K., Wohlschläger, A., & Haggard, P. (2007). Who is causing what? The sense of agency is relational and efferent triggered. *Cognition, 107*, 693–704.

Engbert, K., Wohlschläger, A., Thomas, R., & Haggard, P. (2007). Agency, subjective time, and other minds. *Journal of Experimental Psychology: Human, Perception, and Performance, 33*, 1261–1268.

Farah, M. J. (2000). The neural bases of mental imagery. In M. S. Gazzaniga (Ed.), *The cognitive neurosciences* (2nd ed., pp. 965–974). Cambridge, MA: MIT Press.

Fodor, J. A. (1983). *Modularity of Mind: An Essay on Faculty Psychology*. Cambridge, MA: MIT press.

Fourneret, P., & Jeannerod, M. (1998). Limited conscious monitoring of motor performance in normal subjects. *Neuropsychologia, 36*, 1133–1140.

Fried, I., Katz, A., McCarthy, G., Sass, K. J., Williamson, P., Spencer, S. S., et al. (1991). Functional organization of human supplementary motor cortex studied by electrical stimulation. *Journal of Neuroscience, 11*, 3656–3666.

Goodale, M., & Milner, D. (2004). *Sight Unseen: An Exploration of Conscious and Unconscious Vision*. New York: Oxford University Press.

Gould, S. J. (1977). *Ever Since Darwin: Reflections in Natural History*. New York: Norton.

Gray, J. A. (1995). The contents of consciousness: A neuropsychological conjecture. *Behavioral and Brain Sciences, 18*, 659–676.

Gray, J. A. (2004). *Consciousness: Creeping up on the Hard Problem*. New York: Oxford University Press.

Greenwald, A. G. (1970). Sensory feedback mechanisms in performance control: With special reference to the ideomotor mechanism. *Psychological Review, 77*, 73–99.

Grossberg, S. (1999). The link between brain learning, attention, and consciousness. *Consciousness and Cognition, 8*, 1–44.

Haggard, P., Aschersleben, G., Gehrke, J., & Prinz, W. (2002). Action, binding and awareness. In W. Prinz, & B. Hommel (Eds.), *Common Mechanisms in Perception and Action: Attention and Performance* (Vol. XIX, pp. 266–285). Oxford: Oxford University Press.

Haggard, P., Clark, S., & Kalogeras, J. (2002). Voluntary action and conscious awareness. *Nature Neuroscience, 5*, 382–385.

Hallett, M. (2007). Volitional control of movement: The physiology of free will. *Clinical Neurophysiology, 117*, 1179–1192.

Harleß, E. (1861). Der Apparat des Willens [The apparatus of the will]. *Zeitschrift für Philosophie und philosophische Kritik, 38,* 499–507.

Hazy, T. E., Frank, M. J., & O'Reilly, R. C. (2006). Banishing the homunculus: Making working memory work. *Neuroscience, 139,* 105–118.

Hommel, B. (2009). Action control according to TEC (theory of event coding). *Psychological Research, 73,* 512–526.

Hommel, B., & Elsner, B. (2009). Acquisition, representation, and control of action. In E. Morsella, J. A. Bargh, & P. M. Gollwitzer (Eds.), *Oxford handbook of human action* (pp. 371–398). New York: Oxford University Press.

Hommel, B., Müsseler, J., Aschersleben, G., & Prinz, W. (2001). The theory of event coding: A framework for perception and action planning. *Behavioral and Brain Sciences, 24,* 849–937.

Jackendoff, R. S. (1990). *Consciousness and the Computational Mind.* MA: MIT Press.

James, W. (1890/1950). *Principles of Psychology* (Vol. 2). New York: Dover.

Jeannerod, M. (2006). *Motor Cognition: What Action Tells the Self.* New York: Oxford University Press.

Kern, M. K., Safwan, J., Arndorfer, R. C., & Shaker, R. (2001). Cerebral cortical representation of reflexive and volitional swallowing in humans. *American Journal of Physiology: Gastrointestinal and Liver Physiology, 280,* G354–G360.

Kimberg, D. Y., D'Esposito, M., & Farah, M. J. (1997). Cognitive functions in the prefrontal cortex—Working memory and executive control. *Current Directions in Psychological Science, 6,* 185–192.

Lashley, K. S. (1942). The problem of cerebral organization in vision. In H. Kluver (Ed.), *Visual Mechanisms. Biological Symposia* (Vol. 7, pp. 301–322). Lancaster, PA: Cattell Press.

Lashley, K. S. (1951). The problem of serial order in behavior. In L. A. Jeffress (Ed.), *Cerebral Mechanisms in Behavior. The Hixon Symposium* (pp. 112–146). New York: Wiley.

Levelt, W. J. M. (1989). *Speaking: From Intention to Articulation.* Cambridge, MA: The MIT Press.

Libet, B. (2004). *Mind Time: The Temporal Factor in Consciousness.* Cambridge, MA: Harvard University Press.

Livnat, A., & Pippenger, N. (2006). An optimal brain can be composed of conflicting agents. *Proceeding of the National Academy of Sciences, USA, 103,* 3198–3202.

Logan, G. D. (2003). Executive control of thought and action: In search of the wild homunculus. *Current Directions in Psychological Science, 12,* 45–48.

Lorenz, K. (1965). *Evolution and the Modification of Behavior.* Chicago: The University of Chicago Press.

Lotze, R. H. (1852). *Medizinische Psychologie oder Physiologie der Seele [Medical Psychology or Physiology of the Soul].* Leipzig: Weidmann'sche Buchhandlung.

Lynn, M. T., Berger, C. C., Riddle, T. A., & Morsella, E. (2010). Mind control? Creating illusory intentions through a phony brain-computer interface. *Consciousness and Cognition, 19,* 1007–1012.

MacLeod, C. M., & MacDonald, P. A. (2000). Interdimensional interference in the Stroop effect: Uncovering the cognitive and neural anatomy of attention. *Trends in Cognitive Sciences, 4,* 383–391.

Marr, D. (1982) *Vision.* New York: Freeman.

Maruya, K., Yang, E., & Blake, R. (2007). Voluntary action influences visual competition. *Psychological Science, 18*, 1090–1098.

Mayr, E. (2001). *What Evolution Is.* London: Weidenfeld & Nicolson.

McGurk, H. & MacDonald, J. (1976). Hearing lips and seeing voices. *Nature, 264*, 746–748.

Melcher, T., Weidema, M., Eenshuistra, R. M., Hommel, B., & Gruber, O. (2008). The neural substrate of the ideomotor principle: An event-related fMRI analysis. *NeuroImage, 39*, 1274–1288.

Merker, B. (2007). Consciousness without a cerebral cortex: A challenge for neuroscience and medicine. *Behavioral and Brain Sciences, 30*, 63–134.

Molapour, T., Berger, C. C., & Morsella, E. (2011). Did I read or did I name: Diminished awareness of processes yielding identical "outputs." *Consciousness and Cognition, 20*(4), 1776–1780.

Morsella, E. (2005). The function of phenomenal states: Supramodular interaction theory. *Psychological Review, 112*, 1000–1021.

Morsella, E., & Bargh, J. A. (2010). What is an output? *Psychological Inquiry, 21*, 354–370.

Morsella, E., & Bargh, J. A. (2011). Unconscious action tendencies: Sources of "un-integrated" action. In J. T. Cacioppo, & J. Decety (Eds.), *The Handbook of Social Neuroscience* (pp. 335–347). New York: Oxford University Press.

Morsella, E., Berger, C. C., & Krieger, S. C. (2011). Cognitive and neural components of the phenomenology of agency: A meta-analytic view. *Neurocase, 17*, 209–230.

Morsella, E., Gray, J. R., Krieger, S. C., & Bargh, J. A. (2009a). The essence of conscious conflict: Subjective effects of sustaining incompatible intentions. *Emotion, 9*, 717–728.

Morsella, E., Krieger, S. C., & Bargh, J. A. (2010). Minimal neuroanatomy for a conscious brain: Homing in on the networks constituting consciousness. *Neural Networks, 23*, 14–15.

Morsella, E., & Lanska, M., Berger, C. C., & Gazzaley, A. (2009b). Indirect cognitive control through top-down activation of perceptual symbols. *European Journal of Social Psychology, 39*, 1173–1177.

Nagel, T. (1974). What is it like to be a bat? *Philosophical Review, 83*, 435–450.

Neisser, U. (1967). *Cognitive Psychology.* New York: Apple-Century-Crofts.

Norman, D. A., & Shallice, T. (1980). Attention to action: Willed and automatic control of behavior. In R. J. Davidson, G. E. Schwartz, & D. Shapiro (Eds.), *Consciousness and Self-Regulation* (pp. 1–18). New York: Plenum Press.

Öhman, A., Carlsson, K., Lundqvist, D., & Ingvar, M. (2007). On the unconscious subcortical origin of human fear. *Physiology & Behavior, 92*, 180–185.

Öhman, A., & Mineka, S. (2001). Fears, phobias, and preparedness: Toward an evolved module of fear and fear learning. *Psychological Review, 108*, 483–522.

Ortinski, P., & Meador, K. J. (2004). Neuronal mechanisms of conscious awareness. *Neurological Review, 61*, 1017–1020.

Pacherie, E. (2008). The phenomenology of action: A conceptual framework. *Cognition, 107*, 179–217.

Perky, C. W. (1910). An experimental study of imagination. *American Journal of Psychology, 21*, 422–452.

Prinz, W. (2003). How do we know about our own actions? In S. Maasen, W. Prinz, & Roth (Eds), *Voluntary action: Brains, minds, and sociality* (pp. 21–33). London: Oxford University Press.

Raymond, J. E., Shapiro, K. L., & Arnell, K. M. (1992). Temporary suppression of visual processing in an RSVP task: An attentional blink? *Journal of Experimental Psychology: Human Perception and Performance, 18*, 849–860.

Riddle, T. A., & Morsella, E. (2009). *Is that me? Authorship processing as a function of intra-psychic conflict.* Proceedings of the Annual Convention of the Association for Psychological Science, San Francisco, CA.

Rizzolatti, G., Sinigaglia, C., & Anderson, F. (2008). *Mirrors in the Brain: How Our Minds Share Actions, Emotions, and Experience.* New York: Oxford University Press.

Roepstorff, A., & Frith, C. D. (2004). What's at the top in the top-down control of action? Script-sharing and "top-top" control of action in cognitive experiments. *Psychological Research, 68,* 189–198.

Rosenbaum, D. A. (2002). Motor control. In H. Pashler (Series Ed.) & S. Yantis (Vol. Ed.), *Stevens' Handbook of Experimental Psychology: Vol. 1. Sensation and Perception* (3rd ed., pp. 315–339). New York: Wiley.

Rossetti, Y. (2001). Implicit perception in action: Short-lived motor representation of space. In P. G. Grossenbacher (Ed.), *Finding consciousness in the brain: A neurocognitive approach* (pp. 133–181). Netherlands: John Benjamins Publishing.

Sato, A. (2009). Both motor prediction and conceptual congruency between preview and action-effect contribute to explicit judgment of agency. *Cognition, 110,* 74–83.

Sergent, C., & Dahaene, S. (2004). Is consciousness a gradual phenomenon? Evidence for an all-or-none bifurcation during the attentional blink. *Psychological Science, 15,* 720–728.

Schacter, D. L., & Addis, D. R. (2007). The cognitive neuroscience of constructive memory: Remembering the past and imagining the future. *Philosophical Transactions of the Royal Society of London, Series B: Biological Sciences, 362,* 773–786.

Shepard, R. N. (1984). Ecological constraints on internal representation: Resonant kinematics of perceiving, imagining, thinking and dreaming. *Psychological Review, 91,* 417–447.

Skinner, B. F. (1953). *Science and Human Behavior.* New York: Macmillan.

Stroop, J. R. (1935). Studies of interference in serial verbal reactions. *Journal of Experimental Psychology, 18,* 643–662.

Suhler, C. L., & Churchland, P. S. (2009). Control: Conscious and otherwise. *Trends in Cognitive Sciences, 13,* 341–347.

Synofzik, M., Vosgerau, G., & Newen, A. (2008). I move, therefore I am: A new theoretical framework to investigate agency and ownership. *Consciousness and Cognition, 17,* 411–424.

Taylor, J. L., & McCloskey, D. I. (1990). Triggering of preprogrammed movements as reactions to masked stimuli. *Journal of Neurophysiology, 63,* 439–446.

Wegner, D. M. (2002). *The Illusion of Conscious Will.* Cambridge, MA: MIT Press.

Wegner, D. M. (2003). The mind's best trick: How we experience conscious will. *Trends in Cognitive Science, 7,* 65–69.

Wegner, D. M., & Wheatley, T. P. (1999). Apparent mental causation: Sources of the experience of will. *American Psychologist, 54,* 480–492.

Wenke D, & Haggard P. (2009). How voluntary actions modulate time perception. *Experimental Brain Research, 196,* 311–318.

Williams, M. A., Morris, A. P., McGlone, F., Abbott, D. F., & Mattingley, J. B. (2004). Amygdala responses to fearful and happy facial expressions under conditions of binocular suppression. *Journal of Neuroscience, 24,* 2898–2904.

Wohlschläger, A. (2000). Visual motion priming by invisible actions. *Vision Research, 40,* 925–930.

Zeki, S., & Bartels, A. (1999). Toward a theory of visual consciousness. *Consciousness and Cognition, 8,* 225–259.

18 The Function of Consciousness in Controlling Behavior
Sara Steele and Hakwan Lau

HOW WELL DO we control our actions? The Western tradition is founded on beliefs in rationality and the ability to consciously reason through decisions; however, philosophers have argued for centuries over whether we truly possess "free will," or whether our actions are all predetermined by our circumstances. The modern age presents us with a number of circumstances that challenge the integrity of our agency. In mass media, advertisers have developed a number of strategies to compel target demographics to buy goods and services. Substance abuse counselors try to understand the conflicting motivations that underlie addiction and to develop strategies for liberating patients from compulsive and self-destructive behaviors. Lawmakers must decide when behaviors should be left to personal choice versus when they must be regulated, and how best to influence the population to make collectively profitable decisions. The United States criminal justice system recognizes circumstances when people are not responsible for their actions, based on evaluations of whether they were "in control" of themselves at the time of the crime. Clearly, perceptions of agency inhabit a rich and complicated place in the ideology of our society. But what are its psychological bases within an individual?

In 1978, researchers Richard Nisbett and Timothy Wilson of the University of Michigan conducted a series of studies on the higher-level cognitive processes underlying the production of responses to decision-making tasks. They came to the conclusion that subjects often fail to recognize when a particular feature of their experimental condition has had a crucial effect on their decisions; rather, they instead draw from personal beliefs to reconstruct plausible explanations for their own behavior. For instance, high school students who had been surveyed about divisive social issues were placed into groups with highly persuasive confederates. Many students were converted to the opposite stance, but no subject reported that the discussion had any effect in changing or modifying his position; experimental subjects, when questioned, actually misremembered their original opinions as being sympathetic to their new outlook (Nisbett & Wilson, 1977). Interestingly, the flawed explanations proffered by subjects about which factors had been crucial for their turnarounds usually match predictions by outside observers on how they *would* respond in similar circumstances. In another example, Latane and Darley (1970) examined the bystander effect, in which observers are less likely to help a victim in distress as the number of witnesses increases. Even when subjects were presented with experimental results, participants vehemently denied that the presence of others had had an impact on their behavior, in contrast to the responses of control group subjects asked to predict how they might act in a similar situation. Accurate attribution of causality fails in a number of experimental manipulations, including the role of a previously administered vocabulary test on free associations or the influence of the position of pieces of clothing in a department store on judgments of their quality. These findings suggest that what we intuitively understand about agency, or the ability to perform deliberate actions that affect the world around us, may be derived more from our beliefs about how decision making should work than from any privileged knowledge we actually experience firsthand. Thus, a more structured approach must be taken to understand the relationship between subjective reports of conscious intentions and the goal-directed behaviors that are produced.

The Feeling of Will

Within rich ecological contexts, it might be difficult for an experimenter to isolate the role of conscious decisions in guiding behavior. The studies previously mentioned from Nisbett and Wilson, for instance, were carried out in peculiar circumstances wherein it was believed that the decision-making processes would be heavily influenced by outside stimuli and might for argument's sake be viewed as idiosyncratic illusions, akin to illusions in the visual system. Furthermore, they did not monitor volitional processes in isolation but rather mediated by metacognition and memory, for the responses were collected some seconds to minutes after the action was performed.

Studies of spontaneous motor initiation, however, have captured the formation of very simple self-generated actions on a fine temporal scale. Spontaneously initiated motor actions are those that are not made in immediate or direct response to external stimuli. For instance, one may choose to casually flex one's wrist while sitting in a dark room, out of one's free choice and timing, not in reaction to anything in particular. Some philosophers have argued that in such cases, it should seem obvious that the action is caused by one's conscious intention (Searle, 1983). Whereas one may argue that fast reactions to external stimuli may be driven by an unconscious reflex (e.g., a runner leaping forward upon hearing the starting gun), spontaneous actions do not presuppose any immediate cause but the conscious intention itself. Scientists and philosophers disagree as to what constitutes "consciousness" and how to measure it, but we will restrict ourselves to the relatively uncontroversial stance that "conscious" states are those internal states that a subject can report explicitly (e.g., through verbal report), whereas "unconscious" states are those that a subject cannot explicitly report. Stripping away the confounding elements of outside stimuli, social circumstances, and much of the burden of memory encoding and recollection, we are left with the sequential pairing of a subjectively reportable urge and a simple, stereotyped motor act—a molecule of volition, or the smallest particle of the experience of willful action that can be isolated and still possess its basic properties. We will begin with a series of investigations that examine the role of the perception of agency in spontaneously initiated motor actions.

THE READINESS POTENTIAL

One of the most perplexing findings in cognitive neuroscience was originally reported by Kornhuber and Deecke in 1965. They placed electrodes on the scalp to measure electroencephalography (EEG) while subjects made spontaneous movements at their own timing. The EEG data were time-locked to the point of motor execution as measured by muscle contraction indicated by electromyography. They were averaged over many trials, which produced an event-related potential (ERP) known as the *Bereitschaftspotential*, or readiness potential. This activation pattern is a slowly rising potential, peaking around the point of action execution and starting from 1 to 2 seconds before that (Fig. 18.1). The readiness potential is most pronounced at electrodes near the vertex (Cz in the EEG coordinate system), which is directly dorsal to the medial premotor areas including the supplementary motor area (SMA), the presupplementary motor area (pre-SMA), and the cingulate motor areas below them. It is generally believed that one major source of the readiness potential lies in the medial premotor areas (Ball et al., 1999; Cunnington et al., 2003; Erdler et al., 2000; Weilke et al., 2001).

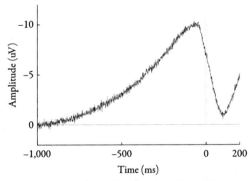

FIGURE 18.1 A schematic depiction of the readiness potential preceding spontaneous movements. The readiness potential is usually recorded at the top of the scalp, above medial frontal premotor areas. It gradually ramps up, beginning about 1–2 seconds before movement and peaking around the time of movement execution (marked as time = 0 above).

The demonstration of the readiness potential calls into question whether spontaneous movements are really caused by the preceding conscious intentions. Conscious intentions appear to cause motor actions almost immediately—certainly much faster than 1 to 2 seconds. This could mean that the brain starts to prepare for actions quite a long time before a subject experiences the urge to initiate them.

Benjamin Libet and colleagues invented a technique to record the time scale of subjects' feelings of intention in relation to the readiness potential and the action initiation (Libet et al., 1983). To measure the onset of conscious intention, he invented a creative but controversial paradigm, which is sometimes called the "Libet clock paradigm." In those studies, subjects watched a dot revolving around a clock face at a speed of 2.56 seconds per cycle while they flexed their wrist spontaneously (Fig. 18.2). After the action was finished, subjects were required to report the location of the dot when they "first felt the urge" to produce the action (i.e., the onset of intention). The subject might, for instance, say it was at the 3 o'clock or 4 o'clock position when they first felt the intention. This created a framework by which subjects could time and report the onset of their intention. The experimenter could thereby work out the temporal distance between the recorded "urge" and when the action was actually produced. Libet and colleagues found that on average, subjects report the onset of intention to be about 250 ms before motor execution.

Many people feel uncomfortable with the fact that the onset of the readiness potential is much earlier than the reported onset of intention, and some have tried to explain away the gap. Libet and colleagues have tried to study the onset of the readiness potential more carefully, discarding trials which might have been "contaminated" by preplanning well before the action (for instance, by counting to ten and then triggering the movement), as reported by the subjects. By only looking at the trials in which the actions were seemingly spontaneous, Libet and colleagues reported that the onset of

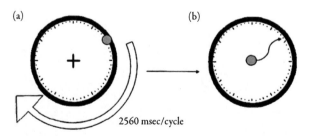

FIGURE 18.2 The Libet clock paradigm. a. The subject views a dot rotating slowly (2.56 seconds per cycle) around a clock face and waits for an urge to move to arise spontaneously. When the urge arrives, the subject makes a movement such as a key press. b. After making the movement, the subject estimates the earliest time at which the intention to move was experienced. To carry out this time estimate, the subject either verbally indicate the location of the dot where the intention was first felt, or move a cursor to that location (as in this example). In a common control condition, the subject uses the clock to estimate the time of movement rather than the onset of intention. Figure edited and adapted from Lau et al., 2007.

the readiness potential is only about 500 ms before action execution (Libet et al., 1983). However, this is still clearly earlier than the average onset of intention at 250 ms. And by discarding so many trials, it may simply be that the analysis lacked the power to detect an earlier onset.

Some have argued that the onset of readiness potential might be an artifact caused by the averaging needed to produce the ERP (Miller & Trevena, 2002). However, the original Libet experiment collected readiness potentials for each block of 40 trials, each of which was almost never preceded by the onset of intention in any trial within that block. Romo and Schultz (1987) have recorded from neurons in the medial premotor areas while monkeys made self-paced movements. It was found that these neurons, in fact, fired as early as 2.6 seconds before movement onset. It is difficult to tell with any certainty what the temporal relationship should be between any experience of intention and the monkey's behavior, or even if monkeys might have analogous subjective states. However, such findings corroborate the extended timescale for premotor activity. One recent study has reported that the spatial pattern of fMRI activity from this region, at up to 5 seconds before action, can statistically predict the timing of action above chance level (Soon et al., 2008). One probabilistic model proposes that the delay in onset of intention may actually be a statistical strategy for reliable perception of the readiness potential (Nikolov et al., 2010), because its slowly rising activation would deviate significantly from baseline noise mostly at later time points and not early on while its signal is relatively weak. This supports the account that the subject's perception of the urge to act is actually a response to ongoing premotor activity.

Others argue that the readiness potential may not actually reflect the specific and causal aspects of motor initiation. However, as mentioned earlier, it is likely that the readiness potential originates partly from the medial premotor areas. Lesions to these areas can abolish the production of spontaneous actions (Thaler et al., 1995). These areas also contain neurons that code specific action plans (Shima & Tanji, 1998; Tanji & Shima, 1996). Furthermore, when people use the Libet clock paradigm to time their own intentions, there is attentional modulation of activity in the medial pre-SMA (Lau et al., 2004), as if people were reading information off the area, which is likely to be a source of the readiness potential.

The Libet clock method has also received considerable criticism. It involves timing across modalities and could therefore be susceptible to various biases (Gomes, 2002; Joordens et al., 2002; Klein, 2002; Libet, 1985; Trevena & Miller, 2002). However, it is unlikely that all of these biases are in the direction that would help to narrow the gap between the onsets of the readiness potential and intention. Some have actually suggested that the different biases may point to different directions and, thus, cancel each other out (Klein, 2002). Also, in the original experiments by Libet and colleagues, there were control conditions that tested for the basic accuracy of the clock. They asked subjects to use the clock to time either the onset of movement execution or, in another condition, to time the onset of tactile stimuli presented externally by the experimenter. Because the actual onsets of these events are objectively measurable, they could estimate the subjective error of onset reports produced by the clock method. They found the error to be on the order of about 50 ms, for instance, people misestimate the time of action execution to be 50 ms earlier than it actually is. This size of error is considerably smaller than the gap between the onsets of the readiness potential and intention.

The basic results of Libet and colleagues have been replicated in several different laboratories (e.g., Haggard & Eimer, 1999; Lau et al., 2004; Soon et al., 2008). In general, a consistent pattern is found; the onset of intention is around 250 ms before action execution. These findings seem to confirm our intuition that conscious intentions are followed by motor actions almost immediately. In fact, given that the readiness potential starts as early as 1 to 2 seconds before action execution, it is hard to imagine how the onset of intention could coincide with or precede the readiness potential, unless one thinks of intention as a kind of prior intention (Searle, 1983), meaning the general plan that is formed at the beginning of the experimental session when the subject agrees to produce certain actions in the next half-hour or so. However, the intention we are concerned with here is the immediate "urge" to produce the motor action (Libet, Wright, & Gleason, 1982). The relationship between consciousness and "prior intentions," or the setting up of particular stimulus-response contingencies, will be discussed further in the section on cognitive control.

Taken together, the evidence suggests that conscious intention (i.e., the immediate feeling of motor initiation), is unlikely to be the first unmoved mover in triggering stereotyped motor movements. It is probably preceded by unconscious brain activity that may contribute to action initiation. What, then, is conscious intention for?

CONSCIOUS VETO?

Libet's interpretation of the timing-of-intention results is that although intention may not be early enough to be the first cause of action, the fact that it occurs before action execution means that it could still be part of the causal chain. Maybe the decision to move is initiated unconsciously, but the awareness of intention may allow us to "veto" (i.e., cancel) the action.

This seems to be a possibility. Libet and colleagues (Libet et al., 1983), as well as other researchers (Brass and Haggard, 2007), have performed experiments in which subjects prepare for an action and then cancel it in the last moment, just before it is executed. The fact that we have the ability to "veto" an action seems beyond doubt. The question, however, is whether having the conscious intention is critical. Could the subjectively felt decision to veto be preceded by unconscious activity, in the same way that the intention to act is preceded by the readiness potential? Or perhaps some actions are unconsciously vetoed without entering our awareness at all?

Some recent evidence calls into question whether conscious intention would facilitate the veto function. As mentioned earlier, when people were using the Libet clock to report the onset of their intentions, there was attentional modulation of activity in the pre-SMA (Lau et al., 2004). These data have been subsequently further analyzed, and it has been shown that subjects who showed large degree of attentional modulation tended to also report the onset of intention to be relatively earlier. One interpretation could be that attention biases the judgment of onset to be earlier. It was found in another experiment (Lau et al., 2006) that this was also true when people used the Libet clock to time the onset of the motor execution. The higher the level of fMRI activity modulated by attention, the earlier subjects reported the onset to be. Because, on average, subjects reported the onsets to be earlier than in actuality, a bias to the negative (i.e., early) direction produced more erroneous rather than more precise reports. In general, the principle of attentional prior entry (Shore et al., 2001) suggests that attention to an event speeds up its perception and negatively biases the reported onset. If this were true in the case of the Libet experiments, this could mean that attention might have exaggerated the 250 ms onset, that is, had subjects not been required to attend to their intentions in order to perform the timing tasks, the true onset of conscious intention may well be much later than 250 ms prior to action execution. It is unclear whether we have enough time to consider the veto.

Another study reported that some patients with lesions to the parietal cortex reported the onset of intention to be as late as 50 ms prior to action execution (Sirigu et al., 2004). If the awareness of intention allows one to veto actions, one might expect these patients to have much less time to consciously evaluate spontaneous intentions and cancel the inappropriate ones. This could be quite disastrous to daily life functioning. Yet there were no such reports about these patients. Investigating veto decisions in such cases may shed light on whether the experience of agency is part of the minimum necessary requirements to perform particular tasks.

MANIPULATIONS OF AGENCY

Although the experience of intention is reported to precede voluntary motor actions in every trial of Libet's study, the percept may not be fully formed and is vulnerable to a variety of manipulations. In one study (Lau et al., 2007), single pulses of transcranial magnetic stimulation (TMS) were sent to the medial premotor areas (targeting the pre-SMA). Again, subjects were instructed to produce spontaneous movements and to time the onset of intentions and movement execution using the Libet clock. Surprisingly, although TMS was applied *after* motor execution, it had an effect on the reported onsets. No matter whether TMS was applied immediately after action execution or with a 200 ms delay, the stimulation exaggerated the temporal distance between the reported onsets of intention and movement, as if people reported a prolonged period of conscious intending. One interpretation may be that TMS injected noisy activity into the area and the intention monitoring mechanism did not distinguish this from endogenously generated activity that is supposed to represent intention. However, what is crucial is the fact that the reported onsets can be manipulated even after the action is finished. This suggests that our awareness of intention may be constructed after the facts, or at least not completely determined before the action is finished. If conscious intentions are not determined before the execution of action, they certainly cannot play a role in facilitating veto, let alone causing it.

This interpretation may seem wild, but it is consistent with other proposals. For instance, on the basis of many ingenious experiments manipulating a subject's sense of agency, Wegner (2002) has suggested that the conscious will is an illusion. The sense of agency is often a product of contextual factors. Wegner cites a number of experiments to support these claims, including a study on "facilitated communication" (Wegner et al., 2003). Subjects playing the role of "facilitators" were asked to place their fingers on two keys of a keyboard while a confederate playing the role of "communicator" placed his or her fingers on top of those of the subject. Subjects were given headphones with which they listened to True/False questions of varying difficulty. Confederates were given headphones as well, and subjects were led to believe that the confederates would be hearing the same questions, although in fact the confederates heard nothing. Subjects were told to detect subtle, unconscious movements in the confederate's fingers following each question. When such movements were detected, the subject should press the corresponding key in order to answer on the confederate's behalf. It was found that subjects answered easy questions well above chance levels. If they had performed the task strictly according to the instructions, they should have only performed at chance. Therefore, subjects must have been directing their own key presses. Nonetheless, they attributed a significant causal role for the key presses to the confederate. The degree to which subjects answered easy questions correctly was not correlated with the degree to which they attributed causal responsibility to confederates, suggesting that the generation of action and attribution of action to an agent are independent processes.

A positron emission tomography study captured patterns of brain activation under less deceptive manipulations of perceived control while subjects guided a joystick and watched a cursor move on a screen (Farrer et al., 2003). In some conditions, the joystick controlled the cursor normally; in others, the motion appeared rotated or inverted; and in another, the cursor moved randomly. Subjects were asked to judge whether the control was intact, distorted, or controlled by another person. Activation in the insula corresponded to cases wherein subjects felt they were in control, and activity in the dorsal premotor cortex, the pre-SMA, the right anterior cingulated gyrus, and the inferior parietal lobe, particularly the right side, accompanied feelings that one was not in control. These are the same areas that are implicated in a number of pathological cases involving disorders of the feeling of agency. These areas may underlie the formation of perceptions about causal roles between self and objects in the world.

To summarize, despite speculation that the awareness of intention may play a causal role in allowing us to select or cancel our actions, recent empirical evidence has cast considerable doubt.

CLINICAL APPLICATIONS: ALIEN HAND SYNDROME

One of the most extreme conditions involving the breakdown of volition is the so-called "alien hand syndrome." The syndrome can result from damage to a variety of different brain regions, falling into three subtypes—lesions to the corpus callosum, damage to medial-frontal premotor regions, and damage to posterior (especially parietal) regions (Scepkowski & Cronin-Golomb, 2003). The key feature of such cases is that the patient perceives one of his or her hands to be acting entirely of its own accord, as if some outside force controlled it. Some patients deny ownership of the affected hand. The "rogue" limb is capable of startling behaviors ranging from mimicry of the other hand to "willful" conflict with the unaffected hand's actions, as well as compulsive behaviors such as grasping and utilization of tools. No left-handed patients are reported.

According to those who view conscious will as nothing more than an illusion masking the unconscious processes that drive behavior (Wegner, 2002), the existence of "alien hands" supports the conclusion that there is a dedicated system for constructing the experience of will; when this system breaks down, our ability to consistently attribute the causes of behavior fails, and we are left with no experience of will when performing our own actions. However, advocates of a causal role for experiences of intention might point out that the behaviors of the alien hand are very different from those produced by the conscious system. In this case, production of motor actions occurs without conscious intention and appears to follow a program of action that is unrelated to or contrary to that of the rest of the organism. If this is true, conscious will may play an important role in organizing behavior.

Executive Influence

It is worthwhile to note that up to this point, we have been discussing agency largely in perceptual terms—that is, in terms of the output from other mental processes that allows us to be aware of well-learned voluntary behaviors and the intention to perform them. There has been little success in isolating the role of subjective experience as an *input* for subsequent processes. Our instinctive understanding of agency suggests that the contents of consciousness exert a force on our actions in some way. However, most of the evidence we have discussed so far highlights cases in which the interaction between subjects and stimuli is determined by processes that remain unavailable to consciousness. It is nonetheless possible that consciousness is necessary for some particular type of task, which would give evidence that subjective presence played some causal role in producing behavior. A less intuitive possibility is that the unconscious processes that drive our actions maintain some kind of direct connection with the contents of consciousness, such that the perception of the urge to act arises directly from the same process that produces the act. In this case, our thoughts about actions, while not actually causing them, at least have some direct reference to the way that action is produced. Barring this possibility, a serious, unremitting disjunction between the contents of one's deliberations and the production of action would give credence to the suggestion that sensations of self-control and agency are nothing more than illusions.

There is also the possibility that the feeling of agency is not an illusion altogether, but rather that it is subject to illusion. Just as in the studies by Nisbett and Wilson with complex social phenomena, many of the studies discussed in the preceding section were aimed at producing confusion in the assignment of agency, or dissociating intentions from behavior. In the visual system, investigations of illusions uncovered the strategies and shortcuts that allow for veridical perception of objects in the vast majority of circumstances and that reflect constraints in information processing—but they did not raise the question of whether sight ever provides accurate visual information, even when it became obvious that much of what we see is reconstructed or filled in by the visual system. Similarly, our experiences of both immediate urges and long-term deliberations might be distinct from the empirically determined causal chain in many cases while still providing a useful representation of internal states and enabling specific types of behavior.

A more detailed investigation of the relationship between subjective reports of intentions and the decision-making process (Johansson et al., 2005) illuminates what seems to be a grossly dysfunctional type of illusion: so-called "choice blindness," a paradigm that produces confabulation in normal subjects under fairly normal circumstances while performing a relatively simple task. Subjects chose between paired photographs of female faces based on attractiveness and then answered questions about the reasons behind their choices. On some trials, the selected face was surreptitiously replaced by the rejected face, and the photograph was presented again for the subsequent questioning. Not only did subjects largely remain unaware of the discrepancy between their choices and the presented outcomes, they produced explanations for their choices that were largely similar to justifications for unaltered choices. If perceptions of choices or intentions do not allow us to recognize their outcomes, it is hard to imagine that there is any direct link by which the brain monitors the consequences of a decision against prior intentions (as in Sirigu et al., 2004); the brain might evaluate its progress against some other decision process than the one that is experienced consciously.

This is an unusual but highly problematic illusion—why can't people recognize when their desires have been frustrated? Perhaps conscious intent is a monitor for particular types of situations—an agent that claims to govern "more than it can know" (Nisbett & Wilson, 1978)—but nonetheless crucial for particular types of functions encountered in regular executive functioning.

TOP-DOWN COGNITIVE CONTROL

So far we have discussed acts of volition that are relatively simple, like starting a motor movement, or canceling a particular action. Sometimes we also voluntarily prepare for a set of rules or action plans in order to satisfy a more abstract goal in mind. For instance, a telephone ring usually triggers a particular action: to pick up the phone. However, when one visits friends at their homes, one can deliberately change the mapping between the stimulus (telephone ring) and action; for example, it would be more appropriate to sit still or to ask the host to pick up the phone, rather than picking it up oneself. This volitional change of stimulus-response contingency is an example of top-down cognitive control.

It has been suggested that top-down cognitive control may require consciousness (Dehaene & Naccache, 2001). The idea is that unconscious stimuli can trigger certain prepared actions, as demonstrated in studies in subliminal priming (Kouider & Dehaene, 2007). However, the preparation or setting up of the stimulus–response contingency may require deliberation with the experience of intention as a central component of the process.

Recent studies suggest that this might not be true in the sense that unconscious information seems to be able to influence or even to trigger top-down cognitive control (Mattler, 2003). Lau and Passingham (2007) conducted a study in which subjects had to prepare to do a phonological or semantic judgment based on the shape of a figure they saw (Fig. 18.3). In every trial, if they saw a square, they had to prepare to judge whether an upcoming word has two syllables (e.g., "table") or not (e.g., "milk"). If they saw a

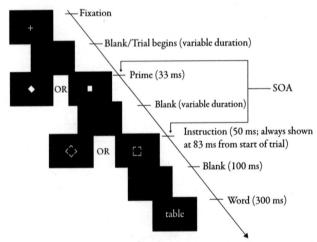

FIGURE 18.3 Experimental paradigm of Lau and Passingham (2007). Subjects view briefly presented words and perform either a phonological task (is the word one syllable or two syllables?) or a semantic task (does the word name something concrete or abstract?). Before word presentation, subjects are instructed which task to perform on a given trial by a visual symbol (a square for the phonological task, or a diamond for the semantic task). The symbolic instruction itself acts as a metacontrast mask for an earlier prime, also a square or a diamond. Because the prime is briefly presented and masked, it is not consciously perceived. On half of trials, the prime is congruent with the instruction and on the other half, incongruent. Behavioral and imaging results suggest that the unconscious primes affected top-down task switching. When primes were incongruent with instructions, accuracy fell, reaction time increased, and brain regions corresponding to the task indicated by the prime were partially activated (all relative to the prime-congruent condition). But when the stimulus onset asynchrony (SOA) between prime and instruction was lowered, such that primes became visible, the priming effect was not evident. This double dissociation suggests that the interference of incongruent primes on task switching cannot be attributed to conscious processing. Figure adapted from Lau and Passingham, 2007.

diamond, they had to prepare to judge whether an upcoming word refers to a concrete object (e.g., "chair") or an abstract idea (e.g., "love"). In other words, they had to perform top-down cognitive control based on the instruction figure (square or diamond). However, before the instruction figure was presented, there was an invisible (masked) prime figure, which could also be a diamond or a square. It was found that the prime could impair subjects' performance when it suggested the alternative (i.e., wrong) task to the subjects (incongruent condition). One could argue that this was only because the prime distracted the subjects on a perceptual level and did not really trigger cognitive control. However, the experiment was performed in an fMRI scanner, and the findings suggest that when being primed to perform the wrong task, subjects used more of the wrong neural resources as well (Lau & Passingham, 2007). That is, areas that are more sensitive to phonological or semantic processing showed increased activity when the explicit instruction figure made subjects perform the phonological and semantic tasks respectively. The invisible primes also seem to be able to trigger activations in task sensitive areas. This suggests that the primes can influence or exercise top-down cognitive control.

Another study examines how unconscious information affects our higher-level objectives by focusing on how the potential reward influences our level of motivation (Pessiglione et al., 2007). Subjects squeezed a device to win a certain amount of money. The harder they squeezed, the more money they would win. However, the size of the stake in question for a particular trial was announced in the beginning by presenting the photo of a coin. The coin could either be a British pound (~2 US dollars) or a penny (~2 US cents), and it signified the monetary value of the maximal reward for that trial. Not surprisingly, people squeezed harder when the stakes were high, but interestingly, the same pattern of behavior was observed even when the figure of the coin was masked so that subjects reported not seeing it. This suggests that unconscious information can influence our level of motivation as well.

If unconscious information alone is sufficient to exercise all these sophisticated top-down control functions, why do we need to exert effort in deliberating our intentions?

EXCLUSION AND INHIBITITON

A well-studied paradigm in memory research (Jacoby et al., 1992) describes a task that can only be performed when a subject can explicitly represent her intentions. This is called the exclusion task. One example would be to perform stem completion while avoiding a particular word. So for instance, the experimenter may ask the subjects to produce any word starting with letter D (i.e., completing a "stem"), but to avoid the word "dinner." So subjects can produce "dog," "danger," "dear," etc., but if they produce the word "dinner," it would be counted as an error. When the target of exclusion cannot be explicitly recalled (ie, lacking a conscious representation that is available for verbal report), they may fail to exclude it. In fact, they tend to produce exactly the word they should be avoiding with a higher likelihood than if they were not presented with the word at all.

The notion that consciousness is required for exclusion is also supported by a case study of a blindsight patient (Persaud & Cowey, 2008). Subject GY has a lesion to the left primary visual cortex (V1), and reports that most of his right visual field is subjectively blind. However, in forced-choice situations he can discriminate simple stimuli well above chance level in his "blind" field (Weiskrantz, 1986, 1997). In one study he was required to perform an exclusion task (Persaud and Cowey, 2008), that is, to say the location (up or down) where the target was *not* presented. Whereas he could do this easily in the normal field, he failed the task when stimuli were presented to his blind field. Note that he was significantly worse than chance in the blind field, as if the unconscious signal drove the response directly and inflexibly, defying exclusion control. This seems to support the account that consciousness is required for exclusion.

The general idea that inhibition requires consciousness seems to be supported by other studies too, including those that do not employ the exclusion paradigm. One study tested subjects' ability to ignore distracting moving dots while performing a central task independent of the distractors (Tsushima et al., 2006). It was found that if the motion of the distractor was above the perceptual threshold, people could ignore the dots and inhibit the distraction successfully. Somewhat paradoxically, when the motion was below perceptual threshold, people could not ignore the dots and were distracted. The results from brain imaging seem to suggest that when the motion of the stimuli was strong, it activated the prefrontal cortex, and triggered it to suppress the motion signal. When the motion of the stimuli was below perceptual threshold, however, the signal failed to trigger the inhibitory functions in the prefrontal cortex, and therefore the motion signal was not suppressed and remained distracting.

HOW CAN WE FIND THE TRUE FUNCTION OF CONSCIOUSNESS?

The notion that flexible control or inhibition of perceptually driven actions requires consciousness is not without its critics (Haase & Fisk, 2001; Snodgrass, 2002; Visser & Merikle, 1999). One problem becomes clear when we consider the motion distractor example above. The "conscious signal" here seems to be the same thing as a strong signal, driven by greater motion strength in the stimuli. For this type of function, signals need to be strong enough to reach the prefrontal cortex in order to trigger the associating executive functions. Do unconscious stimuli fail to be excluded because we are not conscious of them or because the signal is just not strong enough? Or are the two explanations one and the same? Not all studies are subject to this argument. For instance, in the blindsight study mentioned above (Persaud & Cowey 2008), the subject failed to exclude in the blind field even when the contrast level would give a performance that was similar to that in the normal visual field. If we take forced-choice performance as an index of signal strength, the signal to the blind field was not weak in this sense. However, in most other cases, we often take awareness to be the same as accurate performance. Patients like GY suggest a constitutive difference between the ability to perform perceptual tasks and to have perceptual experiences. To prove that a certain function can only be initiated by a conscious act of volition, it is important to dissociate consciousness per se from signal strength.

It is possible to recreate blindsight-like behavior in normal subjects (Lau & Passingham, 2006) by using metacontrast masking, in which a target is followed by a briefly presented non-overlapping mask after a variable duration. This paradigm manipulates discrimination performance as a U-shaped function of the time between the two stimuli, with the strongest impairment occurring when there is a 30 ms gap. After performing the discrimination task, subjects were asked to rate the subjective visibility of the stimuli they had observed. It was found that for matched psychophysical sensitivity, subjects' reports of their subjective experiences varied wildly. This would suggest that when the signals were equally strong for a perceptual task, the subjects were conscious of the target in one case whereas it appeared invisible in the other case. Although technically quite challenging, such a design may be used to "knock-out" consciousness without degrading the strength of the underlying signal.

Conclusion

Acts of volition are accompanied by a sense of conscious effort or intention. The fact that we feel the conscious effort is not in doubt. What is less clear is whether the processes underlying the conscious experience directly contribute to the execution of the actions, in a way that actions could not be accomplished by unconscious processes just as effectively. The general picture seems to be that many sophisticated functions can be performed unconsciously or driven by unconscious information. Does this mean that intention has no special function at all? The answer is not yet clear. It is likely that some psychological functions cannot be performed unconsciously, but experiments have not yet been able to convincingly pin them down.

The experiments discussed above challenge our understanding of the way we exert influence on the world, but it's important to remember that these are far removed from ordinary circumstances and normal modes of processing. In an elevator with an attractive member of the desired sex, one might face the situation where one experiences a great deal of urges, some of which are vetoed consciously or perhaps even rejected before the specific shape of the desire takes form in consciousness. At the same time, one might try to devise a strategy for getting the desired mate's phone number, develop plausible pretenses, and evaluate possible reactions. It is even likely that the premotor activation sequences for forming the question will already be underway before one experiences the decision to go for it—but we know very little about how the preceding contemplation originates and is used within the nervous system to render the appropriate executive strategy.

Some might point out that the processes we feel "in control" of are only a tiny selection among the myriad activities that the brain performs. The drama we experience when wrestling with decisions might simply be an inventory of the internal signals that reverberate above a certain threshold and hence, may comprise a poor representation of the totality of our actual interaction with the world around us. Others might counter that those behaviors that are performed with experienced agency fall into a specialized class and that the same behaviors performed consciously and unconsciously often occur in an entirely different fashion. Despite persistent difficulties in evaluating the specific causal role for subjective experiences, we are making considerable progress in understanding the properties and limitations of experiences of agency within the individual.

Although the exact functioning is yet to be made clear, we should not be too quick to reject perceptions of agency, because they have obvious functions in a variety of social contexts. The legal, therapeutic, and economic concerns outlined at the opening of this chapter illustrate the importance of assumptions about intention in the institutions of our society. The ability to form representations about intentional states may be linked with some of the most defining features of humanity, such as theory of mind (the ability to conceptualize a nonsubjective point of view) and linguistic abilities. Our initial intuitions about the way intention works may not hold up in some experimental contexts; nonetheless, agency remains a fascinating and significant element of human behavior.

REFERENCES

Ball, T., Schreiber, A., Feige, B., Wagner, M., Lücking, C. H., & Kristeva-Feige, R. (1999). The role of higher-order motor areas in voluntary movement as revealed by high-resolution EEG and fMRI. *NeuroImage, 10*(6), 682–694.

Brass, M., & Haggard, P. (2007). To do or not to do: the neural signature of self-control. *Journal of Neuroscience, 27*(34), 9141–9145.

Cunnington, R., Windischberger, C., Deecke, L., & Moser, E. (2003). The preparation and readiness for voluntary movement: a high-field event-related fMRI study of the Bereitschafts-BOLD response. *NeuroImage, 20*(1), 404–412.

Dehaene, S., & Naccache, L. (2001). Towards a cognitive neuroscience of consciousness: basic evidence and a workspace framework. *Cognition, 79*(1–2), 1–37.

Erdler, M., Beisteiner, R., Mayer, D., Kaindl, T., Edward, V., Windischberger, C., et al. (2000). Supplementary motor area activation preceding voluntary movement is detectable with a whole-scalp magnetoencephalography system. *NeuroImage, 11*(6), 697–707. doi: 10.1006/nimg.2000.0579.

Farrer, C., Franck, N., Georgieff, N., Frith, C. D., Decety, J., & Jeannerod, M. (2003). Modulating the experience of agency: A positron emission tomography study. *NeuroImage, 18*(2), 324–333.

Gomes, G. (2002). The interpretation of Libet's results on the timing of conscious events: a commentary. *Consciousness and Cognition, 11*(2), 221–230; discussion 308–313, 314–325.

Haase, S. J., & Fisk, G. (2001). Confidence in word detection predicts word identification: implications for an unconscious perception paradigm. *The American Journal of Psychology, 114*(3), 439–468.

Haggard, P., & Eimer, M. (1999). On the relation between brain potentials and the awareness of voluntary movements. *Experimental Brain Research. Experimentelle Hirnforschung. Expérimentation Cérébrale, 126*(1), 128–133.

Jacoby, L. L., Lindsay, D. S., & Toth, J. P. (1992). Unconscious influences revealed. Attention, awareness, and control. *The American Psychologist, 47*(6), 802–809.

Johansson, P., Hall, L., Sikstrom, S., & Olsson, A. (2005). Failure to detect mismatches between intention and outcome in a simple decision task. *Science, 310*, 116–119.

Joordens, S., van Duijn, M., & Spalek, T. M. (2002). When timing the mind one should also mind the timing: biases in the measurement of voluntary actions. *Consciousness and Cognition, 11*(2), 231–240; discussion 308–313.

Klein, S. (2002). Libet's research on the timing of conscious intention to act: a commentary. *Consciousness and Cognition, 11*(2), 273–279; discussion 304–325.

Kornhuber, H., & Deecke, L. (1965). Hirnpotentialänderungen bei Willkurbewegungen und passiven Bewegungen des Menschen: Bereitschaftspotential und reafferente Potentiale. *Pflügers Archive, 284*, 1–17.

Kouider, S., & Dehaene, S. (2007). Levels of processing during non-conscious perception: a critical review of visual masking. *Philosophical Transactions of the Royal Society B: Biological Sciences, 362*(1481), 857–875.

Latane, B., & Darley, J. (1970). *The unresponsive bystander: Why doesn't he help?* New York: Appleton-Century-Crofts.

Lau, H. C., Rogers, R. D., Haggard, P., & Passingham, R. E. (2004). Attention to intention. *Science, 303*(5661), 1208–1210.

Lau, H. C., & Passingham, R. E. (2006). Relative blindsight in normal observers and the neural correlate of visual consciousness. *Proceedings of the National Academy of Sciences of the United States of America, 103*(49), 18763–187618.

Lau, H. C., Rogers, R. D., & Passingham, R. E. (2006). On measuring the perceived onsets of spontaneous actions. *The Journal of Neuroscience: The Official Journal of the Society for Neuroscience, 26*(27), 7265–7271.

Lau, H. C., & Passingham, R. E. (2007). Unconscious activation of the cognitive control system in the human prefrontal cortex. *The Journal of Neuroscience: The Official Journal of the Society for Neuroscience, 27*(21), 5805–5811.

Libet, B., Wright, E. W., & Gleason, C. A. (1982). Readiness-potentials preceding unrestricted 'spontaneous' vs pre-planned voluntary acts. *Electroencephalography and Clinical Neurophysiology, 54*(3), 322–335.

Libet, B., Gleason, C. A., Wright, E. W., & Pearl, D. K. (1983). Time of conscious intention to act in relation to onset of cerebral activity (readiness-potential). The unconscious initiation of a freely voluntary act. *Brain: A Journal of Neurology, 106* (Pt 3), 623–642.

Libet, B. (1985). Unconscious cerebral initiative and the role of conscious will in voluntary action. *Behavioral and Brain Sciences, 8*, 529–566.

Mattler, U. (2003). Priming of mental operations by masked stimuli. *Perception & Psychophysics, 65*(2), 167–187.

Miller, J., & Trevena, J. A. (2002). Cortical movement preparation and conscious decisions: averaging artifacts and timing biases. *Consciousness and Cognition, 11*(2), 308–313. doi: 10.1006/ccog.2002.0567.

Nikolov, S., Rahnev, D., & Lau, H. (2010). Probablistic model of onset detection explains paradoxes in human time perception. *Frontiers in Psychology, 1*:37.

Nisbett, R. E. & Wilson, T. D. (1977). Telling more than we can know: verbal reports on mental processes. *Psychological Review, 34*(5), 231–259.

Nisbett, R. E. & Wilson, T. D. (1978). The accuracy of verbal reports about the effects of stimuli on evaluations and behavior. *Social Psychology, 41*(2), 118–131.

Persaud, N., & Cowey, A. (2008). Blindsight is unlike normal conscious vision: Evidence from an exclusion task. *Consciousness and Cognition, 17*(3), 1050–1055.

Pessiglione, M., Schmidt, L., Draganski, B., Kalisch, R., Lau, H., Dolan, R. J., et al. (2007). How the brain translates money into force: a neuroimaging study of subliminal motivation. *Science, 316*(5826), 904–906.

Romo, R., & Schultz, W. (1987). Neuronal activity preceding self-initiated or externally timed arm movements in area 6 of monkey cortex. *Experimental Brain Research. Experimentelle Hirnforschung. Expérimentation Cérébrale, 67*(3), 656–662.

Scepkowski, L. A., & Cronin-Golomb, A. (2003). The alien hand: cases, categorizations, and anatomical correlates. *Behavioral and Cognitive Neuroscience Reviews, 2*(4), 261–277.

Searle, J. R. (1983). *Intentionality: An Essay in the Philosophy of Mind*. Cambridge: Cambridge University Press.

Shima, K., & Tanji, J. (1998). Both supplementary and presupplementary motor areas are crucial for the temporal organization of multiple movements. *Journal of Neurophysiology, 80*(6), 3247–3260.

Shore, D. I., Spence, C., & Klein, R. M. (2001). Visual prior entry. *Psychological Science: A Journal of the American Psychological Society/APS, 12*(3), 205–212.

Sirigu, A., Daprati, E., Ciancia, S., Giraux, P., Nighoghossian, N., Posada, A., et al. (2004). Altered awareness of voluntary action after damage to the parietal cortex. *Nature Neuroscience, 7*(1), 80–84.

Snodgrass, M. (2002). Disambiguating conscious and unconscious influences: do exclusion paradigms demonstrate unconscious perception? *The American Journal of Psychology, 115*(4), 545–579.

Soon, C. S., Brass, M., Heinze, H. J., & Haynes, J. D. (2008) Unconscious determinants of free decisions in the human brain. *Nature Neuroscience, 11*(5), 543–545.

Tanji, J., & Shima, K. (1996). Supplementary motor cortex in organization of movement. *European Neurology, 36* (Suppl 1), 13–19.

Thaler, D., Chen, Y. C., Nixon, P. D., Stern, C. E., & Passingham, R. E. (1995). The functions of the medial premotor cortex. I. Simple learned movements. *Experimental Brain Research. Experimentelle Hirnforschung. Expérimentation Cérébrale, 102*(3), 445–460.

Tsushima, Y., Sasaki, Y., & Watanabe, T. (2006). Greater disruption due to failure of inhibitory control on an ambiguous distractor. *Science, 314*(5806), 1786–1788.

Visser, T. A., & Merikle, P. M. (1999). Conscious and unconscious processes: the effects of motivation. *Consciousness and Cognition, 8*(1), 94–113.

Wegner, D. M. (2002). *The Illusion of Conscious Will*. Cambridge, MA: MIT Press.

Wegner, D. M., Fuller, V. A., & Sparrow, B. (2003). Clever hands: uncontrolled intelligence in facilitated communication. *Journal of Personality and Social Psychology, 85*(1), 5–19.

Weilke, F., Spiegel, S., Boecker, H., von Einsiedel, H. G., Conrad, B., Schwaiger, M., et al. (2001). Time-resolved fMRI of activation patterns in M1 and SMA during complex voluntary movement. *Journal of Neurophysiology, 85*(5), 1858–1863.

Weiskrantz, L. (1986). *Blindsight: A Case Study and Implications*. Oxford: Oxford University Press.

Weiskrantz, L. (1997). *Consciousness Lost and Found: A Neuropsychological Exploration*. Oxford: Oxford University Press.

19 Sense of Agency: Many Facets, Multiple Sources
Elisabeth Pacherie

THE STUDY OF metacognition has traditionally been concerned with the processes involved in the monitoring and control of cognitive activities such as learning, remembering, reasoning, problem solving, and decision making. Agency is a very recent addition to the list of topics thought to fall within its purview. This may be in part because, for a long time, agency ranked rather low on the agenda of philosophers and cognitive scientists. However, attitudes about agency have changed rapidly. During the last 15 years we have seen an explosion of interest in the sense of agency, the sense that we are in control of our actions and their effects, that we are the doers of our deeds. This is due in a large part to the development of psychological and neuroscientific methods that have made it possible to study a sense of agency empirically. These empirical investigations have done a lot to rekindle the interest of philosophers who now regard agency as a far more complex phenomenon than previously thought. Although empirical research has uncovered a wealth of cues for a sense of agency, we still need to know the relative influence of these cues and it isn't completely clear how they interact with one another. In particular, there is disagreement as to the nature of agentive content and the reliability of the sense of agency. Using the conceptual tools and distinctions developed within research on metacognition may help clarify some of those issues.

Later, I offer a brief survey of recent models of how and where in the cognitive architecture the sense of agency is generated. I argue that these models should be seen as complementary rather than as rivals and discuss some recent evidence on how different types of agency cues are integrated. I draw a distinction between agentive experiences and agentive judgments and discuss their relation. I also consider the issue of the reliability of the sense of agency in the light of this distinction. I conclude with a discussion of whether and in what sense agentive experiences and judgments should be considered part of meta-cognition. In particular, I discuss the complex relations between action-monitoring and agency-monitoring as well as several different criteria for metacognition.

The Sense of Agency: Sources and Mechanisms

Empirical research on self-agency has explored a variety of potential cues to agency. Those cues have been used to generate different cognitive models of agency, ranging from low-level sensory-motor mechanisms to high-level cognitive mechanisms. A number of researchers have proposed that the monitoring of action execution is crucial for agency and that the sense of agency is generated by low-level mechanisms that exploit performance-related sensory-motor cues. Tsakiris and colleagues have investigated the possibility that efferent signals sent to the motor system while implementing an intention provide such cues. In particular, they have proposed that efferent signals are used to generate accurate temporal and kinematic predictions about how and when particular body parts should move (Tsakiris & Haggard, 2005; Tsakiris, Haggard, Franck, Mainy, & Sirigu, 2005; Tsakiris, Prabhu, & Haggard, 2006). In one study (Tsakiris, Haggard, Franck, Mainy, & Sirigu, 2005), subjects experienced a passive extension of the right index finger, produced via a lever. The lever could be pressed either by the subject's left hand ("self-generated action") or by the experimenter ("externally-generated action"). The visual feedback was manipulated so that subjects saw either their own right hand or someone else's right hand during the passive extension of the index finger. Both hands were covered with identical gloves positioned on identical levers, so that discrimination on the basis of morphological differences was not possible. Participants judged whether the right hand they saw was theirs or not. Self-recognition was significantly more accurate when subjects were themselves the authors of the action, even though visual and proprioceptive information always specified the same posture, and despite the fact that subjects judged the effect and not the action per se. When the displacement of the participant's right index finger was externally generated, and only afferent information was available, self-recognition performance dropped to near-chance levels. These results indicate that self-recognition of one's own bodily movements is much more accurate when these movements are active rather than passive and show the crucial role of efferent signals for self-recognition.

Another line of evidence for the role of efferent signals in generating a sense of agency involves "intentional binding," a phenomenon in which self-produced movements and their effects are perceived as being closer together in subjective time than they actually are (Haggard & Clark, 2003; Haggard, Clark, & Kalogeras, 2002). More specifically, when a voluntary act (e.g., pressing on a button with the right index finger) causes an effect (e.g., a tone), the action is perceived by the agent as having occurred later than it did, and the effect is perceived as having occurred earlier. In contrast, when similar movements and auditory effects occur involuntarily (e.g., the button press is produced by an involuntary movement of the right index finger, induced by transcranial magnetic stimulation over the left motor cortex) rather than voluntarily, the binding effect is reversed and cause and effect are perceived as further apart in time than they actually are. The phenomenon of intentional binding suggests that the sense of agency is constructed at the time of the action itself, that it exploits efferent signals and is an immediate by-product of the motor control circuits that generate and control the physical movement.

Another very influential proposal, the predictor and comparator theory, appeals to internal forward models used for action control (Blakemore & Frith, 2003; Frith, Blakemore, & Wolpert, 2000a,b). According to this proposal, forward models are fed an efference copy of actual motor commands and compute estimates of the sensory consequences of the ensuing movements. The predicted sensory consequences are compared with actual sensory feedback (reafferences). When there is a match between predicted and actual states, the comparator sends a signal to the effect that the sensory changes are self-generated, and when there is no match (or an insufficiently robust match), sensory changes are coded as externally caused. Indirect evidence for this model comes from studies demonstrating that discrepancies between predictions and sensory reafferences affect tactile sensations (Blakemore, Wolpert, & Frith, 1998, 2000) and visual perception of one's own movements (Leube et al., 2003). Thus, in their studies of tickling, Blakemore and colleagues exploited the well-known fact that the intensity of the tactile experience when we tickle ourselves is greatly reduced in comparison with the sensation when someone else tickles us. This phenomenon occurs because self-generated tactile sensation can be predicted from the motor commands that generated the movements creating the sensations. Using functional magnetic resonance imaging, Blakemore and colleagues showed that corresponding to this reduction in tactile sensation is a reduction of activity in somatosensory cortex (Blakemore, Wolpert, & Frith, 1998). They also showed that this prediction is based on a rather precise specification and that the perceived intensity of a self-generated tactile sensation is markedly affected by small deviations in the timing or trajectory of the tactile stimulus from the movement that generated it (Blakemore, Frith, & Wolpert, 1999). For example, if there is a delay of 100 ms between the movement and the tactile stimulation, then the perceived intensity of the tactile stimulation increases even though the subject is unaware of the delay. Direct evidence is also provided by studies demonstrating that the sense of agency is gradually reduced as these discrepancies increase owing to spatial deviations and temporal delays (Fourneret & Jeannerod, 1998; Knoblich & Kircher, 2004; Knoblich, Stottmeister, & Kircher, 2004; Leube et al., 2003; Sato & Yasuda, 2005; van den Bos & Jeannerod, 2002). Two studies (Farrer & Frith, 2002; Farrer et al., 2003) have also shown that the activity of two main brain areas was modulated by the degree of discrepancy between predictions and sensory reafferences. In the inferior part of the parietal lobe, specifically on the right side, the more discrepant the signals were and the less the subject felt in control, the higher the level of activation. A reverse correlation was observed in the anterior insula, with activity at its maximum when the signals were perfectly matched.

However, several authors have argued that the results of some of these studies are open to alternative interpretations in terms of perceptual rather than sensory-motor cues (Gallagher, 2007; Knoblich & Repp, 2009; Pacherie, 2008). It is well known that we have little awareness of the proprioceptive feedback associated with movements or even of the corrections we make during goal directed movements (De Vignemont, Tsakiris, & Haggard, 2006; Fourneret & Jeannerod, 1998). Indeed, passive movements are associated with more activity in the secondary somatosensory cortex than active movements (Weiller et al., 1996). The vast majority of our actions aim at producing effects in the environment and we normally attend to the perceptual effects of our movements rather than the movements themselves. Therefore, it may be that perceptual cues rather than sensory-motor cues are crucial to the sense of agency. Direct evidence for this view comes from an experiment of Fourneret and Jeannerod (1998) in which subjects were instructed to move a stylus on a graphic tablet along a straight line to a visual target. Subjects could not see their drawing hand, only its trajectory being visible as a line on a computer screen. On some trials, the experimenter introduced a directional bias electronically so that the visible trajectory no longer corresponded to that of the hand. When the bias was small (<14°), subjects made automatic adjustments of their hand movements to reach the target but remained unaware that they were making these corrections. It is only with larger biases that subjects became aware of a discrepancy and began to use conscious monitoring of their hand movement to correct for it and reach the target. These results suggest that although discrepancies between predicted and actual sensory feedback are detected at some level because they are used to make appropriate corrections of the hand movement, they are not normally consciously monitored. Rather, the sense of agency for the action seems to rely mostly on a comparison of the predicted and actual perceptual consequences of the action. As long as the trajectory seen on the screen matches the predicted trajectory, proprioceptive information is ignored. Indeed, in view of the fact that proprioceptive information only reaches awareness when it is very discrepant with expectations, Frith (2005) even suggests that a lack of proprioceptive experience may be one possible indicator that one is performing a voluntary act.

Further evidence that perceptual cues may contribute more to the sense of agency than sensory-motor cues comes from pathologies (Jeannerod, 2009). For instance, compared with healthy control subjects, patients with schizophrenia are impaired in explicitly judging whether they are in control of perceptual events but not obviously impaired in automatically compensating for sensory-motor transformations between their movements and the resulting perceptual events (Fourneret et al., 2002). Likewise, frontal patients have a preserved automatic sensory-motor control, contrasting with impaired action awareness and conscious monitoring (Slachevsky et al., 2003).

There is also evidence that higher-level inferential and interpretative processes play a role in determining the sense of agency for an action. Studies of Wegner and colleagues have demonstrated that cognitive cues can alter the sense of agency for an action independently of changes in sensory-motor and perceptual cues. For instance, in their "I-Spy" study (Wegner & Wheatley, 1999), a participant and a confederate of the experimenter had joint control of a computer mouse that could be moved over any one of a number of pictures on a screen. When participants had been primed with the name of an item on which the mouse landed, they expressed a stronger sense of agency for the action of stopping on that object (when in fact the stop had been forced by the confederate). In another experiment, the "helping hand" study, Wegner and colleagues (Wegner, Sparrow, & Winerman, 2004) also demonstrated that it was not even necessary for a subject to actually move to experience a sense of agency. They had participants watch themselves in a mirror while another person behind them, hidden from view, extended hands forward on each side where the participants' hands would normally appear and performed a series of movements. When the participants could hear instructions previewing the movements, their sense of agency for these movements was enhanced, but such vicarious agency was not felt when the instructions followed the movements.

Further studies also suggest that the mere priming of potential action effects enhances the sense of agency for the action (Aarts, Custers, & Wegner, 2005) and that nonconscious priming of goals and outcomes also increases the sense of agency for the corresponding action (Aarts, Custer, & Marien, 2009). Thus, in the latter study, participants first learned to stop a sequence of six colors rapidly presented on the computer screen by pressing a key, which was immediately followed by the presentation of a particular color. Participants were told that this color was the result of their action and corresponded to the stop location. They were then told that during the rest of the experiment the presented color might also be determined by the computer (in reality, they always were) and that after each trial they would have to rate their sense of agency for the presented outcome. Agency ratings revealed that subliminally priming outcomes (with a specific color word) just before the outcome was produced enhanced experienced self-agency. Importantly, priming outcomes relatively far in advance also augmented self-agency, but only if the outcome was attached to positive affect. To explain this effect, Aarts and colleagues argue that coactivating outcome information with positive affect causes that outcome to operate as a motivational goal state. As a consequence, the representation of the outcome would be more likely to be kept active over time and thus could enhance experiences of self-agency when it matches with the observation of the actual outcome, even when the time lag between priming and outcome is relatively long.

According to Wegner's theory of apparent mental causation, the sense of agency is typically inferred retrospectively from the existence of a match between a prior thought and an observed action, in which the thought occurs just before the action, is consistent with the action, and other potential causes of the actions are not present. Wegner also notes, however, that we perform many actions without the benefit of such previews and suggests that "Even when we didn't know what we were doing in advance, we may trust our theory that we consciously will our actions and so find ourselves forced to imagine or confabulate memories of 'prior' consistent thoughts" (Wegner, 2002, p. 146). Here, Wegner goes beyond the causal inferential mechanisms central to the theory of apparent mental causation, suggesting that more holistic, interpretive processes are at work.

According to this interpretive approach, the sense of agency is subserved by a holistic mechanism that is concerned with narrative self-understanding. Our sense of what, if anything, we are up to, is based on the operations of a high-level integrative process that draws on the agent's self-conception. We treat ourselves as entities whose behavior needs to be made sense of in light of an implicit theory of ideal agency and try to put the best spin on things that we can. Our self-conception is also influenced by the social values promoted by our culture. For instance, Western cultures promote individual autonomy, whereas Eastern cultures put more stress on social identity as a member of a group constrained by social rules and conventions than on individual choice and control. Aarts and colleagues (Aarts, Oikawa, & Oikawa, 2010) investigated whether subliminal priming of the outcome of an action prior to their occurrence increased experiences of self-agency in Dutch and Japanese participants. They found that the mere priming of outcome information in an action-outcome task, in which the cause of the outcomes is ambiguous, enhances the experience of self-agency irrespective of culture. However, Dutch participants experienced higher level of self-agency than Japanese participants, and this cultural effect was mediated by differences in beliefs of self-determination as measured by the Self-Determination Scale. These findings suggest that there are two complementary processes that the experience of self-agency emanates from: a basic authorship ascription process (shared across cultures), and a reflective process based on culturally bound beliefs about self-determination that modulates experiences of self-agency.

Religious beliefs have also been shown to have an influence on the sense of agency. Dijksterhuis and colleagues (2008) investigated how subliminally primed thoughts of an agent before action can affect ascriptions of authorship for that action in a task in which participants competed against a computer program to remove words from a computer screen. Participants reported greater feelings of authorship when primed with first person singular pronouns, and lower feelings of authorship when primed with "computer." Authorship feelings could also be affected by priming subjects with a supernatural agent. Feelings of authorship decreased when participants were primed with "God," but only among believers.

Many authors have expressed some sympathy with, and in some cases whole-hearted commitment to, the narrative approach. Interpreting split-brain studies in this light, Roser and Gazzaniga (2004, 2006) have argued that the left hemisphere contains an interpreter whose job it is to make sense of the agent's own behavior. The psychiatrist Louis Sass has suggested that schizophrenic patients with delusions of alien control no longer feel as though they are in control of their actions because "particular thoughts and actions may not make sense in relation to the whole" (Sass, 1992, p. 214) and Stephens and Graham (2000) have further developed his proposal. Incidentally, the role of cultural factors is evident in whom patients with delusions of control will identify as the agent of their actions (e.g., God, a spirit, or the devil for the religiously inclined; robots or aliens; the CIA, the KGB, or in recent years Al Qaeda). Peter Carruthers suggests that "our awareness of our own will results from turning our mind-reading capacities upon themselves, and coming up with the best interpretation of the information that is available to it—where this information doesn't include those acts of deciding themselves, but only the causes and effects of those events." (Carruthers, 2007, p. 199).

Various forms of confabulations provide evidence for the narrative approach. When young children happen to achieve a goal by luck, they will say that they had intended the action that yielded that goal all along (Phillips, Baron-Cohen, & Rutter, 1998). Split-brain subjects are prone to confabulate accounts of actions that are generated by their right hemisphere (Gazzaniga & LeDoux, 1978). Data from subjects in altered states of consciousness also support the narrative approach. For example, bizarre behaviors performed in response to hypnotic suggestion are often accompanied by elaborate rationalizations and confabulations on the part of the agents (Moll, 1889).

Integrative Frameworks

All the models I described share a core idea. They appeal to a principle of congruence between anticipated outcome and actual outcome, or in the case of the narrative approach between action and self-conception. The points on which they differ are (1) whether the cues that are used are primarily cognitive, perceptual, or sensory-motor; and (2) how closely these cues are related to action production and control processes. There is, however, a growing consensus that these different models should be seen as complementary rather than opposed, and that the sense of agency relies on a multiplicity of cues coming from different sources (Bayne & Pacherie, 2007; Gallagher, 2007; Pacherie, 2008; Knoblich & Repp, 2009; Sato, 2009; Synofzik, Vosgerau, & Newen, 2008).

Thus, the conceptual framework I proposed (Pacherie, 2008) distinguishes between three hierarchically ordered intentional levels, corresponding to increasingly detailed specifications of the action to be performed: (1) distal intentions in which the action to be performed (i.e., goals and means) is specified in cognitive terms; (2) proximal intentions that are specified in actional-perceptual terms, that is, in terms of the action schemas to be implemented and the perceptual events that will occur as a consequence; and (3) motor intentions that are specified in sensory-motor terms. To take a simple example, I may intend to startle the thief prowling in the living room (distal intention), to flip down the switch on the right hand side of the switch panel and thus turn on the light in the room (proximal intention), to move my arm along a given trajectory, position my right index on the switch and lower the switch with a certain amount of force (motor intentions). Comparisons of desired, predicted, and actual states at each of these three levels provide different (and sometimes conflicting) cues to agency. For instance, I may move my arm and finger as intended (congruence at motor level), flip down the switch but thus turn on the air conditioning instead of the light (discrepancy at the proximal level), and yet succeed at startling the thief (congruence at the distal level). Or, my movement could be faulty (discrepancy at the motor level), resulting in my flipping down another switch that also happens to command the light (congruence at the proximal level), yet fail to startle the thief who has already left (discrepancy at the distal level).

This framework, as well as other similar integrative frameworks, leaves open a number of questions. How do all these agency cues interact? What is the relative weight of cues at each of the three levels with regard to experiencing agency? To what extent can cognitive expectations overrule perceptual and sensory-motor evidence? To what extent can the relative weight of different agency cues be modulated by the nature of the task, by the attentional state of the agent, or by the agent's level of expertise?

Some recent studies have started probing these issues. In their "space pilot" study, Metcalfe and Greene (2007) had participants play a computerized game where a number of variables affected accuracy. By manipulating these variables (speed, feedback delay, random discrepancy from mouse input), they were able to show that the degree of subjective control reported by their participants was not just a function of their judged performance but was also sensitive to the variables affecting consistency between motor actions and their effects. In a recent study using a similar task and variables, Dewey and colleagues (2010) replicated these findings. In addition, they also found that when the task was framed as a competition (a boat race), both participants' performance and sense of control over their own action were influenced by the performance of the rival. In particular, they rated their own control higher when the computer rival had good control.

Moore, Wegner, and Haggard (2009) investigated the effects that priming subjects with prior thoughts about an effect had on intentional binding. Participants made either a voluntary key press movement, or had an equivalent involuntary movement applied passively to their finger. All movements were followed by either a high or a low-pitched tone, at random. In addition, one of these two tones could be presented as a prime, prior to the movements. The primes aimed to induce an intention ("prior conscious thought") relating to a possible effect of the forthcoming action. The prime was either congruent or incongruent with the effect of the ensuing action. Participants were asked to give verbal estimates of the duration of the interval between a key press movement and a tone. In line with previous research showing that self-generated actions lead to a reduction in the perceived temporal interval between movements and effects compared to non–self-generated movements (this reduction being taken as a correlate of an enhanced sense of agency), intervals initiated by voluntary movements were perceived as shorter than those involving passive involuntary movements. Prime congruence also modulated the sense of agency for both voluntary and involuntary movements, with congruent prime–effect pairings leading to an enhanced sense of agency (lower interval estimates). However, this modulation by prime congruence was significantly stronger for involuntary than for voluntary movements. These results corroborate the idea that the sense of agency depends on a mechanism that uses multiple cues, both intrinsic and extrinsic to the motor system, as to the origin of actions and their effects. They also suggest that extrinsic cues (e.g., conscious intentions evoked by primes) are most effective when intrinsic cues (motor signals) are absent.

Sato (2009) investigated the respective contribution to the sense of agency of conceptual congruence between preview information and actual outcome and of sensory-motor congruence between prediction and actual sensory feedback. He found that both of these factors contributed to the sense of agency, but that sensory-motor congruence appeared to have a more robust impact. Knoblich and Repp (2009) investigated how skill level and task difficulty can affect the relative weight that is given to different types of agency cues. Their results indicated that subjects appear to rely more on perceptual cues if a task is difficult or unfamiliar, but that they become more sensitive to sensory-motor cues when the task is less challenging or their expertise with it greater.

Van den Weiden et al. (2010) investigated the role of behavior representation level in priming effects on the experience of self-agency over behavior. Their investigation was premised on the idea that action can be represented at different levels (e.g., movements vs. outcomes) and that an agent's preferred level of action representation varies as a function of both context and individual differences. According to Action Identification Theory (Vallacher & Wegner, 1985, 1987), any behavior can be represented at multiple levels. People who represent their behavior at a low level define their behavior in terms of the concrete, mechanistic aspects of their action (how an action is done), whereas people who represent their behavior at a higher level define their behavior in terms of the goals or purposes of their action (why the action is done). Vallacher and Wegner (1989) developed a reliable tool for assessing an individual's preferential level of action identification, the Behavior Identification Form (BIF). In their experiments, Van der Weiden and her colleagues used the BIF to measure participants' preferred level of action representation. In the experimental task, participants had to move a gray square rapidly traversing a rectangular path consisting of eight white tiles in a counterclockwise direction by pressing and holding the S-key. The computer independently moved another gray square along the path at the same speed, but in the opposite direction (clockwise). At a stop signal, participants had to stop the movement immediately by pressing the Enter-key. This action turned one of the eight white tiles black, representing the location of either their square or the computer's at the time they pressed stop. Thus, the black square could be represented as the consequence of their action (although as a matter of fact the stop location was always determined by the computer and actual control was absent). On some trials, the participants were subliminally primed with a location, a black square being flashed on the position on which the square would stop, just before the stop signal. After each stop, participants indicated how much they felt they had stopped the square at the presented position. The results indicated that priming high-level outcome representations (e.g., final location of the square) enhanced experienced self-agency over behavior much more strongly in participants with a high BIF-score (i.e., general tendency to represent their behavior in terms of why an action is done) than in participants with a low BIF-score (i.e., general tendency to represent their behavior in terms of how an action is done).

Although further empirical work is needed to get a better understanding of all the factors that influence the relative weighting of cues, it seems likely that a Bayesian cue integration process is at work and that the sense of agency is determined by an optimal combination of different cues (Hendricks, Wiggers, Jonker, & Haselager, 2007; Lau, Rogers, & Passingham, 2007; Moore, Wegner, & Haggard, 2009).

Agentive Experiences vs. Agentive Judgments

To have a sense of agency for an action is to be aware of oneself as the agent of the action. But what form(s) does this awareness take? The claim that the sense of agency is the result of cue integration processes shouldn't be taken to entail that it can only take one form. Cue integration may well be a multistage process that gives rise to different forms of agentive awareness. One important distinction is between agentive experiences and agentive judgments. In particular, this distinction can help make sense of, and to some extent help resolve, current disputes over how rich the representational contents of states of agentive self-awareness can be.[1]

Conceptions of the representational contents of states of agentive self-awareness (agentive contents, for short) range from the "thin" to the "thick." At the thin end of the spectrum, one may experience oneself as acting rather than being passive and as acting more or less effortfully. For instance, one may be aware of one's bodily movements as active rather than passive, as fluid and harmonious or awkward and jerky. Moving up the spectrum, agentive content may include not merely the representation of a movement as one's own action, but also a representation of its effects in the world as effects one brought about. Moving even further up, agentive content may include a representation of the kind of action one is performing and one's reasons for performing it. For example, one may be aware of oneself as opening a door, and as opening a door in order to (say) leave a building (as opposed to showing someone how to open the door). At the thicker end of the spectrum, it has been suggested that agentive contents represent our mental states as causing our actions (Hohwy, 2004). One might say, for instance, that I am aware not just that I am opening the door in order to leave the building, but that I am also aware of my opening the door as caused by my intention to leave the building.

Not all theorists agree that agentive contents can display such richness. Some hold onto an austere conception that only allows for thin contents. One way to make sense of their reticence is in terms of a distinction between agentive experiences and agentive judgments (Bayne & Pacherie, 2007). Gallagher (2007) draws a similar distinction between two levels of the sense of agency, contrasting them in terms of first-order phenomenal experience of agency and higher-order, reflective attribution, whereas Synofzik, Vosgerau, and Newen (2008) distinguish between feelings of agency and judgments of agency. One important reason to distinguish between agentive experiences and agentive judgments is that they can dissociate. Consider a well-known case from William James' *Principles of Psychology*. A patient with an anesthetized arm is asked to raise it. The patient's eyes are closed, and unbeknownst to him his arm is strapped to the armrest and prevented from moving. Asked whether he has raised his arm, he answers positively. Upon opening his eyes, the patient is surprised to discover that his arm has in fact not moved, for he had experienced himself as moving his arm. He now judges that actually he has not moved his arm. Suppose the patient is asked to close his eyes again and raise his arm. Despite now knowing that his arm is strapped to the armrest and therefore judging that he is not moving it, he may nonetheless still experience himself as moving his arm. Simply judging that one is not moving a limb may not remove the experience of agency. Conversely, in routine actions, agentive experiences are typically very thin and short-lived, if not completely absent, yet we may judge that we are the authors of these routine actions. A friend's looking at you and asking you, "Didn't you say you were done eating chocolates today?" may make you realize that you are just now plunging you hand in the chocolate box. You then judge that you were about to take a chocolate, although until the moment your friend intervened you had no agentive experience for your action. It seems that proponents of an austere conception of agentive content have agentive experiences in mind, for there are certainly limits to what can be represented in experience. There are no obvious limits, on the other hand, to the richness of agentive judgments. Thus, as long as one is willing to countenance both agentive experiences and agentive judgments as complementary forms of agentive self-awareness, the debate about agentive content shouldn't really be about how rich it can be. Rather, the debate should be about how introspective contents are distributed between agentive experience and agentive judgment and about how experience and judgment relate.

It is very much an open question how rich the contents of agentive experience can be. Arguably, there are restrictions on the kind of properties that can be experientially encoded. A strong case can be made for thinking that the contents of agentive experience can go beyond merely representing one's movement as active rather than passive, but also include information about the degree of control one has over the movement and the degree to which the action is effortful. This aspect of agentive experience—our moment-by-moment sense of ourselves as the agents of various movements we control to a greater or lesser degree—is largely based on sensory-motor cues from low-level, comparator-based systems. Evidence suggests that we have little conscious access to the content of the sensory-motor representations involved in the comparator process or indeed to the content of the prediction error signal this comparison may yield. Rather, this aspect of the agentive experience may reflect sensitivity to the absence or presence of error signals and to their strength. Although the exact nature of the mechanisms that monitor error signals to yield conscious agentive feelings has yet to be elucidated, there is evidence that the strength of positive agentive feelings (feelings of control and fluency) correlates with the level of activation in the anterior insula and the strength of negative agentive feelings (feelings of lack of control and disfluency) correlates with the level of activation in the right parietal lobe (Farrer & Frith, 2002; Farrer et al., 2003).

This conception of agentive feelings and their basis has much in common with Koriat's account of metacognitive feelings. As characterized by Koriat and colleagues (1999; Koriat, 2000, 2007), metacognitive feelings are the products of sub-personal, nonanalytical inferential processes from cues that pertain not to the content of the information processed at the object-level but rather to global, structural aspects of the processing of information (e.g., fluency or lack thereof). Koriat also insists on the crossover mode of operation of metacognitive feelings. On the one hand, they are the product of unconscious inferences from subpersonal cues; on the other hand, once formed, these feelings are conscious and can serve as the basis for the conscious control of information processing and action. Basic agentive feelings might have the same kind of crossover nature, being based on implicit sensory-motor information.

It is controversial, however, whether only implicit information can contribute to metacognitive feelings (Metcalfe, 2000). Similarly, as we saw earlier, it is controversial whether agentive experiences have as their sole basis implicit sensory-motor information. As some of the evidence reviewed in the previous sections indicates, matches and mismatches between perceptual predictions and conscious perceptual feedback appear to be important cues to agency and, indeed, their role in determining the sense of agency for an action may be more important than the role of sensory-motor cues. This in turn suggests that agentive experience can access and incorporate information contained in perceptual prediction and feedback and thus participates in the richness of perceptual content (Pacherie, 2011). Similarly, Gallagher (2007) suggests that the sense of agency as a first-order experience is not just the product of efferent signals and sensory feedback, but also incorporates perceptual information linked to the effects of the action in the world.

With respect to the distribution of agentive content over experiences and judgments, another important issue concerns the cognitive penetrability of agentive experience. Some aspects of agentive experience are largely based on sensory-motor cues from low-level, comparator-based systems. These low-level systems are largely modular and as such presumably rather impervious to top-down influences. Yet, perceptual cues may contribute more to agentive experience than sensory-motor cues and there's a better case to be made for the cognitive penetrability of perceptual content. For instance, in one of the classic papers of New Look psychology, Bruner and Goodman (1947) found that poorer children perceived coins as bigger than rich children do. This study, as well as more recent work (see Raftopoulos, 2005), that suggests that high-level information can affect the contents of visual perception. Analogously, insofar as agentive experiences incorporate perceptual information, it might be possible for cognitive expectations to exert a top-down influence on agentive experience at least around the margins. Some of the studies investigating the relative weighting of agency cues reviewed earlier suggest that this is indeed the case, as priming subjects with prior thoughts about an effect was found to significantly modulate the sense of agency (Moore, Wegner, & Haggard, 2009; Sato, 2009).

One important caveat is in order, however. Most studies of agency have used explicit agency judgments that involve participants introspecting upon his or her sense of agency by answering questions such as, "Did you do that?" or at best, "To what degree did you feel that you were the one who did it?" As pointed out by Moore, Wegner, and Haggard (2009), it is unclear whether in answering such questions subjects are relying solely on their agentive experiences or reporting agentive beliefs based on further considerations. To try and circumvent this problem, they used intentional binding as an implicit measure that should be less susceptible to such interferences and thus more likely to capture agentive experience itself. Intentional binding, described earlier, refers to the fact that the interval between a voluntary action and an outcome is perceived as shorter than the interval between a physically similar involuntary movement and an outcome. By asking participants to report when a given effect occurred or to estimate the duration of the interval between a movement and an effect rather than asking them whether they caused this effect, one can implicitly measure the strength of their agentive experience. To better determine how rich the content of agentive experiences can be and more fully assess the degree to which they are cognitively penetrable while avoiding possible confounds, it will be important for future research to develop a range of implicit measures of agency.

Conversely, one may ask how strong the dependence of agentive judgments on agentive experience is. Agentive judgments are typically grounded in and justified by agentive experiences. Often, we judge that we are the agent of a particular action on the grounds that we enjoy an agentive experience with respect to it and our agentive judgments are simply endorsements of our agentive experiences. Correlatively, we normally judge that we are not the agent of a particular event because we lack an agentive experience with respect to it. Yet, our agentive judgments can be more than just endorsements of our agentive experiences. Although my agentive experience might tell me that I performed a certain action, it may not tell me what kind of action it was or what my reasons were for performing it. The job of agentive judgments would then be to provide an interpretation of the action in the light of one's self-conception. This may be done, as Wegner suggests, by either linking the action to some consistent prior thought we had or, if need be, by confabulating reasons for the action.

Furthermore, as the examples of James' patient and of the chocolate addict presented earlier illustrate, our agentive judgments are not beholden to our agentive experiences. Not only can we deny that we are the authors of events toward which we have an agentive experience, we can also assert that we are the authors of events for which we lack such an experience. In general, experiential states do not compel assent, and there is no reason to think that matters are any different with respect to agentive experiences. The agent's narrative self-conception and cognitive expectations might place rich and substantive constraints on whether or not the contents of agentive experiences are to be accepted. It might be the case that agents evaluate their agentive experience (or lack thereof) in light of their narrative self-conception. Agentive experience for an action may be overridden by certain holistic constraints, in instances in which the action makes no sense with regard to our narrative self-conception. Or conversely, we may self-attribute an action despite lacking an experience of agency for that action, if the action makes perfect sense in light of our narrative self-conception. The latter may actually be quite common, as there is reason to think that in many cases the agent won't have any information about agentive experience to draw on in forming retrospective agentive judgments. Such experiences are likely to be labile and short-lived; leaving no trace in long-term memory unless attentional resources are used to probe and consolidate them. Given their short lifespan, our agentive experiences may well have been obliterated by the time we make an agentive judgment. Such "gaps" between agentive experience and agentive judgment might be large enough for processes of narrative reconstruction to exploit, allowing an agent's narrative self-conception to restructure their sense of agency.

Let me close this section with a brief discussion of the reliability and accuracy of our sense of agency for our actions. The question of how reliable states of agentive self-awareness are may yield different answers depending on how much we pack into their contents, on whether we consider agentive experiences or agentive judgments, and on how closely we take the mechanisms involved in the generation of agentive self-awareness to be related to the mechanisms of action production.

The richer we consider agentive content to be, the more possibilities for error we open. Sensory-motor cues are highly reliable cues to self-agency insofar as they have very direct links to action production (efferent signals) and exploit proprioceptive information that is immune to error through misidentification (proprioceptive information can only be information about oneself). If agentive experiences were based only on efferent cum proprioceptive information they would be very reliable indeed, as it is hard to see how one could experience oneself as actively moving when one isn't. Yet, as we also discussed, these cues contribute rather thin agentive content mostly concerned with active bodily movements, the body parts involved and the timing of their movements.

Perceptual cues largely contribute to enriching the contents of agentive experience. We do not just experience ourselves as moving but also as producing effects in the world. Matches between the predicted perceptual effects of our movements and perceptual events in the world may thus play a central role in agentive experience. Yet, perceptual events resulting from one's own and others' actions are not qualitatively different and keeping them apart is not trivial. Similarly, predictions of perceptual consequences arising from actual action preparation may not be easily distinguished from primed representations of action effects. Reliance on perceptual cues therefore opens the possibility of errors that can be either false positives, as when we have an experience of agency for events actually produced by someone else's action, or false negatives, as when we lack an experience of agency for an event we actually brought about. The latter kind of error can also happen because we sometimes fail to correctly predict the perceptual consequences of our action. If I press a switch expecting the light to go on and it doesn't, I may fail to notice that by pressing the switch I turned the air conditioning on and thus lack a sense of agency for that event.

Motivational factors can also induce both false positives and false negatives. We are more likely to take credit for outcomes associated with positive affect (reward) signals than outcomes associated with negative affect signals. Studies into incentive learning and the neurological mechanisms involved in motivation (Berridge, 2007; Robbins & Everitt, 1996; Toates, 1986) suggest that humans readily become motivated to produce an outcome when the outcome is attached to positive affect as a result of rewarding cues. As one of the studies (Aarts, Custer, & Marien, 2009) described earlier shows, associating positive motivational value to an outcome representation will sustain its activation over time, thus increasing the probability that the representation of the outcome is still active at the moment the outcome is produced and therefore that a match is detected, resulting in a feeling of agency for that outcome. Conversely, representations of outcomes with negative motivational value or no motivational value may decay rapidly, decreasing the probability that the match with the produced outcome be detected.

The existence of both false positives and false negatives shows that the mechanisms that generate agentive experiences are not infallible. However, reliability does not require infallibility and in normal environments such errors may not be systematic enough as to make agentive experiences generally untrustworthy.

Those who contend that the sense of agency is deeply flawed tend to attribute richer content to states of agentive self-awareness. Thus, Wegner's claim that the conscious will is an illusion comes with a high-loaded view of what agentive content includes. For instance, he claims that we experience ourselves as acting freely and consciously causing our actions and that these experiences are illusory. He uses the results of Libet's experiments as evidence of the illusory character of our agentive experiences. Libet and colleagues (1983) investigated the timing of the conscious intention to act in a task where subjects had to spontaneously flex their wrist. They found that, on average, subjects report the onset of a conscious intention or "urge" to act to be about 250 ms before movement onset. They also found that these conscious intentions were reliably preceded by several hundred milliseconds by a negative brain potential, the so-called "readiness potential." The existence of this antecedent unconscious brain activity led Libet to the conclusion that the action was initiated unconsciously rather than by the conscious intention and hence that insofar as our conscious intentions do not initiate our actions, we do not have full-blown "free will." Libet's results and the conclusions he derived from them regarding the causal efficacy of conscious intentions and the existence of free will have been widely discussed and criticized (see chapter 18; Pacherie & Haggard, 2010). Libet, however, was concerned with the causal role of conscious intentions not with the sense of agency and its reliability.

Wegner claims that the existence of match between a prior conscious intention and an ensuing action is an important agency cue. As we saw earlier, there is empirical evidence that this is indeed one of the cues used in generating an experience of agency for an action. However, it is one thing to accept that claim but an altogether different one to accept the much more contentious claim that Libet's demonstration that our conscious intentions do not initiate our actions is itself evidence that agentive experiences are illusory. Even granting for the sake of argument that Libet is right that conscious intentions make no direct causal contribution to the execution of our actions, this will support the conclusion that our agentive experiences are illusory only if it is further assumed that agentive experiences have a content that makes reference to the causal role of conscious intentions. When I have a conscious intention prior to an action, is it really the case that I *experience the action as caused by my conscious intention* or is it rather the case that the existence of a match between this prior intention and my ensuing action contributes to my *experiencing the action as mine*?

Given that even nonconscious priming of outcomes can also enhance the sense of agency for corresponding actions (Aarts, Custer, & Marien, 2009), it is surely not the case that all agentive experiences need have contents that refer to the causal role of a prior conscious intention. Given that in both types of cases, it is the detection of a match between prior representation, whether conscious or not, and ensuing outcome that is deemed responsible for the enhanced experience of agency for the action, it is unclear why the contents of agentive experiences should be so different when prior representation are conscious. This leaves open the possibility that when we have an experience of agency for an action and a conscious prior intention is also accessible, we tend to judge that the conscious intention caused the action. But then this causal story would be part of the content of the agentive judgment that interprets the agentive experience in the light of our folk-psychological conceptions of agency and causality rather than part of the content of the agentive experience itself. If so, Libet's results may impugn the veridicality of our agentive judgments without necessarily impugning the validity of our agentive experiences.

Action-Monitoring, Agency-Monitoring, and Metacognition

As I remarked in the introduction, agency is a recent addition to the list of topics found under the heading of metacognition. Although, as we saw, many researchers are now actively investigating the sense of agency and its underpinnings, few of them appear to explicitly think of their work as an investigation of metacognitive processes. One sociological reason for that may be that it typically takes some time for researchers coming from traditionally disparate areas of investigation to realize that they are all working under the same (metacognitive) roof. But some researchers who have done work on both agency and metacognition (Proust, 2003, 2007) appear to explicitly deny that the monitoring and control of our bodily actions qualify as metacognition, indicating that there can be theoretical reasons why researchers working on agency could be reticent to consider their work as pertaining to metacognition.

However, metacognitive skeptics with respect to agency, as we may call them, could have in mind two different things: action-monitoring or agency monitoring.

Action-monitoring and control and agency-monitoring and control are tightly linked, and many of the signals and cues they exploit are the same. Yet, they shouldn't be confused. They use these signals and cues for different purposes. Action-monitoring and control is about ensuring that the action is successfully executed, whereas agency-monitoring is about determining when and whether we are in control of actions and their outcomes.

In principle, then, four stances are possible: (1) claim that both action-monitoring and agency-monitoring are forms of metacognition; (2) deny that either are; (3) claim that agency-monitoring but not action-monitoring is metacognitive; or (4) claim that action-monitoring but not agency-monitoring is metacognitive. I very much doubt that anyone would want to endorse the fourth stance, but cases might be made for each of the other three, depending on one's construal of metacognition. In what follows I consider five different criteria one may want to use to define and circumscribe metacognition: the structural criterion, the consciousness criterion, the self-reflectivity criterion, the epistemic criterion and its weakened-down version, the meta-epistemic criterion. I start with the structural criterion.

The structural criterion characterizes metacognition in terms of a type of cognitive architecture involving layers of processes interconnected in specific ways. This structural criterion is best captured in Nelson and Narens' (1990) very influential conceptual framework. According to their framework, cognitive processes may be divided into those that occur at the object level and those that occur at the meta-level. The object-level includes the basic operations traditionally subsumed under the rubric of information processing and involved in tasks such as learning, reasoning, remembering, decision making, and so on. The meta-level contains a dynamic model of the operations going on at the object-level. These two levels are connected by two relations, defined in terms of the direction of the flow of information. Metacognitive control is exerted when information flowing from the meta-level to the object-level modifies the object-level processes. Metacognitive monitoring takes place when information flows from the object-level to the meta-level to inform and update the model based on what is happening at the object-level (Fig. 19.1).

If the presence of such a layered architecture together with bidirectional information flow is taken to constitute not just a necessary but also a sufficient condition for metacognition, then even the most basic forms of action-monitoring and agency monitoring qualify as metacognition. The predictor and comparator model presented earlier was first developed by engineers and computational modelers interested in action-monitoring and motor control rather than self-agency. This predictor and comparator model can easily be described in terms of Nelson and Narens' framework. At the object level are goals fed to inverse models that compute motor commands that in turn yield sensory feedback when executed. At the meta-level are forward-models that represent the causal flow of the object-level processes and can thus generate a prediction of the consequences of performing these commands together with comparators. Information flowing from

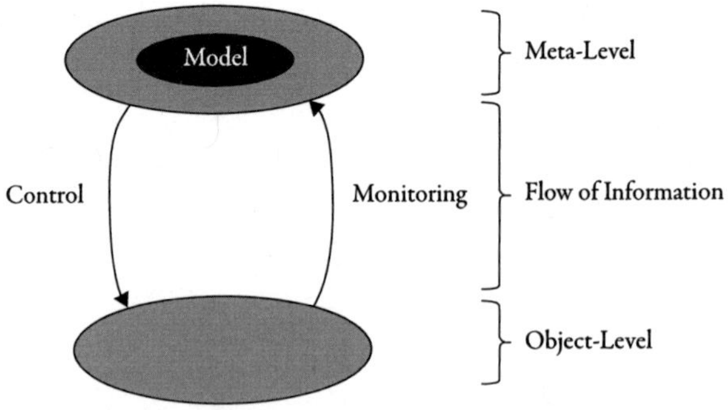

FIGURE 19.1 A theoretical model of metacognition, consisting of two structures (metalevel and object-level) and two relations (monitoring and control) in terms of the direction of the flow of information between the two levels. Adapted from Nelson, T. O., & Narens, L. (1990). Metamemory: A theoretical framework and new findings. In G. Bower (Ed.), *The Psychology of Learning and Motivation: Advances in Research and Theory* (pp. 125–173). New York: Academic Press.

the object-level to the meta-level takes the form of efference copies of the motor commands as well as sensory feedback. At the meta-level, prediction errors derived from the comparison of predicted and actual feedback are used to control and adjust the ongoing activity. Thus, even low-level action monitoring appears to satisfy the structural criterion and on the basis of that criterion should qualify as metacognitive.

But could someone willing to countenance agency-monitoring but not action-monitoring as metacognitive justify their stance in terms of a modified version of the structural criterion? One may want to claim that agency-monitoring is one level up from action-monitoring and control, that agency-monitoring is in effect a monitoring of action-monitoring. There is indeed something to be said in favor of this claim. Action-monitoring exploits efference copies of motor commands and sensory feedback, that is, information flowing from the object-level. Agency-monitoring in contrast takes as input the results of comparisons between sensory predictions and actual sensory feedback, that is, information flowing from the meta-level of action-monitoring. Nelson and Narens' (1994) framework can easily be generalized to more than two levels and could therefore accommodate this picture of the relation between action-monitoring and agency-monitoring.

But this generalization of the framework will only allow us to claim that agency-monitoring is a higher form of metacognition than action-monitoring; it won't allow us to reject the claim that action-monitoring is a metacognitive process. On the basis of the structural criterion alone, nothing justifies saying that metacognition starts only with the third layer of the cognitive cake. Moreover, even if we were to make such a stipulation, we wouldn't be out of the woods. Action-monitoring and control are themselves a hierarchical, multi-layered affair. As I argued elsewhere (Pacherie, 2008), we monitor and control actions not just at the motor level, but also in terms of their predicted and actual perceptual consequences in the world (proximal level), and in terms of their goals and outcomes as characterized in conceptual terms (distal level).

Thus, besides being arbitrary, such a stipulation would not be sufficient to push action-monitoring outside of the metacognitive picture. We are therefore led to the conclusion that if metacognition is defined solely in terms of the structural criterion, both action-monitoring and agency-monitoring qualify as metacognitive. It may still be argued, however, that this criterion provides a necessary condition but not a sufficient condition for metacognition.

One further criterion one may want to consider is the consciousness criterion. It is often assumed and sometimes explicitly claimed that metacognition is a conscious activity. For instance, Koriat (2000, 2007) holds that both metacognitive feelings, which serve to interface between the implicit and the explicit, and metacognitive judgments are an integral part of conscious, explicit cognition and enter into a conscious control process that is necessary for controlled behavior. This view of metacognition and consciousness as tightly linked is not universally accepted. Several authors have argued that there is nothing inherent in metacognitive monitoring and control that demands consciousness (Kentridge & Heywood, 2000; Spehn & Reder, 2000). Suppose, however, that we take consciousness to be a necessary condition on metacognition, would that rule out action-monitoring as a metacognitive activity? It would perhaps rule out low-level action-monitoring, in which control appears to be automatic and to take place below the threshold of consciousness, as evidenced by some of the experiments reported earlier (Fourneret & Jeannerod, 1998; Slachevsky et al., 2003). But, as the same experiments also show, when discrepancies between predicted and actual outcomes increase, subjects become aware of these discrepancies and switch to conscious control strategies. Thus, supplementing the structural criterion with a consciousness criterion doesn't suffice to completely do away with action-monitoring as a form of metacognition.

As we saw, one important difference between action-monitoring (and control) and agency-monitoring is that the former is about assessing progress toward the goal and ultimately ensuring that the action is successfully completed, whereas the latter is about assessing the extent to which one controls the action outcome and thus the extent to which the action is one's own. One way to directly target this difference is in terms of a self-reflectivity criterion. According to the self-reflectivity criterion, a belief, a judgment, or a feeling is metacognitive if it not only is directed at cognitive states and processes of the cognizer, but also does so under the aspect of their being one's own. Metacognition thus defined is restricted to what Graham and Neisser (2000) call self-reflective metacognition. Working with the self-reflectivity criterion, we can readily dispose of action-monitoring as a form of metacognition. The problem though is that we also dispose of many other things, and in effect pretty much throw the metacognitive baby out with the bathwater. Much of metacognition research on memory, decision making, or problem solving is not so much concerned with how people assess their memories, decisions, or answers to problems as their own as with how they assess how good their memories are, how easily they can learn something, and how likely their decisions and answers are to be correct (see Dunlosky and Metcalfe [2009] for a review of these issues). Thus, although it is certainly right to consider self-reflective metacognition as metacognition, it seems unwarranted to view it as the whole of metacognition rather than as a special form of metacognition.

Finally, one may want to consider epistemic criteria. Metacognition is sometimes characterized as knowledge about knowledge and sometimes as cognition about cognition. The first characterization is overly restrictive, at least if knowledge is used in the strict sense in which it implies truth, as both our metacognitive assessments and the cognitive states being assessed may be inaccurate. The second characterization is vague, as more or less restrictive definitions of cognition and cognitive processes can be given. Cognitive processes can be defined as referring to epistemic processes, that is, as processes *aimed at* acquiring, preserving or amplifying knowledge, or, more generally as referring to all processes traditionally subsumed under the rubric of information processing. Cognitive processes understood as epistemic processes centrally include perceptual processes concerned with knowledge acquisition, memory processes concerned with knowledge preservation, and reasoning processes concerned with knowledge preservation (deductive reasoning) and ampliation (inductive and abductive reasoning). They do not include "pragmatic" or "practical" processes aimed at bringing about changes in the world, for although their success at doing so may depend on the truth of some of the agent's beliefs and the changes they bring about may put agents in a position to acquire new knowledge, this is not what these processes are primarily about.[2] In contrast, a more comprehensive definition of cognition as information processing would include both epistemic and "pragmatic" processes as cognitive processes.

One possible epistemic criterion for metacognition would state that a process counts as metacognitive only if it monitors and controls epistemic processes. By making satisfaction of this epistemic criterion part of the definition of metacognition, one rules out both action-monitoring and agency-monitoring as forms as metacognition, for in both cases the object-level processes being monitored are pragmatic rather than epistemic processes. A middle course is possible however, one that imposes the epistemic condition not on object-level processes, but on meta-level processes. We can call that the meta-epistemic criterion. A process would then count as metacognitive if it is an epistemic process directed at object-level cognitive processes, whether the latter are epistemic or not. On that definition of metacognition, agency-monitoring processes would qualify as metacognitive processes insofar as they aim at a certain form of self-knowledge, knowledge of one's own agency. Action-monitoring and control processes would not count as metacognitive, however, for their purpose, keeping actions on course, is practical rather than epistemic.

Of the five criteria just reviewed, the structural criterion, taken as both necessary and sufficient, lets us embrace both action-monitoring and agency-monitoring as forms of metacognition. The consciousness criterion, besides being disputed, excludes only low-level action-monitoring from the realm of metacognition. The self-reflectivity criterion rules out too much, demoting from their metacognitive status many of the processes traditionally studied under that rubric. The epistemic criterion alone gives us a principled way or rejecting both action-monitoring and agency-monitoring as forms of metacognition, and its watered-down version, the meta-epistemic criterion gives us a principled way of ruling out action-monitoring while preserving the metacognitive status of agency-monitoring. I haven't tried here to motivate accepting or rejecting these criteria, only to lay down what their acceptance or rejection would imply with regard to the delimitation of the field of metacognition. Presumably, all would agree that a structural criterion is necessary, if not sufficient, and that the self-reflectivity criterion is overly restrictive. Whether disputes over the remaining criteria are merely verbal or more substantive, I cannot say.

It is clear, however, that researchers in the domain of agency and in more traditional domains of metacognitive enquiry are faced with very similar challenges, such as identifying the various cues that contribute to our agentive or metacognitive assessments, understanding their interactions and relative weighting, and characterizing the ways in which these assessments can help regulate the processes assessed. It is clear also that similar conceptual tools are needed to help us meet those challenges, like concepts of metacognitive knowledge and agentive knowledge, distinctions between agentive or metacognitive experiences and judgments, and between prospective and retrospective judgments. So, whether or not one thinks it fit to adopt the label "metacognition of agency," the two traditions can only benefit from reinforced mutual interactions.

Acknowledgment

This work was supported by the Agence Nationale de la Recherche in France (ANR Grant 07-1-191653). I am grateful to Joëlle Proust for many conversations and discussions on the relationship between agency monitoring and metacognition, to Frédérique de Vignemont for her comments on a draft of this chapter, and to Janet Metcalfe and Herb Terrace for many useful comments and suggestions.

NOTES

1. For more extensive discussions of these issues, including further dimensions of variation among states of agentive self-awareness, see Bayne and Pacherie (2007), Bayne (2008), and Pacherie (2010).

2. One way to frame the distinction between epistemic states and processes, on the one hand, and pragmatic or practical states and processes, on the other, is in terms of Searle's (1983) notion of direction of fit. In his terminology, cognitive states have a world-to-mind direction of fit if in achieving success of fit the world is altered to fit their content and they have a mind-to-world direction of fit if their success depends on their contents fitting the world. States with a mind-to-world direction of fit and the processes that yield them would count as epistemic processes, whereas states with a world-to-mind direction of fit and the processes yielding them would count as pragmatic or practical.

REFERENCES

Aarts, H., Custers, R., & Wegner, D. (2005). On the inference of personal authorship: Enhancing experienced agency by priming effect information. *Consciousness and Cognition, 14*, 439–458.

Aarts, H., Custers, R., & Marien, H. (2009). Priming and authorship ascription: When nonconscious goals turn into conscious experiences of self-agency. *Journal of Personality and Social Psychology, 96*, 967–979.

Aarts, H., Oikawa, M., & Oikawa, H. (2010). Cultural and universal routes to authorship ascription: Effects of outcome priming on experienced self-agency in The Netherlands and Japan. *Journal of Cross-Cultural Psychology, 41*, 87–98.

Bayne, T. (2008). The phenomenology of agency. *Philosophy Compass, 3*, 182–202.

Bayne, T., & Pacherie, E. (2007). Narrators and comparators: The architecture of agentive self-awareness. *Synthese, 159*, 475–491.

Berridge, K. C. (2007). The debate over dopamine's role in reward: The case for incentive salience. *Psychopharmacology, 191*, 391–431.

Blakemore, S., & Frith, C. (2003). Self-awareness and action. *Current Opinion in Neurobiology, 13*(2), 219–224.

Blakemore, S., Frith, C., & Wolpert, D. (1999) Spatiotemporal prediction modulates the perception of self-produced stimuli. *Journal of Cognitive Neuroscience, 11*, 551–559.

Blakemore, S., Wolpert, D., & Frith, C. (1998). Central cancellation of self-produced tickle sensation. *Nature Neuroscience, 1*, 635–640.

Blakemore, S. J., Wolpert, D., & Frith, C. (2000). Why can't you tickle yourself? *Neuroreport, 11*, R11–R16.

Bruner, J., & Goodman, C. (1947). Value and need as organizing factors in perception. *Journal of Abnormal and Social Psychology, 42*, 33–44.

Carruthers, P. (2007). The illusion of conscious will. *Synthese, 159*, 197–213.

De Vignemont, F., Tsakiris, M., & Haggard, P. (2006). Body mereology. In G. Knoblich, I. Thorton, M. Grosjean, M. Shiffrar (Eds.), *Human Body Perception from the Inside Out* (pp. 147–170). New York: Oxford University Press.

Dewey, J. A., Seiffert, A. E., & Carr, T. H. (2010). Taking credit for success: The phenomenology of control in a goal-directed task. *Consciousness and Cognition, 19*, 48–62.

Dijksterhuis, A, Preston, J., Wegner, D. M., & Aarts, H. (2008). Effects of subliminal priming of self and God on self-attribution of authorship for events. *Journal of Experimental Social Psychology, 44*, 2–9.

Dunlosky, J., & Metcalfe, J. (2009). *Metacognition.* Thousand Oaks, CA: Sage.

Farrer, C., Franck, N., Gerogeiff, N., Frith, C. D., Decety, A., & Jeannerod, M. (2003). Modulating the experience of agency: A positron emission tomography study. *NeuroImage, 18*, 324–333.

Farrer, C., & Frith, C. D. (2002). Experiencing oneself versus another person as being the cause of an action: The neural correlates of the experience of agency. *NeuroImage, 15*, 596–603.

Fourneret, P., de Vignemont, F., Franck, N., Slachevsky, A., Dubois, B., & Jeannerod, M. (2002). Perception of self-generated action in schizophrenia. *Cognitive neuropsychiatry, 7*, 139–156.

Fourneret, P., & Jeannerod, M. (1998). Limited conscious monitoring of motor performance in normal subjects. *Neuropsychologia, 36*, 1133–1140.

Frith, C. (2005). The self in action: Lessons from delusions of control. *Consciousness and Cognition, 14*, 752–770.

Frith, C., Blakemore, S., & Wolpert, D. (2000a). Abnormalities in the awareness and control of action. *Philosophical transactions of the Royal Society of London. Series B, 355*, 1771–1788.

Frith, C., Blakemore, S., & Wolpert, D. (2000b). Explaining the symptoms of schizophrenia: Abnormalities in the awareness of action. *Brain Research Reviews, 31*(2–3), 357–363.

Gallagher, S. (2007). The natural philosophy of agency. *Philosophy Compass, 2*, 347–357.

Gazzaniga, M., & LeDoux, J. (1978). *The Integrated Mind.* New York: Plenum.

Graham, G. & Neisser, J. (2000). Probing for relevance: What metacognition tells us about the power of consciousness. *Consciousness and Cognition, 9*, 172–177.

Haggard, P., & Clark, S. (2003). Intentional action: Conscious experience and neural prediction. *Consciousness and Cognition, 12*, 695–707.

Haggard, P., Clark, S., & Kalogeras, J. (2002). Voluntary action and conscious awareness. *Nature Neuroscience, 5*, 382–385.

Hindriks, K. V., Wiggers, P., Jonker, C. M. & Haselager, W. F. G. (2007). Towards a computational model of the self-attribution of agency. In P. Olivier and C. Kray (Eds.) *Proceedings of the Artificial Intelligence and Simulation of Behaviour Annual Convention 2007* (pp. 350–356).

Hohwy, J. (2004). The experience of mental causation. *Behavior and Philosophy, 32*, 377.

Jeannerod, M. (2009). The sense of agency and its disturbances in schizophrenia: A reappraisal. *Experimental Brain Research, 192*, 527–532.

Kentridge, R. W., & Heywood, C. A. (2000). Metacognition and awareness. *Consciousness and Cognition, 9*, 308–312.

Koriat, A. (2000). The feeling of knowing: Some metatheoretical implications for consciousness and control. *Consciousness and Cognition, 9*, 149–171.

Koriat, A. (2007). Metacognition and consciousness. In P. D. Zelazo, M. Moscovitch, & E. Thompson (Eds.), *The Cambridge Handbook of Consciousness* (pp. 289–325). Cambridge, UK: Cambridge University Press.

Koriat, A., & Levy-Sadot, R. (1999). The processes underlying metacognitive judgments: information-based and experience-based monitoring of one's knowledge. In S. Chaiken, & Y. Trope (Eds.), *Dual Process Theories in Social Psychology* (pp. 483–502). New York: Guilford.

Knoblich, G., & Kircher, T. T. J. (2004). Deceiving oneself about being in control: Conscious detection of changes in visuomotor coupling. *Journal of Experimental Psychology-Human Perception and Performance, 30*, 657–666.

Knoblich, G., & Repp, B. H. (2009). Inferring agency from sound. *Cognition, 3*, 248–262.

Knoblich, G., Stottmeister, F., & Kircher, T. (2004). Self-monitoring in patients with schizophrenia. *Psychological Medicine, 34*, 1561–1569.

Lau, H. C., Rogers, R. D., & Passingham, R. E. (2007). Manipulating the experienced onset of intention after action execution. *Journal of Cognitive Neuroscience, 19*, 1–10.

Leube, D., Knoblich, G., Erb, M., Grodd, W., Bartels, M., & Kircher, T. (2003). The neural correlates of perceiving one's own movements. *Neuroimage, 20*, 2084–2090.

Libet, B., Gleason, C. A., Wright, E. W., & Pearl, D. K. (1983). Time of conscious intention to act in relation to onset of cerebral activity (readiness-potential). *Brain, 106*, 623–642.

Metcalfe, J. (2000). Feelings and judgments of knowing: Is there a special noetic state? *Consciousness and Cognition, 9*, 178–186.

Metcalfe, J., & Greene, M. (2007). Metacognition of agency. *Journal of Experimental Psychology: General, 136*, 184–199.

Moll, A. (1889). *Hypnotism.* London: Walter Scott.

Moore, J. W., Wegner, D. M., Haggard, P. (2009). Modulating the sense of agency with external cues. *Consciousness and Cognition, 18*, 1056–1064.

Nelson, T. O., & Narens, L. (1990). Metamemory: A theoretical framework and new findings. In G. Bower (Ed.), *The Psychology of Learning and Motivation: Advances in Research and Theory* (pp. 125–173). New York: Academic Press.

Nelson, T. O., & Narens, L. (1994). Why investigate metacognition? In J. Metcalfe, & A. P. Shimamura (Eds.), *Metacognition: Knowing about Knowing* (pp. 1–26). Cambridge, MA: MIT Press.

Pacherie, E. (2008). The phenomenology of action: A conceptual framework. *Cognition, 107*, 179–217.

Pacherie, E. (2011). Self-agency. In S. Gallagher (Ed.), *The Oxford Handbook of the Self*. Oxford, UK: Oxford University Press.

Pacherie, E., & Haggard, P. (2010). What are intentions? In, L. Nadel, & W. Sinnott-Armstrong (Eds.), *Conscious Will and Responsibility. A Tribute to Benjamin Libet* (pp. 70–84). Oxford, UK: Oxford University Press.

Phillips, W., Baron-Cohen, S., & Rutter, M. (1998). Understanding intention in normal development and in autism. *British Journal of Developmental Psychology, 16*, 337–348.

Proust, J. (2003). Perceiving intentions. In J. Roessler, & N. Eilan (Eds.), *Agency and Self-Awareness* (pp. 296–320). Oxford, UK: Oxford University Press.

Proust, J. (2007). Metacognition and metarepresentation: Is a self-directed theory of mind a precondition for metacognition? *Synthese, 2*, 271–295.

Raftopoulos, A. (Ed.). (2005). *Cognitive Penetrability of Perception*. New York: Nova Science.

Robbins, T. W., & Everitt, B. J. (1996). Neurobehavioral mechanisms of reward and motivation. *Current Opinion in Neurobiology, 6*, 228–236.

Roser, M., & Gazzaniga, M. (2004). Automatic brains—interpretive minds. *Current Directions in Psychological Science, 13*, 56–59.

Roser, M., & Gazzaniga, M. (2006). The interpreter in human psychology. *The Evolution of Primate Nervous Systems*. Oxford, UK: Elsevier.

Sass, L. (1992). *Madness and Modernism: Insanity in the Light of Modern Art, Literature, and Thought*. New York: Basic Books

Sato, A. (2009). Both motor prediction and conceptual congruency between preview and action-effect contribute to explicit judgment of agency. *Cognition, 110*, 74–83.

Sato, A., & Yasuda, A. (2005). Illusion of sense of self-agency: Discrepancy between the predicted and actual sensory consequences of actions modulates the sense of self-agency, but not the sense of self-ownership. *Cognition, 94*, 241–255.

Searle, J. (1983). *Intentionality, an Essay in the Philosophy of Mind*. Cambridge, UK: Cambridge University Press.

Slachevsky, A., Pillon, B., Fourneret, P., Renie, L., Levy, R., Jeannerod, M., & Dubois, B. (2003). The prefrontal cortex and conscious monitoring of action: An experimental study. *Neuropsychologia, 41*, 655–665.

Spehn, M. K., & Reder, L. M. (2000). The unconscious feeling of knowing: A commentary on Koriat's paper. *Consciousness and Cognition, 9*, 187–192.

Stephens, G., & Graham, G. (2000). *When Self-Consciousness Breaks: Alien Voices and Inserted Thoughts*. Cambridge, MA: MIT Press.

Synofzik, M., Vosgerau, G., & Newen, A. (2008). Beyond the comparator model: A multifactorial two-step account of agency. *Consciousness and Cognition, 17*, 219–239.

Toates, F. (1986). *Motivational Systems.* Cambridge, UK: Cambridge University Press.

Tsakiris, M., & Haggard, P. (2005). The rubber hand illusion revisited: Visuotactile integration and self-attribution. *Journal of Experimental Psychology-Human Perception and Performance, 31*, 80–91.

Tsakiris, M., Haggard, P., Franck, N., Mainy, N., & Sirigu, A. (2005). A specific role for efferent information in self-recognition. *Cognition, 96*, 215–231.

Tsakiris, M., Prabhu, G., & Haggard, P. (2006). Having a body versus moving your body: How agency structures body-ownership. *Consciousness and Cognition, 15*, 423–432.

Vallacher, R. R., & Wegner, D. M. (1985). *A theory of action identification.* Hillsdale, NJ: Erlbaum.

Vallacher, R. R., & Wegner, D. M. (1987). What do people think they're doing? Action identification and human behavior. *Psychological Review, 94*, 3–15.

Vallacher, R. R., & Wegner, D. M. (1989). Levels of personal agency: Individual variation in action identification. *Journal of Personality and Social Psychology, 57*, 660–671.

van den Bos, E., & Jeannerod, M. (2002). Sense of body and sense of action both contribute to self-recognition. *Cognition, 85*, 177–187.

van der Weiden, A, Aarts, H., & Ruys, K. I. (2010). Reflecting on the action or its outcome: Behavior representation level modulates outcome-priming effects on self-agency experiences. *Consciousness and Cognition, 19*, 21–32.

Wegner, D. (2002). *The Illusion of Conscious Will.* Cambridge, MA: MIT Press.

Wegner, D. M., Sparrow, B., & Winerman, L. (2004). Vicarious agency: Experiencing control over the movements of others. *Journal of Personality and Social Psychology, 86*, 838–848.

Wegner, D. M., & Wheatley, T. (1999). Apparent mental causation: Sources of the experience of will. *American Psychologist, 54*, 480–492.

Weiller, C., Juptner, M., Fellows, S., Rijntjes, M., Leonhardt, G., Kiebel, S., et al. (1996). Brain representation of active and passive movements. *Neuroimage, 4*, 105–110.

Index

behavioral evidence, neuroimaging, 226
behavioral studies, joint attention, 226–227
Behavior Identification Form (BIF), 329
behaviorism
  animals and causal knowledge, 65–67
  animals and relation between acts and world, 67–68
  animals forming representations, 64–65
  reinterpretation hypothesis, 63
  theory of evolution, 22–24
behaviorist, 63
behavior reader, 63
behavior-reading hypothesis, 64–65
behavior-rule explanations
  behavior-rule hypothesis, 82–84
  comparative simplicity, 88–91
  mindreading and infants, 91–93
  rules, 94–95
  stage 1 vs. stage 2 mindreading, 86–87, 90–91
Bereitschaftspotential, readiness potential, 306–309
binocular rivalry paradigm, voluntary action, 287–288
bipedal organisms
  sun, mitigating effects of exposure, 21*f*
  visual perspective of, 22*f*
black box arguments, behavior, 88–90
blind fold, gaze following test, 131
blind imitation, 144
body orienters, 129
bonobos
  declarative gestures, 55–56
  joint attention, 55
  lexigrams, 56
brain imaging
  behavioral studies, 182–183
  observing actions of others, 259
broadcast ability, 8, 296
Brown, Roger, 29

canonical neurons, 181, 182
catch the mouse, interactive game, 224
chaining theory
  sentence, 25
chimpanzees
  color of pigment of sclera, 22*f*
  gaze following, 66
  joint attention, 54–57
  learning American Sign Language (ASL), 28, 29–33
  lexigrams, 56
  teaching, 15
Chimpsky, Nim, 29–33
choice blindness, intention, 313
cognition
  comparing human and nonhuman, 74–75
  relational reinterpretation hypothesis, 75–77
cognitive control
  direct and indirect, 298
  top-down, 313–315
cognitive opacity
  cultural learning, 142
  cultural skills, 140–142
  presumption of relevance, 145
cognitive revolution, animal cognition, 34–35
collaborative dialogue, 106, 118
common ground, communication, 171–172
communication. *See also* ostensive communication
  animal, 14–17
  apes, 57–58
  declarative and informational pointing, 4
  defining, 165–166
  facilitated, 311
  human, as epistemic cooperation, 139
  infant-mother, 39–40
  language, 5
  language adding to, 17
  modalities of, 108
  production and comprehension, 43*n*.1
  social learning and, 148
communicative acts
  components of, 168
  detecting, 166–167
  directional signaling, 168, 170
  functions of, 167–168
  mutually readable formats, 168, 170–171
  referential specificity, 168, 171–172
  shared intentionality, 168–169
communicative demonstration contexts, 143
comparative psychology, mentalistic hypothesis, 62
comparator model, discrepancy cue, 239–240
comprehension, communication, 43*n*.1
comprehensive model, sense of agency, 261–262
computers, mental processes, 34